OXFORD TELEVISION STUDIES

General Editors **Charlotte Brunsdon**
John Caughie

British Television

A Reader

PUBLISHED IN THE OXFORD TELEVISION STUDIES SERIES

British Television

A Reader

Edited by **Edward Buscombe**

Clarendon Press · Oxford

OXFORD
UNIVERSITY PRESS

Great Clarendon Street, Oxford OX2 6DP

Oxford University Press is a department of the University of Oxford.
It furthers the University's objective of excellence in research, scholarship,
and education by publishing worldwide in

Oxford New York

Athens Auckland Bangkok Bogotá Buenos Aires Calcutta
Cape Town Chennai Dar es Salaam Delhi Florence Hong Kong Istanbul
Karachi Kuala Lumpur Madrid Melbourne Mexico City Mumbai
Nairobi Paris São Paulo Singapore Taipei Tokyo Toronto Warsaw

with associated companies in Berlin Ibadan

Oxford is a trade mark of Oxford University Press
in the UK and in certain other countries

Published in the United States
by Oxford University Press Inc., New York

British Library Cataloguing in Publication Data
Data available
Library of Congress Cataloging in Publication Data
Data available
ISBN 0–19–874265–7

Typeset in Frutiger and Minion
by RefineCatch Limited, Bungay, Suffolk
Printed in Great Britain by
T.J. International, Padstow, Cornwall

Oxford Television Studies

General Editors
Charlotte Brunsdon and **John Caughie**

OXFORD TELEVISION STUDIES offers international authors—both established and emerging—an opportunity to reflect on particular problems of history, theory, and criticism which are specific to television and which are central to its critical understanding. The perspective of the series will be international, while respecting the peculiarities of the national, it will be historical, without proposing simple histories; and it will be grounded in the analysis of programmes and genres. The series is intended to be foundational without being introductory or routine, facilitating clearly focused critical reflection and engaging a range of debates, topics, and approaches which will offer a basis for the development of television studies.

Contents

Acknowledgements

For help of various kinds with this volume I would like to thank:
Manuel Alvarado, Charlotte Brunsdon, John Caughie, John Hartley,
Annette Hill, Andrew Lockett, Tom O'Regan, Garry Whannel, and
at Oxford University Press Ruth Marshall and Angela Griffin.

Ed Buscombe

List of Contributors

LORD BRIGGS, author of many books in the nineteenth and twentieth centuries, has written five volumes on the *History of Broadcasting in the United Kingdom*. He has also written *A Social History of England*, a new edition of which appeared in 1999. He was formerly Vice-Chancellor of the University of Sussex and from 1976–91 Provost of Worcester College, Oxford. He was Chancellor of the Open University from 1978 to 1994. He is a Fellow of the British and American Academies.

CHARLOTTE BRUNSDON is Reader in Film and Television Studies at the University of Warwick. She is co-editor (with Julie D'Acci and Lynn Spigel) of *Feminist Television Criticism: A Reader* (OUP, 1997) and general editor (with John Caughie) of the Oxford Television Studies series.

DAVID BUCKINGHAM is Reader in Education at the Institute of Education, London University. His books include *Children Talking Television* (1993), *Moving Images* (1996), *The Making of Citizens* (1999), and *After the Death of Childhood* (2000).

JOHN ELDRIDGE is Professor of Sociology at the University of Glasgow. He is a founder member of the Glasgow Media Group with whom he has published extensively. With Lizzie Eldridge he is co-author of *Raymond Williams: Making Connections* (1994).

CHRISTINE GERAGHTY is Senior Lecturer in Media and Communication at Goldsmiths College, London. She has written extensively on film and television and is the author of *Women and Soap Opera* and the co-editor of *The Television Studies Book* (Arnold, 1998).

SYLVIA HARVEY teaches film and media at Sheffield Hallam University. She has written about broadcasting policy, Channel 4 television, and British independent cinema. She is on the Board of the International Documentary Festival and is co-editor of *Television Time* (1996).

ANNETTE HILL is Senior Lecturer in Mass Media at the Centre for Communication and Information Studies, University of Westminster. She is the author of *Shocking Entertainment: Viewer*

Response to Violent Males (1997) and the co-author of *TV Living: Television, Culture and Everyday Life* (1999). She is also the editor of *Framework: The Journal of Cinema and Media.*

FRANK KRUTNIK is the author of *In a Lonely Street: Film Noir, Genre, Masculinity* and with Steve Neale, *Popular Film and Television Comedy.* He has published numerous articles in such leading international film journals as *Screen, Film Quarterly, The Velvet Light Trap* and *Journal of Popular Film and Television.* Currently based in London, he has also lectured in the US, Canada, Scotland, and Spain.

ANDY MEDHURST teaches Media Studies at the University of Sussex. He is the co-editor of *Lesbian and Gay Studies* (Cassell, 1997) and author of *A National Joke: Popular Comedy and English Cultural Identities* (Routledge, 2000).

GRAHAM MURDOCK is Reader in the Sociology of Culture at Loughborough University and Professor II in Media Studies at the University of Bergen, Norway. He has previously held Visiting Chairs in California, Mexico City, Brussels, and Stockholm. He is internationally known for his extensive writing on communications and contemporary culture. He is Head of the Political Economy Sector of the International Association for Media and Communications Research.

STEVE NEALE is Research Professor in Film, Media and Communication Studies at Sheffield Hallam University. He is the author of *Genre* (1980), *Cinema and Technology* (1985), and *Genre and Hollywood* (forthcoming). He is also co-editor of *Contemporary Hollywood Cinema* (1998).

ROBIN NELSON is Principal Lecturer and Research Co-ordinator in Contemporary Arts at the Manchester Metropolitan University. His most recent book on television culture is *Television Drama in Transition* (Macmillan, 1997).

TOM O'REGAN is Associate Professor of Communication Studies and Director, Centre for Research in Culture and Communication, Murdoch University, Western Australia. He has written and edited books on Australian cinema and television in its international contexts. These include *Australian National Cinema* (1996), *Australian Television Culture* (1993), *The Australian Screen* (1989), and *An Australian Film Reader* (1985). In 1997 he was Visiting Research Fellow in the Tom Hopkinson Centre for Media Research, Cardiff University of Wales.

PADDY SCANNELL is Director of the Graduate Centre, and also Director of Research in the School of Communication, Design and

Media at the University of Westminster. He is the author or co-author of a number of books including *Radio, Television and Modern Life: A Phenomenological Approach* (1996), *Broadcast Talk* (1991), and *A Social History of British Broadcasting, Volume 1: 1922–1939* (with David Cardiff, 1991). He is one of the founding editors of *Media, Culture and Society*. His research interests include phenomenology, broadcast talk, and the media in Southern Africa.

MICHAEL TRACEY is Director of the Centre for Mass Media Research, University of Colorado at Boulder. From 1981 to 1988 he was Director of the Broadcasting Research Unit in London. His last book was *The Decline and Fall of Public Service Broadcasting* (OUP, 1998).

GARRY WHANNEL is a Professor of Media Arts at the University of Luton. He is the author of *Fields in Vision: Television Sport and Cultural Transformation* (Routledge, 1992) and is currently writing a book on images of sports stars, with specific reference to discourses of masculinity and morality.

Introduction

Edward Buscombe

FOR ALL ITS FAULTS (and pointing them out is a national pastime), British television has been a success. To a degree rare in other fields of cultural endeavour, British television stands comparison with that of any other country. For over half a century it has excited the admiration, even emulation, of other nations, and the loyalty of its domestic viewers. It's worth making such a bald statement at the outset, because academic writing about television can be churlishly critical, grudging even when conceding merit, and often giving the impression of being written by people who don't much like television—or perhaps don't even watch it. This is a strange phenomenon which might repay investigation. One wouldn't be inclined to say that writers on the cinema don't watch films, for instance, or that opera critics don't care for music. What is it about television that attracts so much hostility—the politicians, ever ready to chip away at its independence in the cause of footling party advantage, the prudes quick to condemn 'outrages' they haven't even seen? Even television practitioners often claim not to watch 'the box', as if viewing might be evidence of a lack of gravity, or of underemployment. Important people have better things to do is the implication.

Not all the writing in this book is unreservedly enthusiastic. This is not a celebration of British television; rather it is an attempt to lay out some of its chief institutional characteristics and take a careful look at some of its representative programmes. But I think that all the writers included here afford television the respect of paying attention, of taking it seriously; which is the least we should expect for a piece to be worth including in an anthology intended for those who are making a systematic study.

The structure of the book is simple. It proceeds from the bottom upwards—or, as the Marxists used to say, from the base to the superstructure. Part I collects together a number of accounts of British television institutions, tracing how they evolved to their present form of organization, and what fundamental principles inform them. Part II then moves to accounts of programmes, the actual products of those institutions. The principle of selection in this second part is based upon attempting a fair representation of the major genres or types of programmes (fiction of various kinds, news, sport, etc.); and also on selecting writers whose accounts situate programmes in relation to a range of constraints, influences, or determinations. In choosing each piece of writing for this section, I have asked myself not only what it tells us about a particular programme, but what it tells us about British television.

There is a particular reason for beginning the book with accounts of television institutions. Whatever the triumphs of individual programmes, what distinguishes British television in relation to the rest of the world is the structural model which it adopted at a very early stage in its development. This model, usually referred to as public service broadcasting, is what has given British television many of its strengths, and perhaps some of its weaknesses. It has undoubtedly been a major source of its political independence and intellectual ambition, but on occasion also a cause of its stuffiness, even of a degree of self-satisfaction. Public service broadcasting has often been regarded as a peculiarly British phenomenon; though in fact it has been successfully exported to some other countries,[1] it has not been an easy model to copy. Americans, for example, seem to have great difficulty grasping that the BBC is not simply a version of their own PBS, a provider of worthy fare for underprivileged intellectuals, instead of a producer of mainstream programming. The idea that a government would finance through a form of direct taxation a medium of entertainment (as it seems to Americans) which advertisers would be willing to provide for free is not conceivable within their frame of thought. Conversely, authoritarian regimes of whatever description find it hard to accept that a television service which is publicly owned and operated could be allowed to escape political control. The first step, then, towards understanding what makes British television tick is a grasp of the precise nature of 'public service broadcasting'.

For this reason, a great deal of what has been written about British television takes the form of describing and analysing the history of its institutions. Though much work remains to be done, there is now a substantial body of writing about the BBC, the institution which unquestionably dominates British television, and indeed much of British cultural life. Asa Briggs's multi-volume

---

1 Principally to the English-speaking countries of the Commonwealth and to parts of north-western Europe. Sometimes, as in the case of Germany after the war, the export was at the point of a gun, as German radio in the British-occupied sector was modelled along the lines of the BBC, in large part by Hugh Carleton Greene, later to be the BBC's director-general. See Asa Briggs, *The History of Broadcasting in the United Kingdom*, iv: *Sound and Vision* (Oxford: Oxford University Press, 1979), 151–3, and Hugh Carleton Greene, *The Third Floor Front: A View of Broadcasting in the Sixties* (London: Bodley Head, 1969).

history of the BBC[2] is an account of its internal workings, and the interaction of government policy and other external pressures with the personalities and objectives of its administrators. Though it is less successful as a history of the BBC's actual programmes,[3] the book shows, in massive detail, how over the years the practical realities of running a public service operation were negotiated. Other accounts of the BBC have filled in more detail of its ideologies, assumptions, and working methods.[4]

One of the distinctive features of the British system is that even when commercial broadcasting has been permitted, it has been closely regulated according to principles derived from the notion of public service. As various accounts of ITV and Channel Four show,[5] the operations of the free market have been carefully regulated in order to ensure that television, even when produced for profit, should make some contribution to the public good. This notion, that television might have a function beyond mere entertainment, and that the nation might have a collective interest in seeing it fostered, has been extraordinarily tenacious in British public life. Television's continuing high approval rating with the public owes something to the success with which the balancing act between popularity and purpose has been maintained. But it is also doubtless because the idea of public service television is consonant with other structures within British public life. For example, the idea that the government, representing the people, has a perfect right to involve itself in funding a service which could be provided by private finance finds an echo in the National Health Service; while the model of a service which, while funded

2 Asa Briggs, *The History of Broadcasting in the United Kingdom*, i: *The Birth of Broadcasting*; ii: *The Golden Age of Wireless*; iii: *The War of Words*; iv: *Sound and Vision*; v: *Competition, 1955–74* (Oxford: Oxford University Press, 1961, 1965, 1970, 1979, 1995).

3 See Edward Buscombe, 'Broadcasting from Above', *Screen Education*, 37 (1980), 73–8.

4 See Greene, *The Third Floor Front*; Andrew Boyle, *Only the Wind will Listen: Reith of the BBC* (London: Hutchinson, 1972); Tom Burns, *The BBC: Public Institution and Private World* (London: Macmillan, 1977); Burton Paulu, *Television and Radio in the United Kingdom* (London: Macmillan, 1956; rev. 1981); Michael Leapman, *The Last Days of the Beeb* (London: Allen & Unwin, 1986); Steven Barnett and Andrew Curry, *The Battle for the BBC: A British Broadcasting Conspiracy?* (London: Aurum Press, 1994); Tom O'Malley, *Closedown? The BBC and Government Broadcasting Policy 1979–92* (London: Pluto Press, 1994).

5 Stephen Lambert, *Channel Four: Television with a Difference* (London: BFI Publishing, 1982); Bernard Sendall, *Independent Television in Britain*, i: *Origin and Foundation, 1946–62*; ii: *Expansion and Change, 1958–68* (London: Macmillan, 1982, 1983); J. Potter, *Independent Television in Britain*, iii: *Politics and Control, 1968–80*; iv: *Companies and Programmes, 1968–80* (London: Macmillan, 1989, 1990); David Docherty, *Running the Show: 21 Years of London Weekend Television* (London: Boxtree, 1990); Andrew Davidson, *Under the Hammer: The ITV Franchise Battle* (London: Heinemann, 1992); Paul Bonner with Lesley Aston, *Independent Television in Britain, ITV and the IBA, 1981–92: The Old Relationship Changes* (London: Macmillan, 1998).

by government edict, is administered at arm's length and not directly by politicians has been applied in many areas, particularly to such cultural agents as the Arts Council and the various heritage bodies.

The (relative) uniqueness and complexity of its structures are in themselves a reason why so much that has been written about British television should be concerned with institutional questions. The concept of public service itself is nowhere defined in the laws which regulate broadcasting, and has had to be teased out down the years by a succession of commentators, as well as tested by broadcasters and politicians alike. But there is another reason why commentators should have dwelt so much on questions of organization, one which derives not from the nature of television itself but from the history of television studies. In the 1970s interest in institutional matters was greatly stimulated by the radical intellectual currents which derived their political impetus from such events as the Paris *événements* of 1968, the Prague Spring, and the demonstrations against the Vietnam War, and drew their ideas from Marxism, especially the new varieties which flowered in the work of Louis Althusser, Antonio Gramsci, and others. The emphasis given within Marxism to the role of economics in determining cultural development seemed especially relevant to broadcasting, which in contrast to such forms of expression as the theatre or literature could not be carried out without the expenditure of a great deal of money. On the other hand, British broadcasting was far more carefully controlled by the state than other mass media such as the cinema or newspapers, and this seemed to pose in their sharpest form problems about the extent to which freedom was compatible with stage regulation and public finance. The new Marxists had much to say about the role of the so-called ideological state apparatuses, of which broadcasting was a pre-eminent example. To many writers broadcasting seemed the ideal arena in which to test out hypotheses about just how the economic base of society, and the particular form in which it organized production, might govern other areas of activity such as culture which could not be understood solely as material 'products'.

At this time film studies, which itself had become not uninterested in questions of power and money, began to develop an intense concern with the textual operations of the cinema, finding new ways of explaining how film 'language' worked, how a film actually generated the meanings it communicated. Structuralism, semiotics, and later, psychoanalysis were all ransacked for help in understanding how a film achieved its effects. Some of this work crossed over into the analysis of television, and a number of studies of British television programming were produced which sought to make use of these advances.[6] But somehow this never became the dominant mode of writing about television. As is well represented by the readings in the present volume, the analysis of programmes, while by no means theoretically unsophisticated, has rarely aspired (or descended?) to the kind of minute examination of the image or soundtrack that became all the rage in film studies. None of the pieces collected in this anthology require the possession of a technical language, or indeed any specialized knowledge beyond that of the average intelligent viewer.

Nevertheless, the analysis of actual television programmes in Britain was deeply affected by the politicization of cultural theory. The literary culture in which so many of the 1970s generation of media scholars were steeped had a generally hostile attitude towards the mass media, including the cinema and television. Influential figures such as Raymond Williams and Richard Hoggart struggled to find redeeming features in the culture that was actually consumed by the working classes to whom they owed emotional and political allegiance, while the more aggressively left-wing ideologues regarded television with undisguised contempt, as little more than the opium of the masses. For many students drawn to the media such a sweeping condemnation created acute contradictions, for if television was contemptible, why bother to study it? Some of those who persisted in doing so were motivated by the knowledge that whatever their own judgement, the working classes consumed television in vast quantities. A responsible social analysis could not simply ignore this. And some in the field of cultural studies were held by a fascination with media production which they simply could not repress, even if they found many actual programmes distasteful. Within the increasingly politically conscious field of media studies, such contradictions could not simply be ignored.

One way to deal with this problem was to write exhaustive analyses of television programmes which, even if it were conceded that they displayed some mitigating virtues, were shown to be ultimately the products of bourgeois ideology; in the words of Geoffrey Hurd, 'going beyond what a programme intends to be or say (entertaining, perhaps, realistic certainly), to the more important meanings that are embedded in its structures'.[7] Thus though 'people do find the programmes pleasurable', in police series such as *The Sweeney*

---

6 Edward Buscombe (ed.), *Football on Television* (London: BFI, 1974); Glasgow University Media Group, *Bad News* (London: Routledge & Kegan Paul, 1976); Stephen Heath and Gillian Skirrow, 'Television, a World in Action', *Screen*, 18/2 (1977), 7–59; Roger Silverstone, *The Message of Television: Myth and Narrative in Contemporary Culture* (London: Heinemann Educational Books, 1981).

7 Geoffrey Hurd, 'The Television Presentation of the Police', in Tony Bennett, Susan Boyd-Bowman, Colin Mercer, and Janet Woollacott (eds.), *Popular Television and Film* (London: BFI Publishing, 1981).

or *Z Cars* 'the drama is emptied of its potentially disruptive conflict by divorcing the activity of policing from any class analysis of power relationships within society'. In other words, however much fun the programmes might be, ultimately they are a sell-out.

All too easily this mode of analysis could descend to a kind of point-scoring system, whereby programmes might be awarded consolation marks for any features that were adjudged 'progressive' even if all were ultimately compromised by their accommodation to the overarching ideology of the system.[8] More fundamentally, this approach allowed no way out of the Catch-22 into which Marxist theory delivered television programmes. If, as a Marxist, you rejected the existing state of society on the grounds that it was irredeemably bourgeois, you were bound ultimately to reject all its cultural manifestations on the grounds of their ideological complicity. Thus the only television programmes which could receive the seal of approval were by definition those which would never appear, since bourgeois society, especially in the form of such a politicized entity as the BBC, could not allow such programmes to be made. Of course, the cynical might remark, this was not without a certain advantage, in that one was never called upon to defend any actual example of the good, only to criticize the bad; always an easier task.

Another strategy for reconciling left-wing politics with a continuing interest in media productions involved opening up a space between the ideology embedded within a particular programme (held to be inevitably determined by its origination within an ideological state apparatus such as the BBC, and ultimately from social hegemony itself) and the ideological readings which actual audiences might derive from it, based on their own class positions. A programme might be rescued from its origins by being read against the grain, as it were. If at times this strategy strayed dangerously close to saying a television programme could mean anything you liked, at its most sophisticated it did explore the demonstrable fact that viewers did not all see things the same way.

This strategy, sometimes known as the 'encoding/decoding' approach after an influential article by Stuart Hall,[9] can be seen as originating in two widely differing intellectual sources. On the one hand was the influence of semiotic theory derived from the writings of Roland Barthes and Umberto Eco. Over and beyond the relatively small number of actual semiotic analyses of British television,

8 Let it not be thought I am merely scoring cheap points here, let me admit to doing my fair share of this kind of thing, for example in an essay entitled '*The Sweeney*: Better than Nothing?', *Screen Education*, 20 (1976), 66–9.

9 Stuart Hall, 'Encoding/Decoding', in Stuart Hall, Dorothy Hobson, Andrew Lowe, and Paul Willis (eds.), *Culture, Media, Language* (London: Hutchinson, 1980).

there was at a certain moment in the 1970s a more general influence of this current of thought, which allowed an important advance in the theorization of television. Up until that time it had been difficult for those writing about television to grasp any sense of 'television-ness'. All too often analysis collapsed back into a discussion of what programmes were 'about', what they were 'saying' rather than how they said it. The medium itself was assumed to be transparent, a 'window on the world', to use the tag adopted by the BBC's flagship current affairs programme *Panorama*. Semiotics did at least allow a focus on the specific operations of the television text as opposed to its referential content. More particularly, this centred around the notion of television being essentially an encoding process through which its content was represented in a kind of language. In order to make sense of the programme, audiences had to be able to decode it. But in the process of decoding, a range of meanings might be generated which, though not completely unstable, since anchored in the text itself, were to an extent open to negotiation. Audiences might refuse some of the meanings the text seemed to offer, and construct others.

The second influence was from a quite different source. The Marxist tendency within British media studies has been largely hostile to the tradition deriving from orthodox sociology, especially from the mass communications work done by sociologists in America. This was rejected wholesale on the grounds that it was, to use a particularly pejorative term in the Marxist vocabulary of the time, 'empirical'. This meant that it relied too much on observation and too little on theory. But the so-called 'uses and gratifications' model which emerged from this tradition seemed to offer, from a quite different perspective from that of semiotics, a way of breaking down the monolithic and unidirectional model of media communication in which audiences received and digested a message from on high.[10] 'Uses and gratifications' proposed an interactive model of television viewing in which audiences took from programmes, if perhaps not just what they wanted, then still only that which was consistent with their needs, so finding 'alternative satisfactions in the same televised material'.[11]

This move away from text-centred towards audience-centred readings, while an attractive way out of the straitjacket within which political commitment seemed to have confined television analysis, has been criticized as ultimately an abnegation of the scholar's responsibility to have an opinion about the material he or

10 See Denis McQuail, Jay G. Blumler, and J. R. Brown, 'The Television Audience: A Revised Perspective', in McQuail (ed.), *Sociology of Mass Communications* (Harmondsworth: Penguin, 1972).

11 Ibid. 153.

she analyses, and not simply interrogate others' responses from the vantage of some lofty, disengaged eminence.[12] A political commitment ought surely to imply that one wants to make a difference. The point, as Marx famously said, is not just to understand the world but to change it. In other words, the point of studying British television is, at the end of the day, to see how it can be made better. This would seem to require the scholar to make judgements about what is good or bad television, and not merely to wave it all through on the grounds that people will make their own use of it.

This brings us to the question of 'quality', seemingly one of the most intractable which can be asked about television.[13] British television has been described as 'the least worst television in the world', a tribute, albeit grudging, to its quality.[14] But what exactly is good television? How will we know it when we see it? Surprisingly little attention has been paid to this question. None of the chapters selected for inclusion in this book is principally concerned to invoke aesthetic criteria in respect of the programmes discussed. All, at least by implication, make judgements about them, but they are ultimately judgements about the political and social tendencies the programmes embody, not about their artistic success. The Marxist tradition seems to have left British television criticism ill equipped to approach such matters. Even when there have been debates about aesthetic strategies, as in the lengthy discussions about realism and *Days of Hope*,[15] it was the political effect of such strategies that was in dispute, not their artistic success. Of course Marxists may reply that ultimately art, if not reducible to politics, is inextricably interwoven with them. But this is surely begging the question. How can we explain the evident enjoyment of television by millions of people? Is this not an aesthetic effect, rather than a political one? Isn't it because the programmes are good that people like them?

It is easy enough now, with the collapse of Marxism's political support systems, to see the limits of an approach to television which confines itself to the medium's ideological operations. But at the time this was a bracing corrective to the vacuousness and complicity of much that passed for television criticism. At the very least, it took television seriously, and at its best it had considerable explanatory power, as for example in uncovering much of the

---

12 See Charlotte Brunsdon, 'Television: Aesthetics and Audiences', in Patricia Mellencamp (ed.), *Logics of Television* (London: BFI Publishing, 1990).

13 See Geoff Mulgan (ed.), *The Question of Quality* (London: BFI, 1990).

14 By Milton Shulman in *The Least Worst Television in the World* (London: Barrie & Jenkins, 1973).

15 See Colin McArthur, 'Days of Hope', *Screen*, 16/4 (1975–6), 139–44; Colin MacCabe, '*Days of Hope*: A Response to Colin McArthur', *Screen*, 17/1 (1976), 98–101.

mystification that surrounded television's claims to objectivity and balance in the area of news. If the Marxist tendency within television studies has skewed or stunted our understanding of its cultural accomplishments, it has to be admitted that the almost complete absence of vigorous and intelligent reviewing of television has deprived us of any countervailing force to the overly politicized discourse of academic writing. Cinema studies have benefited from a long-standing, informed, and accomplished tradition of film reviewing. The so-called auteur theory, the major driving force behind the best criticism of American cinema for the past half-century, originated not in academia but in the pages of a monthly reviewing magazine, *Cahiers du Cinéma*. The pantheon of great directors which *Cahiers* established, Hitchcock, Hawks, Sirk, Ray, *et al.*, was able to survive the successive waves of intellectual asteroids which battered against it. However much *Vertigo* or *The Big Sleep* or *Written on the Wind* was 'deconstructed', their appeal to succeeding generations of cineastes, thus established, never wavered.

In contrast, as Mike Poole has shown, television criticism in Britain, when it is not simply a part of television's own promotional activities, is more about showing off the personality of the reviewer than about arriving at any critical insights.[16] With the benefit of hindsight, one can see that the sad decline of Clive James from newspaper critic to celebrity jokester was always inherent in the frivolity of his television writings. The pity is that so many reviewers still clearly feel the need to imitate him. No other model for dealing with the daily output of television, beyond making jokes at its expense, has emerged. As a result, once Marxist theory had undermined the ideological foundations of *Coronation Street* or *The Sweeney* or *Bruce's Big Night*, their critical standing collapsed for want of any other support.

Television is a mature medium; over sixty years have elapsed since the first regular British transmissions. It ought by now to be getting the criticism its many remarkable achievements deserve. Its news and current affairs programmes still by and large earn the trust and respect of their audiences, even in an age as cynical as ours. Its drama has consistently been impressive in its range, seriousness, and inventiveness. There is a wealth of entertainment and enlightenment in the many programmes for niche audiences, ranging from gardening and cookery to archaeology, wildlife, and art. British children's programmes are unsurpassed. And then there is comedy, the glory of British television. To my mind, *Fawlty Towers* is the greatest achievement of British comedy since Dickens.

16 Mike Poole, 'The Cult of the Generalist: British Television Criticism 1936–83', *Screen*, 25/2 (1984), 41–61.

But whereas books on Dickens are many, and yet more appear every year, where is the book that gives *Fawlty Towers* its due?[17]

Of course practitioners of television, who are mostly indifferent, or even hostile, to academic criticism, may well retort that this does not matter very much. If television has, by and large, been a success story without the benefit of a developed critical discourse, then surely it will get along without one in the future. And maybe it will. The relation between criticism and production can only be very indirect, certainly not one of cause and effect. But there are grounds for wondering, all the same. For one thing, the slide towards measuring everything in public life by its cost to the taxpayer now poses a bigger threat to public service broadcasting that anything that has threatened it in the previous three-quarters of a century. Already we are seeing the effects: in the remodelling of the BBC along 'Birtian' principles;[18] in the lower budgets for programme-makers, especially in the 'commercial' sector; in the general 'dumbing-down' of programmes. If this tendency is to be resisted (and the survival of the BBC depends upon that), then the case for public service broadcasting will have to be made, clearly, incisively, and repeatedly, by those who best understand its history, its achievements, and its justification. Not all of those people, and increasingly less of them, are to be found within broadcasting itself. The BBC will need allies, and its political friends will need arguments. Academics can supply them.

Secondly, and this is not unrelated, recent scandals concerning faked scenes in television documentaries and actors impersonating real people on talk shows have revealed the effects of the present intense pressure to achieve ratings. Equally, they have uncovered considerable confusion in television about the difference between truth and reality, about what is at stake in the reconstruction of events, and what it takes to achieve credibility on television. These confusions may have serious consequences; if television loses the confidence of its audience, it will take a long time to get it back. Academics are not the only people to have an understanding of these issues, but they can bring a necessary sense of history (most of these issues have, after all, been debated before). They can also offer a disinterested discussion of the public interest, of why it matters that television is honest and truthful. If television believes it can ignore this, it will ultimately pay the price by losing the interest of the public.

17 Though see Jerry Palmer, *The Logic of the Absurd* (London: BFI Publishing, 1987).

18 Sir John Birt, director-general of the BBC until 1999, has introduced a variety of modern management practices aimed at increasing efficiency.

Part I   There was nothing inevitable about the form which broadcasting took in the United Kingdom. Though its development was profoundly affected by a range of social and political determinations, at the same time a chance combination of personalities and political circumstances had a profound influence on its future. While not wishing to resurrect the great man theory of history, one cannot ignore the role of John Reith. As Michael Tracey makes clear in Chapter 1, the way in which Reith positioned the fledgling BBC during the British General Strike of 1926 was to have far-reaching consequences for the relationship between broadcasting and political power. By exploiting the contradictions in the government's position, its need to exert control over the dissemination of information about the strike, while at the same time not wanting to appear dictatorially to suppress opposition, Reith was able to open up a space within which the BBC could operate with a sufficient degree of independence to guarantee its own credibility. Tracey shows that this decisive piece of manœuvring by Reith was not achieved without an element of casuistry ('Assuming the BBC is for the people, and that the Government is for the people, it follows that the BBC must be for the Government in this crisis too'). Whether this lets the cat out of the bag with regard to the BBC's role within the state, or whether it merely demonstrates that a certain element of *realpolitik* is inevitable in such matters, is an argument which is as much worth having as it ever was. The episode of the General Strike did not define for all time the relation between broadcasting and the British state, since it is in the nature of such vital national concerns that they will be in a state of constant renegotiation. In a number of subsequent national crises (the Second World War, the Suez affair, Northern Ireland, the Falklands–Malvinas War) the independence of the BBC and other broadcasters has been put under severe pressure. But the arguments and strategies deployed by both sides have been remarkably consistent since 1926, and the BBC's relation to the government of the day has remained one which Reith would have recognized, and approved.

   The need to define the boundaries of political independence from the government arises not only from its inherent desirability but also from the fact that within a public service broadcasting system there must be an element of government regulation, not least to secure its finances. Once this intervention by government is accepted, in the interests of maintaining public provision, then it becomes necessary to find structures which will effectively ensure not only that the broadcasters are independent of the government, but that they are seen to be so. However, the achievement of independence is not by any means the only goal of public service broadcasting. Indeed, from one perspective this can be seen as merely the means to an end. Independence is necessary so that a more fundamental purpose may be achieved, that of providing the public with the kind of information which they need in order to discharge to the full their roles as citizens. As Paddy Scannell shows (Chapter 2), the concept of public service is one which has been refined and developed down the years, although John Reith was one of its principal propagators. Its essence is the idea that there are certain public benefits which will accrue if broadcasting is organized along public service lines. Principally these benefits are social, educational, cultural, and civic. If regulated in the public interest, broadcasting can be used to increase social cohesion, improve the general level of cultural consumption, and raise standards of civic responsibility. As Scannell shows, a particular set of policies, such as ensuring equal access to the system, is then required in order for these goals to be achieved. In his conclusion Scannell acknowledges that the concept of public service is under threat. With the increasing intrusion of the 'market' into even such formerly protected areas as health and education provision, in which cost-saving becomes the primary objective and the public good a hoped-for by-product rather than a primary goal of social activity, it is not surprising that there are pressures to subject broadcasting to competition. Whether the kinds of competition that are now emerging can be compatible with the ideals of public service is the major question about the future of television in Britain.

One of the most remarkable things about the broadcasting system is the fact that it has managed to admit so much competition into the system already without the principles of public service being seriously eroded. Asa Briggs shows, in his account of the formation in the mid-1950s of Independent Television, the first commercial television service in Britain (Chapter 3), that it was precisely the fear that a commercial television service would eat away at the BBC's ability to maintain a public service that drove much of the early opposition to commercial television. The long debate about whether such competition should be allowed laid bare the assumptions of the public service ideal. But it also exposed some of its possible drawbacks. Monopoly, even such a high-minded one as the BBC, always tends to breed complacency and arrogance, two characteristics which the BBC has never entirely been free from. Looking back, there is no doubt that the introduction of ITV was an enormous kick up the backside for the BBC, which may have saved it from its own hubris. The ingenuity of those designing the new duopoly lay in devising a structure which permitted competition from advertising-funded television while not opening the door to the unregulated pursuit of the lowest common denominator in audiences.

In her account of the formation and the first ten years of Channel Four (Chapter 4), Sylvia Harvey shows how the public service principle continued to be a major force in the development of new channels, ensuring that even though Channel Four was to be funded by advertising, its specific remit, written into the broadcasting act which established it, was to 'encourage innovation and experiment'. Such goals could only make sense, indeed could only be achievable, in a public service environment where the pursuit of profit was not paramount. The great irony of Channel Four, of course, is that it was established during the heyday of a Conservative government dedicated to rolling back the frontiers of the public sector and replacing it with privately owned services. Not for the first time in British broadcasting there was an historic compromise between ideologically incompatible forces. Channel Four was sold to the Tories on the basis that its small-scale entrepreneurial producers represented a healthy breeze of competition blowing through the previously complacent public service duopoly. It is not the least amusing contradiction of capitalism that in the name of economic *laissez-faire* it permits many flowers to grow which get right up the nose of its more socially conservative supporters. The outrage of many fuddy-duddy free-marketeers when the new network's more explicit programmes aired greatly added to the fun of its opening few months. Whether its role of *enfant terrible* can be sustained now the channel is a teenager is a question which is already being debated.

The establishment of Channel Four may turn out to be the high-water mark of public service broadcasting in Britain. Graham Murdock argues (Chapter 5) that the early 1980s saw not only the birth of the new station but a fundamental shift in government attitudes towards funding the development of television services. In future not only would new channels be financed by commercial means, as Channel Four was, but the public service obligations hitherto imposed on commercial channels would be substantially lifted. At the time when Murdock was writing, the new cable and satellite channels had made only a small impact on the broadcasting audience. But Murdock (and his near-namesake, Rupert Murdoch) was prescient enough to see that it was only a matter of time before these new services, freed from the financial handicap of public service obligations, would mount a serious challenge to the established broadcasters. Simultaneously, and not coincidentally, there has been a concerted attempt both by the Conservative Party and by those in the communications industries with a financial interest at stake to tunnel under the BBC, the rock on which the whole edifice of public service broadcasting was built. As the new service-providers eat into the BBC's audience it ceases to be incontestably the default channel, and so its claims to the licence fee, a tax which falls equally on those who watch its programmes and those who don't, suffers an inevitable loss of legitimacy. At least, that is what some hope for. As Murdock restates it, the argument in favour of public service broadcasting is still compelling; but it will have to be uttered with strength and clarity if it is to resist the constant chipping away of the vested interests and free-market ideologues.

Part II Even more than popular cinema, television programming is ruled by a regime of genres. Programmes which escape generic categorization are very few indeed; perhaps because television production itself is so rigidly divided into generically segmented departments: drama, children's programmes, news and current affairs, etc. But whereas within the cinema one meta-genre, the approximately two-hour-long 'feature' or fiction film, is overwhelmingly dominant, with the most successful genres (the Western, the musical, the crime film, etc.) being variants of that basic format, within television the genres are much more various. Here there are two meta-genres, one based on reality, the other on fiction. The rules and conventions which govern news, for example, are quite different from those governing drama. Within drama itself there are a range of genres: classic serials, soap operas, docu-dramas, etc. And these genres can exist in a variety of formats: the single play, the series, the serial. Thus programmes as different as *Dad's Army*, *Casualty*, and *Cracker*, examples respectively of the sitcom, hospital melodrama, and crime drama, are all technically series; i.e. they have characters who remain much the same week after week, but the narrative of each episode is relatively self-contained.

In the spread of its genres, British television does not differ significantly from other countries. And as in most other countries, it seems, soap opera is, from the perspective of the audience, the queen of genres. Week in, week out it is the soaps that dominate the ratings on British television. For this reason if for no other, this is a good place to begin our selection of readings on programmes. Precisely because they can generate such huge audiences, soap operas are crucial to the economics of present-day television. The story of why and how a new soap opera is commissioned, the thinking that goes into choosing its setting, inventing its cast of characters, deciding its characteristic tone and style, and even its slot in the schedule, can be very revealing of the forces that drive the system. All programmes, of course, are consciously willed into existence. They do not spring ready-made out of the ether. The process of their making, if it can be accessed, is always instructive of both the nature of television and the wider society within which it exists. But because of their strategic position within the schedules, the thinking behind soaps lays bare the most basic truths about the system.

David Buckingham's account of the creation of *EastEnders* (Chapter 6) is an exemplary case-study in the relation between institutions and the programmes they produce. The programme-makers themselves (Julia Smith and Tony Holland) prefer, as programme-makers often do, to preserve the mystique of individual creativity. No one told them what to do: they simply made up the programme out of their own observations and experience. But the testimony of the BBC executives such as Michael Grade and Jonathan Powell tells another story. The BBC needed a programme of exactly this type for both short-term and long-term purposes. In the short term it needed to boost its morale by securing its competitive position in the ratings vis-à-vis the other channels. In the longer term, it needed to maintain its audience share if it was to preserve the legitimacy of its claim to the licence fee. In making *EastEnders* it was thus embarking on a paradoxical but wholly understandable venture: to use public money to make the most popular programme on British television. In doing so it demonstrated an essential truth about the BBC: that only by being very popular can it make programmes for minorities too.

Christine Geraghty's analysis of the theme of community within British soap operas (Chapter 7) looks in the other direction, not inwards to the production base but outwards at the society for whom the programmes are made. The book from which her essay is taken is a comparative study of British and American soaps (or more precisely *Dallas* and *Dynasty*; she leaves to one side American daytime soaps such as *Days of Our Lives* and *As the World Turns*). Geraghty's contention is that British soap opera is especially concerned with constructing a community, a social group to which the characters display a loyalty and which in turn supports them. Unlike most other genres, women play a dominant, even *the* dominant, role. This observable fact about British soaps, and its implications, has attracted considerable numbers of women to write about this genre.[19] A sexual division among television genres is evident enough.

19 Women have dominated academic writing about soaps both in Britain and abroad. See, among others, Richard Dyer, Christine Geraghty, Marion Jordan, Terry Lovell, Richard Paterson, John Stewart, *Coronation Street* (London: BFI Publishing, 1981); Dorothy Hobson, *'Crossroads': The Drama of a Soap Opera* (London: Methuen, 1982); Muriel G. Cantor and Suzanne Pingree, *The Soap Opera* (Beverly Hills, Calif.: Sage, 1983); Ien Ang, *Watching 'Dallas': Soap Opera and the Melodramatic Imagination* (London: Methuen, 1985); Christine Geraghty, *Women and Soap Opera: A Study of Prime Time Soaps* (Cambridge: Polity Press, 1991); Martha Nochimson, *No End to Her: Soap Operas and the Female Subject* (Berkeley: University of California Press, 1992); Mary Ellen Brown, *Soap Opera and Women's Talk: The Pleasure of Resistance* (Thousand Oaks, Calif.: Sage, 1994); Laura Stempel Mumford, *Love and Ideology in the Afternoon* (Bloomington: Indiana University Press, 1995); Jane Feuer, *Seeing through the Eighties* (Durham, NC: Duke University Press; London: BFI Publishing, 1995).

Certain forms of programming, for example sport and to a considerable extent news and current affairs, have a predominantly male address; others, such as certain kinds of drama (besides soaps, the classic serial, say), are more orientated towards women viewers. This division, despite the energetic and doubtless sincere anti-sexism of many academics, seems to reproduce itself in the commentaries on those forms. Few women write about the news or sports; few men have written about soaps.[20] David Buckingham is of course an exception; but it is perhaps not accidental that his study of *EastEnders* is as much concerned with the institutions of broadcasting as it is with the programme *per se*, thus illustrating a further aspect of this sexual division: that on the whole few women have concerned themselves with questions of television economics, structures, and policy.[21]

It might be supposed that if any genre were male-orientated it would be crime fiction. But whereas in the cinema crime movies have been overwhelmingly the domain of the male (the *femme fatale* of *film noir* notwithstanding), in television crime there are important distinctions to be made, as Charlotte Brunsdon shows (Chapter 8). In particular, she contends that all three of the programmes she deals with in detail, *Inspector Morse*, *Prime Suspect*, and *Between the Lines*, can be seen as responding to issues of sexuality as they cohere around the question of 'equal opportunities'. The British television audience is certainly not unique in its taste for crime programmes; indeed, many of the most popular ones on British television have been imported from abroad, especially from America. But, as Brunsdon shows, British crime series reveal not just the enduring popularity of crime fiction as a source of entertainment (something that has been a feature of popular culture for a hundred years). The programmes also demand to be read symptomatically, focusing as they do a whole variety of current issues and problems. Perhaps because of its highly collectivized manner of production, television, more than other forms of popular culture, seems particularly absorbent of communal anxieties. One may speculate too that the public service ethos encourages some programme-makers to be socially responsive, and responsible.

But if some drama producers and writers have antennae peculiarly attuned to what is happening in the world outside, a contrary

20 Notable exceptions are Robert C. Allen, *Speaking of Soap Operas* (Chapel Hill: University of North Carolina Press, 1985); Allen's edited collection *To Be Continued . . . Soap Operas around the World* (New York: Routledge, 1995) contains several essays by women; John Tulloch and Albert Moran, *'A Country Practice': Quality Soap* (Sydney: Currency Press, 1986). And, vice versa, Gillian Skirrow, in Stephen Heath and Skirrow, 'Television, a World in Action', and Paula Skidmore, 'Telling Tales: Media Power, Ideology and the Reporting of Child Sexual Abuse in Britain', in David Kidd-Hewitt and Richard Osborne (eds.), *Crime and the Media: The Postmodern Spectacle* (London: Pluto, 1995).

21 There are a few exceptions: Sylvia Harvey, as instanced in Ch. 4 of this volume; see also Caroline Heller, *Broadcasting and Accountability* (London: BFI, 1978).

movement is also a feature of contemporary television, in which programmes ostensibly concerned with actuality ape many of the characteristics of drama. The formerly rigid distinction between those genres which are orientated towards fiction and entertainment and those which, attempting to represent the real, hold to a regime of truth and objectivity is increasingly being eroded, especially by the relentless pressure of the ratings, itself a production of the move towards increased competition, lighter regulation, and a possible challenge to the public service principle itself. Annette Hill describes a new breed of programmes which, essentially, make entertainment out of real-life emergencies, often involving crime (Chapter 9). Such programmes appear to operate on a dual axis with regard to the 'reality effect'. On the one hand, they seek to heighten audience involvement by deploying the full range of techniques traditionally associated with news and documentary: hand-held cameras, direct sound, location shooting, and so forth. Because the audience believes what they are seeing is true, its interest is reinforced by such techniques and made more immediate. On the other hand, the programmes borrow from fiction the techniques of dramatic construction: actors, scripted dialogue, studio lighting. Reality can be confused and mundane; such techniques can shape it and so make it more graspable. But once the line is crossed in reconstructing reality, the audience has only the guarantee of the broadcasting authorities that truth is still paramount. Some recent well-publicized cases in which the makers of documentaries are alleged to have tampered with and even concocted evidence shows that retaining the trust of the audience will require vigilance.

The genre in which truth is most crucially at stake is news. The capacity to deliver reliable and responsible news and current affairs programmes is surely at the heart of public service television in its role as the stimulator of good citizenship. On the whole, British television has been remarkably successful in retaining the trust of its viewers, certainly in comparison with the credibility of newspapers. This despite the fact that television news has received intense scrutiny from academics over the past thirty years, during which concepts such as 'objectivity', 'balance', and 'agenda-setting' have been exhaustively interrogated, and news programmes and programmer-makers put under the microscope.[22] The highly

---

22 Richard Collins, *Television News* (London: BFI, 1976); Glasgow University Media Group, *Bad News* (London: Routledge & Kegan Paul, 1976); *More Bad News* (London: Routledge & Kegan Paul, 1980); *Really Bad News* (London: Writers and Readers, 1982); *War and Peace News* (London: Open University, 1985); Stan Cohen and Jock Young (eds.), *The Manufacture of News: Social Problems, Deviance and the Mass Media* (London: Constable, 1973; rev. 1981); Philip Schlesinger, *Putting 'Reality' Together: BBC News* (London: Constable, 1978); John Hartley, *Understanding News* (London: Methuen, 1982); Brian McNair, *News and Journalism in the UK* (London: Routledge, 1994).

politicized nature of much that has been written about news has thrown into relief some awkward questions about the relationship between television and government, or more generally between television and the state. But at times it has threatened to throw the baby out with the bathwater. As academic critics relentlessly demonstrated, balance and objectivity could never be absolute. Who decides where to place the fulcrum which sustains the balance? From which point of view does a report appear objective? The intrusion of postmodernist notions, undermining the prestige of master-narratives, emphasizing instead heterogeneity and cultural relativism, seemed to loosen further the mooring ropes of news as the flagship of broadcasting organizations. John Eldridge's chapter (10) is an astute and salutary reminder that even if television news has been forced to concede some of the high ground of its authority, it can still regroup around the redoubt of accuracy.

Like any other kind of programming, television news has been forced to take account of the competition for audiences. However much the BBC may foster its own self-image as the repository of the eternal verities ('Nation shall speak truth unto nation', as it says at Broadcasting House), it cannot ignore the fact that its newsreaders are personalities whose popularity affects the ratings. News, like the rest of television, appears increasingly subject to the forces that make packaging a priority over content, and star quality is perhaps the most available way of layering some gloss over the show. Andy Medhurst's chapter on Gilbert Harding (Chapter 11) is a reminder that the television personality is by no means a recent invention. In taking us back to the barely recoverable era of the 1950s, he traces the rise of a career that evokes many uncomfortable echoes of more recent times. Famous mainly for being famous, Harding's was the prototype for many contemporary careers, not least in its small tragedies. The culture of celebrity is now so deeply embedded in our sense of what television is that it is hard to imagine it any other way. And perhaps it never was any other way. But the story of Gilbert Harding shows a key moment in this formation.

Medhurst's chapter is also exemplary in its attempt to excavate television history. It has been often observed that television, though in many ways obsessed with history, has little sense of its own past. Until recently it paid little heed to the preservation of programmes once transmitted, with the result that tapes of such classics of British comedy as *Dad's Army*, *Not Only But Also*, and *Steptoe and Son* were wiped.[23] In this respect television was merely following the practice of the cinema, which has had a similarly feckless attitude to its achievements. And, as with the cinema, this institutional dis-

23 See Steve Bryant, *The Television Heritage* (London: BFI Publishing, 1990).

regard for the past has found its echo in the comparative lack of any sustained effort by academics to retrieve the history of the medium. A quarter of a century ago the authoritative British film journal *Screen* could remonstrate that 'The study of the history of the American film industry has scarcely begun.'[24] Today the lack of an adequate history of Hollywood has been amply filled, with a spate of solidly researched and intellectually sophisticated accounts. But writing the history of British television still has a long way to go. Apart from the weighty tomes dealing with the BBC and ITV there is little; as yet, no comprehensive histories of television news, or documentary, or sport, or comedy.

Without doubt one of the foremost achievements of British television has been its drama. The roll-call of outstanding work is a long one, which stands comparison with that in the other arts in post-war Britain. Writers such as Alun Owen, David Mercer, John McGrath, Trevor Griffiths, Dennis Potter; producers such as Sydney Newman, Tony Garnett, Kenith Trodd; directors such as Ken Loach, Alan Clarke, Mike Leigh, are major figures in our culture. This history too has yet to be written,[25] but a thread which runs through much of what has so far been said about this tradition is the lament for the decline of the single play. A television form that had a brief bright flowering in American television in the 1950s, never to bloom again on that side of the Atlantic, it became within British television a kind of talisman, a test by which to measure the moral fibre of British television institutions and their supposed decline. In fact, of course, drama has always flourished in a variety of contexts, and virtually all the names listed above have worked in series, even serial, formats, and many have produced not only original writing for television but adaptations too. Robin Nelson's chapter (12) comes from a book which not only takes seriously the drama which has existed outside the single-play format but assesses it in relation to such American productions as *Hill Street Blues* and *Twin Peaks*, not always to the advantage of the British productions. The section reprinted here, on *Oranges Are Not the Only Fruit* and *Middlemarch*,

---

24 Edward Buscombe, 'Notes on Columbia Pictures Corporation, 1926–41', *Screen*, 16/3 (1975), 65–83: 83.

25 Though a start has been made by George Brandt (ed.), *British Television Drama* (Cambridge: Cambridge University Press, 1981); Mike Poole and John Wyver, *Powerplays: Trevor Griffiths in Television* (London: BFI Publishing, 1984); John Caughie, 'Before the Golden Age: Early Television Drama', in John Corner (ed.), *Popular Television in Britain: Studies in Cultural History* (London: BFI, 1991); George Brandt (ed.), *British Television Drama in the 1980s* (Cambridge: Cambridge University Press, 1993); John Cook, *Dennis Potter: A Life on Screen* (Manchester: Manchester University Press, rev. edn. 1998); W. Stephen Gilbert, *Fight and Kick and Bite: The Life and Work of Dennis Potter* (London: Hodder & Stoughton, 1995); Sean Day-Lewis, *Talk of Drama: Views of the Television Dramatist Now and Then* (Luton: University of Luton Press, 1998); Humphrey Carpenter, *Dennis Potter: A Biography* (London: Faber & Faber, 1998).

makes its arguments about the aesthetics of drama through a comparison with *X-Files* (though for reasons of space the comments on the American series have been omitted). In reviving the issue of realism, Nelson manages to move things beyond the point at which they seemed to have got stuck during the debate about *Days of Hope* in the 1970s. He also shows that so-called 'heritage' drama, period plays based upon Britain's literary heritage, often with one eye on the export market, need not necessarily lack relevance to contemporary society.

Sitcom too is a form of drama; perhaps the most difficult form of all, and certainly the one on which the audience makes the most implacable demands. Other kinds of drama can be judged by a variety of criteria; they may move, excite, inform, all to a greater or lesser degree, and still be judged a success. But if a sitcom does not make us laugh, it is a flop. Yet if writing sitcom is demanding, so is writing about it. Trying to make the audience laugh is perhaps not much more difficult than trying to explain why it laughs. In the course of their book *Popular Film and Television Comedy*, Steve Neale and Frank Krutnik do in fact make a noble effort to explain how and why humour works. But in their section dealing with one of the classics of British sitcom, *Steptoe and Son* (Chapter 13), they are more concerned with situating the programme in its social context. It's often been observed that television is above all a domestic medium. Not only is it by and large consumed within the home; to a very great extent it constructs its viewers as domestic subjects, addressing them especially in their roles of private rather than public individuals, and particularly in their position as members of a family. Sitcom is therefore perhaps the television genre *par excellence*, since almost invariably the 'situation' upon which the drama is founded is that of a family or quasi-family, even if often a highly dysfunctional one. The relationship between parent and child is worked out in *Steptoe* with the kind of excruciating honesty that only laughter can deal with. Neale and Krutnik also analyse the way in which the show deals with that other great obsession of the British sitcom, the class system. They suggest that the very structure of the sitcom, in which, whatever disruptions may occur during the weekly episode, the 'situation' will always return to 'normal' by the end, is inherently a conservative one, in which the possibilities of individual development are inevitably blocked. The family, and the British nation (which George Orwell memorably described as a family with the wrong members in control), is essentially unchanging, and unchangeable. Yet if each sitcom depends structurally on stasis, this does not mean that there cannot be development from one sitcom to another. There are clearly very different things going on in *Absolutely Fabulous*, not least in relation to the family (who are the children and who are the adults?), from what transpires in *Steptoe*.

Whatever the truth of this, it is evident that television itself is changing fast. Nowhere is this more evident than in the area of sport. For years the authorities who govern British sport kept television at arm's length, in the belief that if audiences were allowed too much access, the appetite would sicken and so die. It was only in the 1990s that television managed to convince the guardians of football that their product had much in common with Shakespeare's Cleopatra, who 'makes hungry where most she satisfies'. The more sport the viewers have been given, the more they appear to want; and, more importantly, the more they will pay for it. It is sport that is the motor that has driven the onward movement of satellite and cable channels, whose exclusive deals for the transmission of cricket, rugby, boxing, and especially football have transformed the terrain of British broadcasting. Despite desperate attempts to shore up the bulwarks of public service by creating a list of protected events which may not be exclusively sold to pay-channels, the tide of sport-driven privatized services is rising ever higher. The threat to the entire concept of public service broadcasting is serious: not only are these new channels eating away at the audiences, both of the BBC and of the regulated terrestrial commercial channels, threatening their finances either through undermining the case for the licence fee or by taking away advertisers; the claim of the BBC in particular to be the true national broadcaster will suffer severe damage if it can no longer deliver to its audience such quintessentially national events as the Cup Final, Wimbledon, or the Test matches.

These matters have already been much discussed, and as the pressure mounts on majority broadcasters more will be said.[26] Garry Whannel provides a further dimension to our understanding of the strategic role of sport within the television schedules (Chapter 14). Increasingly, the satisfactions and indeed the values of sport have spread throughout television in general, providing material and models for quiz shows, game shows, and entertainment of all kinds. Just as the new breed of crime reconstructions blur the dividing-line between fact and fiction genres, so new programmes such as *Gladiators* and *Fantasy League Football* run together showbiz and the aggressively masculine ethos of strenuous competition which derives from sport. At one level, Whannel shows, such programmes can be viewed as instances of the postmodern, in their play with the codes and conventions of television itself; at another they are

26 See e.g. Steven Barnett, *Games and Sets: The Changing Face of Sport on Television* (London: BFI Publishing, 1990); Garry Whannel, *Fields in Vision: Television Sport and Cultural Transformation* (London: Routledge, 1993).

further evidence that all television aspires towards the culture of celebrity. But, as Whannel argues, perhaps most importantly of all these shows reveal some of the stress points in our society, especially the backlash against the perceived rise of feminism. Though sport itself continues to be one of the most politically backward parts of our society, sport on television cannot be indifferent to the forces of change. Even if its response is often to dig itself in deeper, it finds the need to overlay itself with the protective mantle of blokeish good humour.

With the last reading we end back where we started, with general institutional questions, and a reminder that, despite its often parochial concerns, its long-standing traditions of self-sufficiency, leading at times to insularity, British television is increasingly connected to the world market. In certain parts of the world, especially Canada and Australasia, the BBC has long enjoyed a special place within local schedules. If this secure niche is now under pressure in an ever more competitive environment, Tom O'Regan reminds us (Chapter 15) that British television still retains the immense advantage of being made in English, the dominant language of cultural exchange. British television producers are also adapting both to financial constraints at home and to new opportunities abroad by exploring a variety of forms of co-production. This can be a risky strategy, especially for the BBC. In such deals there is always a price to pay; as in any marriage, there will be a more or less subtle adjustment by each to the sensibilities of the other partner. But any dilution of the 'Britishness' of the BBC's programme content will be quickly seized upon, both by its friends intent on defending the principle of public service, and by its enemies as evidence that the BBC is now a commercial broadcaster like any other and should be treated as such, forced to make its way on a strictly business basis without the protection of the licence fee. Negotiating a space in which the necessary co-production monies can be found without compromising its role as the bastion of the British public service sector will be a tricky exercise; but then, the BBC has spent its life performing a series of balancing acts.

I
Histories, Structures, Economics

1

The BBC and the General Strike: May 1926

Michael Tracey

[Reith] put his native guile to good use at the time of the General Strike of 1926, when he had to walk as delicately as Agag between asserting the independence of the BBC too strongly (and perhaps losing it for ever) and surrendering it on the spot. The compromises which he then accepted made it possible for his successors to be much more firm and uncompromising when they faced the anger of governments about the BBC's treatment of such crises as Suez 16 years ago and Northern Ireland today.

(Greene 1972)

In time of national crisis the Government, as it did during the Strike, rightly takes over the conduct of broadcasting.

(*Morning Post*, 26 May 1926)

THE HISTORICAL TREATMENT of the concept of 'impartiality'—its initial formulation and subsequent utilization—provides an insight into the precise meaning the social environment can have for the process of production. At no time was this more apparent than in the period of the General Strike in May 1926. At that time the fledgling British Broadcasting Company and its dominant and irascible general manager, John Reith, made it clear to parliamentarians that their interpretation of 'impartiality' in 'controversial' broadcasting would not offend the established political orders.

Times of severe political crises—the General Strike, Suez, Northern Ireland after 1969—have created considerable problems for broadcasting in defining its position *vis-à-vis* the crisis, and have thrown into sharp relief the nature of the relationship with the state

First published in Michael Tracey, *The Production of Political Television* (London: Routledge & Kegan Paul, 1977), 142–56.

(Smith 1972; Hill 1974). The previous chapters indicated the continued importance, and difficulties of interpretation, of impartiality in the production activities of programme-makers. As will become apparent from the present discussion, the precise nature and elements of the concept of 'impartial broadcasting' were argued over and established in the very earliest days of broadcasting, but the importance for this discussion was the way in which the precise meaning of impartiality was clarified by the looming presence of Baldwin's government during the days of the strike—notably in the shape of Churchill.[1]

When the British Broadcasting Company was formed in 1922, one of the main concerns was the possible danger of 'controversial broadcasting', though there is actually no specific reference to 'controversy' or to 'controversial broadcasting' in the original licence of January 1923. There is, in fact, a good deal of obscurity about the veto on controversial broadcasts and on the attitudes of different governments to it during the early years, and yet it was always assumed to exist during the period leading up to the General Strike of 1926. The director of telecommunications of the Post Office told the Ullswater Committee in 1935 that from 1922 onwards a general veto had been imposed by the Cabinet on all subjects of political and religious controversy (BP5). Despite protestations to the contrary by the postmaster-general (PMG) in the period 1923–6, the BBC was wise to act with circumspection, even though, as far as can be detected, there were no specific instructions on the matter: 'foolishness would be followed by withdrawal of the Licence' (Briggs 1961: 170). The BBC's attitude was that a 'broadcasting service which contained no reference to politics could not claim to be a balanced service, or an informative or educative one'.

Equally difficult in this period before the strike was the question of news broadcasting. The licence granted to the BBC on 18 January 1923 included a clause which said that the BBC should not broadcast any news or information except that obtained and paid for from the news agencies (Briggs 1961: 133). It was the major newspaper interests in the shape of the Newspaper Proprietors' Association which were to be the severest baulk to the BBC's developing any kind of news organization. From the beginning of the negotiations with the companies which were eventually to form the BBC, the PMG had made it perfectly clear that the press interest should in no way be alienated (Briggs 1961) or financially embarrassed by the new organization. Despite protracted negotiations during the 1923–6 period,

---

1 The following account is based mainly on the collection of General Strike files which the BBC keeps at its Written Archives Centre (WAC) at Reading, and on a number of secondary sources. The main file concerned at the archives is WAC 45567, News Arrangements.

and despite one or two minor concessions by the press interests (see Briggs 1961: 263), it was possible for Briggs (1961: 267) to sum up the situation by saying that 'throughout the whole period when the BBC was a company . . . it was subject to such severe restrictions on the broadcasting of news and outside events that the ordinary listener had only the remotest idea of what the shape of future broadcasting would be'.

The subject of controversial broadcasting was first brought to a head in April 1923, when a question was raised in the House concerning a broadcast by the editor of *Building News* in which he had asked that a threatened building strike be called off, appealing to the parties involved to accept arbitration. In reply to the concerned questions of various Labour MPs, the PMG, Sir William Joynson-Hicks, stated: 'I think it is undesirable that the broadcasting services should be used for the dissemination of speeches on controversial matters, and I have had the attention of the BBC called to the incident' (quoted in BP5)—something which Reith interpreted as a direct order. That year saw several attempts by the BBC to have controversial programmes broadcast: for example, a request was made for the BBC to be allowed to broadcast the king's speech at the opening of Parliament and for the leaders of the three main parties to broadcast during the forthcoming election. Both requests were refused by the PMG.

The restrictions imposed on broadcasting in the years up to the General Strike were severe and wide-ranging, news, for example, effectively being limited to a 7 p.m. bulletin (when all the papers were deemed to have been sold) with material provided by the news agencies.[2] The restrictions reflected both the economic anxieties of the newspaper publishers and the political anxieties of the government. As Briggs (1961: 267) puts it: 'the Derby and political speeches alike were taboo'. The BBC was pressed on both sides by the newspaper owners and the politicians, and it was in this context of a badly underdeveloped news service that the BBC found itself in the May of 1926 the major national source of news.

Prior to that, however, there were a number of events which were to highlight the position of the BBC: a sense of growing confidence in some circles that the BBC could to an extent be trusted politically even though it still could not be allowed to infringe the economic interests of the newspaper and news agency owners. In 1923 a committee of inquiry had been set up by the government under the

---

2 News bulletins could not broadcast before 7 p.m. but there was no restriction to one bulletin each day. The National Programme broadcast two news bulletins each evening, one at 7 p.m. and one at 10 or 10.30 p.m.

chairmanship of Sir Frederick Sykes to examine all the issues of finance, organization, and control which remained unresolved. It reported on the question of controversial broadcasting and declared that the BBC should be allowed to broadcast on controversial affairs, particularly since there was really no subject on which controversy would not arise at some point.[3]

Following the committee report, a broadcasting board was established to 'advise the Postmaster-General on matters connected with broadcasting' (Briggs 1961: 247), and at the meeting of 14 May 1924 the question of the broadcasting of speeches on controversial matters was raised. Reith suggested that the exclusion of such matters tended to reduce the interest and value of broadcasting (BP5). He proposed that the BBC should be allowed to broadcast speeches by members of each of the three main parties during important debates in the House or at the time of elections. The choice of the speakers was to be entirely a matter for the parties. Other members of the board argued that this would create difficulties in that there would be too many requests to broadcast and that it would be difficult to know what should and should not be broadcast, impartiality would be difficult to sustain, and the great danger would be the misuse of broadcasting by the party in power. In June 1924 the board reported to the PMG, Vernon Hartshorn, that while the restrictions on political speeches should be retained, in other areas previously thought of as 'controversial' a more liberal attitude should be adopted (BP5).

The initial breach had been made, then, in the restrictions on content, but at the same time the basic elements of the whole discussion about political broadcasting were also being developed. What I want to suggest is that the essence of the restrictive concern was rooted in the fact that no one quite understood how things would work out in practice; they were politically unsure as to the consequences of granting permission to the BBC for 'controversial broadcasting', though it has to be added that among most MPs there was a remarkable lack of concern with the new medium (Briggs 1961: 350–1).

In 1924 Reith entered the fray once more by seeking permission to broadcast a debate between the party leaders. Permission was not forthcoming, although Ramsay MacDonald, Baldwin, and Asquith did, in fact, broadcast during the election of October 1924. In 1925 the government, as intransigent as ever, employed the excuse that, as the Crawford Committee was to consider the whole issue, the making of a premature decision would be wrong. The BBC's

---

3 Sykes Committee, *Broadcasting Committee Report*, Cmd. 1951 (London: HMSO, 1923).

memorandum to the committee declared in passionate terms[4] that the restrictions on talks and political broadcasts be reduced. The memorandum argued that the BBC should be allowed to broadcast 'controversial matters' always under the 'adequate safeguards for impartiality' and added that 'naturally there are certain subjects which the broadcasting authority would not desire to handle at all, but it is not difficult to draw the line'.

Apart from the central argument of Reith that the BBC should be transformed from a commercially based enterprise to a publicly owned body (Briggs 1961: 331–2), he was pressing for an expanded news service and greater freedom to cover controversial matters, and it was on these matters that the bulk of the opposition to the BBC rested. When the Crawford Committee reported on 5 March 1926, its major recommendation was that the BBC become a public corporation, but it also recommended that there be a 'moderate amount of controversial matter'.[5] The attitude in Parliament to 'controversial broadcasting' was that 'each "side" complained of the advantage given to the other, and both parties had to be reassured by the PMG (with only a few members expressing uneasiness) that all kinds of political broadcasting were being prohibited' (Briggs 1961: 352).[6] On 14 July 1926 the PMG announced that the main recommendations of Crawford were being accepted by the government. He was later to add, on 15 November 1926, in response to the expressed anxieties of many MPs, that 'he had instructed the Corporation that, when it began its operations, it was not to broadcast its own opinions on matters of public policy nor was it to broadcast on matters of political, industrial, or religious controversy' (Briggs 1961: 359). To soothe the disappointed Reith some of the restrictions on news programming were removed. In the debate of 15 November on the BBC's new charter, Lord Wolmer, the assistant PMG, declared: 'I want to make this service not a Department of State, and still less a creature of the Executive, but as far as is consistent with ministerial responsibility, I wish to create an independent body of trustees operating the service in the interests of the public as a whole' (Briggs 1961: 360). That, however, was said in November 1926, nine months after the publication of the Crawford Report. In the meantime the BBC had been through the events of May. It is perhaps important to note that the inhibitions imposed on the broadcasting of political material seem to have derived not from a concept

---

4 For example, it referred to 'the chains which now impede or nullify progress' in controversial broadcasting.

5 *Report of the Broadcasting Committee*, Cmd. 2599 (London: HMSO, 1925), 14–15, para (o)

6 The statement to this effect was made in the Commons on 22 Mar. 1926.

of the possible threat this would pose to state power but rather from the touchy sensibilities of politicians concerning party advantage. It would be made clear, however, during the period 3–12 May that the central question in crises of that order would be the relationship of the BBC to the state and therefore to the political and moral order which that structure was deemed to represent. The BBC entered these events with a severely limited scope in what it could do, no experience of the news process, and no proper news organization. Nevertheless, Reith saw the strike as a 'stupendous opportunity to show what broadcasting could do in an emergency' (Reith 1963).

Developments were afoot not only in the legislation of broadcasting; drastic developments were also taking place in the economics of mining, which were to have almost as significant an effect on broadcasting as they were on the mining industry. From 1924 Britain had been governed by Baldwin's Conservative government. In the face of mounting economic difficulty the government had revalued the pound sterling. The coal industry had been particularly hard-hit by this, since the increase in the value of sterling increased the price of exports, unless the producer was willing deliberately to cut the price of his goods. Since the cost of labour was such a large part of the production of coal, the only way the owners saw of cutting prices was by reducing the wage bill and increasing the number of hours spent earning the smaller wage (Symons 1957; Lloyd 1970). On 31 July 1925 a commission had been established under the chairmanship of Sir Herbert Samuel which reported on 11 March 1926. The report satisfied neither the owners nor the miners. In April 1926 negotiations within the industry broke down completely and led to renewed calls for the general council of the Trades Union Congress (TUC) to organize a general strike. During that month and into May the government and the TUC were locked in negotiations over the dispute, but when, on 1 May, the government subsidy which had underpinned the miners' wages ended, the strike effectively began. The actual spark or signal that the General Strike was on was provided by the printers of the *Daily Mail*, who, on the evening of 2–3 May, refused to print an anti-strike editorial. On hearing the news in the early hours of 3 May, Reith sent a message to the prime minister asking for a personal message to the people; 'It came quickly: "Keep steady; remember that peace on earth comes to men of goodwill" ' (Reith 1963).

Though the collapse of the newspapers was by no means as total as is sometimes imagined, particularly in the provinces where many papers operated almost as normal (Symons 1957), the BBC became overnight the single most important source of national news. On 3 May Reith arranged with the Home Office that BBC property would be protected, and got authorization from Davidson[7] for bulletins to be broadcast at any time;[8] he also arranged with the news agencies that for the duration of the emergency copyright could be suspended. Reith also arranged for all official news to come from the headquarters of the chief civil commissioner and from the ten government centres around the country. He states: 'I had the Chief Civil Commissioner and the Home Secretary and Davidson agree that the BBC should not be commandeered, meaning that it or I should be trusted to do what was right' (Reith 1963). Reith's self-assurance that he could do what was right was aided by his overall view of the pros and cons of the strike. Symons (1957) states:

> Four years earlier he had written to Clynes, feeling that in the Labour Party there was most chance of finding the essence of his own beliefs about a practical application of Christian principle to national and international affairs. But although, like many other liberals, he might have supported the miners against the coal owners, he was certainly not prepared to support the strikers against the government.

Reith's position was in tune with that of Baldwin: the strike was a threat to constitutional government and therefore had to be defeated.

A three-shift system of BBC personnel was organized so that the newsroom, receiving most of its information from Reuters and from Davidson's office at the Admiralty, was manned round the clock. The real question facing the BBC was not, however, whether it could function adequately during the strike but rather on whose side it would function. The position adopted was that it was 'impartial' and 'objective'. For example, in the first news bulletin on 4 May, having pointed to the difficulties which people would experience in turning from newspapers to the limited radio bulletin, the bulletin declared:

> The BBC fully realize the gravity of its responsibility to all sections of the public and will do its best to discharge it in the

---

7 J. C. C. Davidson, financial secretary to the Admiralty, appointed deputy chief commissioner, who not only liaised with Reith to oversee the BBC's output but also had overall editorial control of the *British Gazette*, Churchill's propaganda sheet. He could and did overrule Churchill (James 1969; Pelling 1974).

8 They were in fact broadcast at 10 a.m. and 1, 4, 7, and 9.30 p.m. It is of course difficult to capture the essence of what the programmes were like, but a report in *The Times* of 19 May 1926 gives some indication: 'The bulletin began with special messages, followed by comments on the state of things, made by the BBC and official communications from government departments, after which a summary of the general situation of the country was broadcast, beginning with news from the Home Office and Civil Commissioners, then that received from agencies and winding up with information received by their own means. The second part of the bulletin consisted of a précis of the daily measures taken by Parliament, and news from home and abroad.'

most impartial spirit that circumstances permit. In the last issue of the newspapers, allusion is principally made to the possibility of wholesale oscillations.[9] As to that we express no opinion, but we would ask the public to take as serious a view as we do ourselves of the necessity of plain objective news being audible to everybody. . . . We shall do our best to maintain our tradition of fairness, and we ask for fair play in return.[10]

The question of the actual status and role of the BBC was, however, posed in the sharpest possible form and illuminates the details of the relationship with the state. Constitutionally the BBC's position was quite clear. Not only could the minister order the BBC to broadcast particular messages; he could, if he so desired, take over the running of the organization. There was a continuous debate within the Cabinet as to whether they should in fact commandeer the BBC for the duration of the strike, Churchill, then chancellor of the exchequer, being the main advocate of such a move, Baldwin arguing that this would not be necessary. Reith first heard of Churchill's desire to take over the company on 5 May, and on 6 May he sought a clarification from Baldwin, who agreed to 'leave the BBC with maximum autonomy and independence' (Reith 1963). He might well leave the affairs of the BBC in the capable hands of Reith since the clarity with which Reith and his senior personnel saw their position *vis-à-vis* the government is vividly portrayed in the internal documents of the period. A memo dated 6 May was entitled 'Suggestions for the Policy of the Broadcasting Service during the Emergency'.[11] It states that the BBC has a 'duty' to broadcast anything that the civil commissioners or the government require, that they should 'maintain an objective news service', and that 'we should make a particular point of emphasizing statements calculated to diminish the spirit of violence and hostility'. The memorandum made three main points: that consultations should be the basis for the relationship between the government and the BBC; that if the BBC were overtly partisan then the strikers could cripple

---

9 Deliberate technical interference with radio reception.

10 Transcripts of radio broadcasts, BBC Archives. In this situation the BBC, which had previously been at the mercy of the newspapers, was now the benevolent bestower of copy. On 2 May the BBC received a typical request from Northumberland and Berwickshire Newspapers Ltd., which asked: 'In view of the pending strike of the Printing Trade and the non-publication of newspapers, will you please inform us per return by wire if we have permission to publicly broadcast all items of news broadcast by the BBC stations. We understand that it is with a view to suppressing propaganda as news that the TUC has taken this step and no doubt it will prove of great use to the country if such permission is granted.' Permission was granted.

11 WAC 45567, News Arrangements. Both Briggs (1961: 362) and Boyle (1972: 193) attribute this memo to Reith. The actual memo is in fact signed by Lord Gainford, chairman of the BBC.

the service; and that the BBC had a 'positive' conciliatory role to play (Briggs 1961: 362–3). It is ridiculous to suggest that the BBC had no opinions in the strike, apart from the obvious point that the very notion of conciliation is itself an opinion. The 6 May memo declared that they should

> try to convey to the minds of the people generally that the prolongation of the general stoppage is the one sure process calculated to reduce wages and the standards of living which it is the avowed endeavour of the Trade Unions to maintain and improve; and to try to make it clear that the sooner the General Strike is satisfactorily terminated the better for wage earners in all parts of the country.

The memo concluded with the famous argument that:

> As the Government are sure that they are right both on the facts of the dispute and on the constitutional issues, any steps which we may take to communicate the truth dispassionately should be to the advantage of the Government.

Similar sentiments were echoed in a 'Note for Mr. Davidson: The BBC and the emergency'.[12] In this Reith argues that the value and virtue of the BBC lay in its being seen to be 'independent' from the government and continues: 'Assuming the BBC is for the people, and that the Government is for the people, it follows that the BBC must be for the Government in this crisis too.' The rest of the memo was of the same order as the 6 May memo, and it was clearly the case that the overall policy, albeit in a sophisticated and oblique manner, was at one with Baldwin's, though its general tone may have been slightly more conciliatory than the prime minister's. The position was made even clearer in the 'Managing Director's Report to the Board of Directors' dated 18 May. In this Reith declared:

> Under the Emergency Regulations Act the Government could have commandeered the BBC, but definite action of this kind was actually not necessary since a clause in our Licence made it obligatory on us to broadcast official announcements at any time. They could therefore use us to a considerable extent without definitely commandeering.

He continues:

> There could be no question about our supporting the Government generally, particularly since the General Strike had been declared illegal. . . . We could not therefore permit anything which was contrary to the spirit of that judgement, which might

---

12 WAC 45566, General Strike. Briggs dates this 6 May, whereas it is in fact dated 8 May.

have prolonged or sought to justify the strike, but we were able to give authentic impartial news of the situation throughout. Apart from the clause in our Licence the broadcasting of official communiques would have been demanded irrespective of the political complexions of the Government.[13]

This was similar in content and tone to a memo Reith sent to senior members of his staff on 15 May 1926.[14] Reith's fervent acceptance of the 'illegality' ruling was rather hasty since it was subsequently shown that the precise validity of the ruling was in some doubt. At this stage Reith felt that the BBC's position was one of being 'neither commandeered nor free' but was adamant that the BBC could do nothing which would support the strike (Reith 1963).

By 6 May the connection between the BBC and the government had become a physical one in the sense that Reith and other staff, at Davidson's request, moved into the Admiralty building on 4 May. Gladstone Murray, deputy managing director of the BBC, shared an office with Captain Gordon Munro, one of the assistants to Davidson, where together they drafted news bulletins (James 1969: 246).

What one can see in these internal documents is Reith-as-the-BBC defining quite clearly what he understands to be the bounds of legitimate political activity within which the impartiality of the BBC must fit. Given competing definitions of the situation offered by the strikers and the state, the Reithian logic was to acknowledge the latter. The rationale behind that logic derived partly from the perilous position of the BBC and partly from a genuine attachment by Reith and his senior personnel to the government's course.

There was a quite clear institutional imperative for the actions taken by Reith, which effectively meant that the ability of the company to fulfil its function was only as great as Davidson (for the government) was willing to allow. This resulted in the remarkable situation where the leader of the official opposition in Parliament and the archbishop of Canterbury were refused permission to broadcast during the strike.

On the morning of 5 May Reith had met a deputation of the parliamentary Labour Party and on 7 May was approached by the Labour MP William Graham, who had served on the Crawford

---

13 WAC 45566, General Strike. In the House of Commons on 6 May Sir John Simon, a Liberal lawyer, declared that the General Strike was illegal because the Trade Disputes Act of 1906 did not cover it and that therefore the leaders of the strike were liable for damages 'to the utmost farthing' of their possessions. On 11 May a high court judge, Mr Justice Astbury, confirmed this opinion on the grounds that no trade dispute had been shown to exist in any of the unions involved except the miner's union (Hyde 1973). This view was subsequently challenged; see Briggs (1961: 366 n. 2) and Symons (1957).

14 WAC 45594, Staff Arrangements.

Committee, with a request that a Labour member be allowed to broadcast (Briggs 1961: 376). The Labour Party became more adamant when on 9 May Viscount Grey broadcast on behalf of the Asquithian Liberals and 'included some bitter strictures on the action of the trade unions' (1961: 376). Ramsay MacDonald, the Labour leader, approached Reith personally on 10 May and even sent a copy of the transcript of his proposed text. Reith's inclination was to allow the broadcast, but Davidson and Baldwin refused the request, ostensibly on the grounds that it would set Churchill off again. Reith's diary indicates that he was rather disturbed at this, particularly since the BBC was 'to a certain extent controlled' and following government policy and decisions, while Reith had the unsavoury task of implementing the policy: 'I do not think that they treat me altogether fairly.'[15]

On 7 May Reith received the text of a proposed broadcast by the archbishop of Canterbury. The gist of the speech was conciliatory, proposing that the strike be cancelled, the government subsidy be renewed for a period, and the mine-owners withdraw their suggested wage scales. In other words, all the points of contention should be removed so that negotiations could then take place. Lord Gainford, the BBC's chairman, replied to the archbishop that various changes might be made but added that the decision was ultimately Reith's.[16] This was not true: Reith showed the text of the speech to Davidson, who told him that it could not be broadcast, again arguing that this would set Churchill off on his attempts to commandeer the BBC. Reith informed the archbishop of the decision and told him that they could broadcast nothing that would embarrass the government. On 8 May Reith received a letter from the archbishop expressing surprise at the decision. On the letter Reith pencilled: 'I made it quite clear that (the broadcast) was dependent on what the message was' and that whatever the bishops and clergy wished to say, 'it must not embarrass the government. The greater the authority the more the embarrassment.'[17] In his letter of 8 May to the archbishop, part of which is quoted in Briggs (1961: 279), Reith makes the point that he felt justified in his decision not to permit the broadcast because 'it was a great relief to me to find from you that he [Baldwin] had said that he would prefer the message not to be broadcast' on the basis of a respect for Baldwin's judgement 'not *qua* Prime Minister but *qua* himself'.[18]

Reith was later to write that both men should have been allowed to

15 Reith's diary, 10 May, quoted in Briggs (1961: 376).
16 WAC 45587, Archbishop of Canterbury.
17 Ibid.
18 Ibid.

broadcast: 'neither of them would have done the slightest harm to the position of the government'. His rationale for arguing that they should have been allowed to speak was on the grounds that their speeches would have made no difference to the situation. Thus his apparent liberality on this question rested on pragmatic considerations rather than on principle. He added:

> I was justified in not letting them speak, in terms of what would have happened, or anyhow was likely to have happened, if I had. The BBC could not say, nor permit to be said, anything that might have helped to continue the General Strike, neither could it operate as a strike breaker. It was on the side of the Government, and should have been, and should be to the extent of supporting the cause of law and order, and helping in the maintenance of essential services. (Reith 1963)

It seems likely that the actual reason for the refusal of the request by the archbishop was that he was arguing that a compromise was necessary between the two sides, whereas Baldwin's policy, despite its later more conciliatory tones, demanded nothing less than total surrender by the TUC:

> 'The issue is really quite simple', [Baldwin] remarked to Davidson . . . 'This is an attempt to take over the function of the Government by a body that has not been elected. If they succeed it will be the end of parliamentary democracy which we have taken centuries to build. There can be no negotiations. It can only end in a complete surrender.' (Hyde 1973: 269)

Briggs (1961: 379) describes this as the 'low-water mark' of the BBC because it was so clearly existing on 'sufferance'. It might be more correct to view it as exemplary, the starkest evidence of the general situation of the BBC *vis-à-vis* the government. Basic decisions on content were in effect being made by the deputy chief civil commissioner, Davidson, rather than by Reith. In later explaining his decisions, Davidson was to write that:

> The publication of the Archbishop's statement was not in line either with the general view of the public or the policy of the Government. . . . When the Archbishop suggested that negotiations should be started, I think he failed to realise that the contest was fundamentally a Constitutional struggle. (James 1969: 249)

The commitment of the BBC to the government side was not just a function of the preservation of the 'organization': there was another dimension altogether. There was in effect a distinct ideological imperative to support the government—a genuinely held belief by Reith that the General Strike could under no circumstances be justified. Reith was a neighbour of Davidson's not only in their residences[19] but also in their thinking about the strike and the political crisis that it induced. Davidson wrote in a memorandum after the events:

> It has got to be made absolutely clear, in everything which is written about Baldwin and the General Strike, that his vision and his judgement were clear and decisive, and that he didn't waffle. The idea was always put about that he was under pressure. But there was no question of pressure; he saw the thing as clear as crystal. The decision he took was that there should be no parley . . . the Constitution would not be safe until we had won the victory, and the victory depended on the surrender of the TUC. There were many people . . . running about the streets like dogs, trying to do something about it, but nothing deflected the simple man—he was simple in this, having come to a decision on principle; he just said 'No, I will not accept anything but the surrender of the TUC and the calling off of the strike.' (James, 1969: 232)

In the memo of 15 May Reith states:

> since the BBC was a national institution, and since the Government in this crisis was acting for the people, apart from any Emergency Powers or clause in our Licence, the BBC was for the government in the crisis too; and that we had to assist in maintaining the essential services of the country, the preservation of law and order, and of the life and liberty of the individual and the community. . . . Had we been commandeered we could have done nothing in the nature of impartial news, nor could we have in any way helped inspire appreciation of the fact that a prolongation of the stoppage was a sure means of reducing the standard of living, which it was the avowed intention of the Trade Unions to improve. Nor could we have initiated or emphasized statements likely to counteract a spirit of violence and hostility. We felt we might contribute, perhaps decisively, to the attitude of understanding without which goodwill could not be restored. (Briggs 1961: 365)

What Reith was doing was defining the BBC as an 'organization within the Constitution'[20] and thereby effectively defining

---

19 Of their physical proximity during the strike period, Reith stated: 'We were often on the telephone, or meeting in his house or mine—near the Abbey and within a few yards of each other or in his office or mine, during the next ten days and nights' (Reith 1963).

20 A phrase he was to use on a number of occasions: see Briggs (1961: 366 n .3).

impartiality—for specific institutional and ideological reasons—in such a way as to make it synonymous not with a particular party line but with a particular political and moral order within which that line rested and which for the duration of the strike was deemed to coexist with the Baldwin government. He was clear as to the overall political implications of the situation:

> if there had been broadcasting at the time of the French Revolution, there would have been no French Revolution; the Revolution came from Marseilles to Paris as a rumour. The function of the BBC was fully as much to kill falsehood as to announce truth; and the former can derive automatically from the latter. (Reith 1963)

The observation of the events of May 1926 by Reith and the BBC involved a distinction between the national interest as represented by the government, and the 'threatening forces' of the strikers as represented by the TUC. Some would observe that that situation is not dissimilar from the situation today in which the general inflexion of, for example, industrial coverage is couched in an amorphous notion of the 'national interest' which operates as an absolute value in relation to which all else is subordinate.

At one level the subservience to the wishes and needs of one side was far from total. Messages from both sides were broadcast: reference was made to the *British Worker* as well as to the *British Gazette*; a conscious effort was made to distinguish between agency copy and government copy; and many of the items broadcast were objective in the sense that they were accurate reports of verifiable events. As Hood (1972: 417) points out, though, 'accuracy is not in itself proof of objectivity or neutrality', and what was left out was often more important than what was included. There was the refusal to allow certain broadcasts, most notably the MacDonald and Canterbury ones, the failure to rectify factual errors,[21] the broadcasting of requests for volunteers (i.e. strike-breakers; Symons 1957), and the general line of the news programmes as characterized, for instance, in a unique form of content, the editorials, which were to lead to a description of the BBC as 'too loquacious'. On 26 April B. E. Nicholls, the organizer of programmes, wrote a memo to Reith and the director of educational broadcasting suggesting that 'if the strike comes off we should make arrangements for some public person to give a short message each night, just three or four minutes, after the second general news, on the usual lines of

---

21 For example, it was broadcast that engine men and firemen were returning to work at Oxford, that the strike was breaking down at Salisbury, and that food ships were being discharged at Grimsby. Even though these reports were false and were corrected by the unions, and even though the BBC was informed of these corrections, they were not broadcast (Briggs 1961: 373).

appealing to people to keep their heads and so on, quite non-political'.[22] On 4 May the news announcer was to state:

> Many of you will be missing the editorial chat in your favourite newspapers, and I hope you will not think we are presuming if we venture to supply in its place a few words of advice to the ordinary good citizen. You will not expect from us any comments on the merits of the present controversy.

During the strike the editorial broadcasts were bland and non-controversial, but after 12 May they were to be continued in a far more politicized form. During the days of the strike they were 'designed to have a soothing effect on the nation's nerves and to reassure them', and they dealt with such subjects as transport arrangements, how to keep calm, how to behave, and so on. They were largely written by Major C. F. Atkinson in his capacity as assistant director of publicity and head of the emergency news service.

Whether the view that the effect of the BBC's broadcasts during the strike was actually to dispel rumours and to spread intelligence and good cheer is correct is necessarily in some doubt. What is beyond doubt is that this was the intended role of the BBC—the consequence of its relationship with the government. This was high-lighted by the use of the editorials during the period immediately following the end of the strike, when the miners were still out. There was detailed co-operation between the government and the BBC to get the miners back to work. The interests served in this relation-ship worked both ways. While it was clearly necessary from the government's point of view to get the miners back by whatever means was available, it was also in the overall institutional interests of the BBC to have this new form of programme content developed. This was noted in a memo on 19 May from Murray to Atkinson in which Murray stated that the idea of having an identifiable editorial form was 'to develop the new machinery gradually' which would help to sustain the influences which the BBC had developed during the strike.[23] Reith certainly saw the editorials as a means of further-ing the BBC's interests, and in a letter on 28 May to one of the governors, Basil Binyon, he said that press criticism of the editorials was 'jealousy of the position we had to occupy during the Strike' and that the press 'object to anything which would seem to indicate an increasing importance on the part of Broadcasting'[24] On 25 May the PMG complained about the editorials, whose title was therefore

22 WAC 45567, News Arrangements.
23 Ibid.
24 Ibid.

changed, first to 'Editorial Reviews' and then to just 'Reviews'. The objections remained, however, and the PMG demanded to see the scripts before they were broadcast. As these then had a habit of piling up in his wastepaper basket, the BBC took the hint and abandoned the whole idea of editorials.

Nevertheless, they were used by the government to 'get at' the miners. In a memo to Reith on 21 May Gladstone Murray outlined the details of a meeting he had had with Davidson, who had requested that the BBC do an editorial on the miners' dispute. He wrote that Davidson had suggested that the BBC

> might do a valuable service in the holiday period by using our editorials to give an accurate and authoritative account of the exact position, explaining for instance that the present position in the mines is neither a strike nor a lock-out and also giving some account of the statistics of the actual amount of wages paid in the mining industry, emphasising the very small proportion of miners who are on the lower scale. He thought that we might also go so far as to call attention to the sort of creeping paralysis effect which the continued mining deadlock had on the whole of the industry in the country.

He added that:

> [the] government want to get at the miners over the heads of their leaders. We would only be justified in countenancing this kind of thing if we are convinced that the national interest demanded the short-circuiting of the miners' leaders. . . . They [the government and Davidson] feel that we might do some good now by preaching the doctrine of cooperation, even *ad nauseam*.[25]

In a quite remarkably explicit document written about this meeting with the deputy chief civil commissioner and the implementation of his suggestions, Murray wrote on 25 May:

> I took away from my interview with Mr. Davidson a very strong feeling that while we were to keep clear of controversy over Whitsun, we were nonetheless to establish the status of our editorial reviews and to get people into the habit of listening to them. . . . I agreed to a series of editorials commencing on Friday and including last night, which may be summarised as follows: *Friday 21 May* . Lockout or Strike—A simple definition of the position for general information following the lines of my interview with Mr. Davidson. It should also be noted that Friday's editorial concluded with the following sentence: 'The cold fact that we must deal with is the fact that somehow our

25 WAC 45567, News Arrangements.

basic industry has been allowed to come to a standstill and must be restarted.' Then on Saturday our editorial was entitled 'Coal and Countryside'. Herein we stressed the creeping paralysis point which I called attention to in the account of my interview with Mr. Davidson. . . .

On Saturday night we linked our editorial with the topical spirit of the Feast of the Church of Whit Sunday. The whole idea in this was to convey the 'bring together' conception and to get people thinking of fundamental issues such as: 'More results for given coal, and more comfort for given wages'. It should be noted that we keep constantly to the text of the Samuel Report, a point specifically emphasised by Mr. Davidson. Then we come to the editorial last night, May 24. The underlying idea of this was to stimulate confidence in the miners. *We definitely set out so to construe the recent utterances of the leaders of the miners to give the impression that they were moving in the direction of settlement.* . . . In pursuance of the atmosphere of restoring confidence, we camouflaged the interpretation of the miners' leaders' utterances by suggesting on purely humanitarian grounds and apart from the immediate issues, a Government declaration of goodwill towards family allowances and both.[26]

The General Strike certainly left the BBC as a major news source, and it was during this period that the first significant definitions began to emerge from politicians of the power of broadcast media. In his diary of 4 May Reith notes:

I went with the Admiralty Deputy Secretary to lunch at the Travellers' Club . . . the Prime Minister was there and immediately he saw me he left the people he had been talking with and came over. I mention this because it showed that he knew what was what, and who was who, at this time of crisis. (Reith 1963)

As we have seen in some detail, Baldwin was not the only one who knew what was what and who was who. Reith further recognized that the crisis was a unique opportunity to make significant and irredeemable excursions into the news monopoly of the press and into the realm of 'controversial broadcasting'—it was an opportunity he did not let slip by. More than anything the events of May 1926 clarified the context within which 'impartiality' functions— involving an almost total, if oblique, accommodation to government needs and interests.

When the end of the strike was announced on 12 May, Reith read a message from the king and then the traditional hymn 'Jerusalem' was played. Nothing was more appropriate to the role of the BBC in

26 Ibid.; emphasis added.

the strike than the manner of this announcement. To turn to such established features of an established order was a metaphorical sigh that the crisis had passed and that the political and moral order with which the BBC had identified throughout remained intact.[27]

Appreciation of the BBC's role was quick to follow. There was much appreciation within government circles for the efforts of the BBC. On 17 May Reith received a letter from the prime minister which thanked him for his help during the emergency and added: 'you and all the members of your staff may rest assured that your loyal service has earned the warm appreciation of the government'.[28] Davidson, the civil commissioner, wrote to Gladstone Murray that: 'For myself I can only thank you again for your help without which our department could not have stood the strain that was imposed upon it throughout the Strike.'[29] To which Murray replied: 'I feel very strongly that in the national interest it is more than desirable that your contact with our service, both official and unofficial, should become permanent.'[30] Numerous newspapers expressed their own appreciation of the BBC: 'For our news, for the dispelling of false rumour and for the pronouncements of great public men upon the situations we thank the Voice from the Air' (*Herts and Essex Observer*, 15 May 1926). There were, one might add, no such appreciations from the TUC side.

The overall conclusion to be drawn from the General Strike as a case-study is looked at in the light of the general conclusions to this discussion of the external context of broadcasting. There is, however, a very important point to be made about the role of the BBC. The BBC's claim was, and indeed still is, that it was impartial because it only related news and *ipso facto* told the 'truth'. This claim was, anyhow, overstated, with, for example, the failure to correct errors, the refusal to allow particular personalities to broadcast, and the general line of the broadcasts and the editorials. It is also true, however, that telling 'the truth' via the straightforward relating of facts can have an important propaganda role to play. There is no doubt from reading through the various memos and numerous expressions of intent that the BBC's coverage was specifically aimed towards a particular end, which was the defeat of the strike. Hugh Greene (1969: 20) once defined propaganda as 'an attempt to impose your own way of thinking, your own views of the situation, on the [opponents] ... and then, this having been

---

27 On 20 May 1926 a 'service of reconciliation' was held in the BBC studios. The bishop of Southwark read the text and concluded with the thought that the 'success of the Strike would have had quite incalculable results on the life and prosperity of the nation' (*Guardian*, 21 May 1926).

28 WAC 45566, General Strike.

29 Ibid.

30 Ibid.

achieved, lead them to behave in the way you desire'. Greene was connected with propaganda against Germany, the Malayan communists, and the Arabs. Crucially he adds: 'There would not be much doubt either about the means to be used: to tell the truth within the limits of the information at our disposal and to tell it consistently and frankly' (Greene 1969: 21). Illusions and allusions to concepts of truth and impartiality, far from indivisible concepts, have always figured prominently in British political propaganda.[31]

It is clearly wrong, however, to move from the appearance of impartial or balanced coverage to the argument that this somehow 'proves' that the organization and the programmes it produces are pristine and unpolluted by the views and needs of particular interests within society. Clearly in wartime it would not be denied that the intent of the broadcasting, whatever its form, was to serve a specific interest, that is, the national interest. Yet in the context not of international peace but of intranational strife the purpose and function of broadcasting was also to serve particular interests: those of the state, and therefore the interests which identified with or were represented by that structure. I think it is clear from the preceding account that the actual relationships of power and commitments of ideology in a crisis throw into sharp relief the actual as opposed to the assumed meaning of broadcasting's 'impartiality'. The potential for partiality within the broad framework of apparent impartiality was ably summed up by R. H. S. Crossman, one of Britain's foremost propagandists during the Second World War:

> We discovered, after many experiments in Dr. Goebbels' technique, that the truth pays. It is a complete delusion to think of the brilliant propagandist as being a professional liar. The brilliant propagandist is the man who tells the truth, or that selection of the truth which is requisite for his purpose, and tells it in such a way that the recipient does not realise that he is receiving any propaganda. . . . From what I am saying there arises this conclusion—if the art of propaganda is to conceal that you are doing propaganda then the central substance of propaganda is hard, correct information. (Crossman 1952)

References Bennett, J. (1966), *British Broadcasting and the Danish Resistance Movement 1940–1945: A Study of the Wartime Broadcasts of the BBC Danish Service* (Cambridge: Cambridge University Press).

31 In its white variety. The 'black' version is altogether more nefarious. On this see Delmar (1962) and Bennett (1966).

Boyle, A. (1972), *Only the Wind Will Listen: Reith of the BBC* (London: Hutchinson).

BP5 (Broadcasting Policy 5): 'The Broadcasting of Controversial Matter (Excluding Religious Broadcast): History and Present Practice', BBC Archives, Nov. 1942.

Briggs, Asa (1961), *The History of Broadcasting in the United Kingdom*, i: *The Birth of Broadcasting* (Oxford: Oxford University Press).

Crossman, R. S. S. (1952), 'Psychological Warfare', *Journal of the Royal United Service Institution*.

Delmar, S. (1962), *Black Boomerang* (London: Secker & Warburg).

Greene, Hugh Carleton (1969), *The Third Floor Front: A View of Broadcasting in the Sixties* (London: Bodley Head).

Greene, Hugh Carleton (1972), 'The Future of Broadcasting in Britain', *New Statesman*, 20 Oct. 1972.

Hill, Charles (1974), *Behind the Screen: The Broadcasting Memoirs of Lord Hill* (London: Sidgwick & Jackson).

Hood, Stuart (1972), 'The Politics of Television', in Denis McQuail (ed.), *Sociology of Mass Communications* (Harmondsworth: Penguin, 1972).

Hyde, H. M. (1973), *Baldwin: The Unexpected Prime Minister* (London: Hart-Davis, MacGibbon).

James, R. R. (1969), *Memoirs of a Conservative: J. C. C. Davidson's Memoirs and Papers, 1910–1937* (London: Weidenfeld & Nicolson).

Lloyd, T. O. (1970), *Empire to Welfare State: English History, 1906–1967* (Oxford: Oxford University Press).

Pelling, H. (1974), *Winston Churchill* (London: Macmillan).

Reith, Lord (1963), 'Parliamentary Affairs', *Forsan* (Winter, 1963–4).

Smith, Anthony (1972), 'Internal Pressures in Broadcasting', *New Outlook*, no. 4.

Symons, J. (1957), *The General Strike* (London: Cresset Press).

2

Public Service Broadcasting: The History of a Concept

Paddy Scannell

IT IS WELL KNOWN that broadcasting in Britain is based on the principle of public service, though what exactly that means, on close inspection, can prove elusive. The last parliamentary committee to report on broadcasting—the 1986 Peacock Committee—noted that it had experienced some difficulty in obtaining a definition of the principle from the broadcasters themselves. A quarter of a century earlier the members of the Pilkington Committee on broadcasting were told by the chairman of the BBC's board of governors that it was no use trying to define good broadcasting —one recognized it. Maybe. Yet for the sake of reasonable discussion of the relevance or otherwise of public service broadcasting today it is worth trying to pin down the characteristics that define the British system. A useful starting-point is to distinguish between public service as a responsibility delegated to broadcasting authorities by the state, and the manner in which the broadcasting authorities have interpreted that responsibility and tried to discharge it.

Government intervention to regulate broadcasting has been, in many cases, the outcome of wavelength scarcity and problems of financing. The portion of the electromagnetic spectrum suitable for broadcasting is limited and governments have had to assume responsibility for negotiating international agreements about wavelength allocations to particular countries as well as deciding how to parcel out the wavelengths available in their own country amongst the competing claims of broadcasting and those of the armed forces, merchant shipping, emergency services, telecommunications, and so on. The problem of financing arises because it is not immediately obvious how people are to be made to pay for a

First published in Andrew Goodwin and Garry Whannel (eds.), *Understanding Television* (London: Routledge, 1990), 11–26.

broadcast service. Most forms of culture and entertainment are funded by the box-office mechanism—people pay to enter a special place to enjoy a play, concert, film, or whatever. But radio and television are enjoyed in people's homes and appear as natural resources available, at the turn of a switch, like gas, water, or electricity. The two means of financing broadcasting in universal use, until recently, have been either a form of annual taxation on the owners of receiving sets (the licence fee), or advertising.

The British solution, back in the early 1920s, was the creation of a single company, the British Broadcasting Company, licensed to broadcast by the Post Office and financed by an annual licence fee charged on all households with a wireless. How the concept of public service came to be grafted onto what were originally a set of *ad hoc*, practical arrangements, and the shifting terms of debate about what it has meant, can best be traced through the various committees on broadcasting set up by successive governments from the beginning through to the present. These committees, usually known by the name of their chairmen, have been given the task of reporting to Parliament on the conduct of the broadcasters, the general nature of the service provided, and its possible future development. They have been the means whereby Parliament has kept an eye on the activities of those to whom it has delegated responsibility for providing broadcast services in this country.

The very first broadcasting committee, set up by the Post Office in 1923 under the chairmanship of Major-General Sir Frederick Sykes, was asked to consider broadcasting in all its aspects and the future uses to which it might be put. In the minuted proceedings of this committee and its report we find the earliest attempts to formulate what the general purposes of broadcasting should be. A crucial move was the definition of broadcasting as 'a public utility' whose future should be discussed as such.

> The wavebands available in any country must be regarded as a valuable form of public property; and the right to use them for any purpose should be given after full and careful consideration. Those which are assigned to any particular interest should be subject to the safeguards necessary to protect the public interest in the future. (Sykes Committee 1923: 11)

Bearing in mind the cheapness and convenience of radio, and its social and political possibilities ('as great as any technical attainment of our generation'), the committee judged that 'the control of such a potential power over public opinion and the life of the nation ought to remain with the state' (Sykes Committee 1923: 15). The operation of so important a national service ought not to be allowed to become an unrestricted commercial monopoly.

The report rejected direct government control of broadcasting. Instead, it argued, indirect control should be operated through the licence which by law must be obtained from the Post Office for the establishment of any broadcasting station. The terms of the licence would specify the general responsibilities of the broadcasters and hold them answerable for the conduct of the service to that state department.

Thus the definition of broadcasting as a public utility, and the mandate to develop it as a national service in the public interest, came from the state. The interpretation of that definition, the effort to realize its meaning in the development of a broadcasting service guided by considerations of a national service and the public interest, came from the broadcasters and above all from John Reith, the managing director of the British Broadcasting Company from 1923 to 1926, and the first director-general of the British Broadcasting Corporation from 1927 to 1938. The Sykes Committee had made only short-term recommendations about the development of a broadcasting service and the BBC had been granted a licence to broadcast for only two more years. The Crawford Committee was set up in 1925 to establish guidelines for the future of broadcasting on a more long-term basis. Reith was invited by the committee to present it with a statement of his views about the scope and conduct of broadcasting and he did so in a memorandum which he wrote as an impartial statement, presented in the interests of broadcasting not the British Broadcasting Company, and intended to show the desirability of the conduct of broadcasting as a public service.

In Reith's brief and trenchant manifesto for a public service broadcasting system there was an overriding concern for the maintenance of high standards and a unified policy towards the whole of the service supplied. The service must not be used for entertainment purposes alone. Broadcasting had a responsibility to bring into the greatest possible number of homes in the fullest degree all that was best in every department of human knowledge, endeavour, and achievement. The preservation of a high moral tone—the avoidance of the vulgar and the hurtful—was of paramount importance. Broadcasting should give a lead to public taste rather than pander to it: 'He who prides himself on giving what he thinks the public wants is often creating a fictitious demand for lower standards which he himself will then satisfy' (Reith 1925: 3). Broadcasting had an educative role and the broadcasters had developed contacts with the great educational movements and institutions of the day in order to develop the use of the medium of radio to foster the spread of knowledge.

Here we find a cogent advocacy of public service as a cultural, moral, and educative force for the improvement of knowledge, taste, and manners, and this has become one of the main ways in which the concept is understood. But radio, as Reith was well aware, had a social and political function too. As a national service, broadcasting might bring together all classes of the population. It could prove to be a powerful means of promoting social unity particularly through the live relay of those national ceremonies and functions— Reith cited the speech by George V when opening the British Empire Exhibition: the first time the king had been heard on radio—which had the effect, as he put it, of 'making the nation as one man' (Reith 1925: 4). By providing a common access for all to a wide range of public events and ceremonies—a royal wedding, the FA Cup Final, the last night of the Proms, for example— broadcasting would act as a kind of social cement binding people together in the shared idioms of a public, corporate, national life.

But, more than this, broadcasting had an immense potential for helping in the creation of an informed and enlightened democracy. It enabled men and women to take an interest in many things from which they had previously been excluded. On any great public issue of the day radio could provide both the facts of the matter and the arguments for and against. Reith had a vision of the emergence of 'a new and mighty weight of public opinion' with people now enabled by radio to make up their own minds where previously they had to accept 'the dictated and partial versions of others' (Reith 1925: 4). The restrictive attitude of the Post Office, which, at the time, had forbidden the BBC to deal with any matters of public controversy, was severely restricting the development of this side of broadcasting, and Reith bitterly denounced the shackles imposed on radio's treatment of news and politics. Only when freed from such chains would broadcasting be able to realize one of its chief functions. The concept of public service, in Reith's mind, had, as a core element, an ideal of broadcasting's role in the formation of an informed and reasoned public opinion as an essential part of the political process in a mass democratic society.

Finally, Reith argued strongly for continued 'unity of control' in broadcasting—that is, for the maintenance of the BBC's monopoly of broadcasting in the United Kingdom. The monopoly granted to the BBC in 1922 was merely for the administrative convenience of the Post Office—it found it easier to deal with one licensed broadcasting service than several. At first there had been a considerable outcry (particularly from the popular press) against this 'trade monopoly' as a restrictive practice which inhibited the development of a range of competing programme services for listeners to choose from. But Reith defended what he later called the 'brute force of monopoly' as the essential means of guaranteeing the BBC's ability to develop as a public service in the national interest. The monopoly was, Reith argued, the best means of sorting out a technically efficient and economical system of broadcasting for the whole population—and universal availability was the cornerstone of the creation of a truly national service in the public interest. Secondly, unity of control was essential ethically in order that 'one general policy may be maintained throughout the country and definite standards promulgated' (Reith 1925: 10).

Reith favoured changing the status of the BBC from a company in the private sector, set up originally in the interests of the British radio industry, to a corporation in the public sector under the authority of the state, because he believed it would give broadcasting a greater degree of freedom and independence in the pursuit of the ideals of public service. On the one hand, it was necessary to be freed from commercial pressures. If radio continued to be part of a profit-orientated industry, then the programme service would be influenced by commercial considerations and the need to appeal to popular demand. Entertainment, a legitimate aim of broadcasting, would become a paramount consideration to the detriment of other kinds of programming with a more educative or culturally improving aim. On the other hand, broadcasting needed to be free of interference and pressure from the state in order to develop its political role as a public service.

Reith's advocacy of a public service role for broadcasting in 1925 had the support of Post Office officials. Public opinion too had come round in favour of continuing broadcasting as a monopoly in the custody of the BBC, and there was no opposition to its transformation into a corporation at the end of the following year. Thereafter, for nearly thirty years, secure in its monopoly, the BBC was uniquely empowered to develop a service along the lines envisaged by its first director-general.

There were two crucial decisions made by Reith and a handful of senior BBC staff about how to organize and deliver the programme service. The mandate of national service was interpreted most basically as meaning that anyone living anywhere in the United Kingdom was entitled to good-quality reception of the BBC's programmes. They should be universally available to all. To achieve this a small number of twin transmitters were set up in strategically chosen locations to deliver two programmes to listeners: a regional programme produced from a handful of provincial centres, and a national programme produced from London. Wherever they lived listeners had the choice of either the national or their own regional programme. Secondly, the policy of mixed programming offered listeners on either channel a wide and varied range of programmes over the course of each day and week. Typically it included news, drama, sport, religion, music (light to classical), variety, and light entertainment. This mix catered not only for different needs (education, information, entertainment), but for different sectional interests within the listening public (children, women, farmers, businessmen, and so on).

These decisions had far-reaching consequences. In the first place, they brought into being a radically new kind of public—one commensurate with the whole of society. On behalf of this public the broadcasters asserted a right of access to a wide range of political, cultural, sporting, religious, ceremonial, and entertainment resources which, perforce, had hitherto been accessible only to small, self-selecting, and more or less privileged publics. Particular publics were replaced by the *general* public constituted in and by the general nature of the mixed programme service and its general, unrestricted availability. The fundamentally democratic thrust of broadcasting—of which Reith was well aware—lay in the new kind of access to virtually the whole spectrum of public life that radio made available to everyone. It equalized public life through the common access it established for all members of society—and it is worth noting that initially in nearly every case the broadcasters had a hard fight to assert that right on behalf of their audiences. In one particular case—the access of TV cameras to the House of Commons—the principle has only just been won.

In the long run these structural arrangements for the distribution of the service and the range of programmes on offer were far more important than the actual style and content of particular programmes at the time. The BBC soon succeeded in winning a reputation for itself as a purveyor of moral and cultural 'uplift' in the well-established tradition of improvement for the masses. It was far less successful in establishing its news and political programmes. The monopoly, a source of strength in some areas of programming such as music, was a source of weakness in relation to parties, governments, and state departments. Throughout the era of its monopoly the BBC's independence of government was frail and it was widely regarded (especially overseas) as government's semi-official mouthpiece.

In the decade after the Second World War the monopoly came under increasing pressure, and the first post-war committee of inquiry into broadcasting—the 1950 Beveridge Committee—made the question of the monopoly its central concern. The BBC produced a classic defence of its position in its written submission to the committee. To introduce competition for audiences into broadcasting by establishing other programme services would inevitably lead to a lowering of programme standards: by that the BBC meant 'the purpose, taste, cultural aims, range and general sense of responsibility of the broadcasting service as a whole'.

Under any system of competitive broadcasting all these things
would be at the mercy of Gresham's Law. For, at the present stage
of the nation's educational progress, it operates as remorselessly
in broadcasting as ever it did in currency. The good, in the long
run, will inevitably be driven out by the bad. It is inevitable that
any national educational pyramid shall have a base
immeasurably broader than its upper levels. The truth of this can
be seen by comparing those national newspapers which have
circulations of over four millions with those whose circulations
are counted in hundred-thousands. And because competition in
broadcasting must in the long run descend to a fight for the
greatest number of listeners, it would be the lower forms of mass
appetite which would more and more be catered for in
programmes. (Beveridge Committee 1950, para. 163)

In the event, the Beveridge Committee endorsed the BBC's monopoly, but its days were numbered. Within a couple of years a general
election returned a Conservative government that rejected the
recommendations of Beveridge and opted to establish commercial
television, funded by advertising, in competition with the BBC's
television service.

The British system is sometimes presented as a mixture of public
service and commercial broadcasting as represented respectively by
the BBC and Independent Television (ITV) but this is misleading.
The terms under which commercial broadcasting was established
by government made it part of the public service system from the
beginning. A public corporation, the Independent Television
Authority (ITA), was created by Act of Parliament with general
responsibilities to establish a commercial television service that
would inform, educate, and entertain. This service was subject to
state regulation and control by an authority charged with maintaining high standards of programme quality. It was an extension of
public service broadcasting, not an alternative.

Even so, when the next committee on broadcasting, chaired by
Sir Harry Pilkington, set about examining the impact of commercial television in 1960 and comparing its programme service
with that of the BBC, it found much to complain of in the doings of
ITV. If the main concern of Beveridge had been with the monopoly,
Pilkington was concerned with programme standards and the
ominous threat of 'triviality'. Pilkington defined the concept of
public service broadcasting as always to provide 'a service comprehensive in character; the duty of the public corporations has
been, and remains, to bring to public awareness the whole range of
worthwhile, significant activity and experience' (Pilkington Committee 1962: 9). Against this criterion the committee noted the

widespread public anxiety about television which had, in the last few years, taken over from radio as the dominant broadcasting medium. The commonest objection was that television programmes were too often designed to get the largest possible audience, and that to achieve this they appealed to a low level of public taste (Gresham's Law again). There was a lack of variety and originality, an adherence to what was safe, and an unwillingness to try challenging, demanding, and, still more, uncomfortable subject-matter.

The committee had no hesitation in identifying commercial television as the culprit. The BBC was praised for its responsible attitude to the power of the medium of television. In the review of the BBC's performance there was a short paragraph on triviality—'The BBC are aware of the liability of TV to fall into triviality, but have not always been successful in preventing this happening' (Pilkington Committee 1962: 42)—but a whole page and a half were devoted to the problem of triviality in commercial television. The ITA was scolded for equating quality with box-office success, and was scathingly condemned for its ability to 'understand [neither] the nature of quality or of triviality, nor the need to maintain one and counter the other' (Pilkington Committee 1962: 65). In short, commercial television was regarded as failing to live up to its responsibilities as a public service. It was not fit, in its present form, to extend its activities, and the plum that the committee had on offer—a third television channel—was unhesitatingly awarded to the BBC.

By the mid-1970s the terms in which the role of broadcasting in society was discussed had changed again, and the representations made to the committee on the future of broadcasting chaired by Lord Annan raised issues that would have seemed astonishing fifteen years earlier. The Annan Report, published in 1977, noted a marked shift in the social, political, and cultural climate in Britain since the deliberations of its predecessor.

> For years British broadcasting had been able successfully to create, without alienating Government or the public, interesting and exciting popular network programmes from the world of reality as well as the world of fantasy—programmes on the arts and sciences, international reportage, political controversy, social enquiry, local investigation. These now began to stir up resentment and hostility, and protests against their political and social overtones.
>   Hitherto it had been assumed—apart from the occasional flurry over a programme—that Britain had 'solved' the problem of the political relations of broadcasting to Government,

Parliament and the public. Now people of all political persuasions began to object that many programmes were biased or obnoxious. But some, with equal fervour, maintained that broadcasters were not challenging enough and were cowed by Government and vested interests to produce programmes which bolstered up the *status quo* and concealed how a better society could evolve. (Annan Committee 1977: 15)

Pilkington had praised the BBC and blamed ITV. Annan found both wanting—and the BBC rather more than ITV. The old monopoly had given way to a cosy 'duopoly' between the BBC and ITV, who had both come to terms with competition by providing a broadly similar programme service with a roughly equal share of the audience. A significant spectrum of opinion, both among politicians and among the general public, was now calling a plague on both broadcasting houses. Broadcasting had become 'an over-mighty subject' answerable neither to its political masters nor the general public. It was no longer representative of the increasingly diverse tastes, interests, and needs of an increasingly diverse society. Perhaps the only way to deal with the problem was to break up the existing broadcasting institutions.

The committee's response to the barrage of conflicting opinion it encountered was to opt for 'pluralism'—'Pluralism has been the *leitmotiv* of all of us in this Report,' it noted (Annan Committee 1977: 108). It wanted to create a wider range of programmes that spoke not to the mass audience addressed by the existing duopoly but to those minorities and social groups whose needs and interests were not adequately served under the existing arrangements. It therefore recommended that the available fourth television channel should go to neither of the existing authorities but should be given to an independent Open Broadcasting Authority charged with the responsibility to develop a service that catered for all those interests presently under-represented or excluded in the output of the BBC and ITV. The new authority would not produce any of its own programmes but, like a publishing house, would commission its programmes from a wide range of sources, including independent programme-makers. The essential basis of what, in 1980, became Channel Four was contained in Annan's concept of the Open Broadcasting Authority.

If hitherto public service broadcasting had been widely accepted in a largely unquestioning way, from Annan onwards old certainties crumbled. The defence of the original monopoly had been linked to a claim to a unified policy for programming that rested on a presumed social, cultural, and political consensus whose values were widely shared. But when that consensus collapsed, what case could there be for a monopoly or a duopoly, or even the modest pluralism advocated by Annan? In the last decade there have been striking technological developments in broadcasting and telecommunications which, coupled with a sharp change in the political climate, have undermined all the old arguments in favour of public service broadcasting.

Today the key topic in debates about broadcasting is deregulation. Should the state cease to control and regulate broadcasting, and let market forces shape its future development? State regulation, the argument goes, was necessary from the beginning through to the end of the 1970s because in that period the scarcity of suitable wavelengths for broadcasting necessitated the intervention of the state to regulate their allocation and use. In this country there are at present only four national television channels, regulated by two authorities, broadcasting to the whole population, but change is only just around the corner. As the Peacock Report puts it:

> We are now in an unusually rapid technological advance in broadcasting. People can buy video recorders and watch films whenever they choose. Cable networks are beginning to develop in various parts of the country. There is already some broadcasting by satellite and, although it is impossible to predict its future precisely, it seems certain that its effects will be very large. . . . There is no reason why a large—indeed an indefinitely large—number of channels should not be brought into use. In the case of cable television fibre optic communication techniques allow for two way communication and make pay TV a live possibility. (Peacock Committee 1986: 2)

What will soon be available—at a price, it is argued,—is multichannel access to a wide range of different video services and television programmes supported either by advertising, or by a fixed monthly charge or on a pay-as-you-view basis. Whatever the precise mix of ways in which these services are financed and paid for, it will not be by the licence fee method which has always been the means of financing the BBC. In this context why should people go on paying for the BBC as they do at present? It will become, after all, only one service out of many. It was this question that the Peacock Committee was asked by the government to consider in 1985, and its report was published the following year.

Other committees had considered broadcasting in social, cultural, and political terms. Peacock, set up to consider alternatives to the licence fee as a means of financing the BBC, applied a stringent economic approach and in doing so completely shifted the grounds of discussion. For Peacock, broadcasting was a commodity—a marketable good like any other—provided for consumers, and the establishment of consumer sovereignty in broadcasting through a sophisticated market system was the aim of the report. It defined a satisfactory broadcasting market as offering 'full freedom of entry for programme makers, a transmission system capable of carrying an indefinitely large number of programmes, facilities for pay-per-programme or pay-per-channel and differentiated charges for units of time' (Peacock Committee 1986: 134). Consumer sovereignty meant the greatest freedom of choice for individuals via the widest provision of alternative broadcast goods. Neither the state nor delegated broadcasting authorities should continue to determine the nature and scope of the available broadcasting services. In future consumers should be the best judges of their own welfare.

Peacock envisaged a three-stage transition to a free market in broadcasting. In the crucial second stage (some time in the 1990s) it recommended that the BBC should be financed by subscription. Eventually, in the next century, a full market for broadcasting, with a very wide range of services via geostationary satellites and fibre optic cable systems as well as traditional terrestrial broadcast services, would be based wholly on direct payment for either particular channels or particular programmes.

The committee recognized that these proposals might well lead to the erosion of public service broadcasting, and it was concerned to identify how the essential elements of public service broadcasting—which it defined as the production of a wide range of high-quality programmes—might be retained. It wanted to protect those programmes of merit which, it acknowledged, would not survive in a market where audience ratings were the sole concern. To this end it suggested—though only in general terms—the establishment of a Public Service Broadcasting Council to secure the funding of public service programmes on any channel from stage two onwards. In spite of this gesture, the whole tenor of the Peacock Report reversed the thinking of all previous parliamentary committees on broadcasting. Hitherto commercial considerations had taken second place to a public service commitment. Peacock, however, placed public service a long way second to commercial considerations and consumer choice. Public service broadcasting would no longer be the definitive feature of the British system.

Raymond Williams has identified the idea of *service* as one of the great achievements of the Victorian middle class, and one that deeply influenced later generations (Williams 1961: 313–17). It was certainly a crucial component of the ideal of public service as grafted onto broadcasting in its formative period from the 1920s to the 1950s. The Victorian reforming ideal of service was animated by a sense of moral purpose and of social duty on behalf of the community, aimed particularly at those most in need of reform—the lower classes. It was institutionalized in the bureaucratic practices of the newly emerging professional classes—especially in the reformed civil service of the late nineteenth century, whose members saw themselves as public servants. At its best this passion for improving the lot of those below was part of a genuinely humane concern to alleviate the harsh consequences of a newly industrialized society. But it did nothing to change the balance of power in society, and maintained the dominance of the middle classes over the lower ranks.

One strand in this general concern for the conditions of the poor focused on their educational and cultural needs. A key figure in this development was Matthew Arnold (an inspector of schools for most of his working life), who believed that everyone was entitled to the enjoyment of those cultural treasures which, in his day, were available only to the educated classes. Arnold defined culture as 'the best that has been thought and written in the world' (quoted in Williams 1961:124), a definition echoed by Reith in his advocacy of public service broadcasting. The radical element in Arnold's thinking was this claim that the state should use its authority to establish a fully national education system with a curriculum that included the study of the arts and humanities. Culture, for Arnold, was a means of alleviating the strain and hostility between classes in a deeply divided society, and the task of 'civilizing' the masses had a prudent political basis. It was a means of incorporating the working classes within the existing social and political order, and thus preventing the threat of revolt from below. Arnold's best-known essay, *Culture and Anarchy*, expressed that fear in its very title.

The idea that the state should intervene in the terrain of culture and education, so daring in Arnold's time, had won a much wider acceptance some fifty years later, at the time that broadcasting was established. Indeed, government intervention to control and regulate broadcasting and to define its general purposes is an early and classic instance of state intervention to regulate the field of culture. Victorian ideals of service laced with Arnoldian notions of culture suffused all aspects of the BBC's programme service in the thirty years of its monopoly. Such attitudes, in broadcasting as elsewhere, did not outlast the 1950s—or at least not with the degree of unselfcritical certainty that they had hitherto possessed. 'The ideals of middle class culture', as the Annan Report put it, 'so felicitously expressed by Matthew Arnold a century ago . . . found it ever more difficult to accommodate the new expressions of life in the sixties' (Annan Committee 1977: 14). Even so, it noted that at some levels the 'old Arnoldian belief in spreading "sweetness and light" still inspired the BBC' (Annan Committee 1977: 80).

Underlying Arnoldian ideals of sweetness and light was a concern for social unity mingled with national pride. In the epoch of the BBC's monopoly both concerns were central to its role as a public service in *the national interest.* The linking of culture with national-ism—the idea of a national culture—was given new expression in broadcasting through those kinds of programme that had the effect of, in Reith's words, 'making the nation as one man'. From the 1920s through to today the BBC has continued this work of promoting national unity through such programmes. Sir Michael Swann, chairman of the BBC's board of governors, told the Annan Com-mittee that 'an enormous amount of the BBC's work was in fact social cement of one sort or another. Royal occasions, religious services, sports coverage, and police series, all reinforced the sense of belonging to our country, being involved in its celebrations, and accepting what it stands for' (Annan Committee 1977: 263). The report described the BBC as 'arguably the most important single cultural institution in the nation', and recommended preserving it as 'the natural interpreter of [great national occasions] to the nation as a whole' (Annan Committee 1977: 79, 114).

Such occasions—exemplified by, say, the wedding of Prince Charles and Lady Diana Spencer—may indeed be moments of national unity in which all sections of society participate. But what of moments of crisis? The question then arises as to whose interests, in the last resort, broadcasting is there to serve—those of the state or the people? Governments claim the right to define the national interest and expect the broadcasters, particularly in a crisis, to uphold their definition of it. To defend the public interest may mean challenging the government of the day—a risky thing for institutions who derive their authority to broadcast from the government.

This politicized concept of the public interest has a very different history from that of public service, for the former relates to the news function of modern media and was elaborated in struggles for press freedom from the late eighteenth to the mid-nineteenth cen-tury. Against the power of the state, radical publics—bourgeois and proletarian—emerged to claim universal political and civil rights; the right to vote, to free speech and free assembly. A new kind of 'public sphere' was formed, independent of church and state, claiming the right to criticize both and committed to the establishment of public life, grounded in rational discussion, in which all members of society might participate (for a discussion of this concept in relation to broadcasting, see Garnham 1986). The struggle to establish an independent press, both as a source of information about the activities of the state and as a forum for the formation and expression of public opinion, was part of this process, and an important aspect of the long battle for a fully democratic representative system of government.

The establishment of broadcasting coincided with the moment that the vote was finally conceded to all adult men and women, and the development of mass democracy is closely connected with broadcasting's role in that process. Reith was well aware of the importance of radio as a new organ of public opinion and as an instrument of democratic enlightenment, and was keen to move it in those directions. If the BBC was slow to develop a robust independence from the state, it was not, as some have argued, the fault of its first director-general. Nevertheless, it is true to say that the political independence of broadcasting goes back no further than the mid-1950s. The introduction of strictly limited competition for audiences between the BBC and ITV gave the BBC something else to worry about other than its political masters. Competition in the sphere of news and current affairs had the effect of detaching the BBC from the apron strings of the state. Deference to political authority was replaced by a more populist, democratic stance as the broadcasters asserted the public's right to know by making politicians answerable and accountable to the electorate for their conduct of the nation's affairs. In news interviews, studio discussions and debates, current affairs magazine programmes, documentaries, and documentary dramas a whole clutch of political and social issues came onto the agenda through the medium of television—became part of the public domain, matters of common knowledge and concern. In this way broadcasting came to fulfil—never without difficulty, always under pressure—its role as an independent 'public sphere' and a forum for open public discussion of matters of general concern.

The extent of 'openness' is, however, something that varies according to the social, economic, and political climate. The thresholds of tolerance are not fixed. It is arguable, for instance, that television was more 'open' in the mid-1960s than the late 1970s. It is notable, however, that a Conservative government enhanced the 'public sphere' role of broadcasting at the beginning of the 1980s by authorizing Channel Four to give special attention to the interests of minority groups and to commission a significant amount of its programmes from independent programme-makers. The establishment of Channel Four must be seen as the expression of a continuing political commitment to regulating broadcasting as a public good and in the public interest.

The pursuit of these aims has to date been underpinned by a disregard for commercial considerations as either the only or the primary objective of the broadcast services. This has manifested itself in two ways that are crucial to the realization of public service objectives: a policy of mixed programming on national channels available to all. Where commercial motives are primary, broadcasters will go only for the most profitable markets—which lie in densely populated urban areas that can deliver large audiences without difficulty. The markets for cabled services are likely to prove even more selective: the affluent districts of major towns and cities will be wired up, while the poorer areas will be neglected. More sparsely populated, remoter areas will be ignored entirely. The long-term commitment of the BBC and IBA to make their services available to all has meant an investment out of all proportion to the returns in order to reach those regions that strictly economic considerations would simply neglect. The BBC set up sixty-five new transmitting stations in order to extend its service from 99 per cent of the population to the 99.1 per cent it reaches at present.

The alternative to mixed programming is generic programming —a channel that provides a service in which all or most of the programmes are of the same kind. Typically this has—on radio— meant particular kinds of music channel: classical, top forty, country and western, reggae, or whatever. More recently, in the United States, generic TV channels have been established in cable services —Home Box Office (mainly movies), MTV (music videos), CNN (Cable News Network), as well as pay-per-view channels that offer mainly sporting fixtures. Generic programming fragments the general viewing public as still constituted, for instance, in the mixed programme service offered on the four national UK television channels. In doing so it destroys the principle of equality of access for all to entertainment and informational and cultural resources in a common public domain. The hard-won 'public sphere' created over the last thirty years on national television may shatter into splinters under the impact of deregulated multi-channel video services.

The Peacock Report has redefined broadcasting as a private commodity rather than a public good. Individual consumers, in the media universe of the next century as envisaged by Peacock, will choose what they want and pay for what they get. But consumers are not all equal in their purchasing power. The privatization of informational and cultural resources may well create a two-tiered society of those who are rich and poor in such resources. Such a development would undercut the fundamentally democratic principles upon which public service broadcasting rests.

In the political climate of today public service broadcasting may seem a concept that has outlived its relevance. I do not think so. The history of its development in Britain has undoubtedly been coloured by the patrician values of a middle-class intelligentsia, and a defence of public service broadcasting in terms of quality and standards tied to prescriptive and élitist conceptions of education and culture is no longer feasible. But that has proved to be a contingent historical feature in the development of the BBC. Far more crucial has been the political will, until very recently, to maintain, against the grain of economic considerations, a commitment to properly public, social values and concerns in the system as a whole, that is, in the services provided by both the BBC and the IBA. In my view equal access for all to a wide and varied range of common informational, entertainment, and cultural programmes carried on channels that can be received throughout the country must be thought of as an important citizenship right in mass democratic societies. It is a crucial means, perhaps the only means at present, whereby a common culture, common knowledge, and a shared public life are maintained as a social good equally available to the whole population. That was the basis of public service broadcasting as envisaged by John Reith, the much misunderstood first director-general of the BBC. It is the basis of the present system. It should continue to be so in the future.

Postscript
Andrew Goodwin
and Garry Whannel

Since this chapter was written the government White Paper *Broacasting in the '90s* has been published. Among its main recommendations are:

—— The present ITV system to be replaced by a regionally based third channel, which would have to include quality news and current affairs.
—— The IBA and the Cable Authority to be replaced by a new Independent Television Commission, which would provide 'lighter touch' regulation.
—— Channel Four's remit to be preserved but its advertising sold separately from ITV.
—— The establishment of a fifth channel, starting in 1993, to be followed by a sixth if technically feasible.
—— Franchises for Channel Three and Channel Five will run for ten years and will be auctioned to the highest bidder.
—— The BBC will be encouraged to progress towards the introduction of subscription-based services.

As this book goes to press [1990] there is clearly still much to be decided. Three things are already clear. The preservation of Channel Four's remit is a significant victory for public service broadcasting, but the changes in the conditions by which it receives revenue could be a crucial blow that will make following the remit very difficult. The new ITV system will inevitably be far more concerned with costs and far less concerned with programme quality. The BBC comes out relatively well—there has been no move as yet to dismantle its structure by statute, only a nudge, not a hefty shove.

Indeed one likely result of the expansion of broadcasting due to satellite and the reorganization of ITV will be the short-term strengthening of the BBC. The BBC currently makes fairly expensive programmes that for the most part are watched by large audiences. The cost per hour of the new satellite channels is much lower, and they could end up locked in a struggle with the new ITV companies for half of the audience, while the BBC remains fairly secure with its own 50 per cent.

But the more long-term outlook may be grimmer. In order to create the conditions for satellite and other new channels to thrive, it may eventually be necessary to attack the present structure of the BBC. In particular the licence fee might be abolished to force the BBC to adopt a subscription system.

The underlying basis for current broadcasting policy stems, of course, from the shift, evident in the Peacock Report, away from a consideration of broadcasting as a social and cultural service for the community to broadcasting as the production of commodities, with viewers seen as consumers making choices in the market-place.

There is little evidence so far that more will mean better. Everything suggests that the cost per hour of broadcasting as a whole will inevitably decrease considerably. Underlying the policy initiative is a desire to weaken the power of the broadcasting unions and increase casualization, both of which help to reduce the unit costs of independent production.

While it would be naïve to adopt a simple cost = quality formula, there can be little doubt that the two have a close relation. Quality television can be made for £100,000 per hour or £25,000 per hour, and one can also spend £100,000 and make rubbish. However, it is very hard to make television of any quality at an average cost of less than £10,000 per hour. The irony of this new economistic approach to broadcasting is that, by supposedly opening up the market to free consumer choice, it will precisely destroy the ability of the broadcasting industry to offer the range of choice currently available.

References   Annan Committee (1977), *Report of the Committee on the Future of Broadcasting* (Annan Report), Cmnd. 6753 (London: HMSO).

Beveridge Committee (1951), *Report of the Broadcasting Committee, 1949* (Beveridge Report), Cmnd. 8116 (London: HMSO).

Garnham, N. (1986), 'The Media and the Public Sphere', in P. Golding, G. Murdock, and P. Schlesinger (eds.), *Communicating Politics*, Leicester: Leicester University Press, 1986.

Peacock Committee (1986), *Report of the Committee on Financing the BBC* (Peacock Report), Cmnd. 9824 (London: HMSO).

Pilkington Committe (1962), *Report of the Committee on Broadcasting, 1960* (Pilkington Report), Cmnd 1753 (London: HMSO).

Reith, J. (1925), *Memorandum of Information on the Scope and Conduct of the Broadcasting Service*, BBC Written Archive, Caversham, Reading.

Sykes Committee (1923), *Broadcasting Committee Report* (Sykes Report), Cmnd. 1951 (London: HMSO).

Williams, R. (1961), *Culture and Society* (Harmondsworth: Penguin).

Further Reading   Crawford Committee (1926), *Report of the Broadcasting Committee* (Crawford Report), Cmnd 2599 (London: HMSO).

Home Office (1988), *Broadcasting in the '90s: Competition, Choice and Quality* (London: HMSO).

MacCabe, Colin, and Stewart, Olivia (eds.) (1986), *The BBC and Public Service Broadcasting* (Manchester: Manchester University Press).

Scannell, Paddy, and Cardiff, David, *Serving the Nation: Public Service Broadcasting before the War* (Milton Keynes: Open University Press).

For a fuller discussion of the wider implications of this chapter, see Paddy Scannell, 'Public Service Broadcasting and Modern Public Life', *Media, Culture and Society*, 11/2 (Apr. 1989), 135–66.

3

The End of the Monopoly

Asa Briggs

·

THE NATIONAL TELEVISION COUNCIL to resist commercial television was formally inaugurated at a meeting in the home of Lady Violet Bonham Carter on 18 June. At this meeting, which [Christopher] Mayhew thought went 'splendidly', Lady Violet, 'magnificent in the Chair', was appointed chairman for the future and Lord Waverley honorary president (his office was to be no sinecure), and an organizing committee was set up which Mayhew did not consider to be 'really powerful and representative enough' in its first guise.[1] It included several MPs, among them Mayhew, Edward Shackleton, and the Liberal D. W. Wade. The vice-presidents and supporters, whose names figured on the letterhead, included Sir Michael Balcon, Beveridge, E. M. Forster, Frank Gentle, Julian Huxley, Lord Horder, Violet Markham, Lord Moran, Harold Nicolson, Lady Palmerston, W. F. Oakeshott, Bertrand Russell, Viscount Samuel, Mary Stocks, and Henry Willink.

The committee met thereafter every two weeks in an interview room in the House of Commons. From the start it placed a great deal of emphasis on evoking 'the weight of authority', even though some of its members felt that 'the high moral tone is the one calculated to make the government obstinate'.[2] In private and public, emphasis was placed on the need for 'pressure and publicity' to counter the 'pressure' from vested interests. 'We express our sincere hope', the council wrote, 'that the government will yield no further to the intense pressure to which they have been subjected by a comparatively small number of interested parties'.[3]

First published in *The History of Broadcasting in the United Kingdom*, iv: *Sound and Vision* (Oxford: Oxford University Press, 1979), 903–36 by permission of the author, the British Broadcasting Corporation, and Oxford University Press.

1 Mayhew to Simon, 19 June 1953, Mayhew Papers, in private possession. 'This can be changed,' he added.
2 Barnes to the bishop of Bristol, 20 Nov. 1953, bishop of Bristol to Barnes, 28 Nov. 1953, Barnes Papers, in private possession.
3 Mayhew to Simon, 19 June 1953, Mayhew Papers; National Television Council, organizing committee, minutes, 18 June 1953; Mayhew stressed that the council should be 'positive' in its approach and William Clark suggested—with general approval—that the BBC should not be regarded as 'perfection'. For an early council pamphlet, see *Britain Unites against Commercial TV*. Cf. the Popular Television Association's *Britain Unites to Demand Competitive TV*.

The council set out deliberately to appeal to 'thinking' people everywhere and sponsored a pamphlet by Mayhew, *Dear Viewer*, which sold 60,000 copies. 'I ask you', Mayhew's text concluded, 'to exercise all the influence you have, as a free citizen of the most democrat country in the world, to prevent this barbarous idea being realised.' Mayhew gave all the royalties of *Dear Viewer* to the council.

The 'weight of authority' was represented not only by names like that of Lady Violet herself, Lord Waverley, Lord Brand, or Lord Halifax, but by those of church leaders—the two archbishops and, as a member of the organizing committee, the Revd E. Rodgers of the department of Christian citizenship of the Methodist Church—and of the vice-chancellors of universities and leading representatives of teachers' organizations.[4] Fourteen vice-chancellors, including those of Oxford (C. M. Bowra), Cambridge (Lionel Whitby), and London (H. Hale-Bellot), all signed a letter to *The Times* in which they warned that if television was placed on 'a commercial basis', 'the power of television for good' would be lost, never to be recovered.[5] The sense of a 'moral responsibility' for television output went further than the protection of the rights of 'the young'. 'Once sponsored radio and TV are admitted,' the *Daily Sketch* thundered, 'nothing is sacred.'[6] This was the 'high moral tone' at its most suspect.

If the National Television Council was the first off the mark—in public—in June 1953 and within a few weeks had agreed on a constitution, within a fortnight of the government statement on 2 July a rival organization, the Popular Television Association, was set up. Its object was 'to awaken the national conscience to the dangers,

---

4 Many bishops made statements on the subject, e.g. Dr Greer, the bishop of Manchester, as reported in the *Manchester Guardian*, 25 June 1953. Their views were strongly criticized in the *Recorder*, 4 July 1953, and the members of the rival Popular Television Association (see below) included Canon L. J. Collins and Canon C. B. Mortlock. In Oct. 1953 the bishop of Durham, Dr A. M. Ramsey, said he was startled by the dogmatism of some of his colleagues and had not made up his mind. Christian Action deliberately stood aside as a body (Mayhew to L. J. Collins, 18 Dec. 1953, 28 Jan. 1954; Collins to Mayhew, 8 Apr. 1954; both in Mayhew Papers). Mrs Dorothy M. Roberts proposed a concentration on headmistresses at the first meeting of the council after Lord Samuel had complained that not enough women were represented. For a National Union of Teachers statement, see *Schoolmaster*, 10 July 1953. *Education*, l0 July 1953, reported the unanimous adoption by the Association of Education Committees of a resolution hostile to commercial broadcasting 'whether by sound or sight'. It was proposed by J. L. Longland. For protests from the Workers' Educational Association, see *Liverpool Daily Post*, 22 June 1953. The council itself recognized that it was short of businessmen (organizing committee, minutes, 18 June, 1 July, 1 Oct. 1953). Sir Miles Thomas, then chairman of BOAC, was an enthusiastic supporter (Thomas to Mayhew, 25 Nov. 1953, Mayhew Papers).

5 *The Times*, 1 July 1953. The vice-chancellors referred to the different treatments of the coronation on the two sides of the Atlantic. Appleton at Edinburgh was a dissenter.

6 *Daily Sketch*, 4 June 1953.

social, political and artistic, of monopoly in the rapidly developing field of television' and 'to provide the public at the earliest possible moment with alternative programmes which are in keeping with the best standards of British taste'. 'Almost overnight,' the earl of Derby, its president, promised of commercial television, 'the owner of a television set becomes a richer man.'[7] Its vice-presidents included Alec Bedser, the cricketer, Collin Brooks, Professors George Catlin and John Coatman, Sir Ian Fraser, Rex Harrison, Valerie Hobson, the Marquis of Londonderry, Somerset Maugham, the Duke of Northumberland, Viscount Nuffield, and A. J. P. Taylor.

There had also been an immediate reaction to the Government statement in the Conservative parliamentary party. The day after it was made, the Broadcasting Group met to discuss future tactics and pressed for the speediest possible end to the BBC's monopoly. They went on to convey this view to R. A. Butler, the chancellor of the exchequer, who assured the 1922 Committee on 9 July that the government firmly intended to go ahead with its plan.[8] They also secured the formal setting up of a new Radio and Television Committee—this time the official committee which they had hoped for—with Walter Elliot as chairman and Sir Robert Grimston as vice-chairman.[9] Elliot was an experienced broadcaster, who had been a well-known member of the old BBC *Brains Trust* as well as an experienced politician, and on 8 August he wrote to Sir Ian Jacob, director general of the BBC, suggesting a broadcast debate on whether 'the uses of advertisement are sweet or nasty'. 'I shall be quite willing to take the part of Daniel,' he added, 'and there are an almost unlimited number of candidates for the lions.'[10] Jacob had his own stock of images: advertising mixed with programmes he compared with coal being carried in a railway train compartment full of passengers.

Whatever the outcome of such an open debate might have been—and the governors procrastinated in deciding whether to stage it[11]—there was little doubt on either side in July 1953 about the important uses of 'public relations'. Principles mattered, particularly to the influential members of the National Television Council, but efficient presentation of the case for or against was known to matter too when large sections of the public were ignorant

7 Press statement, 13 Nov. 1953; repr. in *Britain Unites to Demand Competitive TV.*

8 *Daily Telegraph*, l0 July 1953. The matter had not been discussed at the meeting of the 1922 Committee on 2 July, the day of the announcement.

9 *The Times*, 9 July 1953.

10 Walter Elliot to Sir Ian Jacob, 8 Aug. 1953, BBC Written Archives Centre (WAC), Reading.

11 BBC Board of governors, minutes, 3 Sept. 1953, WAC. The board of management (minutes, 14 Sept 1953, WAC) felt that a debate in a public hall might be more suitable. See Briggs, *Sound and Vision*, 946.

or apathetic. Mayhew was very well known to viewers as a BBC television personality, and he could draw on the part-time services of Sydney Lewis, the public relations officer of the Associated British Pictures Corporation, one of the film interests which, like the newspaper interests, opposed commercial television.[12] The Popular Television Association, however, had the big battalions on its side: it included so many public relations experts, indeed, that it was embarrassed by their presence, as it was also by the claim of Lord Woolton, the great public image maker, that, although he was ill in 1953, he had created the association from inside the Conservative Party's central office.[13] Years later, Harold Harris, writing in the *Evening Standard*, recalled how he had been approached on 11 July 1953 by Anthony Fell MP with the offer of 'a public relations job' in connection with 'a short sharp public relations campaign' to secure the speedy introduction of commercial television. 'The complete support' of Aims of Industry, which had been fighting battles against nationalization, would, he was told, be made available.[14] It was. Kenneth Mason and Gordon McIvor were seconded to the association and worked as paid officials. The full-time secretary was Ronald Simms, who had been employed by the agency W. H. Gollings & Associates. Simms was later to succeed Mark Chapman-Walker as publicity director for the Conservative Party, and when he left the Conservative Party he was to be associated with a campaign for commercial radio.[15]

Before turning in more detail to the two pressure groups which struggled to influence government in 1953, it is necessary to consider again the material presented by Professor Hugh Wilson in his detailed but controversial study of the advent of commercial television in 1955, one of the few monographs at the disposal of a historian of British broadcasting. 'A future scholar, looking at the struggle over commercial television,' wrote a reviewer in *The Economist* of Wilson's book when it appeared in 1961, 'will find that though some new papers may be available, others will have been destroyed and that fewer and less accurate memories will be at his disposal for consultation.'[16] The words ring true, for it is already difficult to substantiate some of Professor Wilson's detail. His monograph is only one source, however, and part of its controversial

---

12 Dr Eric Fletcher, Labour MP for East Islington, was deputy chairman of the Associated British Pictures Corporation, which also gave financial support to the National Television Council. Fletcher represented Warner Brothers. For differences in the board, see Howard Thomas, *With an Independent Air* (London: Weidenfeld & Nicolson, 1977), 143–4.

13 H. H. Wilson, *Pressure Group* (London: Secker & Warburg, 1961), 165.

14 *Evening Standard*, 18 July 1961.

15 *Daily Express*, 16 May 1962.

16 *The Economist*, 26 Aug. 1961

quality sprang not so much from its revelations of 'cloak and dagger' detail, but from the fact that it was something of a *livre d'occasion* which appeared at a time when both the BBC and its competitor, not yet created in 1953, were under further official review by the Pilkington Committee.[17] Old battles were still being fought as the new battle proceeded. Eight years had already elapsed since the passing of the Television Act of 1954, but there were two threats of court action when the book was published; and Lord Reith drew attention to it in a remarkably frank and vituperative speech in the House of Lords which shocked many of his fellow peers at least as much as the introduction of commercial television in 1954 had done. 'Hunched, mountainous and speaking with a kind of controlled ferocity,' as one observer described him, Reith moved a resolution calling attention to the lesson of Wilson's study. In return, he was attacked by a hurt as well as indignant Woolton and accused somewhat inadequately of offering merely 'a torrent of vulgar abuse'.[18]

Reith's speech was far more than that: he packed into it the feelings of a lifetime, and still felt at the end that he had not 'damn-blasted Woolton as forcefully' as he ought to have done.[19] By 1962, however, few shared his forthright values which had once dominated a generation. A more generally acceptable defence of Professor Wilson's account was made in 1962 by R. H. S. Crossman, who began a review with the characteristic (and prophetic) words, 'I have always maintained that there is trouble in store for anyone who strips off the legend and gives the first truthful account of British Parliamentary politics since 1945.'[20]

Vantage-points from which to study recent history have changed many times since 1962, and in this chapter . . . attention is focused on what at the time was thought, said, and done about commercial television and its prospects, not on what has been thought, said, and done since. Neither the National Television Council nor the Popular Television Association in 1953 was in a position to forecast accurately either the pattern or the consequences of competitive television in Britain, and neither was to win a complete victory. This was clear even by 1955. Professor Wilson had little to say of the final act of Parliament—the 1954 Television Act. He had little to say also about the protracted debates leading up to it or of the complex structure of broadcasting which eventually emerged and which diverged so strongly from many of the most recent predictions. A. J. P. Taylor, who was an active member of the Popular Television

17 Cmd. 1753 (1962). The committee, with Sir Harry Pilkington as chairman, had been appointed in July 1960.

18 *The Times*, 10 May 1962, commenting on Wilson, *Pressure Group*.

19 Lord Reith, *The Reith Diaries*, ed. C. Stuart (London: Collins, 1975), 9 May 1962.

20 *Guardian*, 8 June 1962.

Association, saw the eventual outcome both as participant and historian in very different terms from those of Wilson. 'I gave no
endorsement to the present system of commercial television, mis-
takenly called "independent",' he wrote, 'indeed, I specifically condemned it.'[21] Others, however—the majority in Parliament then
and later—preferred the 'new system' to all the alternatives. It
seemed a wiser outcome than any which had at first been likely.

Because there are so many layers of later history, it is necessary to
recall that during the period of history covered in this chapter the
only recent official inquiry into the BBC which was on the record
was that of the Beveridge Committee[22] and that Lord Hailsham
complained bitterly in Parliament that members of the government
and most of his fellow peers had not even read the Beveridge
Report.[23] It is necessary to recall, too, that Robert McKenzie, already
well known as a broadcaster,[24] had not yet published his *Political
Parties*, the first of a number of studies in political science which
introduced into this country from across the Atlantic conceptions
of 'pressure politics',[25] and that Henry Fairlie had not yet publicized
the term 'the Establishment' nor J. K. Galbraith the concept of 'the
affluent society'.[26] Not everyone in 1954 attributed the advent of
alternative television solely to the sinister machinations of a small
group of 'nominally insignificant Conservative backbenchers'
working from inside the Conservative Party, although the idea was
certainly already current and was expressed frequently in Parliament by Herbert Morrison, one of the Labour Party's chief
spokesmen.[27]

Most of the debate centred, like 'the rehearsal' of 1952, on 'commercialism' and its present and possible influence on social and
cultural life. 'In that subtle way that is unique to this Island,' wrote
The Economist, 'it is not so much stated as taken for self-evident that
only cads would want to have advertising on the air.'[28] Yet the real
issue to others, a minority which included *The Economist*, was the

21 *New Statesman*, 28 July 1961.

22 See Briggs, *Sound and Vision*, ch. 3.

23 *House of Lords, Official Report*, vol. 188, col. 384, 1 July 1954.

24 See Briggs, *Sound and Vision*, 669, 811.

25 R. T. McKenzie, *British Political Parties* (1955). See also S. E. Finer, *Anonymous
   Empire* (1958); J. D. Stewart, *British Pressure Groups* (1958); H. Eckstein, *Pressure
   Group Politics, The Case of the British Medical Association* (1960).

26 *Daily Mail*, 29 Oct. 1958. Fairlie bracketed Haley with Lady Violet Bonham Carter
   and John Sparrow, the warden of All Souls, as 'cardinals' of the 'Establishment'.
   J. K. Galbraith's *The Affluent Society* also appeared in 1958.

27 See Briggs, *Sound and Vision*, 441, and *News Chronicle*, 10 Oct. 1953: 'The handful
   of Tory backbenchers who started a revolt over commercial television less than
   eighteen months ago have travelled a long way.' Cf. *Hansard* vol. 527, col. 207, 4
   May 1954: 'All that has happened is that about twenty hon. Members on the back
   benches opposite have thrust their will down the throats of the Government.'

28 *The Economist*, 15 Aug. 1953.

same as it had always been since 1944 and 1945. Why should broadcasting be treated in a different way from 'other media', including the press? Was there not an overwhelming objection *in principle* to leaving television in the hands of a single corporation? For *The Economist*, Beveridge had not settled the issue, and it was still prepared to envisage in the summer of 1953 not commercial television but either a second public service corporation modelled on the BBC or a whole host of alternative models falling far short of what the major commercial interests wanted.

The Economist said very little—far less than Wilson was to do— about the financial interests which stood to gain (perhaps not at first) from the advent of commercial television.[29] Yet it recognized more than Wilson did, even though he was writing in retrospect, that the ultimate outcome would depend on 'a compromise'. Indeed, the very idea of introducing competitive television and leaving sound broadcasting as a monopoly was already an initial compromise, at least as far as principle, if not profit, was concerned, and the government showed itself willing throughout to compromise on basic questions of control. 'It is probably fair to say', the *Tablet* had written as early as April 1953, 'that the solution will be found by trial and error, in the empirical fashion of the English, and that it will not be found at either extreme,' while it was before the government statement was made in July that *The Economist* itself had urged the government 'to explore the possibility between the two extremes'.[30] *The Economist* was already anticipating Wilson, however, in pointing to the significance of pressures. If the BBC's monopoly were to be broken and a better scheme devised in this country than either that of the present monopoly or 'the pure commercialism of America', this would not be because 'wise men have sat down together and thought it out as an ideal system and had then commended it to their fellow citizens by reasoned persuasion. . . . It will be because the subject happened, by accident, to fall among politicians, who then found themselves pushed by the

29 For stress on the financial interests, see e.g. Ness Edwards in the *Daily Herald*, 19 June 1953; *Church Times*, 3 July 1953; and, above all, *Daily Worker*, 7 July 1953, and *Sunday Tribune*, 26 June 1953. Aspects of the story were summed up in C. Jenkins, *Power behind the Screen* (1961). For the comparative finances of American television during this period, see Chester and Garrison, 44–6 and ch. 7. For the three years 1948–50 aggregate operating losses of $48 million were reported to the Federal Communications Commission. For an American comment on British financial prospects, see *Advertisers' Weekly*, 2 July 1953. Cyrus Ducker, the chairman of the television advertising panel of the Institute of Incorporated Practitioners in Advertising, said modestly in Oct. 1953 that he believed that 'five hours of commercial television a day' would guarantee a revenue 'enabling advertisers to produce excellent programmes which would certainly measure up to those of the BBC' (*The Times*, 20 Oct. 1953).

30 *Tablet*, 25 Apr. 1953; *The Economist*, 20 June 1953. Cf. *The Times*: 'Compromise is seen, by anyone who understands the reality of so-called competitive television, to be valueless' (quoted in *Punch*, 2 Sept. 1953).

pressures to which they respond along a path which may perhaps, if our speculations are well founded, turn out to be fairly satisfactory.' It is doubtful whether *The Economist* had A. J. P. Taylor in mind when it added, 'This will not be very pleasing to the practitioners of reason. But it is the way of the world.'[31]

The two pressure groups tried to use 'reason' as well as the arts of public relations, although according to at least one provincial evening newspaper, 'the vast majority of people', when they considered commercial television, were not 'swayed by reason' but by 'a sentiment which has something in it of the idea that an Englishman's home is his castle': 'they heartily dislike a commercial foot in the door' and 'feel that freedom to switch off is no freedom at all'.[32] Such a sentiment could be related, of course, to a principle. Ending the BBC's monopoly might give 'freedom from the BBC', as Maurice Cranston put it, only 'in exchange for bondage to the powerful advertisers, the makers of razor-blades, deodorants, malted milks, tonic wines and so on'. There was a difference even in popular entertainment between that which was 'prompted by some sense of public service' and that which was prompted only by 'the desire for material gain': commercial television was 'intrinsically debasing'.[33]

As the debate continued, the National Television Council saw and depicted its rival as a tool of vested interests—many of them monopolists themselves—and as 'professional, audacious, mercenary and ruthless' in its methods, while the Popular Television Association dwelt on the 'holier-than-thou' do-goodism of its opponents, 'the rule of the high-minded', or, as the marquess of Linlithgow was to describe them, 'the Patriarchs'.[34] 'Let us prefer the long competitive spoon with the Devil', John Grierson, the documentary film maker begged, 'to the milk-and-water hand-outs of this episcopal clinic.'[35] 'I hope and pray that commercialisation of television will, throughout the country, be decisively defeated,' wrote the bishop of Manchester.[36]

There was thus a contrast of styles as well as of purposes between the two pressure groups, with the National Television Council emphasizing its poverty and the Popular Television Association its freedom from cant. Both bodies attempted to secure a wide range of representation and participation, although the former knew from

31 *The Economist*, 15 Aug. 1953.

32 *Yorkshire Evening Post*, 2 Sept. 1953.

33 *Time and Tide*, 27 June 1953; letter to the *Manchester Guardian*, 20 May 1953.

34 C. Mayhew, 'Pressure Groups and Television', *Guardian*, 17 July 1961; *House of Lords, Official Report*, vol. 188, cols. 242–4, 30 June 1954.

35 Quoted in the Popular Television Association pamphlet *The Fundamentals of Competitive Television*.

36 Address to the Manchester Diocesan Conference, 24 June 1953, quoted in *Britain Unites against Commercial TV*.

the start that it could rely on the support of a very large number of voluntary groups already in existence. The National Television Council was very anxious to secure its donations from 'as many representative bodies as possible, with not too much money from any one source'.[37] When it was suggested, however, that an appeal might be made to Conservative Party organizations, Waverley thought that it might be treated as an 'unwarrantable intrusion'. 'We are in a period', he went on, 'in which the excesses and mala-droitness of our opponents are likely to do our cause more good than any *vigorous* activity on our part.'[38] The Popular Television Association felt from the start that it had to 'stump the country' and to invade the press both with articles and with letters. Indeed, guid-ance in drafting letters was given to members of the Association who desired it, and many identical letters appeared in scattered newspapers. So, too, did identical articles. A twelve-minute film, *Television Choice*, featured Alec Bedser and the film star Joan Griffiths; and there were public rallies (well planned but sometimes very sparsely attended) in London, Birmingham, Liverpool, Man-chester, York, Cardiff, Edinburgh, and Glasgow.

Like the National Television Council, the association tried to emphasize that it was 'a non-party body', and it always made the most of non-Conservative writers and speakers, like David Hard-man, a former Labour parliamentary secretary to the ministry of education, Lord Winster, a former Labour minister for civil avia-tion, and Professor Catlin, one of its vice-presidents. If there were Conservative undertones in slogans like 'setting television free', A. J. P. Taylor could be relied upon to translate them into the lan-guage of 'the freedom of the mind'. The members also included Gillie Potter, the comedian, who had made his reputation before the war with sound broadcasting, Ted Kavanagh, scriptwriter of *ITMA*, Malcolm Muggeridge, one of the signatories of its first letter to *The Times*, Maurice Winnick, bandleader and owner of the broadcasting rights in Britain of *What's My Line*, Professor Arnold Plant, the economist, and a second Collins, Canon John, best known for his leadership of the Campaign for Nuclear Disarmament.

Common to the whole campaign—although not to all the campaigners—was a certain animus against the BBC, just as experi-ence with the BBC and its governing bodies was a very strong bond in the leadership of the National Television Council. There were many inconsistencies. Gillie Potter, who had been made by the BBC, claimed that it was now flogging foul films and 'boosting bawdy books', while at the same time A. J. P. Taylor, who blamed George

---

37 National Television Council, organizing committee, minutes, 5, 19 Aug. 1953.

38 Ibid., 3 Sept.1953. A draft pamphlet by a professional journalist was turned down on 17 Sept.

Barnes for turning *In the News* into 'a balanced forum of ortho-
doxy', was condemning the corporation as a bastion of 'respectability'.[39] Norman Collins attacked its 'Brahmin caste', while Ted
Kavanagh was claiming that it was not offering Roman Catholics
enough Roman Catholic programmes. Catlin believed it was not
doing enough for adult education—and much else besides—while
Winnick, backed by Lord Derby, maintained that it was not offering
the right kind of popular entertainment.[40] This was variety of critique enough, but there were many other appeals *ad homines*. Thus,
Scotland was offered priority when commercial licences were
granted and Wales was promised its own television service.[41]

There was also a very special appeal to technicians, script writers,
artists, and performers, who were tempted with the prospects of
alternative employment. 'Songwriters ready for the rush,'
announced *Melody Maker*, which gave its wholehearted support to
the campaign. 'Commercial TV would mean more work for thousands' was another newspaper headline.[42] One television star who
stood on the sidelines was Gilbert Harding. When asked to join the
National Television Council by Lady Violet Bonham Carter he
replied that 'whilst he was almost wholly persuaded that commercial
radio and television are bad, he could not make up his mind about
the desirability of associating himself openly with the NTC'.[43]

The influence on opinion of the Popular Television Association is
very difficult to measure. What is certain, however, is that the public
debate between the council and the association, intermittent and
faltering though it was,[44] revealed many cross-currents and
counter-currents within the political parties. Most Labour MPs
were opposed to any change and did not need whips to tell them so.
They could be accused (by a fellow socialist) of clinging to 'a mixture of Socialist doctrine and Puritanism'.[45] Yet at the same time
they were deeply suspicious of commercial pressures and of the
association with the Popular Television Association of a body like

39 See his article 'Freedom of Speech and Television' in the *Contemporary Review*,
   Dec. 1953, where he called the BBC 'highly tolerant in whatever does not matter'.

40 *New Statesman*, 21 July 1961.

41 *Daily Mail*, 29 Oct. 1953; *South Wales Echo and Express*, 10 Nov. 1953.

42 *Melody Maker*, 8 Aug. 1953. See also (for other kinds of musicians) *Music Teacher*
   (Sept. 1953), and (for magicians) *Abra Cadabra*, 8 Aug. 1953; *Glasgow Evening
   Times*, 23 Sept. 1953.

43 National Television Council, organizing committee, minutes, 11 May 1954.

44 Both 'sides' knew this. The National Television Council decided in Nov. 1953
   (minutes, 18 Nov. 1953), for example, to cancel a Dec. meeting in Manchester, to
   be addressed by Dr Stephen Taylor, on the grounds that 'the Popular Television
   Association had recently held a meeting in Manchester at which the attendance
   had been very poor'.

45 *Tribune*, 26 June 1953. Cf. *The Economist*, 13 Mar. 1954, where it was stated that
   many Labour MPs were afraid that commercial television would spread jokes
   against socialism and consider jokes against Churchill as 'rather bad taste'.

Aims of Industry. One Labour Party pamphlet described the government's proposals as 'commercialism run mad' (a phrase of Morrison's) and attacked 'the Conservative TV (too vulgar) policy'.[46] 'Our programmes would be full of concealed propaganda for "free enterprise", for commercialism, for all the values of big business.'[47] By contrast the Conservative Party, which appealed to many elements besides 'big business', was split, and every view about television, including the most extreme, seems to have been held inside it.

The Times was right to say in retrospect that 'the Conservative Party, which was in power, could without weakening in the least its hold on the country have set its face against the change'. But it was wrong in following Morrison in suggesting that the party 'shirked responsibility' only 'because a few resolute and astute men who knew their own minds drove them down the road'.[48] Certainly 'resolute and astute men' were always active, particularly inside the Conservative central office, and it was under the 'party' imprimatur and not that of the Popular Television Association that Chapman-Walker produced a summer pamphlet in 1953, *There's Free Speech, Why not Free Switch?* Certainly, too, the section in the pamphlet on 'moral critics' of commercial television referred to some influential members of Chapman-Walker's own party. Yet in the constituencies Conservative opinion was changing in the summer and autumn of 1953, and the more the Labour Party thundered against 'commercialism', the more there was a revulsion inside the Conservative Party against critics like Halifax and Hailsham. It was felt increasingly that if the party introduced commercial television before a general election and the Labour Party then tried to 'take it away', the issue would greatly favour the Conservatives.

As early as June 1953 many Conservatives had felt uneasy when Attlee described 'Lord Halifax and so on' as 'the best minds in the Conservative Party'.[49] The next Conservative prime minister, Anthony Eden, did not like the idea of commercial television, but he did not speak out. As the summer went by there were many Conservative backbenchers who had hitherto taken no part in parliamentary debates on radio and television who now declared that they no longer opposed competitive television and had been won over to a belief that an acceptable British compromise was possible. The shift in support was plain at the Conservative party conference at Margate early in October. Of five resolutions on television submitted to the conference, four supported the government and the fifth asked for a free vote on the issue. Sir Robert Grimston called

46 VH 6394: 'Keep our TV and Radio Standards'.
47 Labour Party, *Talking Points*, 28 June 1952.
48 *The Times*, 11 May 1962.
49 *Observer*, 14 June 1953.

competitive television 'a fundamental principle of Conservative policy', and eventually a resolution was carried fully approving the government's decision to permit an element of competition. There were only a few scattered votes against, and one speaker, eschewing all moderation, warned that a continuing BBC monopoly of television would imperil 'the free society'.[50]

The Conservative party conference had been invited, however, to support government proposals which were very different in substance from those which it might have been called on to accept a year before. The parliamentary recess had been a time for 'careful thinking'; and at the end of August the postmaster-general in an important statement told the country that the government did not now intend to adopt the American system of dependence on sponsoring—it would substitute commercial programme contractors—that it was not 'in any way altering the present method of working of the BBC', and that it recognized 'the misgivings' expressed by 'thoughtful and serious people' about its first proposals.[51] The last point was underlined also by R. A. Butler, who said in a widely quoted speech that he did not wish to discount 'the sincere feelings of those who genuinely think that this new and powerful force should be kept as a monopoly of an already tried and trusted organisation'. Even the promised White Paper, he said, should not be the last word. It should focus attention on 'practical issues' so as 'to help the Government to reach a final decision'.[52]

Such comments had not shifted the attitudes of the opponents of commercial television. The *Manchester Guardian* condemned the biggest of the 'compromises' being canvassed by De La Warr—that of issuing 'a number of syndicates' with licences to provide commercial television programmes and with the advertisers being kept out of programme-making—as 'at only one remove' from sponsored television;[53] and a related point was taken up on the eve of the publication of the White Paper by Lord Radcliffe, whose letter of 16 October to *The Times* triggered off a new controversy. Noting that no one talked any longer of 'sponsorship', Radcliffe asked why anyone should put more trust in the owners of commercial stations than in advertisers.[54] And if, as Lord Derby had suggested, the

50 *The Times*, 9 Oct. 1953.

51 Ibid., 31 Aug. 1953.

52 *Manchester Guardian*, 31 Aug. 1953.

53 Ibid., 1 Sept. 1953.

54 When the government made its July statement, Collins stated categorically, 'the issue of the sponsorship no longer arises' (*Daily Telegraph*, 3 July 1953). Cf. Lord Foley, a vice-president of the Popular Television Association (*News Chronicle*, 20 Oct. 1953), who said 'sponsored television in Britain is a dead issue', and Sir Frederick Sykes (*The Times*, 27 Oct. 1953), who claimed, 'That chimera has been definitely laid.'

government through 'safeguards' could take away the licences of any such station owners who broke 'a code of practice', would not this be a far more serious threat to 'freedom' than any restrictions at present imposed by ministers on the BBC? Moreover, if a new 'Authority' were to be set up to deal with the supervision of commercial television—and he insisted that it should be called 'commercial'—it would be 'a great deal less free and independent than the BBC itself'.[55]

Radcliffe spoke of a 'confused . . . struggle for liberty', although Malcolm Muggeridge, who had been engaged in an interesting controversy with Mayhew earlier in the summer, claimed, not entirely convincingly, that the confusion existed largely in Radcliffe's own mind.[56] Advertising revenue, Muggeridge said, would make possible 'free' television just as it made possible a 'free' press. 'Whoever controlled' a future television station would, 'like the controllers of a newspaper, do their best, in their own interests to ensure that the material presented was "palatable" to the public.' Once installed, competitive television would become 'varied and manifold'.

The adjective 'palatable' raised all the old issues—about the press (very unpopular at this time in many Labour Party circles) as much as about television—and obviously there was no guarantee that if there were more stations there would be greater variety of output.[57] Muggeridge was wrong, too, to speak of the alternative being 'a continuance forever of all television and sound radio being directed by one agency under Government control'. First, the BBC had never been under direct 'government control' in the sense that he implied, and, second, it was unlikely that any government, least of all the particular Conservative government in power in 1953, would allow commercial television to be entirely free from control. Muggeridge was right to insist, however, as Boothby had demanded and as the government had already conceded, that politics and religion would have to come within the programming arrangements of the new commercial stations if there were to be any advance in freedom.

Three important points were made in this last burst of correspondence, with Edward Shackleton drawing attention to the differences between 'commercial television' and a 'commercial Press' and Benn Levy enlarging upon them. First, they said, the press

---

55 In a letter to *The Times*, 24 Oct. 1953, Edward Shackleton claimed that 'the commercializers', having got rid of the word 'sponsored', were now trying to get rid of the word 'commercial'.

56 Ibid., 20 Oct. 1953.

57 See ibid., 27 Oct. 1953, for a response to this point in a letter from an American reader: 'Whatever else may be said of it, the BBC offers a far more varied fare than American commercial radio. Commercialism reduces all to the dead level of majority taste, as nothing shows better than your evening newspapers.' Cf. Barnes, note of 7 Aug. 1953: 'We may fail, but we shall not do it [broadcasting] better by having to compete with a service whose object is to sell goods' (Barnes Papers).

derived income from both advertising and sales; commercial tele-vision would derive income from advertising only. Secondly, they went on, commercial television would be controlled from the start by fewer people than the press, even the press of 1953, which had been reduced by newspaper failures and had ended in mergers. If there were many complaints about the decline in the number of newspapers, it had to be recognized that commercial television would actually begin with an oligopoly. Thirdly, they concluded, genuine freedom of expression depended on 'a multiple market' and on attention being paid to minority opinions and tastes. It was unlikely, in their opinion, that commercial television would be as responsive to such tastes as the BBC. 'The issue', as they saw it, was not whether television should be 'run by "Whitehall" or by "the people"', but whether it should be 'run by persons answerable to the representatives of us all or to the representatives of what is compendiously called "big business"'.[58]

Correspondence in newspapers gives some idea of the strength of feeling late in 1953, at least among a minority who cared. So, too, do articles in periodicals. Some writers, however, tried not to argue one case or another but to place what was happening in perspective. 'It may be safely forecast', one of them began, 'that no one will attempt to impose the American pattern of competition on this country.' It might be safely forecast also, he thought, that 'there would be a large measure of support for the creation of a second Television Corporation not dissimilar to the BBC'. 'The respective Licences might allocate certain specific functions to each,' but each would include programme-makers and administrators.[59]

The forecast was only partially correct, for while the main point in the new White Paper (Cmd. 9005), which appeared on 13 November 1953, was that a 'second Authority' was necessary, it was stated that the new authority was not to engage in daily programme-making itself. It was to supervise the commercial sys-tem through ownership and operation of transmitting stations and the renting out of its facilities to commercial companies—the number was not mentioned—which would be responsible not only for selling time to advertisers but for securing balanced programme output in each station. This, the White Paper stated, was 'a typically British approach to this new problem'. A considerable degree of freedom was to be combined with what potentially, at least, was a stringent degree of control. 'In practice,' however, the White Paper added, 'the fewer rules and less day-to-day interference the better; the need would be for a continuing friendly and constructive con-tact between the Corporation and the companies'. The monopoly

58 *The Times*, 24, 30 Oct. 1953.
59 A Correspondent, 'Solving the TV Controversy', *Fortnightly* (Nov. 1953).

would be broken, but control would not go. 'As television has great and increasing power in influencing men's minds, the Government believes that its control should not remain in the hands of a single authority, however excellent it may be.'

Doubts about the extent of 'control' remained. There were supporters of 'freedom' who objected to the 'conception of running advertising TV on the lines of a Kindergarten school or the Cheltenham Ladies College'.[60] 'This is not competitive TV,' one advertiser complained, 'this is a minuscule BBC operating under handicaps which even that august body has never had to face.'[61] 'It is strange', wrote the *Scotsman*, 'that the Government has succumbed to the theory that the public cannot be trusted to choose their own entertainment and that there is some moral superiority about a Corporation.'[62] Yet at least one newspaper, which found the government's proposals worthy of careful study, thought that 'in the wider interests of the community as a whole it is vital' (particularly given the lifting of the ban on religion and politics) 'that the new Corporation shall exercise its full power to discipline any company which permits any lowering of the standards to which the viewing public has been accustomed'.[63]

Most commentators found the government's proposals 'ingenious', if not disarming,[64] although there was still no change of front on the part of those opponents of commercial television who condemned it on principle. In a letter addressed to *The Times*, Sydney Lewis, writing as honorary secretary of the National Television Council, noted that while the government appeared to be making 'a serious effort to meet the storm of protest raised against its earlier proposals', there was no basic change. 'Every penny of the revenue for providing programmes under the new system will come from advertisers,' and 'even the proposed Corporation, which is meant to supervise the system, is in the last resort financially dependent on the advertisers.'[65] For the *Observer*, as for *The Times*, pressure on the programme companies by their 'backers'—whatever the promised controls—would inevitably 'deliver up a mass audience, happily

60 *Daily Sketch*, 16 Nov. 1953.

61 'TV without Trust', *World's Press News*, 20 Nov. 1953. For American critical comment, see *Broadcasting-Telecasting*, 19 Nov. 1953: 'The restrictions they propose to throw about the new commercial operations would make our wildest-eyed rigid regulationists cringe.'

62 *Scotsman*, 14 Nov.1953.

63 *Birmingham Post*, 14 Nov. 1953.

64 *Financial Times*, 16 Nov. 1953; *Daily Telegraph*, 14 Nov. 1953.

65 S. K. Lewis to the editor of *The Times*, 15 Nov. 1953. Several drafts of this letter exist. One includes the phrase 'TV advertisements are sheer loss to the viewers—a useless and irritating hindrance to their enjoyment; and from the economic point of view their only effect is likely to be to increase home sales at a time when we need to increase our exports.'

relaxed and prepared to accept the suggestions of the advertiser';[66] while the *Daily Worker* suggested that both 'the advance of the working class' and 'the preservation of peace', two very large objectives, were both 'imperilled' by the new policy which could best be described as 'dope unlimited'.[67] For *The Economist*, which continued to favour its own plan (still in line with those envisaged by Geoffrey Crowther and the Beveridge Committee), the postmaster-general had devised not an ideal 'framework', but 'a scheme that fulfilled the Government's promise to a group of its backbenchers to introduce some element of competition . . . while offending as little as possible the influential and vociferous element within the Conservative Party that is perfectly content with things as they are'.[68]

The Economist was not alone in questioning whether there would be sufficient profit within the system to make it work. 'Whether advertisers will find this new medium worthwhile and will pay enough to make the hiring companies solvent,' wrote the *Daily Telegraph*, 'only experience will show.' The new corporation's initial capitalization of £500,000 seemed inadequate in respect both of capital and of potential revenue, and there was a strong case, many argued, for it to be able to secure income from another source than advertising. As for the companies, given their overheads and programme expenses, who would be able to afford to undertake such a venture?[69] *The Times* envisaged the possibility of only one new company taking up all the available time, 'if indeed under the arrangements envisaged by the White Paper it can find the money to keep a full service going'.[70] The *Manchester Guardian* thought that the three, four, or six minutes of advertising to be allowed each firm was too 'miserly [an] allowance' to support the finances of a competitive system.[71] All these were mistaken judgements. Yet Kingsley Martin was even further away from the mark. He quoted an American who had told him that American television companies were beginning to find it difficult to make profits. 'You people in England look like starting commercial television just when we in the United States look like giving it up.'[72]

66 *Observer*, 15 Nov. 1953; *The Times*, 14 Nov. 1953. The same point was made in newspapers as different as the *Yorkshire Post*, 14 Nov. 1953, and *Reynolds News*, 15 Nov. 1953.

67 *Daily Worker*, 14 Nov. 1953.

68 *The Economist*, 21 Nov. 1953; see also Briggs, *Sound and Vision*, 891.

69 *Daily Telegraph*, 14, Nov. 1953.

70 *The Times*, 14 Nov. 1953.

71 *Manchester Guardian*, 14 Nov. 1953.

72 *New Statesman and Nation*, 14 Nov. 1953. Kingsley Martin assumed also that 'the new companies will not as a rule be able to put on serious or informative programmes'.

When it reported on the 1953 White Paper, *The Economist* believed that it was not the last word. 'The very defects of the scheme proposed make it certain that the Government and the public will soon have to think again, and go on thinking, about the right framework for broadcasting in a democracy.'[73] Whatever new was being thought, however, very little that was new was said, in the two-day parliamentary discussions on the White Paper in the House of Lords, on 25 and 26 November, or in the House of Commons on 14 and 15 December.

Originally, the House of Lords would have discussed the White Paper on a motion tabled by Reith, which would not have forced an immediate division. Instead, a motion by Halifax was placed before the House, with Reith's blessing, and Reith attended the debate, without speaking, only on the first day. 'Whilst recognising the desirability of an alternative television system,' it ran, 'this House regrets that it cannot approve the proposals of Her Majesty's Government as outlined in the memorandum on television policy.' The debate attracted a very large audience and at the end tempers were frayed, particularly that of Lord Hailsham, who was one of the most fervent opponents of commercial television. He had taken Halifax's place as mover and final speaker when the latter was ill with influenza, and he roundly condemned, in a style very different from that of Halifax—some critics called it a House of Commons speech delivered in the House of Lords—'the shoddy disreputable politics' leading up to the initiation of competitive television and the 'muddle-headedness' of the proposed solution. No such measure should ever have gone forward, he claimed, 'without being included in an election manifesto'. He did not spare Salisbury, and this was thought to have lost votes; indeed, Simon thought the speech 'noisy and emotional'.

Simon's comment on his own speech—'I knew much more about the problems than the rest of the House of Lords put together'—suggests that the speech cannot have been very productive either; and as he said, it was, in fact, 'completely ignored by Ministers'. Simon thought that the best short speech was by Lord Rochester, the Methodist peer, who had packed 'a lot of moral conviction into it'; but he was appalled both by the archbishop of Canterbury, who was concerned, in his opinion, only with 'expediency', and by the lord chancellor, who 'mouthed

---

73 *The Economist*, 21 Nov. 1953. A National Television Council broadsheet, *Commercial Television: The Government's White Paper*, ended with the words, 'The government has already shown that it is sensitive to public opinion on this question. The National Television Council urges that all men of goodwill will again press on the government their opposition to commercial television. We earnestly hope that the government will have second thoughts on this matter, and that it will allow a free vote of both Houses of Parliament.'

platitudes'.[74] Principles were certainly felt to be at stake on 25 November. 'A political or economic issue on which the fate of the nation depended could hardly have provoked a controversy in which conflicting issues were combined with such deep feelings,' wrote the parliamentary correspondent of the *Manchester Guardian*.[75]

The Liberal and Labour Parties did not attempt to whip their members, although Lord Salisbury, the Conservative leader, sent an official message to the government peers 'earnestly requesting their attendance' and urging them to be in their places 'to support the Government in the Division'. The National Television Council had sent out a similar message to several hundred peers with the approval of Lord Halifax.[76] Some of the arguments had been rehearsed less than three weeks before during the debates on the address, when the lord chancellor, Lord Jowitt, had stated that advertising would still dictate programming even if direct sponsoring was no longer to be a feature of the system, and when Woolton questioned everyone, Labour, Liberal, or Conservative, who had criticized advertising. 'I fail entirely to understand the argument,' he began, 'that if you have advertisements, then the advertisements will inevitably determine the nature of the programmes. Look at our greatest newspapers: full of advertisements, indeed able to keep alive only because of the advertisements; and yet, as your Lordships are well aware, big business is not allowed to determine their policy.'[77]

The final vote in favour of the government on 26 November was 157 to 87. Salisbury, like Butler earlier in the year, had been irritated by some crude arguments, and had made it clear in what Simon thought was a 'brilliant' speech that the government would look again at the financing of its scheme and some of its other features; he had assured the House, too, that the new system would be totally different from the American.[78] Only about twenty Conservatives and National Liberals went into the lobbies to vote with Halifax—they included the duke of Wellington, Viscount Simon, and Lord

---

74 Note by A. Gordon, 27 Nov. 1953, Simon to Mary Stocks (letter not sent), 28 Nov. 1953, Manchester Public Library, Simon Papers.

75 *Manchester Guardian*, 27 Nov. 1953.

76 *House of Lords, Official Report*, vol. 184, cols. 741–3, 26 Nov. 1953. 'The Whip', Salisbury told the House, was 'not an order'. It was an 'indication of the way the Government would like its supporters to vote'. See P. A. Bromhead, *The House of Lords and Contemporary Politics* (1958), 189. There is a draft note from S. K. Lewis in the Mayhew Papers: 'Lord Halifax has asked me to state that he hopes you will find it possible to attend this debate and to support his motion if a division is called.' The response was noted in the National Television Council, minutes, 2 Dec. 1953.

77 *House of Lords, Official Report*, vol. 184, cols. 39–40, 52–53, 94–95 Nov. 1953.

78 Ibid., cols. 556–7, 568, 25 Nov. 1953; 731–8, 26 Nov. 1953.

Moyne—but there were many abstentions (some said over a hundred) and it was obvious that most of the lords were accepting with reluctance what the government had to offer.[79]

'Who wants this TV?' the *Daily Herald* had asked before the debate. The November Gallup poll, announced on the same day, showed that nearly half the electorate was now in favour.[80] The change in support since the previous poll was accounted for by a 13 per cent shift among Conservative voters—still not quite *the* big switch, but big enough to confirm Mark Chapman-Walker in his belief that the introduction of commercial television by the Conservatives could be a 'vote-winner' at the next election.[81] Forty-eight per cent now wanted BBC *and* commercial television and 48 per cent BBC only, and the Labour and Conservative shares of each group were the same. An overwhelming majority of the sample was in favour of a choice of programmes, but the idea of commercial companies providing them without any restraints did not appeal. Only 15 per cent thought that TV stations offering choice should be in the hands of private companies: 32 per cent favoured the BBC and 34 per cent a 'public Corporation'.

The Commons debate on the White Paper revealed that whatever the public might think, some of 'the resolute and astute' were still dissatisfied both with the timetable and with the terms of reference of the proposed operating 'stations'. Lord Derby might call the White Paper 'a step in the right direction',[82] but Anthony Fell, for example, found it 'the most depressing document' he had ever read. He objected particularly to the power of the new authority to withdraw licences from the contracting companies and to the power of the postmaster-general to determine the hours of broadcasting. Nor, in his view, should there be any more unnecessary waiting. The timetable, he and others felt, should involve the speedy clearing of all necessary legislation by the end of February 1954, the setting up of a new authority in March, and the beginning of commercial programming—after a year of preparations—in March 1955. Such a timetable would be right in relation to the general election

79 Before the debate Samuel had asked Farquharson to send him a copy of the Latin motto in Broadcasting House (or a translation) since he might wish to quote it (letter of 20 Nov. 1953). Broadcasting House was described as 'a temple of the arts and muses'. It had been the prayer of the first governors that 'good seed sown may bring forth a good harvest, and that all things hostile to peace or purity shall be banished from this place'.

80 *Daily Herald*, 16 Nov. 1953; *News Chronicle*, 16 Nov. 1953. The *Daily Herald* added that American interests would gain a share of control. 'They already have TV films waiting to be dumped here.' 'It is monstrous that public money should be used', it concluded, 'to upset the present thoroughly British system, which has stood the test of years with such success.'

81 Memorandum of 9 Nov. 1953, quoted in Wilson, *Pressure Groups*, 196–7.

82 Memorandum of the Popular Television Association, 10 Mar. 1954.

timetable, Conservatives like him concluded, since there were hopes
that the first few months of commercial television would give the
public programmes of 'a spectacularly high quality' and these
would be bound to influence popular attitudes at the elections.[83]

From the other side of the House Herbert Morrison, supported
by Gordon Walker, Wedgwood Benn, and three Liberal MPs,[84] continued before, during, and after the debate to press for an all-party
conference to deal with the issues and for a free vote in Parliament
itself. It is difficult to see, however, that there was any room for such
a conference, and the time was long since past for a free vote. Selwyn
Lloyd, who had played such an important role at the very beginning
of the story,[85] was not alone in arguing that the only possibility of
arranging a conference depended on the Labour and Liberal Parties
not only accepting the principle that the BBC's monopoly should
be broken but the further proposition that the means of financing
any alternative system should be based on advertising. As for the
free vote, political calculations were already deeply influencing the
issue. Both political parties were inclined during the winter of
1953–4 to look for political advantage in their stand for or against
the introduction of commercial television, although differences
inside each party remained, with a section of the Conservatives
continuing to resist blandishments or compromises (Hailsham
joined the organizing committee of the National Television Council as late as February 1954) and with some Labour MPs being
prepared to concede, as Morrison would not, that second programmes should be provided by a quite different agency from the
BBC.

Meanwhile the pressure groups were active also. The National
Television Council, arguing that the government's scheme involved
'a fatal division of responsibility between the advertising and commercial interests on the one hand and the National Corporation
on the other', produced a large number of leaflets and sent a
deputation, or exploratory mission, led by Lord Waverley and Lady
Violet Bonham Carter to meet Lord Woolton, Lord De La Warr,
and Sir David Maxwell Fyfe on 25 January 1954.[86] The mission
received some assurances that the position of the proposed new

83 Memorandum of 9 Nov. 1953. Wilson also quotes (*Pressure Group*, 197) a
backbench memorandum of 18 Nov. 1953.

84 The Gallup poll had shown that Liberal voters were most in favour of the continuation of the BBC's monopoly—54 per cent to 44 per cent, although the
comparable figures had been 61 per cent and 37 per cent in June 1953.

85 See Briggs *Sound and Vision*, 390–2.

86 National Television Council, minutes, 2 Feb. 1954. Gammans had been in touch
earlier with Mayhew about the government's plans. Thus, on 12 Dec. 1953 he
wrote to him saying that in his opening remarks in Parliament he would probably
refer to Mayhew's speech at an Oxford Union Society debate. He had sent
Mayhew tactful comments on *Dear Viewer* on 21 May 1953.

authority would be strengthened *vis-à-vis* the commercial companies. If the presence of Lord Beveridge among the National Television Council's deputation cannot have been a help (Mayhew was the fourth member of the group), the presence among the government's four of Captain Gammans, the assistant postmaster-general, was a guarantee that not too many compromises could be made.[87]

The real but limited extent of the government's concessions became plain on 4 March 1954, when the Television Bill was published. It had been prepared in what Wolstencroft, a Post Office official later to be seconded to serve as first secretary of the new Independent Television Authority, called 'a staggeringly short space of time'.[88] The new commercial stations, to be managed by companies licensed on contract, were to provide programmes which had to be predominantly 'British' and which were not to be offensive to 'good taste or decency'. It would be the duty of the new Independent Television Authority to ensure this. The news service had to be 'accurate and impartial', political broadcasting had to be responsible, and religious broadcasting, like BBC religious broadcasting, had to be 'representative of the main streams of thought' and under the control of a 'religious advisory committee'. Neither 'religion' nor 'politics' would be able to advertise directly. 'Advertisers' comments' would not be allowed to take up more than five minutes in any hour; they would have to be 'clearly distinguished from the programmes' and would not be permitted to detract from the programmes. Moreover, in selecting advertisements, the 'programme contractors' were to be expected not to show 'unreasonable discrimination either against or in favour of one particular advertiser'. The most substantial difference from the earlier White Paper, however, was the provision of an annual grant of £750,000 from public funds to the new authority, along with an authorization to the postmaster-general (with treasury consent) to lend the authority up to £2 million.

This concession, which *The Economist*—in favour of it—called a 'subsidy against advertisers', had been advocated in November 1953 by Lord Waverley and the archbishop of Canterbury.[89] It was strongly attacked, however, both by opponents of commercial television, who objected to money being taken from viewers' licence

---

87 The organizing committee of the National Television Council agreed on the membership of the deputation on 19 Jan. 1954. For the deputation and its results, see *The Times*, 26 Feb. l954.

88 Alan Wolstencroft, 'Setting up the Independent Television Authority', Jan. 1955 IBA Archives. This is an excellent summary of the story.

89 *The Economist*, 6 Mar. 1954: 'The "subsidy" is, of course, a protection against advertisers, not a buttress for them.' There were some doubts in the National Television Council, as an undated note on the parliamentary debate brings out. It had never been revealed 'for what precise purpose this money is intended'.

fees 'to pay for commercial television',[90] and by some of the leading figures in the Popular Television Association, which was unhappy about the whole chain of concessions and compromises insisted upon by the government. Why tamper with the market? To critics of 'controls', the government's plans suggested that an attempt was being made 'to infuse the sordid commercial world with a shot of the Third Programme': the 'initial ideas' had been 'lost in a maze of restrictions'.[91] For Sir Herbert Williams, an implacable opponent of all 'Butskellite' versions of Conservatism (and, indeed, of all 'intellectuals' in politics), 'the bulk of this Bill has been invented to placate a whole lot of sloppy-minded people who do not wish to get on with the job'.[92]

The government seemed to its critics to be 'giving something with one hand and taking back three-quarters of it with the other'.[93] For the *Glasgow Herald*, the bill read like the bill of rights of one of the newer democracies, and for the *Scotsman* the government by trying to please everybody was running the risk of satisfying nobody in the end: 'we shall have commercial television in the sense that advertisers will pay for most of the programmes. But it is doubtful whether this can be called competitive television except in a very restricted sense.'[94] The *Financial Times* claimed that the bill was as stuffed with guarantees as the woolsack was of wool; and the *Daily Mail* that ITA would be *ITMA* and that commercial TV would be 'tonsured TV'.[95] 'In view of the Socialist party's opposition,' one journalist asked, 'is it really politically expedient that a Conservative government should draft a Bill so uncompromisingly divorced from the White Paper?'[96]

Many of these points and others were made in a memorandum presented to De La Warr by the Popular Television Association. 'Some of the clauses and provisions contained in the bill,' it stated flatly, 'unless amended or clarified, are contrary to the original intention of the Conservative Government, and this Association, of

---

90 For the licence fees argument, see a speech by Dr Maldwyn Edwards, the superintendent minister of the Birmingham Methodist Mission, who flatly dissapproved of the archbishop of Canterbury's approach (*Birmingham Post*, 6 Mar. 1954). The *Yorkshire Post*, 6 Mar. 1954, referred to 'a loss of millions of pounds of taxpayers' money'. Cf. the *Daily Express*, 6 Mar. 1954: 'The Bill for commercial TV will not stop there. . . . The burden will grow. . . It happened with the Road Fund. It will happen with TV.'

91 *Birmingham Mail*, 6 Mar. 1954; letter to the *Birmingham Post*, 25 Mar. 1954.

92 *Hansard*, vol. 527, col. 209, 4 May 1954.

93 *Recorder*, 6 Mar. 1954.

94 *Glasgow Herald*, 6 Mar. 1954; *Scotsman*, 6 Mar. 1954.

95 *Financial Times*, 6 Mar. 1954; *Daily Mail* 6 Mar. 1954.

96 K. Mason, 'Thirty Questions on the Television Bill', *Recorder*, 20 Mar. 1954. Cf. *Leicester Mercury*, 6 Mar. 1954: 'Any relationship the present Television Bill has to the Government's first ideas on the subject is purely accidental.'

breaking the state-controlled monopoly of television.' They might be used by a future government 'to reduce commercial television to the status of a state-owned and government-subordinated corporation'. Another BBC would have been brought into existence.[97] A whole schedule of amendments was presented, therefore, most of them of substance; and on the basic question of the contractual terms relating the new companies to the authority—not dealt with in the bill itself—strong objections were raised to any sharing of one single national commercial network by different companies on a days-of-the-week basis. This would be monopoly under a new name. Yet the new programme contracting companies should have reasonable security of tenure, and should be able to establish their identity with their viewers.[98]

The contractual terms were challenged elsewhere, not least by Norman Collins, who feared that under the proposed system all the contractors—for reasons of administration and economy—would be London-based and that the chance to produce local programmes would be lost. So, too, would the sense of competition. 'Our Association', Simms added, 'envisages the day when each large centre has two or three transmitters.'[99] There were serious technical difficulties, according to the Post Office, in the way of such competition. The BBC was already using all the available frequencies on band I, and the continuing limitations on band III meant saying 'goodbye for the time being to any idea of a fine free-for-all of small private stations competing with one another and with the BBC'.[100]

There was certainly little salute to 'enterprise' in the draft bill, which contained far more don'ts than dos. Not surprisingly, therefore, it continued to be attacked from the other side also until it received the royal assent on 30 July. Herbert Morrison thought of it as a plot; Mayhew called it a sell-out. The *Manchester Guardian* asked for a 'twenty-third hour' repentance. Why not admit a 'well-intentioned error' and offer enough money to the BBC to enable it to provide alternative services which would be 'competitive between themselves'?[101] In a letter from Lady Violet Bonham Carter to De La Warr on behalf of the National Television Council nine objections were raised;[102] they ranged from the estimate that only 55

97 Cf. *Hansard*, vol. 529, col. 289, 22 June 1954. Even the *Manchester Guardian*, 6 Mar. 1954, called it a 'rival BBC'.

98 Memorandum presented by the Popular Television Association, 18 Mar. 1954.

99 *Daily Telegraph*, 16 Mar. 1954.

100 Wolstencroft, 'Setting up the Independent Television Authority'.

101 *Manchester Guardian*, 1954. The organizing committee of the National Television Council spent a good deal of time on the question of how much a second BBC channel would cost (minutes, 14, 27 Apr., 11 May 1954). There was correspondence on the subject between Mayhew and Sir Ian Jacob.

102 A claim by Simms that the National Television Council was divided on the nine points was denied in a Lewis letter to the *Daily Telegraph*, 17 Mar. 1954.

per cent of the population would be able to see an alternative programme to a sharp criticism of the 'subsidy'. On the much publicized question of standards it was argued that 'if the Authority uses
the powers conferred on it by the Bill, it will result in division of
responsibility and administrative chaos; if it does not use these
powers standards will decline'. No possible amendments could get
round the first objection, however, that the 'the Bill infringes the
fundamental principle that programmes should not be dependent
for their revenue on advertisements'. The council strengthened
its organization during the period of debate, appointing a
parliamentary committee with a drafting subcommittee.[103]

All in all, there were 206 amendments to the bill, few of which the
government felt that it could accept. No single Labour amendment
was carried, and there was strong feeling behind the Labour Party's
view that 'a Government which represents a minority in the country [was] forcing through a Bill which, it is common knowledge,
would have been defeated had there been a free vote of the
House'.[104] The fact that government used the guillotine during the
committee stage certainly did not contribute to any intelligent
cross-bench discussion.

The parliamentary Labour Party began by criticizing the very
name of the new Authority—why should it be called 'Independent'
(as if the BBC were not)?—and the opposition ended by mustering
265 votes on the third reading against the government's 291, when
the Liberal Jo Grimond voted with the government and the Liberal
Clement Davies against. It was Gordon Walker who wound up for
the opposition, reiterating Herbert Morrison's assertion that the
Labour Party reserved the right 'to abandon the entire scheme' after
the next election and might well choose to eliminate advertising.
Thus, while Conservative members were pressing for an early start
for commercial programmes—Captain Orr spoke of September
1955, a perfect forecast—Morrison and Gordon Walker warned
possible programme contractors that they might well 'find in due
course that they are put out of business'.[105] Whatever 'supports' the
government offered to prop up the new authority, they could never
satisfy Labour opponents of commercial television who believed
that even if advertisers were strictly prohibited from communicating directly or indirectly with a programme producer, their interests and wishes would still be the dominant factor in programme

103 National Television Council, minutes, 25 May 1954.

104 *Hansard*, vol. 529, col. 369, 22 June 1954; Lady Violet Bonham Carter to De La
Warr, 12 Mar. 1954. A private National Television Council note read that if there
had been a free vote on the second reading, 'there would have been enough
abstentions, and even a few votes against the measure from the Government
side, sufficient to make its carrying doubtful in the extreme'.

105 *Hansard*, vol. 525, col. 1473, 25 Mar. 1954; vol. 529, cols. 333, 370, 22 June 1954.

production.[106] There was an enormous gulf between them and those Conservative MPs like Ian Harvey who asked for 'full-blooded advertising' as 'a natural part' of programming.

Some of the most interesting speakers in the Commons debates were those who diverged slightly from party lines. Thus, George Darling spoke from the Labour benches as an opponent of the BBC's monopoly and as an author of the Fabian Society's evidence to the Beveridge Committee,[107] while Squadron-Leader A. E. Cooper stated from the Conservative benches, even at the end of the debates, that he had found it 'very hard to give support to my hon. and right hon. friends'.[108] In the House of Lords there were, of course, far more privileged 'rebels' than there were in the Commons, and the most forceful opponents of the measure were not the Labour peers but the bloc led by Halifax, Waverley, and Hailsham.

Little said, however, which was 'startlingly new or original'[109]—to use a phrase of Lord De La Warr, the postmaster-general—during the Lords' initial two-day debate. Samuel and Jowitt made it clear from the start—as did Halifax—that they would continue to oppose the bill to the last. They were strongly backed in their resistance by the National Television Council, which had decided late in May 'to persuade the Peers to be militant', and not to accept a timetable in the House of Lords: 'it was thought essential to convince the Peers of the scandalous way in which Government had "railroaded" the amendments'.[110]

Samuel quoted the *Advertisers' Weekly*, an unlikely journal for him to read, and Jowitt ventured into unusual parliamentary territory when he described himself as a 'keen viewer', but Halifax kept to the familiar landscape and reiterated that 'so long as the main principle on which the scheme is drawn is wrong, the matter is not greatly affected, one way or the other by minor modifications'.[111]

The 'principles' still seemed clear. On the one side, the opponents of the bill followed *The Times* in claiming that commercial television would play down 'to the least common denominator' and enthrone vulgarity; more was made of the 'vulgarity' and less of the 'commercialism' than in the Commons. On the other hand,

---

106 Star, 26 Mar. 1954. Cf. a statement of the National Television Council: 'There are no effective sanctions to enforce the application of the various standards, and the programme contractors will remain completely at the mercy of the advertisers.'

107 See Briggs, *Sound and Vision*, 357 ff.

108 *Hansard*, vol. 529, cols. 292–3, 22 June 1954.

109 *House of Lords, Official Report*, vol. 188, col. 185, 30 June 1954.

110 National Television Council, minutes, 25 May 1954.

111 *House of Lords, Official Report*, vol. 188, cols. 197, 210, 224, 30 June 1954. In his summing up Lord Salisbury (col. 413, 1 July 1954) referred to the Lords as 'this rather antique and detached body' and said that few except Lord Hailsham were frequent viewers or even owned a set. 'Those long streets of small houses in our great towns' were 'the real home of television' (col. 412).

supporters of the bill talked of the necessary 'abandonment of the monopoly' and were not in the least discouraged when De La Warr refused to reveal any more clearly than Gammans or Maxwell Fyfe had done in the Commons precisely what form competition would take within the ITA set-up.[112] That, the postmaster-general insisted, was a matter for the ITA.

Issues of 'monopoly' and 'competition' arose time and time again during the debates, with many different points of view being expressed. For Beveridge, effective competition would only be possible if licence fees were divided between the ITA and BBC and both parties were free to accept or reject advertisements, but for his fellow Liberal Lord Layton, who was to become one of the first members of the board of the new authority, the government's 'new and exciting proposals' allowed at the same time 'competition before the viewer' and 'competition within the profession'.[113] For Lord Kenswood, formerly Ernest Whitfield, formerly a BBC governor, the BBC already offered 'a great measure of competition within itself', and for Hailsham, winding up the debate, 'you do not break a monopoly by creating two bodies each with an exclusive franchise'.[114] Hailsham went on to broaden the economic argument: 'In place of a great public service, [the proposal] . . . is erecting the statue of the tycoon all over the land.'[115] For the bishop of Bristol, chairman of the BBC central religious advisory committee, there was a great danger of 'unseemly competition'; and for Reith there was as much need for monopoly as there always had been on moral grounds. It was sad, he said, that 'the altar cloth of one age' had become 'the doormat of the next'.[116]

There were many charges and counter-charges. Woolton accused Beveridge of 'a peculiar strain of dictatorship' and the archbishop of Canterbury chided the postmaster-general for forgetting that he had once been minister of education. Lord Winterton was very strongly rebuked by Viscount Samuel, Lord Hailsham, and others for suggesting that the BBC had created 'the most successful lobby' in his twenty-five years' experience, and had to withdraw the remark.

In concentrating on the 'pressures' in 1953 and 1954, Professor

112 In the Commons Maxwell Fyfe said that duopoly or a four-power 'opoly' would be better than monopoly, but he did not say how the ITA would actually 'work the system'. Gammans said that 'there is no conceivable reason why we should put in a Bill how this point was to operate' (*Hansard*, vol. 529, col. 290, 22 June 1954).

113 *House of Lords, Official Report*, vol. 188, col. 270, 30 June 1954; col. 394, 1 July 1954.

114 Ibid., col. 273, 30 June 1954; col. 394, 1 July 1954.

115 Ibid., col. 394, 1 July 1954.

116 Ibid., col. 262, 30 June 1954; col. 355, 1 July 1954.

Wilson underplayed the parliamentary debates themselves, their many interesting undercurrents, and the ultimate compromises on many points which ensured that even after the end of the BBC's monopoly Britain would still retain within a dual system provision for a single basic approach to the regulation and control of broadcasting. Nor did he note how the Post Office, with its strong views not only about technical but about organizational restraints, actually strengthened its position in 1954 despite the fact that the assistant postmaster-general was such a committed believer in 'commercialism'. The powers of government as a whole had certainly not been curtailed in 1954. Some Conservative MPs asked why it was necessary to have any legislation at all in order to break the monopoly. Was there not a natural 'freedom of the waves'? Yet this was no more the view of the Post Office or the government in 1954 than it had been in 1922. The government demonstrated, if very falteringly, that whatever was happening elsewhere to television, 'the unknown force', in Britain an attempt would be made to keep it under control. Gammans himself had told Mayhew in May 1953 that it was his 'genuine belief' that 'television in this country will have its own British stamp and we in the Government will do all we can to bring this about'.[117]

The constitutional structures of the new authority drew very heavily on BBC models. The ITA, like the BBC, was to have governors appointed by the crown through the postmaster-general, and he could dismiss them at pleasure; and the ITA, like the BBC, was to be required by charter to broadcast 'any matter with or without visual images' which the government might specify. Indeed, it was not to have the right, which the BBC possessed, to inform its public that specific broadcasts were being made or withheld at the request of the government, and in this respect it was even more under the tutelage of the Post Office than the BBC itself. As for the programme-operating companies, *The Economist* suggested that, given that the ITA could 'cut off their livelihood at a whimper', they were more likely to be frightened of 'authority' than any individual BBC producer would ever be.[118]

The BBC in a sense was 'the victim' of the legislation of 1954, although it was praised by ministers and by backbenchers, and it was eventually to adapt itself to an entirely new situation in such a way that many of its leading officials were to come to the conclusion that the introduction of competition was right. Perhaps the main significance of the change constitutionally was that while the corporation had survived all the Beveridge tests carried out behind

117 Gammans to Mayhew, 21 May 1953, Mayhew Papers.
118 *The Economist*, 13 Mar. 1954.

closed doors, it had not been able to deal effectively with a frontal political attack in public. The third of the nine objections raised by the National Television Council to the new bill was that, 'while purporting to set up an Independent Television Authority, Section 6 of the Bill opens the way to complete political control of this new Authority by the Party in power'.[119] There was no guarantee that the BBC's position, buttressed as it had been by convention, not by statute, would be any more secure.

The National Television Council decided to remain in existence after the new bill received the royal assent on 30 July. The 'gallant resistance', as Mayhew called it, was over. So, too, was the spate of words: more had been spoken on the subject in Parliament, it was claimed, than in the whole of the Old Testament.[120] But there were still hopes of 'a change of government'. There was obvious political danger here, too, although it was not for Mayhew as a Labour MP to point to it. For him and for the council 'the whole controversy' might still be stirred up again in more favourable circumstances. After all, 'television can hardly be said to have been "introduced" until it has actually been started'. The government scheme might 'simply not work', because programme companies might not be able 'to operate profitably on terms acceptable to the ITA'.[121] The council, Mayhew believed, could provide 'watchdog' machinery for the future: it had provided 'a remarkable link between diverse elements in the public life of the country, and has shown that it can exert considerable influence on events'.[122]

What future events would be no one knew. There were, in fact, many doubts about profitability in 1954, most of them expressed in the press. 'It is perhaps an unfortunate coincidence', the *Statist* wrote, 'that efforts to interest advertisers in an expensive broadcast medium may well coincide with an increased flow of newsprint for national and local newspapers.'[123] 'If the commercial money does not flow in,' the *Manchester Guardian* argued, 'then the rival BBC [the term was beginning to stick] will be driven back to ask for still more state aid.'[124]

119 See above, p. 85.

120 Wolstencroft, 'Setting up the Independent Television Authority'.

121 National Television Council, organizing committee, minutes, 28 July 1954. The Pembridge Road premises of the council were vacated on 25 Sept., and the paid staff was disbanded. Letters were sent to members by S. K. Lewis explaining the position on 12 Aug. 1954.

122 National Television Council, organizing committee, minutes, 28 July 1954, includes a statement by Mayhew. A further meeting of the organizing committee was held on 4 Nov. 1954, when there was a discussion on the choice of programme contractors. See Briggs, *Sound and Vision*, 966. This is the last meeting recorded in the minutes.

123 *Statist*, 13 Mar. 1954.

124 *Manchester Guardian*, 6, 25 Mar. 1954.

Such 'ifs' soon became irrelevant. There were to be many dark moments ahead—in 1956—but the most intelligent advertisers already recognized in 1955 that they would be the winners in the future, if not immediately. They knew also, as the Association of British Chambers of Commerce put it, that there was always the possibility of a 'relaxation' in the permitted methods of advertising 'in the light of experience gained'.[125] After all, more than a hundred individuals and organizations had by then applied for operating licences.[126]

The Popular Television Association, which through Lord Derby had welcomed the government's proposals—whatever the reservations felt by many of its members—now hoped that competition between contractors would be 'achieved by multiplying the number of stations' as soon as possible;[127] and Sir Robert Renwick added that while many of the safeguards in the bill would be deplored by 'true supporters of public enterprise', nevertheless, 'free enterprise may be taken as ready to co-operate, provided that the Authority does not in any circumstances become a programme planning or operating corporation'.[128]

Throughout the parliamentary debates the BBC had not been inactive, and it was now ready to face up to competitive television, determined not to change its principles or standards.[129] There was a last flicker of discussion on the eve of the 1955 election as to whether a Labour government would repeal the act—and Attlee said that he intended to do so[130]—but the new Conservative postmaster-general after the election, Charles Hill, made it clear that in his view 'the ITA is now a fact. The clock could not be put back. It was important that the BBC realised this.'[131]

125 Ibid., 25 Mar. 1954.

126 *World's Press News*, 12 Mar. 1954.

127 *Observer*, 7 Mar. 1954.

128 Letter to *Nottingham Guardian and Journal* and *Liverpool Daily Post*, 6 Mar. 1954.

129 H. Grisewood, *One Thing at a Time* (1968), 185.

130 Leonard Miall to Barnes, 13 May 1955, Barnes Papers, reported a conversation with Attlee and Lord Tedder: 'He [Attlee] said it would be impossible to stop ITA once it was on the air but that if the Labour Party were returned they could take action urgently to revoke the ITA legislation. His actual words were "We could put it through by the end of July". Tedder did not believe that the House of Lords would obstruct ' (Barnes Papers).

131 Barnes, note of interview with the postmaster-general, 2 Aug. 1955, Barnes Papers.

4

Channel Four Television: From Annan to Grade

Sylvia Harvey

IN NOVEMBER 1992, as Channel Four celebrated its tenth anniversary and its 10 per cent share of the audience, it seemed as though it had always been there, a venerable landmark, taken for granted and helping to shape the contours of contemporary British television.

But, of course, it is a relative newcomer; and its birth was a complex affair. In order to understand its emergence as an institution, we need to unravel some of the complex threads of historical change and development in the relations between British broadcasting and the state; and to have some sense of the relative weight of individual passions, political priorities, and economic realities in the unfolding of that relationship. This institution did not drop from the skies in response to a few lines in the British Parliament's Broadcasting Act of 1980. It was pushed into existence by many people, acting sometimes together, sometimes at cross-purposes, and under more-or-less favourable conditions. Its birth was no accident, its upbringing carefully planned, and its financial needs were secured in advance. It did not always fulfil the hopes and dreams of its progenitors, but a considerable achievement it none the less was. It was probably the only television channel in the world to combine a legislative requirement to *experiment*, to *innovate*, and to *complement* the service offered by the existing commercial television channel, and all of this on an income guaranteed in advance by its parliamentary godparents, under the direction of a Conservative government.

The Political Context The Channel Four Company was incorporated in December 1980 as a wholly owned subsidiary of the Independent Broadcasting

First published in Stuart Hood (ed.), *Behind the Screens: The Structure of British Television in the Nineties* (London: Lawrence & Wishart, 1994), 102–32.

Authority—the body then charged with regulating commercial radio and television. The date is significant in signalling the birth of a new decade whose social, cultural, and economic character is often associated with the values and beliefs of the 'New Right' and of the new, Conservative prime minister, Margaret Thatcher. One of the continuing problems for British Conservatism in the 1980s was to be that of resolving, or attempting to resolve, a conflict between the values of the 'old' and the 'new' right, between a paternalistic and often authoritarian cultural conservativism, and the demands of economic innovation, of letting the market 'rip'. If the one demanded cultural continuity and respect for heritage and the 'great tradition' (in broadcasting as elsewhere), the other proposed the values of a new enterprise culture, the development of more competitive and cost-effective forms of production, and the absolute sovereignty of individual consumers making choices in the market-place.

This tension between the twin poles of heritage and enterprise can be seen to characterize the formulation of Conservative Party policy in the two Broadcasting Acts (1980 and 1990) that mark the beginning and end of the decade.[1] There is a sense in which Channel Four bears the marks of both tendencies. The idea of public service and public duty, reaching back well over a century into the ethics of the Victorian civil and colonial services, is manifest in the 1980 public service requirement that the new television channel should serve a variety of audience tastes and interests, encourage innovation in programme-making, and show a suitable proportion of educational programmes. Such detailed specification of programme categories, and the emphasis on complementarity—that new tastes and interests should be served by the new channel—had become almost a hallmark of British broadcasting policy. Certainly up to and including the 1980 Broadcasting Act there had been support from both the Conservative and Labour Parties for careful forward planning to ensure choice of programmes not just choice of channels. This commitment to 'public service' principles and to the fostering of a cultural heritage had historically overridden demands for a 'free market' in broadcasting, and sharply differentiated the British approach from that of the United States, where channel proliferation within an essentially commercial or free market framework had been the outcome of a different sort of public policy.

The enterprising tendency, on the other hand, is manifested in the mode of production selected: the Channel Four Company was to commission or 'publish' programmes, not to make them itself.

1 J. Corner and S. Harvey (eds.), *Enterprise and Heritage: Cross Currents of National Culture* (London: Routledge 1991).

Programme-making was to happen predominantly out of house in the new lean, fit, and flexible independent sector, called into being as a consequence of this policy. The old 'vertical integration' that had characterized the industry, allowing the same organizations to both produce and broadcast, would no longer be the only model for production. The new independents, it was argued, would have more innovative attitudes to doing business, and lower overheads than the lumbering giants who were their parents: the BBC and ITV companies. The newcomers, motivated by an anxious desire to deliver programmes at competitive prices, would ultimately transform the industry as a whole, replacing permanent contracts with freelance employment, and doing away with 'over-manning', along with the company pension schemes, subsidized canteens, and childcare facilities, that had indirectly increased the costs of production. From a new right perspective this newly enterprising sector would (quite apart from the more publicly advanced arguments about freedom and diversity of expression) challenge and ultimately change traditional production practices in television.

Before Annan: The Pre-History of Channel Four

The Annan Report of 1977, produced under a Labour government, has been seen as a kind of watershed in the history of Channel Four. It argued the case for a 'third force' in British broadcasting to break the duopoly control then exercised by the BBC and ITV. But the outcome of the twenty-year battle between those who argued for the creation of an ITV2, and those who wanted something completely different, was to be a compromise, formulated by a Conservative government, and expressed in the brief but careful wording of the 1980 Broadcasting Act. In this section I shall explore the 'pre-history' of Channel Four, considering the people, the institutions, and the interests which in both conflict and combination, between the time of the Pilkington Report in 1962 and the Broadcasting Act of 1980, provided the framework for the creation of the new channel.

The BBC monopoly of the airwaves was broken in 1955 with the introduction, by a Conservative government, of the first privately owned television in Britain. This advertising-financed Independent Television (ITV) provided a popular alternative to the existing BBC service, and was placed under the control of a new regulatory body: the Independent Television Authority (ITA). It is perhaps worth remembering, as a preliminary to the lengthy debates about the creation of a fourth channel, what arguments led to the ending of the BBC monopoly. Sir Frederick Ogilvie, a former

Director-General of the BBC, stated the case in a letter to *The Times* in 1946:

> Monopoly of broadcasting is inevitably the negation of freedom, no matter how efficiently it is run, or how wise and kindly the board or committees in charge of it. It denies freedom of employment to speakers, musicians, writers, actors and all who seek their chances on the air. The dangers of monopoly have long been recognised in the film industry and the Press and the theatre, and active steps have been taken to prevent it. In tolerating monopoly we are alone among the democratic countries of the world.[2]

In the 1960s and 1970s a number of distinguished television programme-makers (including figures like Robert Kee, Ludovic Kennedy, Donald Baverstock, Alasdair Milne, and Jeremy Isaacs) had attempted to set up independent production companies, and discovered how hard and financially unrewarding it was to work outside the BBC–ITV duopoly.[3] Many of these figures, concerned about the cultural protectionism of the duopoly, saw the need for a 'third force' in broadcasting in the 1970s.

The 1962 Pilkington Report had been critical of the achievements of ITV, and had advocated that the proposed third television channel be allocated to the BBC. This recommendation was accepted by the Conservative government and BBC2 began broadcasting in 1964. However, in its evidence to Pilkington, the Independent Television Authority (ITA) had spoken up in favour of both competition and the interests of the ITV sector, arguing against the BBC's claim on the new channel, and noting:

> the third service should be independent of the first and second . . . in a free society, control of the means of communications should be diversified not centralized.[4]

This also reflected the view of the ITV companies, among whom the belief in breaking monopolies and introducing increased competition had, at least initially, been strong. Pilkington also envisaged the creation of a fourth channel and believed that this should, in due course, be allocated to independent television. However, this should only be on the basis that it would provide a complementary service (not competition for the same audience through the provision of similar types of programmes). Speaking in the House of Commons in June 1963, the Conservative postmaster-general came

---

2 F. Ogilvie, 'Future of the BBC Monopoly and its Dangers', *The Times*, 26 June 1946.

3 S. Lambert, *Channel Four: Television with a Difference?* (London: BFI, 1982), 34–9.

4 Pilkington Committee, *Report of the Committee on Broadcasting, 1960*, Cmnd. 1753 (London: HMSO, 1962), paras. 878–80.

under concerted pressure from MPs who sympathized with the ITV case, and indicated the government's intention to issue a licence for 'ITA2' within the next two years. However, the debate about the uses of the fourth channel did not gain momentum again until 1971–2. The election of a government less favourable to private ownership (Labour came to power in 1964), and a crisis in television advertising revenue, which dropped by 5 per cent between 1969 and 1970, were to intervene.

Slowly but inexorably, under the pressures of finance and self-interest, the ITV companies, followed by the ITA (with its particular concern for the quality of programmes), came round to the view that 'ITV2', far from being separately owned and controlled in order to bring increased competition to the system, should in fact be under the control of the existing ITV contractors. In 1970 the Conservatives returned to power after a six-year interval, and a flurry of both public and confidential memorandums came to rest on the desk of the new minister, Christopher Chataway. An early indication of the change of heart among the ITV companies came from Hugh Thomas, managing director of Thames Television. Writing in a staff newsletter in 1971 he noted:

> we should want to use ITV2 as a try-out ground for programme experiments and for new concepts and ideas . . . It is essential that ITV2 should be operated by the existing contractors.[5]

In their submission to the minister in December 1971 the ITA accepted, in essence, the view of the ITV companies, proposing that the existing contractors should sell advertising for the new channel in their own areas, and that scheduling should be controlled by a board consisting of all the ITV programme controllers together with representatives from the ITA. Two important additional points were made. Firstly, that the smaller ITV companies should have guaranteed rights to make programmes for the new network, thus diminishing the power of the 'Big Five' (Thames, London Weekend Television, Associated Television, Granada, and Yorkshire). Secondly, that there should be some unspecified amount of airtime made available for programmes produced by outside, independent producers. However, the ITA took a rather lofty and somewhat patronizing view of the abilities of independent producers:

> It would be useful also to see how valid is the proposal that there should be freer access to the medium by particular sections of the community who feel that they have some special message or viewpoint. There are dangers of amateurishness in production and difficulties in incorporating such programmes in a national

5 Lambert, *Channel Four*, 24.

television service without sacrificing impartiality and editorial control.[6]

Criticism of these ITV2 proposals came from a wide range of sources; principally from the broadcasting trade unions, especially the BBC Association of Broadcasting Staff (ABS), and from the Association of Cinematograph, Television and Allied Technicians (ACTT), which organized within ITV. In November the ACTT published its own document prepared by Caroline Heller: *TV 4: A Report of the Allocation of the 4th Channel.* This drew upon some of the rather pessimistic data of a 1970 study conducted by the Prices and Incomes Board. The board noted that the now slow rate of growth of the television audience meant that ITV was facing if not a decline, then at least no increase in advertising revenue. The resultant squeeze on income might make it difficult to finance a second, wholly advertising-supported channel. ACTT members within ITV feared the possible destabilization of the existing commercial system, and the report argued that both job security and programme standards could suffer. Other ACTT freelance members were, however, less sceptical about the new channel and looked forward to its introduction.

Opposition to an ITV-controlled fourth channel was most sharply focused and expressed through a new organization, established in November 1971: the TV4 Campaign. There was by now growing concern on this issue (at least among a media-oriented minority). The *Sunday Times* had published a leader in the previous month expressing its own reservations on the subject:

> Any suggestion that ITV2 would resemble BBC2 should be treated with the blackest scepticism. This is not because the men promoting that idea are dishonest or even because there is necessarily a shortage of talent or idealism. It is because commercial television operates within narrow and demanding constraints, which give priority to profit.[7]

The TV4 Campaign followed this up with even stronger language and a stinging attack on the ITA proposal: 'it represents an arrogant and bland ignorance of the needs of the public'.[8]

The TV4 Campaign was a lively and loose coalition of television producers, media journalists and academics, trade unionists, politicians, and advertisers. Advertisers, of course, wanted lower prices through competition for the sale of airtime on ITV and the

---

6 ITA, *ITV 2: A Submission to the Minister of Posts and Telecommunications* (London: ITA 1971), 17–18.

7 Lambert, *Channel Four*, 44.

8 Ibid. 46.

proposed fourth channel; they therefore opposed the concept of an ITV2 controlled by the existing ITV contractors with a continuing monopoly which they believed would keep the cost of airtime artificially high. Others were moved to attend meetings and write papers with more culturally based motives.

The campaign was agreed upon the following two objectives: 'that a public enquiry should be established as soon as possible . . . and that the fourth television channel should not be allocated to the present independent television contractors'. This view was expressed in an early day motion in the House of Commons, where it attracted the support of about 100 MPs (2 December 1971). The government, however, was more concerned to press ahead with its plan to introduce local commercial radio (finally achieved in the summer of 1972 with the Sound Broadcasting Act) and in January 1972 Christopher Chataway put an end to speculation by announcing that the government did not propose to proceed with the allocation of a licence for the fourth television channel.

Despite this apparent end-of-story, the serious debate was only just beginning. The first major contribution was made by Anthony Smith, who had left the BBC in 1971 to take up a two-year research fellowship at Oxford University; in 1979 he was appointed director of the British Film Institute and subsequently joined the first board of Channel Four. In a letter to the *Guardian* in April 1972 he outlined, in brief, his ideas for a National Television Foundation (subsequently worked up as a submission to the Annan Committee).

The foundation, with a very small staff, would act as a kind of publishing house of the air, buying in and broadcasting programmes from a wide variety of sources. It would be open equally to independent programme-makers with fully worked-out ideas, and to individuals or organizations who had a particular point that they wished to get across to a larger public. Smith argued that the existing broadcasting institutions had become vast and bureaucratic centres of power, corrosive of creative work, inclined to over-careful self-policing, and absorbed in the project of their own institutional survival. Faced with the old-fashioned caution of the duopoly, he argued for something completely different:

> What has to be achieved is a form of institutional control wedded
> to a different doctrine from existing broadcasting authorities, to
> a doctrine of openness rather than to balance, to expression
> rather than to neutralization.[9]

9 A. Smith, 'The National Television Foundation: A Plan for the Fourth Channel', evidence to the Annan Committee on the Future of Broadcasting, Dec. 1974; rep. as app. II in A. Smith, *The Shadow in the Cave: A Study of the Relationship between the Broadcaster, his Audience and the State* (London: Quartet 1976).

Moreover, in a prefiguring of the language of minority television (or of 'niche marketing' in the terms of advertising), Smith identified the possibility of television going beyond the mass audience and towards the discovery of specialized publics, of particular communities of interest.

The philosophy of the foundation, with its sharp critique of the perceived inadequacies of contemporary television, acted as a rallying-point for many who had become disenchanted with the bland or censorious nature of the medium. However, its address to the issue of funding was regarded as problematic in some quarters, relying as it did upon a mixture of sponsorship, grants from educational and other sources, block advertising, and government subvention. Others from within the world of television, and moved by similar concerns, were to develop rather more pragmatic proposals in respect of finance.

In a submission to the minister in 1973, David Elstein and John Birt (then at LWT) argued that the new channel should be developed by the Independent Broadcasting Authority (which had replaced the ITA in 1972) who would appoint a programme controller. The existing ITV contractors should be allowed to sell the advertising airtime for the fourth channel within their own areas, but not be allowed to control the schedule. They would compete with other independent producers to supply programmes; programme ideas would be selected on merit alone. These would be paid for by a levy on the additional advertising revenue, collected by the IBA. Broadly similar proposals were made by Jeremy Isaacs, then controller of features at Thames TV.[10] What Isaacs, Birt, and Elstein shared with Anthony Smith was a desire to liberate the creative people in television from the often stifling effects of bureaucracy, and to find a way to ensure—*systematically*, not, as it were, by accident—that new things could be said in new ways. If they lacked the institutional radicalism represented by the National Television Foundation proposal, they none the less shared its aims, and understood some of the practical means to achieve a greater pluralism and diversity of the airwaves. The best of causes require resources and allies in order to be realized, and their quietly effective memos to the minister acknowledged two key factors: the importance of advertising revenue for the new endeavour, and the need to seek accommodation with (but not surrender to) the barons of ITV. In the absence of a government with a radical, public service bent and money to spend, their pragmatism was ultimately to win the day.

10 Lambert, *Channel Four*, 158–60; J. Isaacs, *Storm over Four: A Personal Account* (London: Weidenfeld & Nicolson, 1989), 200–2.

In 1971 the TV4 Campaign had argued for a public inquiry into the possible uses and structure of a new channel. While this call had not been accepted by the Conservative government of 1970-4, neither had the latter acted to bring a new channel into existence. It was left to the incoming Labour administration of 1974 to invite Lord Annan to chair a committee reporting to Parliament on the future of broadcasting. Labour was to remain in power from 1974 to 1979, though the recommendations of the Annan Report, not available until 1977, were not to be implemented by them. Implementation, as it turned out, was to be the work of the new Conservative government of 1979, which accepted parts of the report while rejecting others.

The committee's brief was wide and demanding and required it to investigate all aspects of British broadcasting. It met, deliberated, and took evidence over a period of two and a half years. I shall consider here only those parts of the final report and its recommendations relating to the fourth channel.

Strongly influenced by one of its members—Phillip Whitehead, a Labour MP who had been active in the TV4 Campaign—and by Anthony Smith, who had been denied membership of the Annan team,[11] the committee outlined four general principles. In their view British broadcasting should be characterized by:

—— accountability through Parliament to a public which is given more chance to make its voice heard
—— diversity of services
—— flexibility of structure
—— editorial independence.[12]

Diversity and programme (as opposed to merely channel) choice were key concepts for the report, and the preamble to the final recommendations took on board one of the ideas that had been developed by Smith: that television should not only be about reaching mass audiences. In a 1977 article Smith had argued:

Beneath the façade of the homogeneous mass audience the cement is cracking . . . a television channel can do something more than try to get the same message across to millions of people . . . it can direct a programme at a highly specialized level, at a large audience of like-minded people.[13]

There is, of course, a continuing problem in an advertising-funded

11 Isaacs, *Storm over Four*, 8.

12 Annan Committee, *Report of the Committee on the Future of Broadcasting*, Cmnd. 6753 (London: HMSO, 1977) 474.

13 Smith, 'The National Television Foundation', 162–3.

system of making programmes for 'like-minded people' who are not, in economic terms, of interest to advertisers. In the past this problem has been solved in Britain by giving regulatory authorities the power to ensure the meeting of broader 'public interest' criteria in the making and transmission of programmes. By the 1990s the almost hegemonic power of 'niche marketing' arguments, combined with the removal of scheduling powers from regulatory bodies, have put in question the future effectiveness of this solution.

The Annan Committee recognized the need to create a space for minority audiences:

> we do not want more of the same. There are enough programmes for the majority . . . What is needed now is programmes for the different minorities which add up to make the majority.[14]

However, not foreseeing the storm of free-market arguments shortly to be unleashed within British political and cultural life, they perhaps failed to confront the issues of cost and control as these relate to serving the interests of minorities, and the implementation of diversity in programming.

In making their recommendations for the fourth channel, the committee effectively combined Anthony Smith's model of a National Television Foundation with the structural radicalism of Phillip Whitehead's concept of a new type of broadcasting authority. Thus it was that the report proposed an Open Broadcasting Authority (OBA)[15] as the institutional midwife who would deliver Channel Four. The OBA would act as a kind of electronic publisher offering an outlet to programmes from a wide variety of sources, some of which, in the words of the report, 'would not be acceptable or appropriate on the existing channels'. While charged with achieving 'overall balance . . over a period of time', it would have much greater freedom than the existing regulatory body, the IBA.[16]

The OBA's programmes would fall into three broad categories: education (including the Open University, though the idea of an exclusively educational channel was rejected); programmes from the ITV companies; and those from independent producers. The committee attached particular importance to this third category as a 'force for diversity and new ideas'.[17] The language of the report on this potential new sector of production helped to create a new discursive field within broadcasting policy; one that went well

---

14 Annan Committee, *Report*, 471–2.

15 For a useful insight into the way in which the committee worked, see Lord Annan's Ulster Television lecture: 'The Politics of Broadcasting Enquiry', Ulster Television, Belfast 1981. This is cited in Lambert, *Channel Four*, 68–9.

16 Annan Committee, *Report*, 236.

17 Ibid. 237.

beyond the fear of parvenu amateurs hinted at in the 1971 ITA submission.

Philosophically, the proposed fourth channel was conceived as more than just a new line in the existing emporium of British broadcasting. The general conclusion of the report stated:

> We see the fourth channel not just as another outlet or even just as a means of giving a more varied service to the audience. It should be the test bed for experiment and symbolise all the vitality, the new initiatives, practices and liberties which could inspire broadcasters.[18]

Cost was the great unresolved issue. In general a diversity of funding sources was regarded as desirable, but the committee recognized that a combination of grant aid, sponsorship, and block advertising might be insufficient, in which case some government subvention might be required. Moreover, in recognition of the difficult financial climate, they recommended that the new channel should not be established 'until the nation's economy will permit the kind of services we have outlined'.[19] Only in Wales, where other political imperatives had emerged, might there be an exception to this gloomy caution. Here the report recommended that some priority should be given to establishing a fourth channel broadcasting programmes in the Welsh language.

From Annan to the 1980 Broadcasting Act

The Labour government was uncertain about the Annan recommendations and took over a year to decide to support the OBA proposal; this support was formalized in the 1978 White Paper on Broadcasting. However, no enabling legislation was formulated and Labour was defeated in the 1979 election. For those who had believed the announcement by a government minister, back in 1963, that Channel Four was imminent, the whole affair had been marked by delay and disappointment.

However, the new home secretary in the incoming Conservative administration, William Whitelaw, had taken a particular interest in the fourth channel project and was sympathetic to some of the aims, if not to the institutional means that had been outlined in the Annan Report. The queen's speech of May 1979 announced the new government's intention to proceed with a fourth channel, to be developed under the aegis of the IBA. The volume of debate and the intensity of campaigning immediately increased.

18 *Report*, 472.
19 Ibid. 240.

A new Channel Four Group had emerged, replacing the old TV4 Campaign, and this was now joined by the Independent Film-makers' Association (IFA), an organization representing experimental and arts grant-aided film-makers who had, until then, regarded themselves as definitively excluded from the world of television. A wide range of film and television programme-makers, together with journalists, trade unionists, critics, politicians, and media policy makers, now made common cause to ensure a crucial safeguard: that of cultural independence for the new institution, arguing that the ITV companies should not control this initiative. In addition, the IFA in a pamphlet circulated at the 1979 Edinburgh Television Festival raised the issue of the relationship between broadcasters and their audiences:

> One of the main aims of TV4 must be to lessen the gulf between the professional communicators (including ourselves) and the public we observe, question and on whose behalf we speak.[20]

The IFA also drew upon aspects of the Annan Report which had advocated provision for the needs of people living in the regions of Britain by calling for the new channel to fund regionally-based, experimental film workshops.

In a speech delivered at the same television festival, Jeremy Isaacs (soon to become Channel Four's first chief executive), outlined his views on the subject:

> We want a fourth channel which extends the choice available to viewers . . . which caters for substantial minorities presently neglected; which builds into its actuality programmes a complete spectrum of political attitude and opinion . . . a fourth channel that everyone will watch some of the time and no one all the time. A fourth channel that will, somehow, be different.[21]

Isaacs had, as I have already noted, communicated his views on both a purpose and a practical structure for the institution in a memo sent some six years earlier to one of William Whitelaw's predecessors. Whitelaw's own views, now the views of government, were outlined at some length in a speech made to the Royal Television Society Convention at Cambridge in the autumn of 1979.

Whitelaw's speech reassured many observers that government was committed to providing 'new opportunities to creative people' and 'new ways of finding minority and specialist audiences'.[22]

20 S. Blanchard, 'Where do New Channels Come From?', in S. Blanchard and D. Morley (eds.), *What's this Channel Fo(u)r?* (London: Comedia, 1982), 17.

21 Isaacs, *Storm over Four*, 19–20.

22 Lambert, *Channel Four*, 93.

Moreover, IBA control was to ensure that Channel Four was not simply the creature of ITV. In response to strong lobbying from the independents (later to develop their case for 25 per cent of programming on all terrestrial channels) the IBA would be required to ensure that 'the largest practicable proportion of programmes' would be supplied from organizations that were not ITV companies. The reward for ITV was the continuation of their monopoly in the sale of advertising. The existing contractors would sell airtime on the new channel, but the IBA would ensure that this income—and if necessary more than this—was made available to meet Channel Four's own costs. It only remained for a change of name to mark the shift of control away from ITV. This happened as the draft Broadcasting Bill made its way through Parliament in the course of 1980. Phillip Whitehead succeeded in changing the reference to 'Service 2' to 'the Fourth Channel Service'.

Only in Wales was Whitelaw's speech met with deep hostility, for it had reneged on the Conservative manifesto pledge to create a Welsh-language channel. A tremendous campaign was developed in Wales as a consequence of this, involving both widespread refusals to pay the television licence fee, the raiding and temporary closing down of transmitters, and, finally, a threat of hunger strike made by the venerable and respected president of the nationalist party, Plaid Cymru. In the face of such angry and widespread protest, the government returned to its original promise, amending the bill in September 1980 in order to create a Welsh Fourth Channel Authority, Sianel Pedwar Cymru (S4C). It would be the task of S4C to create the first prime-time, Welsh-language channel in Wales, drawing its programmes from the BBC, from Harlech Television, and from a soon-to-be-created and vigorous independent sector. The IBA was to ensure that S4C received an adequate amount of advertising revenue: approximately 20 per cent of the total amount collected from the ITV companies. So, for example, from a total of £313.5 million received in 1991 in subscriptions from the ITV companies, £58.4 million went towards the costs of S4C.[23]

The key provisions of the 1980 Broadcasting Act can be briefly summarized (these provisions, with the exception of the ownership arrangements, were carried over almost unchanged into the 1990 Act). The IBA was required to ensure that the Channel Four service would contain 'a suitable proportion of matter calculated to appeal to tastes and interests not generally catered for by ITV' and a 'suitable proportion of programmes . . . of an educational nature'; it was

23 Independent Television Commission, *1991 Report and Accounts* (London: ITC, 1992), 56.

also to 'encourage innovation and experiment in the form and content of programmes'.[24]

It was left to the IBA to decide upon the appropriate institutional form for Channel Four and to collect an annual subscription from all the ITV companies to meet its costs. In return the ITV companies were allowed to sell the advertising airtime on the new channel within their own regions, thus maintaining their monopoly control of airtime sales. This last arrangement had been the method advocated by Birt, Elstein, and Isaacs himself, back in 1973. It would change only with the 1990 Broadcasting Act when Channel Four was established as an independent trust (no longer a subsidiary of the IBA) with board members to be nominated by the Independent Television Corporation (ITC), and with an obligation to meet the costs of its programming by selling its own airtime.

It is clear from the wording in the 1980 act and, more importantly, from the associated financial, administrative, and ownership arrangements (Channel Four was initially to be incorporated as a wholly owned subsidiary of the IBA) that the new institution, if not an 'Open Broadcasting Authority', had the potential to fulfil many of the objectives of innovation and difference proposed by the Annan Committee.

Channel Four: The First Ten Years

■ **A Changing Cultural Context**

Channel Four's programme transmissions began in November 1982, the month after the Falklands–Malvinas victory parade and a year after the riots in Brixton and Toxteth. With the wisdom of hindsight, it is possible to see the Falklands victory parade as in some sense a signal for the passing of an old order. No amount of prime-ministerial rhetoric about Britain being 'great again' in the wake of this war could stop a growing public recognition that the country had lived through its last days of imperial glory, and needed to discover a new economic centre of gravity and a new role in world affairs.

Channel Four was to grow in, and try to reflect, a climate of accelerating social and cultural change, with new attitudes to national identity, family life, public services, sex, and money. In attempting to pull within the frame of television what had previously been either excluded or treated in a bland or simplistic way, it had to represent (in both factual and fictional programmes) a range of contemporary issues from rising female expectations and a rocketing divorce rate, to a growing number of home-owners as well as of homeless people. Its difficult task, with the liberal

24 Broadcasting Act 1980 (London: HMSO, 1980).

encouragement of the new Broadcasting Act behind it, was to give a voice to the new pluralism of the 1980s: that explosive mixture of racial hatred with new multiracial and multicultural tolerance, of the quest for sex equality with the consolidation of new forms of male supremacism, of a new tolerance in matters of sexual orientation with outbursts of homophobic hysteria, of a commitment to the welfare state with the argument that its existence was incompatible with the principle of a free market.

The development of the new channel beyond the moment of its legislative conception was to be fashioned by a culture both more pluralistic and more stratified than that of the two preceding decades: a greater variety of ideas and lifestyles, sharper extremes of wealth and poverty, more ferocious political and ideological disagreements, together with a general lessening of public interest in official politics.

In its early days a greater frankness about the varieties of human sexuality and a more realistic and relaxed representation of everyday speech got Channel Four into deep trouble with sections of the mass circulation press. The tabloids attacked the showing of a programme exploring gay lifestyles, *One in Five*, scheduled for New Year's day 1983, and the *Sun* ran what it called a 'filth count' of the language used in the channel's first month of broadcasting.[25] Subsequently (in 1986) the broadcaster was to experiment with the use of a small red triangle in the corner of the television screen, to indicate material that might be offensive to some. This experiment was discontinued when puritan campaigners persuaded major advertisers to avoid such programmes. But the channel's willingness to engage with its audience's interest in sexual matters, whether in *Out on Tuesday* (1988) or *Sex Talk* (1990), was to expand the horizons of what was possible in television in general. Without its new, often forthright, witty, and imaginative approach it would be difficult to imagine the appearance of Carlton's *The Good Sex Guide* on mainstream ITV at the beginning of 1993. In this sense Channel Four affected the whole ecology of British broadcasting, extending the range of subjects that might be dealt with by television.

In the representation of working life other less sympathetic cultural and political forces could be seen at work. The programme for trade unionists, *Union World* (1984–5), was to disappear in the course of the 1980s. It was not to be replaced by a similar strand.

In political and ideological debates, in respect of 'balance' and 'impartiality', and in the representation of historical and current affairs material, the channel was also to cause offence to some powerful (and less powerful) people. *The Friday Alternative* (1982–3),

25 Lambert, 'Isaacs Still Smiling', *Stills*, 6 (1983), 25, 27.

which had been set up to provide a critical commentary on the week's news from a variety of viewpoints, was axed after less than a year on the grounds of consistent left-wing bias. Jeremy Isaacs recognized a distinction between 'one-off' opinionated programmes and *series* which consistently advanced the same opinions and could therefore be taken to undermine the requirement of balance. The first chairman of Channel Four's board, Edmund Dell, was highly critical of *The Friday Alternative* with its irreverent, witty, and 'straight to the point' attack on traditional news values and approaches; though, interestingly, one outcome of the cutting of this series and of several bruising encounters between the channel's chief executive and its chairman was the policy assertion by Isaacs that:

> We have firmly established the notion that television programmes from a variety of sources may express explicit opinion, without upset to the body politic.[26]

This advocacy and representation of strong opinion was to be furthered through two long-running programme slots: *Opinions*, a thirty-minute slot usually given to well-known speakers, and *Comment*, a three-minute slot after the evening news, given to anyone who had a point of view to put across. One notable blow for opinionated pluralism was struck shortly after the channel went on air, when the socialist historian and anti-nuclear campaigner E. P. Thompson was awarded the *Opinions* platform, having just been turned down for a series of lectures by the BBC.[27]

In other areas, too, the taken-for-granted centrism of British televisual life was challenged: in the development of caustic comedy, whether *The Comic Strip Presents ... The Strike* (1988) or *Crimestrike* (1990); in programmes by women: the original Broadside current affairs series of 1983; or in feature films like *Hush Bye Baby* (1990), delicately considering the issue of unwanted pregnancy in Catholic Northern Ireland; or *Dream On* (1992), exploring the defiant attitudes of working-class women coping with constant crisis on Tyneside; in positive and witty explorations of gay life, *Out on Tuesday* (1989); in the presentation of fact and fiction from the 'Third World' (the *Africa on Africa* season of 1984, the series *South* in 1991), and in a rich variety of films by black British film-makers: *Handsworth Songs* (1987), *Playing Away* (1989), and *Looking for Langston* (1990).

Some historical series were highly innovative, and difficult to fault in terms of balance. For example, *Wales: The Dragon has Two*

---

26 Isaacs, *Storm over Four*, 82–6, 88.
27 Ibid. 53–5.

Tongues (1984) financed by Naomi Sargant, the channel's first senior commissioning editor for education, was a thirteen-part series in which two historians, one Marxist and one more conservative, argued over their conflicting interpretations of Welsh history. Another major series, produced by Central for Channel Four, was *Vietnam: A Television History* (1984), exploring, among other things, Britain's difficult and close relationship with the United States. Other 'people's stories', drawing on a rich new vein of oral history in contemporary historiography, accompanied the major series: two examples of this, from Television History Workshop, were *Making Cars* (1983) and *City General* (1984). A far more controversial history, pushing many of the panic buttons of high-level outrage, was *Greece: The Hidden War* (1986); this offered a critical examination of a little-known aspect of recent British history, namely, the highly partisan role played by the British army in relationship to domestic Greek politics towards the end of the Second World War. Strong complaints were made by powerful figures in the British military establishment.

Isaacs himself offers some useful comments on this novel process whereby entrenched and established views were challenged for the first time *on television*:

> I had never doubted, thinking too much television too unthinking, too bland, that Channel 4 would broadcast programmes that put, as forcibly as possible, a forcible point of view. I had not appreciated, and still find hard to understand, how offensive to some this turned out to be. People had no objection to opinion strongly expressed in a newspaper, in a railway carriage, in a saloon bar. Why object to opinionated television? Perhaps they only enjoyed reading their own opinions in newspapers, and not the other fellow's at all.[28]

It remains to be seen whether or not the new requirements on 'impartiality', written into the Broadcasting Act of 1990, and the subject of much controversy at the time, are used to stifle the expression of strong opinions. In 1991 the conservative Freedom Association had attempted to take Channel Four to court over their screening of a programme putting the view of Americans opposed to the war in the Gulf: *Hell, No, We Won't Go*. The case was not then pursued on the basis of legal advice that the climate would be more favourable to a finding against such programmes after the formal introduction of the new ITC Code on Impartiality in 1993.[29]

---

28 Isaacs, Storm over Four, 53.
29 J. Willis, 'Vague Sense of Unease', *Guardian*, 25 Jan. 1993.

■ **Programmes and Scheduling**

Channel Four's parliamentary remit to 'encourage innovation and experiment in the form and content of programmes', together with the view expressed by Jeremy Isaacs, that it should be for 'all of the people some of the time' seemed to provide the basis for a service that was prepared to edge well beyond the previously established limits of broadcasting expression.

The first ten years of output can be roughly divided into the periods corresponding to the appointments of the first two chief executives: Jeremy Isaacs (1981–7) and Michael Grade (1988–92). The recommendation of the Peacock Report in 1986, that Channel Four should be given the option of selling its own airtime, can also be seen to mark a kind of watershed in the early history of the channel. Certainly the vigorously purposeful reconstruction of the schedule, the judicious buying-in of popular American series (*Thirty-something*, *Cheers*, *The Cosby Show*, *The Golden Girls*), and the continuing success of the Channel's own soap, *Brookside*, has helped to boost the ratings in the Grade era. Viewing figures went up from 8.8 per cent in 1988 to about 10 per cent in 1991.

It was argued in some quarters that, in the late 1980s, Channel Four had 'lost its way' in a populist drive for high ratings.[30] While this does not seem to be confirmed by an examination of the quality and range of programmes commissioned, it might be said the current affairs programming dealing with contemporary Britain had lost something of the 'bite' and range of class voices characteristic of the early to mid-1980s. With the obvious exception of programmes like *The Committee* (1991), which claimed to have uncovered illegal, paramilitary unionist groupings at the highest levels within Northern Ireland, and which led to a fine of £75,000 as the producers and the channel steadfastly refused to divulge their sources to the court, professional distance had, to some extent, taken over from passionate enquiry. Moreover, the loss of the *People to People* slot (1988) and the ending of regional workshop funding in 1991 has tended to concentrate commissions within the metropolitan heartland of London; other voices from and versions of contemporary British life have received little airtime as a consequence. Set against this arguable underdevelopment and retrenchment was the introduction of new peak-time documentary series: *Cutting Edge*, *Critical Eye*, and the access series *Free for All* (1991).

However, many of the structural and generic innovations of Channel Four remain, including *Comment*, the hour-long evening news, *Right to Reply*, *Brookside*, Film on Four and the work of the multicultural and independent film and video departments under

---

30 J. Miller, 'Do We Still Need Channel Four?', *Sunday Times*, 5 July 1992.

their commissioning editors Farrukh Dhondy and Alan Fountain. Dhondy has been responsible for bringing the work of critical black journalists into the intellectual heartlands of British current affairs and arts television with *The Bandung File* (1985–9) and *Rear Window* (1991). His budget also provided the crucial co-production finance for Mira Nair's feature films *Salaam Bombay* (1989) and *Mississippi Masala* (1991).

The independent film and video department, with its Eleventh Hour strand, has fostered experimental work both among British film- and video-makers (*Video 1, 2, 3*, 1985; *Dazzling Image*, 1990) and by introducing work from other countries and cultures: the Godard season of 1985, the Latin American season of 1983, and the screening of work by Chantal Ackerman, Leontine Sagan, Jon Jost, Jan Oxenburg, and Marisol Trujillo. It has also presented and to some extent celebrated gay and lesbian culture before a wider audience in the seasons *In the Pink* (1986) and *Out on Tuesday* (1988). On the fiction front their 'New Waves' season of 1984 remains one of the most impressive collections of low-budget, experimental features by British directors (including *Acceptable Levels, Burning an Illusion, Through an Unknown Land, Brothers and Sisters*, and *Darkest England*).

In the fields of arts and comedy programming, the channel also made a significant contribution to extending the boundaries of these television genres. The first category was distinguished by the development of critical and analytical series such as *Signals, Without Walls*, and *Rear Window*; the latter by an extraordinarily wide variety of material from *Who Dares Wins* to *Drop the Dead Donkey*; from *No Problem* to *Whose Line Is It Anyway?* and the generically extraordinary *Manhattan Cable* (1991).

The drama department under David Rose, and subsequently David Aukin, has developed the Film on Four strand into what is probably one of the most internationally recognized innovations of Channel Four: mobilizing the resources of television to support a starving but still creative British film industry. The aim was to put co-production money into feature films and to encourage a cinema release where possible: building up a reputation and critical profile for the film prior to its television exposure. Where cinema screening was not feasible, an agreement with the Cinema Exhibitors' Association (initially covering films with budgets of under £1.25 million) ensured that the film would not have to wait for the normal three-year period before being cleared for television screening.[31] In this way a relationship of mutual support, not mutual antagonism, was developed between cinema and television.

31 Isaacs, *Storm over Four*, 150.

In his first year of operation David Rose had a budget of £6 million, which, it was hoped, would make, or help to make, up to twenty films—giving an average contribution per film of £300,000. Figures have of course risen since then (by 1991 the channel's annual budget for drama, including Film on Four, had risen to nearly £36 million), but the proportion of money contributed to any one film budget has always varied considerably. Channel Four contributed 100 per cent to the budget of *My Beautiful Laundrette* (1987), 52 per cent to *Another Time, Another Place* (1983), 22 per cent to *Paris, Texas* (1986), 10 per cent to *A Room with a View* (1989), 73 per cent to *Rita, Sue and Bob Too* (1990).[32]

The output of Film on Four—136 feature films by the end of 1991—has been prodigious and varied.[33] 1987, the last of the Isaacs years, was one of the most memorable. In this year Film on Four screenings included: *Letter to Brezhnev*, *My Beautiful Laundrette*, *Caravaggio*, *No Surrender*, *Company of Wolves*, and *She'll Be Wearing Pink Pyjamas*; the last of these won one of the highest audiences of the year for Channel Four at 7.5 million.[34]

Other programmes in the same year (1987) stand out as exemplary of the brief to experiment and innovate. Claude Lanzmann's nine-hour study of the Holocaust, *Shoah*, was shown on two consecutive nights, *Network 7* began a genuinely new trend in factual broadcasting for younger people, *Cinema from Three Continents* challenged the comfortable Anglo-American and Eurocentrism of British film culture, and *The Media Show* was perhaps the first properly researched, dynamically presented, and adequately critical series to appear on British television which explored the medium itself.

■ **Programme Costs, Suppliers, and the Principle of Diversity**

Channel Four might be said to have had two distinct but interrelated purposes: to introduce stylistic and content innovations into British television, and to introduce new industrial structures for the production of programmes. This latter aim was accomplished by the creation of an independent sector, which has grown since the passage of the 1990 Broadcasting Act, with its legal requirement that both BBC and ITV commission 25 per cent of their original output from out of house.

A few general observations about costs may be helpful here. First, Channel Four is a modestly resourced operation. It took about five years to break even (by 1987 the value of the airtime sold on the channel amounted to a little more than its costs; see Table 1). In 1991

32 J. Pym, *Film on Four, 1982–91* (London: BFI, 1992) 116–19.
33 Ibid.
34 Ibid. 64–5.

Table 1. *Channel Four income, hours of transmission, and costs, 1984–1991*

	1984	1985	1986	1987	1988	1989	1990	1991[a]
Income from IBA–ITC (£m.)	105.2	111.0	129.1	135.9	163.4	181.8	217.9	255.2
Annual transmission hours	3,185	3,593	3,913	4,160	5,106	5,818	5,245[b]	7,066
Total costs of programmes (£m.)	89.3	95.4	101.3	114.1	135.1	149.5	179.5	195.2
Average programme costs per hour (£000)	28.0	26.5	25.9	27.4	26.5	25.7	26.3	27.6

Note: the financial figures have not been adjusted for inflation.

[a] In 1991 the financial year changed from Apr.–Mar. to Jan.–Dec. Figures for the full twelve-month period have been given except where noted.

[b] This figure is for nine months only, Apr.–Dec. 1990.

Source: Channel Four, *Annual Report and Accounts*.

its average hourly programme cost was £27,600, and it spent the largest single share of its income on drama, closely followed by entertainment, news, and documentaries (Table 2). By 1991 over half of its originally commissioned programmes were being made in the independent sector (52 per cent as against 48 per cent produced by ITV and Independent Television News), and these were supplied by a total of 668 (mostly small) production companies. Only twenty-eight of these companies received commissions totalling more than £1 million for the year; the majority of them (470) received commissions worth under £100,000.

In the relative disposition of commissions to the independents and to the ITV companies it has been the case since 1984 that the independents have regularly been awarded a greater share of the costs in proportion to the number of hours that they produce. This is almost certainly because the ITV companies are commissioned, on the whole, to produce the cheaper types of programme and not because they are inherently more cost-effective. Table 3 gives the comparative figures on this from 1984 to 1991. (See also Table 4 for a comparison of incomes for the whole of British television in 1991.)

While it is true that Channel Four provides some opportunities for first-time film-makers and for those who would otherwise have no access to television, the problem for the small independents is 'how to survive' in the face of radical uncertainty about the renewal of production contracts. As the individuals who make up the sector

Table 2. *Relative programme costs for Channel Four, 1991*

	Cost of programmes (£m.)	No. of hours
Drama (including Film on Four)	35.9	719
Entertainment	33.3	1,190
News	21.1	638
Documentaries	18.9	494
Current affairs	15.3	613
Education (incl. schools)	14.6	779
Arts and music	13.9	364
Feature films	9.5	1,378
Sport	8.7	569
Quizzes	5.1	148
Multicultural	4.8	98
Religion	3.2	76

Note: In 1991 out of a total of 7,066 transmitted hours, 4,127 were commissioned (i.e. original material for Channel Four) and 2,939 were purchased from other sources.

Source: Channel Four, *Report and Accounts for the Year Ended 31st December 1991.*

Table 3. *Proportion and value of programmes supplied by independent producers and by ITV–ITN, 1984–1991*

Year	Independent production		ITV–ITN production	
	% of hours	% of costs	% of hours	% of costs
1984	29	45	33	39
1985	24	43	34	39
1986	25	43	30	39
1987	25	45	30	34
1988	29	51	30	28
1989	28	55	29	25
1990	54[a]	74	46[a]	26
1991	52	78	48	22

[a] Up to 1989 the percentage figures relate to total hours of programme transmissions. From 1990 they relate only to commissioned programme transmission hours (i.e. only to material originally commissioned for Channel Four, excluding other purchased material).

Source: Channel Four, *Annual Report and Accounts.*

get older, take on domestic commitments, and realize the benefits of secure employment, a predictable income, sick pay, paid holidays, and properly resourced pensions, their commitment to working in a radically insecure sector inevitably diminishes. It is appropriate,

Table 4. *Income for British television: BBC, ITV, Channel Four and S4C, 1991 (£m.)*

BBC (Radio and TV)	ITV	Channel Four	S4C
1,289.6[a]	1,357.5[b]	255.2[c]	58[c]

[a] Licence fee after costs of collection.
[b] Net advertising revenue after deduction of Channel Four and S4C subscription.
[c] Income received from the ITC.

Source: BBC, *Annual Report and Accounts, 1990–91*; ITC, *1991 Report and Accounts*.

therefore, to ask whose cultural and economic interests are served by the maintenance of this sector and this 'miniature' mode of production? And to what extent are freedom and diversity of expression safeguarded for the television audience by this system of production?

Certainly, many independent producers are experiencing almost intolerable living and working conditions, and yet this sector continues to be the preferred free-market policy instrument for implementing the commitment to cultural diversity. There is a tense 'play-off' here between the values of 'heritage' and those of 'enterprise', as discussed at the beginning of this chapter. For that variant of broadcasting heritage which involves a commitment to cultural pluralism is underwritten by the 'enterprising' methods of a dependent–independent production sector which may find it difficult to reproduce itself in the long term.

■ **The Audience**

Across the ten years of its history, from 1982 to 1992, Channel Fours's voices of dissent, difference, and even alarming experiment have gathered and consolidated audiences across the boundaries of class, race, gender, and age. While it remained a minority channel, with its share of the total TV audience rising from 4.7 per cent in 1984 to 9.8 per cent by the end of 1991, it avoided the 'ghetto' trap of always reaching the same small number of people. This is shown by the 'reach' of its programmes, and the number of people who watch it at some time. In its early years some 50 per cent of the television audience viewed something on the channel in any one week; by 1991 that figure had risen to 79 per cent, and it achieved a reach of 93 per cent of the population in the course of an average month.[35]

It may be useful here to indicate some overall shifts in television viewing in a period when British television developed from a

35 Channel Four, *Report and Accounts, 1992*, 10.

Table 5. *Television viewing in the UK as a percentage of the total audience* (%)

Years	BBC1	BBC2	ITV	Channel Four	Other
1980–1	39.0	12.0	49.0	—	—
1990–1	38.0	10.0	43.0	9.0	—
1992	35.8	9.5	41.0	9.8	3.9

Sources: Colin Seymour-Ure, *The British Press and Broadcasting since 1945* (Oxford: Blackwell, 1991), 155; *BBC Annual Report and Accounts, 1990–91*, 80; *Broadcast*, 29 Jan. 1993, 28.

three- to a four-channel, terrestrial system and (as the last column of figures in Table 5 indicates) the new media of cable and satellite have emerged to claim a small but significant share of the television audience. Table 5 allows us to compare the broadcasting landscape just before the arrival of Channel Four with that of ten years later. The figures can of course be read in many different ways, but, in general, it may be worth noting that Channel Four's audience has continued to grow while that of the other terrestrial channels has declined; BBC1, BBC2, and ITV have lost audience to Channel Four and to the other new media.

In social-class terms, as the channel's annual reports regularly point out, a good proportion of its audience is within the 'up-market' socio-economic range ABC1; it also attracts proportionately more younger viewers than ITV.[36] Whether this profile, which is extremely attractive to some advertisers, will ultimately put pressure on the channel to cater principally to the 'up-market' and youth audiences remains to be seen.

Achievements and Future Prospects

The 1990 Broadcasting Act preserved some, but not all, of the features established for Channel Four by the 1980 act. The original programming philosophy was retained. The new act required the channel to encourage 'innovation and experiment in the form and content' of programmes, and to 'appeal to tastes and interests not generally catered for by Channel 3'.

Outright privatization was avoided, though the channel ceased to be a wholly owned subsidiary of the regulatory body. A new corporation was created, whose members were to be appointed by the ITC, and the umbilical link with the ITV companies was broken, as the new corporation was empowered to sell its own advertising.

36 Ibid. 11.

Although this change was designed to inject competition into the sale of airtime (and to end the role of the ITC as 'tax collector' for the channel), none the less some element of symbiosis in the relationship between ITV and Channel Four was retained through the 'safety net' provisions.

Under these arrangements, if the channel's revenue dipped below 14 per cent of total (terrestrial) television advertising revenue, the ITV companies would be required to step in and contribute up to 2 per cent of that total amount. If, however, Channel Four succeeded in aquiring more than 14 per cent, then any surplus would be divided evenly between itself and the ITV companies. Because of this mechanism the ITV companies have some financial interest in the success of their rival, and this is likely to ameliorate the more savage forms of competition for audiences and for the sale of airtime which might otherwise have occurred.

Separate arrangements for Wales ensure the continuation of S4C. A new Welsh Authority has been created for this purpose, receiving direct government funding of 3.2 per cent of total television advertising revenue each year. This figure is not dependent upon the amount of airtime actually sold by S4C, and the Act commits the Secretary of State to paying this amount out of public funds. If S4C had been made dependent upon the value of its own airtime sales, this would have amounted to only a fraction of its costs. In 1991 the value of its airtime was £3.5 million, while the amount which it received through the ITC subscription, then collected from the ITV companies, was £58 million.[37] It is clear that this arrangement is based upon a political recognition of the demands of Welsh cultural nationalism (exemplified by the strong campaign conducted in Wales in 1980) rather than upon free-market principles.

In avoiding both a private shareholding solution for Channel Four and the creation of head-on competition with ITV (for the same audiences at the same time) the long-established public policy principle that audiences should be offered programme choice, not just channel choice, continued to be upheld.

However, it remains to be seen to what extent Channel Four comes under internal or external pressure to maximize its audience, and to prioritize the kinds of programme that attract the kinds of viewer that advertisers most want to reach. The presence of airtime sales staff *within* the institution seems likely to affect commissioning and scheduling decisions (how could it not do so since the advertisers pay for the programmes, however indirectly). It will take considerable managerial skill and a clear cultural vision to hold on to the genuinely pluralistic programming policies established in the

37 ITC, *1991 Report and Accounts*, 46.

1980s. In recognizing both the practical and political difficulties involved in implementing such policies, and their social importance, it may be worth remembering some comments made by Jeremy Isaacs in 1983:

> It is cardinal, surely, to broadcasting in a free, pluralist society, that all sectors of society should be fairly represented on the screen. Tapping those new sources of energy, letting those voices (within an overall obligation to fairness) come through, is both Channel 4's most challenging task, and the practice that evokes most hostility.[38]

38 Isaacs, *Storm over Four*, 76.

5

Money Talks: Broadcasting Finance and Public Culture

Graham Murdock

Broadcasting or
Television?

IN A NOW FAMOUS STATEMENT Mark Fowler, President Reagan's first appointee as head of the Federal Communications Commission (the main regulator of the American media industries), declared that, as far as he could see, 'Television is just another appliance. It's a toaster with pictures.' He spoke for all the men in suits who reach for a calculator whenever they hear the word 'culture'. They regard television as first and last a business, and claim the right to pursue profits with minimal interference from government. Ranged against this is a definition of broadcasting as a public service whose prime responsibility is to develop the cultural rights of modern citizenship. As the screenwriter Dennis Potter insisted in a passionate speech to the Edinburgh International Television Festival in 1993, broadcasting 'is not a business trying to distribute dosh to its shareholders . . . but something held in trust and in law for every citizen'.[1] The contest between these views is increasingly acrimonious.

In November 1991 Gerry Robinson was appointed chief executive of the Granada Group, the conglomerate that controlled Granada Television, one of the leading companies in the ITV system. He had no previous experience of broadcasting, having made his mark as head of the contract caterers Compass. He arrived with a reputation for controlling costs. The television subsidiary was a prime target, and after refusing to implement the measures asked for, David Plowright, the widely respected executive chairman (who had enjoyed a distinguished career as a producer) was forced to resign. For many observers, the incident dramatized the growing

First published in Stuart Hood (ed.), *Behind the Screens: The Structure of British Television in the Nineties* (London: Lawrence & Wishart, 1994), 155–83.

1 Dennis Potter, 'Occupying Powers', *Guardian*, 28 Aug. 1993, 21.

conflict between 'broadcasting' and 'television'. The Directors' Guild of Great Britain dispatched a letter of protest to the *Guardian* signed by many of the country's leading programme-makers. It expressed dismay at Plowright's sacking, and restated their belief that he 'embodied the ideals of quality broadcasting in Britain and that this is therefore a sad day not just for Granada but for British television as a whole'. The comedian John Cleese was less guarded. He sent Robinson a fax which read: 'Fuck off out of it, you ignorant, upstart caterer.' Robinson faxed back: 'Reading between the lines I think I can safely say that I am a bigger fan of yours than you are of mine.' These skirmishes have their roots in the founding moment of modern broadcasting in the 1920s, and in the divergent philosophies and organizational forms that emerged then.

The advent of broadcasting coincided with two profound social changes: the rise of a mass consumer system and the advent of mass democracy; its nascent institutions had to find ways of negotiating these shifts. The American response was to integrate broadcasting into the new consumer market-place. The stations were private companies whose main business was assembling audiences for sale to advertisers. In contrast, the British solution was built round the assumed needs of the new political system, with a view of audiences as citizens rather than consumers. This project was thought to require a public corporation, funded out of the public purse, whose creative decisions would be relatively free of pressure from either government or business, and whose productions would be equally available to everyone. The aim was to create a new kind of shared space in which the cultural rights of citizenship could be developed and refined.

In practice, this space was under continual pressure from governments wishing to secure a favourable hearing for their platforms and policies, and from restrictive definitions of broadcasting's cultural project. Nevertheless, the ideal of providing symbolic resources for citizenship offered a core rationale for public broadcasting that distinguished it sharply from the commercial logic of advertising-funded services.

It became the defining feature of the 'British way' of broadcasting, so that when the BBC's monopoly was finally breached in the mid-1950s, it was transferred relatively painlessly to the new commercial television system. The ITV stations were privately owned and supported by advertising, leaving the BBC with the full licence fee. However, the ITV companies' own 'licence to print money' (as Lord Thompson put it on winning the main franchise for Scotland) was overstamped by a series of public service obligations. They were allowed to employ tried and tested programme formulas to maximize audiences in peak hours, providing they also addressed minorities and extended diversity. Producing programmes that were unprofitable, or at least not as profitable as the alternatives, was the price they paid for enjoying a monopoly of advertising revenue in their franchise areas. This arrangement of non-competitive funding and an overlapping commitment to broadcasting as a public service, produced what critics on the right came to see as a 'comfortable duopoly'[2] long overdue for a strong dose of market discipline. With Mrs Thatcher's election as prime minister they got their chance.

The old adage 'Money talks' applies with particular force to broadcasting. Who gets to speak in this central public space, to whom, about what, and in which ways depends in large part on how the system is paid for. Funding plays a crucial role in organizing production and consumption. It has powerful effects on both the diversity of programming and its availability. The BBC's claim on the licence fee assumes that this is the 'least worst' way to maximize the range of voices in play, and to ensure that their conversations and arguments are accessible to every citizen. The plausibility of this case hinges on whether one sees the continual renewal of public culture as the most productive way to use television technology. Enthusiasts of a market-oriented view of television clearly reject this view. For them there is no 'public', only individual consumers who must be enticed to part with their money. But before we trace the rise of this ethos and the ensuing retreat from public broadcasting, we need a clearer definition of broadcasting's relation to citizenship rights.

Cultural Rights and Complex Citizenship

Recent years have seen a marked revival of interest in the rights of citizenship and their implementation, but definitions vary widely. A number of commentators operate with relatively narrow conceptions. There is, for example, the common-sense view that equates citizenship with participation in the formal political process. Or there is the consumerist definition underpinning John Major's Citizen's Charter, which identifies citizenship with consumer rights in relation to public services. Applied to broadcasting, the first emphasizes the need for 'comprehensive, in-depth and impartial news and information coverage' capable of supporting 'a fair and informed national debate',[3] whilst the second demands adequate

2 Peacock Committee, *Report of the Committee on Financing the BBC*, Cmnd. 9824 (London: HMSO, 1986), ch. 5.

3 BBC, *Extending Choice: The BBC's Role in the New Broadcasting Age* (London: BBC, 1992) 19.

mechanisms of accountability and redress. Both of these elements need to be included in any definition of 'public service', but they do not exhaust it. Over and against attempts to delimit the notion of citizenship, I want to argue for a general definition which identifies it with *the right to participate fully in existing patterns of social life and to help shape the forms they may take in future.* An insistence on a general right to social membership and action allows us to see citizenship in a more complex, multidimensional way. This core entitlement rests, in turn, on four major subsets of rights: civil rights, political rights, social and economic rights, and cultural rights.

Cultural rights are comprised of entitlements in four main areas: information, knowledge, representation, and communication. Information rights consist of rights of access to the information people need to make considered personal and political judgements, and to pursue their rights in other areas, effectively. In particular, it entails a right to comprehensive and disinterested information on the activities and plans of public and private agencies with significant power over people's lives. But information is of only limited use in its raw state. It needs to be placed in context, and its implications teased out and debated. Knowledge rights promote these processes by underwriting the public's access to the widest possible range of interpretation, debate, and explanation.

The third subset of cultural right, rights of representation, revolve around the right to have one's experiences, beliefs, and aspirations adequately and truthfully represented in the major forms of public culture. This is coupled with the right not to be quoted or pictured without informed consent. Finally, communicative rights entail the right to contribute to the circulation of public information, knowledge, and representation, not simply as a consumer but as an active provider—the right to speak as well as to be spoken about.

Even listed baldly like this, it is clear that delivering these entitlements has far-reaching implications for the way in which broadcasting is organized and funded. It must be as open as possible and not subject to undue influence from any one power group. It must promote diversity not plurality, offering the widest possible range of viewpoints, perspectives, and expressive forms, rather than a restricted choice in a variety of packages. And it must be available to everyone at the minimal feasible cost. As we shall see, the various branches of the emerging television industries clearly fail these tests, in whole or in part.

The retreat from public service began with the policy for broadband cable services developed by the first Thatcher government. Cable was not in itself new. The first cable systems were built in the mid-1920s soon after regular broadcast services got under way. Their business was relaying signals to areas where reception was poor or impossible. As well as BBC services, many also carried the transmissions of commercial radio stations based in Europe. This led to a running battle between the BBC, who demanded the right to control what was available over the wires, and the relay companies, who wanted to offer their customers a range of services. Their market orientation was endorsed by the Post Office, which declared in 1932 that 'the choice of programmes should be, as far as possible, regulated by the desire of the subscribers who listen to them'.[4] With the introduction of regular television services, the national broadcasters regained the upper hand and cable was relegated to the subordinate role of relaying their programming. In response, the cable operators renewed their efforts to persuade successive governments to allow them to carry additional services. There was a short-lived experiment with a subscription channel dominated by films in the 1960s and forays into local community services in the 1970s. But at the beginning of the 1980s the cable industry was still confined to a secondary, relay role.

Innovations in technology, however, were breathing new life into arguments for adding a range of subscription services. The new fibre optic networks (using thin strands of glass) had the capacity to deliver a far greater number of television channels than the old wired systems. More importantly, they offered the possibility of developing a wide range of interactive services. It was this second feature that caught the government's attention. It fitted perfectly with their general assumption that information technology would revive the economy, and that developing its potential as quickly as possible was a national priority. Not surprisingly, given this political context, the hand-picked panel that Mrs Thatcher appointed to look into the future of cable systems gave this view their enthusiastic backing. After deliberating for seven months, they duly concluded that cable's 'main role will be the delivery of many information, financial and other services to the home and the joining of businesses and home by high capacity data links'.[5] At the same time they realized that this push would have to wait until the

---

4 Quoted in Ralph M. Negrine, 'From Radio Relay to Cable Television: The British Experience', *Historical Journal of Film, Radio and Television*, 4/1 (1984) 33.

5 *Cable Systems: A Report by the Information Technology Advisor Panel*, Cmnd. 2098 (London: HMSO, 1982), 7

general strategy for deregulating telecommunications services had been implemented. Since both industries shared the same new technologies, their futures were clearly interlinked. As a result, the panel recognized that 'cable systems will go through an initial phase when their attraction will be based on "entertainment" considerations'.[6] They also endorsed the government's growing commitment to privatization in seeing 'no need for any public subsidy to cable systems'.[7] But if private investors were going to pay to install a new cable infrastructure, they would need substantial incentives and a ready source of revenue. The panel's answer was simple: allow entrepreneurs to offer a wide variety of new television channels and get the public to pick up the bill. As they put it, 'private sector funding will only be available if the range of programmes and services permitted on cable systems offers sufficient revenue-earning potential'.[8] This meant that the public service requirements placed on broadcasters had to be suspended or substantially watered down for the new industry.

This fundamental shift towards a philosophy of 'television' was institutionalized in the 1984 Cable and Broadcasting Act. Instead of adding cable to the responsibilities of the Independent Broadcasting Authority (IBA), which regulated commercial television, the act created a separate regulatory agency, the Cable Authority, with the clear expectation that they would apply a 'light touch' in awarding and policing cable franchises. The new body set about their task with relish. They declared in their first annual report that their most important duty 'was to promote cable services'[9] and that, since 'cable was not designed as a public service'[10] many of the areas that had traditionally been the subject of strong regulation within broadcasting—such as the scheduling of advertising breaks, the screening of sponsored programmes, and the amount of foreign programming allowed—'could be left to market forces to decide'.[11]

The major exception was local programming. Since cable systems are installed in bounded geographic areas, enthusiasts had long seen them as an ideal medium for developing local television services, to supplement the programming offered by the main channels, and as a way of involving more people in making programmes. This argument was incorporated into the Cable and Broadcasting Act of 1984. Section 7 required all cable operators to provide programmes

6 Ibid. 48.

7 Ibid. 47.

8 Ibid. 34.

9 Cable Authority, *Annual Report and Accounts* (London: Cable Authority, 1986) 11.

10 Ibid. 17.

11 Ibid.

'calculated to appeal to the taste and outlook of persons living in the area' and to encourage local people and local voluntary groups to participate in their production. However, in line with their chosen role as advocates for the industry, the new authority was quick to argue that 'it is unrealistic to expect substantial amounts of money to be devoted to these services until the basis for a success-ful business has been established'.[12] Given this official indifference, it is not surprising that by July 1992 only ten out of the fifty-five franchises then operating were providing locally made programming.[13]

This situation is unlikely to alter significantly in future for two reasons. Firstly, unlike the 1984 act, the 1990 Broadcasting Act, which replaced it at the beginning of 1991, contains no local or community obligations. Secondly, in an attempt to attract new investment into the industry, the government abolished restrictions on overseas ownership. This has allowed North American com-panies to move in and acquire the majority of UK cable systems. Some of these new owners are companies with interests in cable and entertainment, but most are US telecommunications companies who are using cable to break into the British market for telephone services. As *The Economist* pointed out, the fact that 'Margaret Thatcher deregulated the cable business to an extent unparalleled anywhere in the world' has allowed US firms to use 'Britain as a televisual test-tube for the sorts of programmes and services they will launch in America'.[14]

The American phone company Nynex, which had become Britain's largest cable operator by the end of 1993, is a prime example of this logic. As the firm's chief financial officer has explained, they chose to focus their European efforts on the UK because it is 'one of the few countries open to US corporations and offering the potential to provide telephony'.[15] They have taken full advantage of this 'window of opportunity', building viable geo-graphic markets for telecommunications services by acquiring adjacent cable franchises in selected areas and expanding them through joint ventures. Nynex's network in the Greater Manchester area is due to link up with the networks operated by other com-panies in Liverpool and Yorkshire to form a northern network. This will then link with networks in five other regions to provide a national telecommunications infrastructure that will enable cable

12 *Annual Report and Accounts*, 19.

13 Julie White, 'Survey of Local Channels on UK Cable, 1992', in Dave Rushton (ed.), *Citizen Television* (London: John Libbey, 1993), 140.

14 'You Say You Want a Revolution', *The Economist*, 8 Jan. 1994, 27–8.

15 Nicholas Mearing-Smith, 'Atlantic Alliance', *Spectrum: The Quarterly Magazine of the Independent Television Commission* (Winter 1993), 17.

operators to carry telephone traffic without connecting with either of the established telecommunications operators: BT and Mercury.[16]

These moves change the economics of the cable industry. If financial viability depends solely on establishing a mass subscriber base for entertainment services, offering local and community services can be a useful way of building good public relations in the local area. But if, in the longer term, the main profit centre shifts to telephony, companies are likely to concentrate on attracting relatively affluent subscribers who make extensive use of their telephones and are in the market for other interactive services. Certainly, telephone services are becoming a major growth area for cable operators. In 1991 the number of telephone lines they installed rose from 2,224 to 21,225, and revenues per line generally exceeded forecasts, particularly for business users.[17] The emerging interregional links will also enable cable companies to engage in joint programming. This move towards national networking will place additional pressure on local programming.

Ten years on from the original report on cable systems, the panel's view that they have more to do with telecommunications than broadcasting finally seems to be gaining ground, spurred on by the rapid convergence of the computing, telecommunications, and screen-based industries. Cable operators will continue to offer additional television channels, but most of these will be produced and packaged by companies based outside Britain. They will not provide shared spaces for exploring 'the state of the nation' or negotiating new conceptions of the common good. On the contrary, they will fragment audiences by offering services tailored to saleable interest groups, and they will continue to exclude everyone who cannot afford the entry price. At the end of 1993 subscribers to systems operated by Videotron (one of the leading cable companies) had to pay £30.97 a month to receive all the channels on offer.[18] Even the standard pack, at £9.99, is well beyond the reach of the many poorer families.

Satellite television does nothing to address these problems—which is not surprising since its development is marked by the same rapid retreat from public service principles.

In the spring of 1982 the government announced that it had decided to award two of the direct broadcasting by satellite (DBS) channels allocated to Britain by international agreement, to the

16 Andrew Adonis, 'Cable Companies Plan Rival Telecom Network', *Financial Times*, 5 Dec.1993.

17 Independent Television Commission, *1991 Report and Accounts* (London: ITC, 1992), 37.

18 Torin Douglas, 'Lay your Cards on the Cable', *Marketing Week*, 12 Nov. 1993, 19.

BBC. As with cable, the main impetus was economic rather than cultural. The government wanted to establish a strong British presence in the emerging market for satellite technology, and the BBC's bid provided a convenient way to kick-start a national initiative. The contract to build the satellite went to the Unisat consortium, comprising the newly privatized British Aerospace, the soon to be denationalized British Telecom, and the Marconi Avionics divisions of GEC, one of the country's largest companies. Once again, there was to be no public finance, a ban which included money from the licence fee. Thus in the summer of 1983 the BBC's charter was amended to allow it to borrow on the open market.

The corporation's euphoria at stealing a march on the ITV companies soon wore off as it became clear that the financial burden of the project was far more than they could comfortably carry. Partnership was the only solution, and in the spring of 1984 the government approved a new alliance between the BBC, the ITV companies, and selected 'outside' interests. This soon collapsed, and in 1986 the IBA (who had assumed responsibility for the project) advertised a new franchise for commercial services on three of Britain's national DBS channels. The contract went to the British Satellite Broadcasting (BSB) consortium backed by a mix of leading ITV companies (including Granada and Anglia) and major communications companies, notably Pearson (publishers of the *Financial Times*) and Richard Branson's Virgin group. BSB promised 'quality' programming and committed itself to a substantial amount of original production. It was to be, in part at least, an extension of public service broadcasting, an ambition which led Rupert Murdoch's *Sun* to dismiss it as 'toff's telly'. His motives for attacking the venture were soon to become clear.

Things started to go wrong with BSB almost immediately. Costs soon passed the initial projections. Then, in the summer of 1988, Rupert Murdoch announced that he was leasing four transponders on the Luxembourg-based Astra satellite and launching a new package of television channels in Britain under the Sky brand name. By the time BSB finally went on air, some months after Sky, it was clear that the project was unsustainable. It had been planned on the assumption that it would have a national monopoly on satellite services for long enough to gain a reasonable return. It was totally unprepared for competition. However, Sky was also losing money, and many commentators had already written it off. The solution was a merger. The terms were announced publicly in November 1990. Murdoch emerged with a 50 per cent share of the new group, B Sky B, and overall control. A government initiative which had begun as a planned extension of the BBC's operations had ended up accepting a commercial monopoly relaying transnational programming from an 'offshore' satellite under the strategic direction of an American citizen.

As with cable, these developments represent a substantial shift from 'broadcasting' to 'television'. In place of a universal service committed to diverse representation and open debate, satellite TV offers subscription channels tailored to commercially viable interests and limited to those able to pay. For some, including Rupert Murdoch, this is still a 'public service'. As he told the Edinburgh Television Festival in 1989, 'my own view is that anybody who, within the law of the land, provides a service which the public wants at a price it can afford is providing a public service'.[19] This linguistic twist substitutes a consumerist definition—that public service means offering a service that people want to buy—for a political definition which supports the provision of cultural and information resources needed for full citizenship. Mr Murdoch is not alone. Redefining 'public service' to fit with current practice has become a popular pastime with television executives, not least within ITV.

Despite a good deal of initial scepticism, commentators are now broadly agreed that after an uncertain start, cable and satellite operators have established a significant third force within British television. This new source of competition—for audiences, for advertising, and for programme right—has combined with the impact of new legislation to hasten the retreat from public service values within the ITV system.

The reductive consumerist philosophy of the new television industries requires the established channels to renew their commitment to core public service values so that viewers are offered genuine diversity and choice. The government position, supported by influential figures within ITV, is exactly the opposite. As the 1988 White Paper on Broadcasting put it, 'As the UK moves towards a more competitive, multi-channel broadcasting market, the existing regime for ITV would become increasingly hard to sustain . . . As viewers exercise greater choice there is no longer the same need for quality of service to be prescribed by legislation or regulatory fiat . . . It should be for the operators to decide what to show and when to show it,'[20] subject only to the general law and residual regulatory requirements. In other words, the companies' economic interests in retaining audiences in a harsher competitive environment take precedence over the public interest in sustaining services that guarantee citizens' rights. An increase in the raw number of channels and programmes serves as a pretext for reducing diversity and

19 Quoted in Ian Hargreaves, *Sharper Vision: The BBC and the Communications Revolution* (London: Demos, 1993), 2.

20 *Broadcasting in the '90s: Competition, Choice and Quality*, Cmnd. 517 (London: HMSO, 1988), paras 6.9 and 6.15.

organizing schedules round material that is safe and saleable. Regulation does not disappear in this system; it simply relocates to the corporate boardroom. As one critic of American commercial broadcasting in its early days dryly noted: 'Business succeeds rather better than the state in imposing restraints upon individuals, because its imperatives are disguised as choices.'[21]

By removing many of the regulatory supports for diversity and minority representation, and replacing the IBA with the lighter touch of the Independent Television Commission, the 1990 Broadcasting Act gives these imperatives a good deal more room to manoeuvre. This space is occupied by a strategy that is unashamedly commercial. As Paul Jackson, the director of programmes for Carlton Television (the weekday contractor for London), put it, 'Programmes will not survive in the new ITV if they don't pay their way.'[22]

The one significant exception to this logic is regional programming. Supporters of the ITV original system's decentralized structure, which limits companies to a single franchise covering a specific geographical area, have always seen it as more sensitive to regional interests than the BBC, with its metropolitan base and bias. There is more than a touch of romanticism in this view. The boundaries of the present ITV regions were drawn up on the basis of engineering convenience, to fit the transmitter system. They were not designed to correspond to organic, regional cultures. Added to which, most major ITV companies have long had offices in London and have concentrated on producing programmes for the national network. Even so, by providing spaces for the exploration of specifically local interests and issues, regional programmes at their best have added an important element to the diversity of debate and representation offered by broadcasting.

The 1990 Broadcasting Act appears to strengthen this commitment by making regional programming a statutory duty for the first time. But how far the companies will be willing to meet this obligation, and how far the ITC will penalize them if they don't, is open to question. The larger companies want to establish a stronger presence in the expanding international programme market. But regional productions don't generally travel well, nor do they fit easily into the emerging ownership structure of the ITV system. In an effort to consolidate their commercial position, the major companies lobbied for a relaxation of the rules relating to mergers and

21 Quoted in Robert McChesney, *Telecommunications: Mass Media and Democracy: The Battle for Control of US Broadcasting, 1928–1935* (New York: Oxford University Press, 1993).

22 Georgina Henry, 'ITV Current Affairs Shows "Must Deliver"' *Guardian*, 6 May 1992, 3.

acquisitions. Their efforts met with partial success when the government decided to allow a single company to own any two franchises, apart from the two for London. Almost immediately Carlton proposed a merger with Central, Meridian (which hold the franchise for the south and south-east) bid for Anglia, and Granada moved to acquire London Weekend Television. The long-predicted consolidation of the system had begun. The winners in this competition are more likely to concentrate on producing for the national and international markets and less likely to develop regional programming beyond the minimum necessary to pre-empt sanctions from the ITC. This minimal commitment could be weakened still further if major European companies take up their right to bid for ITV franchises on the same terms as UK companies. If strategic parts of the ITV system follow cable and satellite services and end up being owned 'offshore', by corporations with no allegiance to the core values of 'broadcasting', the shift to 'television' will take a further, massive, step forward.

Marketing the BBC

Given that a market-oriented view of 'television' already underpins the new screen industries and is rapidly reshaping the ITV system, a BBC committed to a complex conception of public service broadcasting is more essential than ever. However, the corporation's ambivalent relation to the new television market-place presents a major stumbling-block.

By the early 1980s it was clear to many observers that the idea of privatizing the BBC was gathering a good head of steam among Mrs Thatcher's advisers. It received strong support from leading think-tanks on the right, including the influential Adam Smith Institute. Their 1984 report on communications policy came out strongly in favour of financing BBC1 by advertising, and funding BBC2 by a combination of advertising, sponsorship and viewer subscriptions.[23] Not surprisingly, the major advertising agencies, led by Saatchi and Saatchi (who had won the Conservative Party account), were quick to endorse the call for advertising. They had been pressing for access to BBC audiences for some time. They also hoped that competition would drive down rates, which they saw as unacceptably high owing to the ITV companies' monopoly on airtime sales.

Although these proposals were radical, they received unexpected and unintended support from the BBC's own moves into the television market-place. As the Adam Smith report gleefully pointed out,

23 Adam Smith Institute, *Omega Report: Communications Policy* (London: Adam Smith Institute, 1984), 41.

'It is wrong to suggest that [they] would unduly "commercialize" the BBC, since it is already heavily commercialized.'[24]

The BBC were faced with a severe dilemma. To compensate for the falling real value of their licence fee revenue they had to become more market-oriented, selling programmes more vigorously overseas and entering the new markets opened up by the video, cable, and merchandising industries. At the same time they had to present these moves as an integral part of their public service remit. As one senior executive explained in 1980, 'These new ventures (or adventures) into profit-making activities must be seen to be, and must actually be, extensions of the public broadcaster's mission. They must ... be profitable enough to finance the development of programme services at all levels to the direct viewer.'[25] The difficulty arises when new services break with the core commitment to universal access.

The BBC's first director-general, John Reith, had made universal access a cardinal principal, insisting that 'There need be no first and third class' and that there should be no element of the service 'which is exclusive to those who pay more, or who are considered in one way or another more worthy of attention'.[26] The corporation had renewed this pledge in 1981 in their evidence to the official inquiry into the future of cable, claiming that: 'All citizens have the right of equal access to the BBC's service of information, education and entertainment provided they are prepared to pay their licence fee.'[27] By proposing subscription services, the ill-fated venture into satellite broadcasting clearly broke with this principle. It established division between the core services, open to all and funded out of the licence fee, and the additional commercial services available only to subscribers.

In recent years the corporation has extended the scope of these 'secondary' ventures. In partnership with Thames Television (the country's largest independent programme-producer) it has established a satellite channel, UK Gold, which is part of B Sky B's subscription package. Through its subsidiary BBC World Service Television, it offers an advertising-funded service on the Star satellite system, which is based in Hong Kong and owned by Rupert Murdoch. And in May 1994, in its most ambitious move to date, it announced an alliance with the Pearson Group to launch a series of new satellite channels around the world starting with two in Europe. It has also established its own domestic subscription

24 *Omega Report*: 4.

25 Robin Scott, 'Public Broadcasting: The Changing Media Scene', *Intermedia*, 86, (1980), 17.

26 John C. W. Reith, *Broadcast over Britain* (London: Hodder & Stoughton, 1924) 218.

27 BBC, *The BBC's Evidence to the Hunt Committee* (London: BBC 1982), 1.

services using the night-time hours to transmit programming to specific professional markets. The core rationale for these initiatives remains the same: raising additional revenues to support programme-making on the two core channels. But by venturing into the market-place so enthusiastically, the BBC runs the risk of undermining its case for a continuation of the licence fee.

The all-party House of Commons National Heritage Committee, which reported on the BBC's future at the end of 1993, seized this cleft stick and brandished it with gusto. On the one hand, 'with great reluctance' they came down in favour of retaining the licence fee for the ten years after the expiry of the corporation's current royal charter in 1986.[28] On the other, they urged the BBC to exploit every opportunity to extend 'its role in the market', but immediately added that 'should the BBC find a new, profitable commercial role . . . it might be very difficult, if not impossible, to justify the existence of a licence fee at all'.[29] The logic of this argument has been taken a stage further by the BBC's former head of news and current affairs, Ian Hargreaves. He argues that the BBC can only become a major player in the emerging transnational television market-place if it is 'free to compete' as a privately owned company relying on advertising and subscription for the bulk of its revenues, topped up with grants for specific projects from a public service broadcasting council.[30] The fact that these proposals come from a former senior insider gives them added force and reopens the case for privatizing the BBC.

The argument for abolishing the licence fee was first given authoritative backing by the Committee on Financing the BBC, chaired by the economist Sir Alan Peacock, which reported in the summer of 1986. They rejected advertising as a means of funding the Corporation but endorsed 'a sophisticated market system based on consumer sovereignty' which gave viewers 'the option of purchasing the broadcasting services they require from as many alternative sources of supply as possible'.[31] In line with this model they proposed phasing out the licence fee and moving the BBC's financing to a subscription base. They envisaged a new social contract in which the corporation would deal with its audiences firstly as consumers and only secondly as citizens. At the same time they recognized that 'There will always be a need to supplement the *direct consumer market* by public finance for programmes of a public service kind supported by people in their *capacity as citizens* and

28 National Heritage Committee, *The Future of the BBC, Report and Minutes of Proceedings*, House of Commons Session 1993–4, (London 1993), para. 78.

29 Ibid., para. 105.

30 Hargreaves, *Sharper Vision*.

31 para. 592.

voters but unlikely to be commercially self-supporting in the view of broadcasting entrepreneurs'[32] (emphasis added). Accordingly they proposed that a new body (analogous to the Arts Council) should dispense public money to worthy programme ideas that advanced 'knowledge, culture, criticism and experiment'.[33] The BBC would be free to compete for these funds but would have no privileged right to them.

When John Major replaced Mrs Thatcher as Prime Minister, a general consensus had emerged that the Peacock Report was the high-water mark of the push to privatize the BBC; that the case for a continuation of the licence fee as the sole source of funding for core services had now been won. This may have been wishful thinking. Certainly there is likely to be fierce argument before such a provision is written into the charter, which takes effect after 1996. Even if this battle is won, the new charter may well usher in the final decade of the corporation's life in the form we know now.

Whilst the government's 1992 consultative document *The Future of the BBC* does not lend its unequivocal support to any particular funding option, equally it does not rule any out, declaring that 'There is no reason why all the BBC's services should be funded exclusively by the licence fee.'[34] In their own manifesto for their future, *Extending Choice*, the corporation partially concede this case, arguing that whilst 'the licence fee remains the best available mechanism for . . . guaranteeing universal access and maintaining a wide range of broadcasting in the UK . . . licence payers will benefit if [the BBC] generates further income from secondary sources'.[35] Not only because 'taken together they can be an important supplement to the licence fee' but because they would 'form part of *a genuinely mixed funding base* for the full range of the BBC's services'[36] (emphasis added). This acceptance of mixed funding opens the way for critics to renew their assault on the BBC's exclusive entitlement to the licence fee and on their resistance to advertising and subscription.

The battle for the future of public service broadcasting, then, is a battle with the BBC as much as a battle with its detractors. To win it, two things are necessary: a clear conception of what public broadcasting stands for now and why it offers an essential counter to the consumerist philosophy of 'television'; and a convincing demonstration of the need to fund this project out of the public purse. The

32 Hargreaves, *Sharper Vision*.

33 Ibid., para. 563.

34 Department of National Heritage, *The Future of the BBC: A Consultation Document*, Cmnd. 2098 (London: HMSO 1992), para 6.25.

35 BBC, *Evidence to the Hunt Committee*, 86–7.

36 Ibid. 67.

plausibility of the second argument depends on the force of the first. Without a convincing philosophical rationale for public broadcasting, arguments about how to finance it become purely technical. Here again, however, the BBC's attempt to define its core project raises a number of questions.

Remaking Public Broadcasting

Public broadcasting must negotiate the new economics of the television market-place, particularly the accelerated move towards a transnational image system. It also needs to respond to significant shifts in the cultural landscape represented by the new politics of difference. The fact that so much of the original rationale for the BBC centred around its role as a national agency with a special relationship to the 'national culture' places the BBC in a problematic relation to both these trends.

In its initial statement of future policy, *Extending Choice*, the corporation argued strongly that it 'should continue to develop its leading position in the international market for television programmes and related services' by promoting programme and archive sales more vigorously and developing new ventures with partners.[37] The House of Commons National Heritage Committee underlined this point, urging the BBC to capitalize on the fact that its 'respected brand name [makes] it an international asset to the UK'.[38] The corporation argued that further moves in this direction would produce a wholly 'virtuous circle of investment yielding high returns for licence payers by allowing domestic programme making to benefit from the additional monies earned in overseas and secondary markets'.[39]

As the Heritage Committee was quick to point out, however, this strategy poses problems of legitimacy. Transforming the corporation 'from being a terrestrial broadcaster into predominantly a supplier of programmes for viewing on demand in the United Kingdom and throughout the world'[40] could provide it with a secure future, but in the process it would have to change 'its role from its present structure and purpose'[41] so that 'the BBC that survived might not be the BBC the Committee admires' and 'might not even be a BBC that could argue for a public sector role'.[42] *The Economist*, with its usual commercial 'realism', drew the obvious

37 Ibid. 39.
38 National Heritage Committee, *Report and Minutes*, para 26.
39 BBC, *Responding to the Green Paper* (London: BBC, 1993), para. 5.9.
40 Ibid., para. 102.
41 Ibid., para.104.
42 Ibid., para. 107.

conclusion, arguing that 'if the BBC is to compete on the world stage, it needs to be free of the restrictions that the charter puts on its commercial ventures. The best way to do that . . . is to privatize it.'[43] But even if the corporation stops short of sawing completely through the philosophical branch supporting its claim to the licence fee, there is still a problem. Any significant increase in its orientation to the transnational television system will exacerbate tensions between the requirements for selling in major overseas markets and the need to address 'the national condition' in a situation where established categories are being challenged by a new politics of difference.

As befits a publication from the Department of National Heritage (which has taken over responsibility for broadcasting from the Home Office), the government's consultative document on the BBC's future lays considerable stress on the fact that it is in a special position to 'celebrate and enhance the national heritage and encourage people to enjoy it'.[44] The BBC accept this role, arguing that they will continue 'to give special prominence to the artistic, sporting and ceremonial events that bring the nation together' and to 'reflect all the dimensions of both popular and minority culture that make us different as a nation'.[45] The problem is that much of what unites 'us' as a nation and defines the 'national culture' is based on our unique experience as a modern imperial power. It is a unity rooted in the supression of difference and the refusal to recognize the claims of 'black Atlantic' culture[46] or the cultures of other areas of the old empire. In a post-colonial polity, notions of 'national heritage' can no longer be evoked or celebrated unproblematically. What we share cannot be taken for granted. It has to be continually renegotiated. The BBC partly recognizes this, and commits itself to portraying 'a multiracial, multicultural society' and responding 'to the diversity of cultures throughout the UK'.[47] But it is not clear what form this response will take. The issue of representation cannot be addressed in full by creating more specialist programmes for ethnic minorities. It must involve a positive engagement at all levels of programming, not only because minorities have a right to see themselves represented in diverse ways within the cultural mainstream, but because such moves are a basic precondition for negotiating a renewed conception of the common good. This same logic applies, in varying degrees, to all minorities.

43 *The Economist*, 8 Jan. 1994, 20.

44 National Heritage Committee, *Report and Minutes*, 17.

45 BBC, *Evidence to the Hunt Committee*, 21

46 P. Gilroy, *The Black Atlantic: Modernity and Double Consciousness*, (London: Verso, 1993).

47 BBC, *Evidence to the Hunt Committee*, 22.

The main difference between public broadcasting and 'television' is not that broadcasting pays more attention to minority interests, but that it represents them across the range of programming, showing people as full subjects, with complexities and contradictions, and not as objects defined by handy stereotypes, be they negative or positive. Public broadcasting at its best is open-ended and dynamic. It does not use overly familiar images to pre-empt uncertainty and close down dialogue. On the contrary, it offers spaces in which the claims of specific interests can be debated, and the relations between unity and difference, solidarity and separation, consent and dissent, continually tested.

This search for a renewed concept of the common good, rooted in an active engagement with difference, is at the heart of public broadcasting's capacity to underwrite cultural rights. But it cannot be pursued successfully unless programmes remain open to the greatest possible range of viewpoints and perspectives, and all viewers have equal access to all the results. This rules out funding from subscription, advertising, and sponsorship.

It also requires that production draws on the full range of available forms and genres. Documentary, current affairs, and discussion programmes are essential, but they are not enough. Fiction and entertainment can offer unique insights and vantage-points. Narratives can go behind closed doors to dramatize the workings of power. They can decentre familiar perceptions, and they can link biography to history in unexpected ways, tracing the intimate repercussions of public events and official policies. To achieve these ends, however, programme-makers need to take risks, not only with new talent and new forms that engage more fully with social and cultural changes, but with audiences. They have to challenge and provoke as well as celebrate and entertain. Whether or not the BBC has the resources and spaces to do this in the future depends on how the corporation is funded.

All forms of finance have drawbacks. But the choice cannot be based on purely economic criteria. The options must be measured against public broadcasting's central role in guaranteeing cultural rights.

Funding the BBC's Future

The case for continuing to fund the BBC's core activities out of the licence fee rests on the claim that all other major sources of funding would produce a less desirable outcome in terms of openness, independence, diversity, innovation, and universal access. But how convincing is this argument?

There are four main sources of possible finance for the BBC:

profits generated by commercial activities in the new television and entertainment market-places; revenues from advertising and sponsorship; direct payments by viewers; and monies granted by government.

There are three main drawbacks to the corporation coming to rely too heavily on profits from its commercial enterprises. First, it generates potential conflicts of interest between the corporation's responsibility to engage with the full diversity of national life and the search for programme ideas that have revenue-earning potential in overseas and secondary markets. The danger here is that this will lead to more productions designed to appeal in America and elsewhere—by celebrating unproblematic, but saleable, visions of national heritage and national life—and fewer that speak to the complex cross-currents of contemporary circumstances. Secondly, funding secondary ventures out of advertising or customer subscriptions erodes the legitimacy of claims to the licence fee and strengthens the hand of those calling for partial or complete privatization. Thirdly, and most importantly, the introduction of subscription services undermines the cardinal principle of universal and equal access by establishing tiers of provision dependent on the viewer's ability to pay.

Consequently, although the idea of maximizing returns on the corporation's investments in facilities and productions has obvious attractions in straitened financial times, it has the clear potential to become a Trojan horse, wheeled through the gates by a government intent on phasing out the licence fee, aided and abetted by BBC personnel aspiring to be major players in the new market-places of the transnational television industry.

The other major pressure comes from advertisers wanting access to the BBC's audiences. Advertising takes two main forms: corporate sponsorship of specific programmes and payments to place conventional advertisements in selected spots in the general flow of programmes. British broadcasters have always been highly suspicious of programme sponsorship, and rightly so. The objections are twofold. First, it acts as a powerful source of potential pressure on creative and editorial decisions that can subordinate the pursuit of diversity and openness to the requirements of corporate image-building. Secondly, and more generally, by giving one specific interest group access which other groups are denied, it reinforces the privileges of corporate speech as against the claims of other voices, commandeering spaces that should remain open. It is therefore clearly inappropriate for a service attempting to maximize the range of viewpoints.

The pressures exerted by spot advertising are less direct but no less damaging to diversity. Indeed, its impact is greater, since it has the potential to reshape general programming strategies, whereas sponsorship is confined to particular productions. Much to the chagrin of many on the right, the Peacock Committee, who were otherwise sympathetic to the case for privatizing the BBC, accepted this argument, conceding that the 'progressive introduction of advertising on the BBC is likely to have effects on the range of programmes available' and that these effects are likely to be mainly negative.[48] In making this point, they drew heavily on research they had commissioned on the impact of advertising on American television. The study's conclusion was unambiguous, arguing that a system mainly supported by advertising

> is inimical to broadcasting range. The combination of dependence on high ratings and uncertainty over what will attract large audiences . . . biases programme offerings toward . . . what does not strain at the leashes of familiarity and acceptability . . . In such a system the implicit terms of the network's 'social contract' with its viewers are relatively narrow: It promises only to grab attention, excite and/or relax and facilitate escape.[49]

These features follow logically from the fact that an advertising-based system must address audiences first and foremost in their role as consumers (of the programmes and goods advertised within them) rather than as citizens with entitlement to the broadest possible range of representational debate.

But, argue supporters of advertising on the BBC, Britain is not America, at least not yet, and they point to the case of Channel Four. Here is a channel with a well-deserved reputation for diversity and innovation that is funded by advertising; why not extend this to the BBC? In many ways this is an attractive argument, but it ignores two very important points. First, Channel Four is not a private corporation. It has no shareholders. It cannot be traded on the open market. It is not obliged to maximize profits. Consequently, although it sells airtime to advertisers, it is not subject to the same demands to deliver the highest possible ratings. It is further insulated from this pressure by the financial safety net provided by the ITV companies. In the present political climate it is very unlikely indeed that any government would be willing or able to secure a similar arrangement for the BBC. The second problem concerns Channel Four's remit. This gives it a special responsibility to address areas and interests that are under-served on the main channels. The BBC, on the other hand, operates two of these channels. It

48 *Broadcasting in the '90s*, para. 327.

49 Jay G. Blumler, 'Television in the United States: Funding Sources and Programming Consequences', in Jay C. Blumler and T. Nossiter (eds.). *Broadcasting Finance in Transition: A Comparative Handbook* (Oxford: Oxford University Press, 1991), 90.

could adopt significant parts of Channel Four's remit, but it would also have to retain a commitment to assembling majorities, and this would expose it to advertisers' demands for audience maximization and the dynamics familiar from the American experience.

Nor is there a strong case for introducing a strictly limited amount of advertising as part of a move towards a mixed funding base. Evidence from countries where this has been tried, such as France, suggests that even a modest dependence on advertising has a marked effect on diversity.[50]

Searching for an entrée to BBC audiences that avoids the usual criticism, the Incorporated Society of British Advertisers (who represent the major companies advertising on television) have proposed separating advertising from programming by 'subletting' one of the corporation's channels at peak hours, 'retaining the off-peak hours for programming financed by the licence fee'.[51] They claim that this arm's-length arrangement would give the BBC the benefit of substantial advertising revenue whilst avoiding direct conflicts of interest. They neglect to mention that it would substantially reduce the cultural space available for public broadcasting and reinforce the privileges of corporate speech as against other voices.

There are substantial question marks, too, against direct funding from viewers. Some commentators have floated the idea of voluntary donations as a useful supplement to the BBC's income. But this has several major drawbacks. First, the amount raised is likely to be small and highly variable, making long-term planning for production highly problematic. Secondly, the likely revenues need to be weighed against the costs of operating and administering appeals to viewers: this should include the opportunity costs of pre-empting resources and broadcast time that could be used for other purposes. Thirdly, and most importantly, the principle of voluntary donation undermines the case for regarding access to public broadcasting as a universal right, to be enjoyed by all as part of an overall entitlement to adequate resources for citizenship.

The case for moving the BBC's funding over to a subscription basis, as proposed by the Peacock Committee and endorsed by a number of subsequent commentators, falls foul of the same basic principle. There is some evidence that people would be prepared to subscribe to BBC services, though the research is by no means clear-cut.[52] But even if viewers did subscribe, and did so at a level

50 McKinsey & Co., *Public Broadcasters around the World* (London: BBC 1993), 13.

51 Incorporated Society of British Advertisers, *The Future of the BBC: The Case for Mixed Funding, including Advertising on BBC Television and Radio* (London: ISBA, 1993), 5.

52 See National Economic Research Associates, 'Subscription', in Tim Congdon *et al.*, *Paying for Broadcasting: The Handbook*, (London: Routledge, 1992), 92–164.

sufficient to replace the licence fee, there would still be the problem that this move would abolish the principle of universal access, and, with it, any principled claim to be underwriting rights of citizenship. BBC services would become another commodity to be purchased or passed over in the television market-place and viewers would be re-created as consumers. Resisting this shift is particularly important now, after a decade that has seen a very significant widening of the income gap between the top and bottom of the class scale, leaving about a quarter of the population living on less than half the average income. The rise of the new television industries has been accompanied by the rise of the new poverty.

In this situation public funding for broadcasting is a necessity, not an option. But what form should it take? Some observers have suggested that the BBC could be funded partly out of the proceeds of the new national lottery. However, this would pitch the corporation into a continual competition with other deserving causes, again making future revenues unpredictable and forward planning impossible. The same objection can be lodged against proposals to fund the BBC through an annual grant out of general taxation. This idea has the advantage of building in a progressive element to public payments, so that the better-off pay more. However, the overwhelming disadvantage is that broadcasting would become a political football to be kicked about in the annual fixture between the spending ministers and the treasury. By opening the BBC to the possibility of more direct and more frequent political pressure, the independence on which diversity depends would seriously be compromised. If the BBC was allocated a fixed percentage of the revenues from income tax or value added tax, the risk of political influence would be substantially reduced. It would also make it more likely that the corporation's finances kept pace with rising costs.[53] However, any such proposals would meet great resistance from the treasury, with their entrenched opposition to any form of 'hypothecation', in which particular segments of taxation income are earmarked for specific purposes.[54]

This leaves the licence fee as the least worst option for public funding in terms of underwriting the core principles of broadcasting. It is also the most feasible politically. But it is not without its drawbacks. Four aspects are particularly open to criticism: equity, efficiency, acceptability, and adequacy.

Because the licence fee is a flat-rate poll-tax which everyone pays regardless of income, it is highly regressive and unfair. This has led

53 David Boulton, *The Third Age of Broadcasting* (London: Institute for Public Policy Research, 1991), 6.

54 See Andrew Graham and Gavyn Davies, 'The Public Funding of Broadcasting', in Congdon et al., *Paying for Broadcasting*, 207.

a number of observers to suggest various kinds of exemption (for pensioners for example) or subsidy (such as incorporating licence payments into the benefits system). These proposals are well-intentioned but flawed since they tie these additions to income to one specific purpose. It could be argued that this places unacceptable limits on personal choice, and that the problem is better addressed by raising the level of pensions and benefits.

The question of efficiency arises when the costs of collection account for an unacceptably high proportion of the revenues obtained. At present, according to one recent estimate, it costs about £3 per household to collect the licence fee (including the costs of anti-evasion campaigns).[55] This is less than many other charges such as telephone bills, and the figure is likely to come down even further with the introduction of more flexible payment by instalment schemes.

More significant, and less easily addressed, is the problem of acceptability. Evidence from other countries suggests that substantial licence fees (of over £50 per household) are 'generally only found in countries where the broadcaster receiving it has an audience share of a third or more'.[56] The BBC's own projections now see a 30 per cent share as the likely norm in future, given the expected growth of cable and satellite services. It could well be even less. The corporation's case looks more positive if the figures for reach and appreciation are highlighted. These show that almost everyone sees some BBC programming in the course of an average week, and that most viewers are satisfied with what they watch. On this basis the corporation could still claim to be providing a service that most people want and value highly, even if the figures for audience share dipped below 30 per cent. But would this argument be generally accepted? Would the majority of people still be willing to pay for a compulsory licence if they spent most of their viewing time watching other channels?

This problem is compounded by the need to set the licence fee at a level that will keep pace with costs and provide for new developments. Linking it to the retail price index is not sufficient, since broadcast costs (which are mainly labour costs) tend to rise faster than the general rate of inflation. To address this, the licence fee would have to be linked to increases in labour costs in the private, service sector.[57] This would allow the BBC to maintain the full scope of its operations, and to invest in developments and innovations without depending too much on other sources of finance, which, as

55 *Paying for Broadcasting*, 203.

56 McKinsey, *Public Broadcasters around the World*, 19.

57 Graham and Davies, 'The Public Funding of Broadcasting', 213.

we have seen, pose problems for the core values of public broadcasting.

This would be the least worst solution from the point of view of the BBC's ability to promote cultural rights, but it would be expensive. It would also exacerbate the problems of equity and efficiency. The alternative is to argue for a lower level of licence fee and to rely on increased income from commercial ventures to make up the shortfall. This is the BBC's present strategy. It is more acceptable to politicians and to the public, but whether it will be able to meet the requirements of complex citizenship is more debatable. But even the BBC's modest proposals are likely to meet vocal opposition from enthusiasts of partial or total privatization. Even among those who support the continuation of the licence fee beyond 1996, there are many who see it simply as an interim solution. As the House of Commons National Heritage Committee put it 'the BBC in its present form will not go on forever. It therefore needs enough time to consider how best to organize for, and operate in, the future.'[58] This conclusion is broadly in line with the Peacock Committee's insistence on a phased shift away from licence funding, culminating in full privatization. As the debate intensifies, supporters of paying for public broadcasting out of the public purse need to insist that what is at stake is the future not only of a major public institution but of the cultural rights of citizenship and with them the quality of democratic life.

58 National Heritage Committee, *Report and Minutes*, para. 54

II
Programmes

6

Creating the Audience

David Buckingham

TELEVISION PRODUCTION involves the creation, not merely of
programmes, but also of audiences. One of the BBC's primary aims in producing *EastEnders* was to build a large
audience at a crucial point in the evening's viewing—even if the
eventual size of that audience appears to have exceeded expectations.
Yet it would be false to suggest that the programme was merely a
calculated or even cynical attempt to grab the ratings, as some
critics have argued; while the ratings are certainly a major consideration, a number of other factors also enter into the equation.

Not the least of these is the BBC's own public service ethos.
In the context of the general crisis in public service broadcasting,
EastEnders' unprecedented success was bound to raise a number of
awkward questions, not merely for critics, but also for the
programme-makers themselves. To what extent is mass popularity
compatible with 'quality' in broadcasting? How can the drive for
ratings be reconciled with the notion of 'responsibility' which is
central to public service? In what ways can we regard a programme
like *EastEnders* as being of benefit to the public at all?

If the BBC's public service tradition represents one set of constraints, the financial risk involved in the undertaking made for
other, more logistical considerations. Decisions about the location
of the serial, the balance of characters, and the kinds of storyline
which could be developed had clear economic implications. The
BBC's long-term commitment to the programme meant devising a
format with considerable, even indefinite, room for future
development—a factor which had to be balanced with the need for
an early success in the ratings.

Finally, the autonomy which is traditionally granted to producers
within the BBC means that particular individuals have a key role in
determining the nature of programmes. Of course, it would be
naïve to regard *EastEnders* as the expression of a 'personal vision':

First published in David Buckingham, *Public Secrets: EastEnders and its Audience*
(London: BFI, 1987), 7–33.

the individuals concerned—in this instance, Julia Smith and Tony Holland—are television professionals with a considerable track record, who could be relied upon to come up with the goods as required. Nevertheless, they do possess a considerable degree of control over the programme, and many of its characteristic concerns derive from their own personal commitments.

In this chapter I shall identify some of the ideas and assumptions about the audience which have informed the planning and production of *EastEnders*. How do those responsible for the programme conceive of their audience and their relationship with it? How far do they use the specific information derived from audience research? To what extent do these ideas influence production decisions? And how do they relate to the public service tradition in broadcasting?

Grabbing the Ratings?

The BBC's decision to produce a new bi-weekly continuing serial dates back to 1981, well before the concern about declining viewing figures became a matter of urgency. The initial 'in principle' decision was made by Bill Cotton, then controller of BBC1, and the early planning was commissioned by his successor, Alan Hart.

Michael Grade, who subsequently inherited *EastEnders*, certainly perceived its value in terms of the competition for ratings, and in particular as a means of increasing the BBC's early evening share, which had slumped to little more than half that of ITV:

> I think it was clear to the BBC that one of the reasons for the discrepancy in the share between ITV's audience and the BBC's audience was down to *Coronation Street*, *Emmerdale Farm* and *Crossroads*. The BBC did not have anything of that kind in its locker. ITV certainly didn't invent the soap opera. The BBC were doing *The Groves* and *Mrs Dale's Diary* and *The Archers* years before. So it was nothing new for the BBC to be in the soap business. But it had somehow gotten out of the soap business over the years, and it seemed the right time to get back into it, as a means also to boost the early evening schedule, which had been languishing for some time.[1]

The choice of a continuing serial as a means of building ratings would therefore appear at first sight to be an obvious one. Yet there were clearly significant risks. A new serial would involve a far greater financial outlay than any of the likely alternatives, such as game shows. While the running costs of a regular soap opera are

---

1 All quotations from Michael Grade are taken from an interview with the author.

comparatively small, it takes many years to recoup the substantial initial investment, and an early exit from the schedules would mean financial disaster as well as public embarrassment.

Furthermore, the number of soaps already being screened led many to doubt whether the public would be willing to accept yet another: indeed, the BBC's first audience research report on the subject in early 1984 concluded that enthusiasm for a new bi-weekly serial was 'at best moderate'.[2] The BBC's own past experience with continuing television serials could hardly be said to inspire confidence either: although 1970s serials like *The Brothers* and *Angels* had done fairly well in terms of ratings, and had lasted for several years, they had not been screened continuously for the full fifty-two weeks. The BBC's only experience in producing continuing serials on television was as long ago as the 1960s, with *Compact* (1962–5), *United* (1965–7), and *The Newcomers* (1965–9), of which only the first had achieved any substantial success in the ratings.

The initial projections of *EastEnders'* potential audience were therefore relatively modest by soap opera standards. Julia Smith and Tony Holland emphasized the continuity between *EastEnders* and their own previous work on *Angels* in this respect:

> TONY HOLLAND: We didn't set out to succeed. We weren't asked to succeed. We weren't asked to be one and two [in the ratings] and get 23 million viewers. We were asked to produce a show of sixty minutes' duration split into two sections of thirty minutes, with the same budget as *Angels* and hopefully to have the same sort of audience rating. . . .
>
> JULIA SMITH: *Angels* at its height had an audience of about 13 million. And everybody thought if we got up there by our third year, that would be quite nice. You see, this is other people imposing things on the BBC. The BBC doesn't work like that. Michael Grade may have tried to hype it up since he came. But basically that is not how the BBC works. . . . We don't see this as being any different from any other programme we've worked on. Our attitudes towards it are exactly the same.[3]

The decision to opt for a continuing serial was thus not merely informed by the desire to reach a large audience. Soap operas possess a symbolic importance for television institutions, above and beyond their function in terms of ratings. By building a loyal audience, often over decades, they can become a highly significant

---

2 BBC, *Bi-weekly Serial: The Appeal of Different Regional and Social Class Concepts*, BBC Broadcasting Research Special Report (London: BBC, Feb. 1984).

3 All quotations from Julia Smith and Tony Holland are taken from an interview with the author, unless otherwise indicated.

element in the way viewers perceive the institutions themselves. *Coronation Street*, for example, can be seen as providing a specific regional identity for Granada Television, despite the fact that the majority of its productions have no such regional flavour. If, as recent research has suggested, popular perceptions of the BBC remain to some extent tied to the rather staid and middle-class 'Auntie' image, a successful soap opera could clearly do much to alter these.[4]

Jonathan Powell, who became head of series and serials in November 1983, and played a key role in the development of *East-Enders*, felt that a continuing serial could also serve as an important training-ground for new talent, just as *Coronation Street* has done at Granada. Using new writers and directors alongside more experienced ones would provide his own department, and the industry in general, with 'a substantial injection of talent'.

While Powell acknowledged *EastEnders'* considerable strategic value in terms of ratings, he also saw it as filling a gap in the overall spread of drama programming:

> It was clearly an area of popular drama in which the BBC wasn't offering something to the public. . . . I think that the point of any department in the BBC as a matter of fact—although it's not my business to say so—is to offer the correct balance of material across the whole spectrum of taste. And I think that a drama department of this size without a bi-weekly is a drama department without a very important linchpin in the panoply of ground that it's covering.[5]

At the same time Jonathan Powell and Michael Grade rejected the suggestion that *EastEnders* was merely a means of keeping the mass audience happy and thereby enabling the BBC to get on with its real business of producing 'serious' television: both were keen to emphasize its dramatic 'quality' and the 'responsibility' with which it dealt with controversial issues. *EastEnders* was regarded as tangible proof that popularity did not necessarily mean 'catering to the lowest common denominator'.

If the drive for ratings was therefore not the only motivation behind the decision to produce *EastEnders*, it certainly assumed a central significance in the period immediately before and subsequent to its launch in February 1985. The Peacock Committee, the latest in a series of government inquiries into the running of the BBC, appeared set to recommend a degree of privatization, which many advocates of public service broadcasting saw as the thin end

4 Laurie Taylor and Bob Mullan, *Uninvited Guests: the Intimate Secrets of Television and Radio* (London: Chatto & Windus, 1986).

5 All quotations from Jonathan Powell are taken from an interview with the author.

of a very thick wedge which would eventually destroy the corporation. More was clearly at stake in the 'Soap Wars' so enthusiastically reported by the tabloid press than the success or failure of individual programmes. If the supremacy of *Coronation Street* was in some sense symbolic of ITV's overall dominance of the ratings, the failure of *EastEnders* would doubtless have been seized upon with relish by the BBC's enemies.

Early Stages Julia Smith was initially approached with a view to producing a new continuing serial in the Autumn of 1983. A veteran drama producer, she had started her BBC career as an assistant floor manager, and later moved on to directing such popular successes as *Dr Finlay's Casebook*, *The Newcomers*, and *Z Cars*, as well as classic serials like *The Railway Children*. Her work as director, and subsequently producer, of *Angels*, a bi-weekly serial set in a hospital, had been widely acclaimed for its realistic and sometimes controversial treatment of contemporary social issues. To assist in the planning, Smith was later able to enlist the help of her long-time collaborator script editor Tony Holland. Their close working partnership had begun on *Z Cars* in the 1960s and had continued through *Angels* and, most recently, *District Nurse*.

A number of potential themes for the new serial had already been identified, and pilot scripts commissioned. Smith's original brief was to investigate their implications in terms of production teams, studio locations, and budgets. The success of *Angels*, and the public protests which repeatedly arose when it reached the end of its thirteen-week run, had led to the suggestion that it should be continued for the full fifty-two weeks. Yet this was eventually ruled out: it would have required too much research and rehearsal time in order to ensure the accuracy of the medical setting. Meanwhile, the other two leading contenders, set in a shopping arcade and a mobile trailer park, also posed significant logistical problems.

In the event, the initial proposal for *EastEnders* was devised in considerable haste. At 6.15 one evening in January 1984 Jonathan Powell contacted Julia Smith by telephone. He was due to meet BBC1 controller, Alan Hart, the following morning at twelve o'clock and wanted to take a definite idea for the new bi-weekly. Could he please have a draft on his desk in forty-five minutes? Across the road in the local wine bar, Smith and Holland rapidly drew up their proposal: it was completed in half an hour. By one o'clock the following day they were given the go-ahead.

The proposal which Smith and Holland produced was in many respects more conventional than some of the other ideas which they had been considering: set in an enclosed working-class inner-city community, it bore more than a passing resemblance to *Coronation Street*. Yet if the BBC was aiming to produce a soap opera for the 1980s, there were considerable risks involved: to depart too far from the tried and tested would be to court disaster.

Locating the Serial

In re-entering the highly competitive 'soap business', the BBC inevitably had to exercise a considerable degree of caution. Key decisions in planning the serial had to be made with extreme care and forethought, as they would for the most part be impossible to reverse once the programme was on the air. The price of failure, in terms of both money and reputation, was very high indeed.

The choice of a location for the serial was clearly crucial, and required a number of considerations to be held in the balance. Julia Smith and Tony Holland were strongly committed to the East End location, for a variety of reasons. Both are Londoners, and felt that the capital city was 'entitled' to have its own soap opera. They also felt that an East End community would possess considerable dramatic potential for a long-running serial:

> TONY HOLLAND: If your brief is to provide a show which can be on twice a week every week of the year, and may go on for more than a year, may go on for two, may go on for twenty-two, you need an incredible amount of mileage. You need a mobile society. You need a lot of story mileage. I don't believe you can do this in a Wimpey home, and I would knock down *Brookside* because of that, because it has no history. . . . You need a society that has a background, a history, and a culture.

As an area which has historically been populated by waves of different immigrant groups, and which has recently begun to be 'gentrified', the East End would provide a setting which could plausibly contain a broad mixture of characters. Furthermore, it would allow a greater potential for turnover of new characters, thus enabling the serial to remain contemporary—a distinct advantage over the relatively static community of *Coronation Street*, which they felt had become stuck in a 'timewarp' of the early 1960s, when it had been originated.

Like Julia Smith and Tony Holland, Jonathan Powell felt that the East End location would provide 'roots' and 'identity', 'an attractive folklore and a sense of history', which was essential for the genre. He also argued that a 'flagship' programme like a continuing serial should provide a regional identity for the BBC, even though the corporation as a whole has a national role. If the independent television companies had soap operas set in their own regions, then the BBC's should, he felt, be set in London.

Logistical factors were also significant here. In 1983 the BBC had purchased Elstree Studios, just outside London, from the independent company Central Television. Although the location of the new serial had not yet been decided at this stage, Elstree was clearly earmarked for it. While it would theoretically have been possible to make the programme at Elstree and set it in Manchester, Julia Smith was strongly opposed to the idea. In order to achieve the degree of authenticity she felt was essential, actors would have to be moved from Manchester down to London, and the cost of this operation would certainly have been prohibitive.

Nevertheless, the choice of London as a location for the new soap opera was regarded with scepticism in certain quarters; none of the long-running soaps prior to *EastEnders* had been set in the south, and there was some concern that the BBC already appeared to be too London-centred.

> JONATHAN POWELL: When I first went to talk to Alan Hart and people, they were very supportive and generally excellent about the whole thing, but the one question they did ask was 'Are you right to set it in the south?' It seemed to me to be a very sensible question. I wanted to be able to say more than, 'Well, I think so because my instinct tells me.' I also rather wanted to be able to say that to myself. As one journalist said, for a producer and a new baby executive, it was a kind of mega banana skin to walk on. So I thought, let's get audience research in, and see what this all means.

Accordingly, in January 1984 the BBC's broadcasting research department commissioned the market research agency Marplan to conduct a national telephone survey to assess the demand for a new serial, and the relative appeal of different locations and settings.[6] On the first point, the findings were relatively gloomy. Only 13 per cent of the sample of 450 people claimed to be 'very interested' in the idea, while 36 per cent expressed moderate interest; a further 50 per cent were either 'not very' or 'not at all interested'. In terms of location, Manchester was selected as the most popular overall, with London a close second and Birmingham a poor third. However, Manchester tended to be unpopular with southerners; Birmingham was unpopular with people in the Midlands; while London was not particularly unpopular in any one region, and thus appeared to have the most widespread appeal. A serial set in a working-class neighbourhood had greater appeal than one set in a middle-class neighbourhood, while a mixed neighbourhood was least popular.

6 BBC, *Bi-weekly Serial*.

Such research clearly has its limitations: it is essentially asking for reactions to a hypothetical concept, rather than to an existing programme, and thus respondents may tend to opt for ideas which are similar to what they already know. Nevertheless, the lack of consumer interest was quite notable, and unlikely to stimulate confidence in the project. In another situation—for example, North American network television—it might never have seen the light of day. The BBC's decision to stand by its commitment in spite of the findings is perhaps symptomatic of its historical refusal merely to 'pander to market forces'—although ironically in this instance it was a decision which had a remarkable pay-off.

In terms of location and setting of the serial, however, the research largely confirmed the producers' feelings. Jonathan Powell interpreted it in this way:

> The crucial bit they came back with really was that the north–south divide seemed to be based around money and class rather than actual geography, and that placing it in an area like the East End, which was inner-city, effectively working-class, cut under the barriers enough to support our instinct that it was right, or that it was a supportable thing to do.

Audience research appears to have been used largely as a means of confirming beliefs which were already held, and as valuable ammunition in arguing the case with senior management. Indeed, where research came up with information which contradicted those beliefs—for example, when it showed very little consumer demand for a new serial—it was to all intents and purposes ignored.

Developing the Concept

With the location agreed, the major logistical problem was the outside shooting. The projected budget of the serial—which had by now acquired the working title *East Eight*—would allow for fifty minutes of studio recording and ten minutes of insert material each week. In the spring of 1984 work began at Elstree on constructing the set which was to become Albert Square. It was the biggest outdoor set the BBC had ever built. What was remarkable to observers even at this stage was the meticulous attention to detail. Although the houses were built of plywood and fibreglass, there were real roads and telephone kiosks, and even real weeds in the gardens. Considerable care was taken to ensure that the shop fronts and houses looked authentically scruffy and dilapidated.

Meanwhile, Julia Smith and Tony Holland had begun devising the characters. After a period of 'research' which reputedly involved touring the East End boroughs of Dalston and Hackney, 'just talking to the people', they eventually found it necessary, as they had earlier done with *Angels*, to escape from London in order to get the job done.

> JULIA SMITH: In a normal office environment, my script editor and myself were making no headway at all; in the end, therefore, we packed typewriters and paper and, at our own expense, flew to Lanzarote. In the space of two weeks we invented twenty-five characters, made families, created a community. We wrote the biographies of the characters up to the time the audience would meet them, starting with what their childhood was like—their whole background prior to the moment we first went on air. Some members of the community we had invented knew each other since childhood; some were very new arrivals and were therefore treated with suspicion. There was the publican, his wife, and their adopted daughter. We had a Bengali shop, a Jewish doctor, a Caribbean father and son, a Turkish Cypriot cafe-owner married to an English girl. There were some older people who remembered the Blitz and found today's world more frightening in some ways. Our youngest character was minus 6 months old, our oldest 70 years.[7]

The forty-seven pages of biographies produced in Lanzarote formed the 'bible' for the team of writers, directors, set designers, wardrobe people, and others who were engaged to work on the serial as its projected starting-date in late 1984 loomed closer.

In developing their characters, and subsequently devising the major storylines for the first two years, Smith and Holland inevitably had to make a number of key decisions about the kind of serial *EastEnders* would turn out to be, and the type of audience it would attract. The possibility of a glamorous British version of *Dallas* or *Dynasty* clearly had to be ruled out, if only on the grounds of cost. Yet while *Coronation Street* certainly provided an influential model of a successful home-grown soap opera, both Holland and Smith felt that it offered a rather outdated and nostalgic view of working-class life. Until recently, the *Street* has rarely featured unemployed or black characters, for example, and it has had difficulty in replacing 'big' characters such as Len Fairclough and Elsie Tanner, or in finding characters with whom younger viewers can identify. In a sense, *Coronation Street* had grown old with its audience, and if *EastEnders* was to achieve similar success it would clearly have to attract a younger, more socially extensive audience, and ensure that it had the mileage to retain it for a good many years to come.

Brookside, British television's newest home-grown soap, provided

7 Julia Smith, 'How to get Started: Creating a Soap Opera from Scratch', *EBU Review*, 36/6 (Nov. 1985), 48.

a further model: as Channel Four's highest-rated programme, with a regular audience of around 6 million viewers, it had attracted critical acclaim for the quality of its acting and for its treatment of contemporary social issues. Yet here again, Smith and Holland were aware of some of the problems which *Brookside* faced. While the setting, in a real housing estate on the outskirts of Liverpool, made for a considerable degree of naturalism, the space restrictions in the houses meant that it was confined to a single-camera approach, which made for a rather laborious visual style. Furthermore, the lack of any central meeting-point for the characters made it difficult for the writers to weave the different storylines together. Smith and Holland also felt that *Brookside*'s coverage of 'social issues' was at times rather self-conscious and didactic.

If *EastEnders* was to stand any chance of long-term survival, it would have to begin, as *Coronation Street* had done in 1960, with a commitment to reflect the realities of contemporary inner-city life—realities which Smith and Holland defined at least partly in terms of 'social problems'. In interviews they have repeatedly argued that the serial is 'a slice of life' which is based in 'documentary realism', and which therefore inevitably confronts 'controversial social issues':

> JULIA SMITH: We decided to go for a realistic, fairly outspoken
> type of drama which could encompass stories about
> homosexuals, rape, unemployment, racial prejudice, etc. in a
> believable context.[8] Above all, we wanted realism.
> Unemployment, exams, racism, birth, death, dogs, babies,
> unmarried mums—we didn't want to fudge any issue except
> politics and swearing.[9]

Smith and Holland have very definite ideas about *how* such 'issues' should be dealt with in a dramatic context, and reject the idea that the programme is 'issue-based'. Nevertheless, as with their work on *Angels*, *EastEnders* was clearly intended from the start to be a programme which would acknowledge 'social problems' rather than sweep them under the carpet.

The initial balance of characters chosen thus meant that certain issues were bound to be raised, given the commitment to a degree of realism. The decision to include a range of ethnic-minority characters, for example, meant that racism was inevitably on the programme's agenda. Likewise, the presence of a number of teenage characters meant that 'teenage problems'—pregnancy, unemployment, family strife—would inevitably be dealt with in some way.

8 *EBU Review*, 47.
9 *Daily Mirror*, 21 May 1985.

The balance of characters also had clear implications in terms of the kind of audience *EastEnders* was attempting to build. Prior to the launch of the BBC's new early evening package its audience at this time of day tended to be predominantly middle-aged and middle-class. In order to broaden that audience, *EastEnders* would have to appeal both to younger and older viewers, and also to the working-class audience which traditionally watched ITV. The choice of a working-class setting, and the broad age range of the characters, thus also made a good deal of sense in terms of ratings.

In addition, *EastEnders* sought to extend the traditional audience for British soaps, which is weighted towards women and towards the elderly. Having a number of strong younger characters, it was argued, meant that the programme would have a greater appeal for young viewers than other British soaps, as well as providing a means of regenerating the narrative in the longer term. Strong male characters would also serve to bring in male viewers, who were traditionally suspicious of the genre. Julia Smith had a definite idea of her potential audience profile:

> I'm not going for the stereotypical middle-class, BBC audience. The professional classes won't get home early enough to see the programme. I expect the audience to consist of working people who watch television around tea-time before going to bingo or the pub. Soap operas traditionally appeal to women, but we have to remember that men watch them too—even if they don't admit to it. And with at least five teenagers in the cast I expect to pick up a lot of young viewers.[10]

Audience research was involved at this stage. The BBC broadcasting research department reduced the biographies which Smith and Holland had produced in Lanzarote to brief, thumbnail sketches which were tested in six small discussion groups held in London and Manchester in February and March of 1984. Participants were asked for their opinions of soap opera in general, before being introduced to the concept of the new bi-weekly; they were then asked to discuss the outlines of the characters, and to anticipate some of the stories in which they might become involved.[11]

The research largely confirmed common-sense wisdom about the appeal of soap opera. 'Credibility', in the form of 'true to life characters' and 'realistic plots and storylines' was found to be an essential ingredient. Viewers enjoyed being able to eavesdrop on the characters' lives, and gossip about them, without having to suffer any of the consequences or difficulties of being involved in 'real'

10 *Broadcast*, 26 Oct. 1984.
11 BBC, *Bi-weekly Serial II*, BBC Broadcasting Special Report (London: BBC, June 1984).

relationships. 'Familiarity' with the characters and with the location was also found to be vital. Viewers liked to feel that they knew the characters well and could predict the ways in which they would react to situations, although there was also a danger of characters becoming too predictable. Significantly, it was noted that viewers' opinions of the home-grown soaps had been influenced by their viewing of US imports such as *Dallas* and *Dynasty*. The glamour of the US soaps had highlighted the mundaneness of serials like *Crossroads* and *Coronation Street*, which many criticized as 'old-fashioned'.

Responses to the idea of the new bi-weekly and to the thumbnail sketches suggested that they connected with a number of familiar stereotypes in viewers' minds. Viewers predicted that the serial would feature large, matriarchal extended families living in run-down and overcrowded accommodation; that it would be based in a small, enclosed community, thereby providing considerable potential for conflict, intrigue, and gossip; and that it would make great play of 'Cockney humour'.

The character sketches themselves were very brief, giving only the character's name, age, and occupation, yet they provided considerable fodder for discussion. Many of the comments were highly stereotyped, but they were in some cases remarkably acute in their predictions. Lou Beale was described as a 'tyrant' who would rule her family with an iron fist; Pauline would have a heart of gold; her daughter Tracey (who subsequently became Michelle) would get pregnant, probably by one of the married characters; Jack Parker, the publican (Den Watts), would be a 'Jack the lad', involved in shady deals, while his daughter Sharon would be spoilt; Ethel would be an Irene Handl-style Cockney and an incorrigible gossip.

In general, respondents expected the new serial to succeed, given the BBC's reputation for high production standards, although some expressed concern that the BBC was 'a bit highbrow', and argued that the scriptwriters should know the locality well if they were to avoid giving an idealized image of East End life. They felt that it should be 'humorous, amusing, and lively' and contain at least some 'larger than life' characters. The influence of US soaps led to considerable discussion of the importance of high production values—an area in which existing home-grown soaps were found to be lacking. Finally, the respondents felt that the new serial should address current social issues, such as unemployment, crime, and racism, but that these should 'grow' out of the characters, rather than being tackled in a more didactic manner.

The potential viewers' ideas corresponded closely to the biographies which Julia Smith and Tony Holland had produced, and it is therefore difficult to assess how far this information influenced their decisions. Vivien Marles, the researcher most closely involved in the project, felt that it did have some influence:

> Because what people had said largely coincided with their own ideas, they warmed to it, and were very keen, and took a lot of it on board. In fact they changed at that point a number of characters, dropped some, and added a few more in.[12]

Nevertheless, she felt that in general the programme-makers used this information very selectively, and largely as a means of confirming their own instincts:

> I am very sensitive to the fact that this programme was not a product of audience research. The producer was very clear right from the beginning about what sort of programme she wanted to make. Although they've been extremely receptive, I could never say that changes were made as a result of audience research. I think it's much more of a working together. Where audience research findings have coincided with the producer's gut feelings, then changes have been made. I actually believe that if all of this research had said something completely different, *EastEnders* would probably be the same as it is today. But it is hypothetical. You can't tell.

This impression was confirmed by Jonathan Powell and Michael Grade: both argued that the research had not been undertaken in order to formulate the programme (as is sometimes the case in US network television), but in order to test out the producers' instincts and to pinpoint any potential problems. While the information might be used in a case where the producers were already uncertain about a particular aspect of the programme, it could equally be ignored if it flatly contradicted their ideas.

Julia Smith and Tony Holland were certainly concerned to refute the idea that they had used audience research in formulating *EastEnders*. Holland was extremely scathing about such research, and asserted that he completely ignored it. Smith argued that audience research was more for the benefit of management than for the programme-makers themselves:

> They used it because they haven't got the confidence, if you like. Or they had to prove to somebody that it was possible to do it. . . . It made it slightly easier for me, that my instincts had been correct. They weren't going to fight me any longer. But I would have gone on fighting if it had turned out the other way.

---

12 All quotations from Vivien Marles are taken from an interview with the author.

The Launch   After almost a year of frenetic activity *EastEnders* was launched at 7 p.m. on 19 February 1985. Julia Smith's original target date of September 1984 had been postponed twice: first, at the instigation of the new controller of BBC1, Michael Grade, who had preferred a January start; and secondly, when *EastEnders'* companion in the BBC's new early evening package, the chat show *Wogan*, had not been ready in time. Julia Smith was certainly uneasy about the late start: *EastEnders* no longer had the long winter months in which to build up a loyal following before the summer downturn in the ratings.

If the initial projections of *EastEnders'* audience size had been relatively modest, the publicity which surrounded its launch was rather less so. In an unprecedented move, the BBC had appointed a publicity officer specifically to promote the new serial. The programme had been trailed in *Radio Times* and on screen for many weeks beforehand, leading many newspaper critics to accuse the BBC of 'hype'. An ostentatious press launch, complete with lavish press pack and 'showbiz walkpast' of the cast, only fuelled their scepticism. The high profile certainly succeeded in giving the programme public visibility—and encouraged as many as 13 million viewers to tune in to the first episode—but it also increased the risks attached to failure. If *EastEnders* was going to make mistakes, it would do so in the public eye, without the opportunity to ease itself in gently.

Michael Grade, fresh from the competitive world of the American networks, was unrepentant:

> I believe in getting as much publicity for programmes as possible. If you say something is wonderful and it isn't, then you pay the price. But in terms of *EastEnders* there is nothing we did in promoting it that I wouldn't do again. The fact that the show is so good justifies the hype. It was a hype, of course. You're launching a £4–5 million project—do you let it creep onto the air?

In retrospect, Grade professed that he had always been confident that the programme would succeed:

> I knew it was going to be a monster hit. All my experience told me so—my professional instincts honed over the years in the heat of battle. I knew from the first three or four minutes it was going to be a monster.

Yet, as Jonathan Powell pointed out, the BBC's investment in the programme meant that it had no option but to be committed to its success:

It was psychologically very important, the fact that we built that lot. It cost a fair amount of money. The fact that we were committed to it, I think some of the success of the programme was due to that, because it was so completely inescapable. It had to succeed. It was important to the programme, to the people who made it, to the organization. . . . We were right to allow ourselves no options. We didn't even allow ourselves the option of failing.

If the confidence of Grade and Powell resembled that of gamblers playing with very high stakes, Julia Smith herself was considerably more cautious. She expected the programme to take as long as two or three years to establish itself with the audience, and anticipated that its strong start would be followed by a significant dip in the ratings over the summer months.

The Ratings War   *EastEnders'* success in the ratings was far from instant, although its eventual rise to prominence in the autumn of 1985 certainly exceeded even the most optimistic expectations. The figures were carefully monitored by the BBC's broadcasting research department, and further qualitative research was undertaken in order to gauge more detailed reactions.

The continuous monitoring showed an interesting pattern of response. As Julia Smith had predicted, the audience size began to fall after the initial burst of interest: after three weeks on air, BBC1's early evening share had returned to the pre-*EastEnders* norm of 7 million, compared with ITV's 13 million. Nevertheless, the show's appreciation indices—which measure the audience's interest and enjoyment of programmes—steadily increased, rising from 58 in February, through 70 in April and 75 in May, to reach 80 by the end of August, a figure which was nearly ten points higher than the average for British soap opera. Although *EastEnders* appeared to be losing the ratings battle, the dramatic rise in its appreciation indices suggested that it was building a loyal following which would provide a firm basis for future growth.

Qualitative research on two early episodes, again using small group discussions, revealed that viewers were able to follow the storylines, and felt that the characters had potential, but found the programme rather dreary and depressing. In particular, they found the conflicts within families rather 'too close to home' and therefore upsetting to watch. This criticism was also reflected in press reviews and in a series of letters published in *Radio Times* in April. Here again, it is difficult to assess the extent to which this information influenced the programme's producers, although it certainly coincided with Michael Grade's own views:

> The only criticism I had of the show in the early days was that it was too strident in tone. There was not enough humour in the show, it was all a bit *Sturm und Drang* in the first weeks. And Jonathan Powell agreed, and we made that adjustment as quickly as we could. We lightened it up a bit here and there and that also helped.

Nevertheless, one major reason for *EastEnders'* eventual success in the ratings was its careful scheduling. Michael Grade had arrived at the BBC with a reputation derived from his work at London Weekend Television of being a scheduling wizard. One of the problems he had identified very early on was the lack of fixed points in the BBC schedule—and in particular in the early evening. *EastEnders* and *Wogan,* in addition to pulling ratings, would also provide a much-needed stability at the start of the evening's viewing. The sheer longevity of a soap opera was also a significant point in its favour: as Grade observed, the BBC's past attempts to dent the ratings for *Coronation Street,* for example by scheduling a popular situation comedy against it, had only proved successful in the short term.

At the same time Grade did not subscribe to the view that 'inheritance' was all-important—the idea that if you caught an audience at the start of the evening, it would stay with you until close down. Particularly in an era of remote-control keypads, this approach was largely outdated. Nevertheless, if *EastEnders* were to be followed by a sequence of popular programmes, it would certainly go a long way to increase the BBC's overall audience share:

> If you've got good programmes that are following it, the audience look at it as a package. They say, 'Right, I'll watch BBC from 7.00 to 9.00 and then I'll switch to ITV because I want to watch their drama.' They'll watch a package of programmes, with a gem like that in the middle which attracts. So there is a package idea, but the pieces around it have to be the right pieces.

Nevertheless, the initial decision to schedule *EastEnders* at 7 p.m. represented something of a gamble since it meant competing with ITV's *Emmerdale Farm,* a rural soap opera with a steady and respectable share of the ratings. Michael Grade described this first phase of the 'Soap Wars' with considerable relish:

> I put *EastEnders* at 7.00 because *Emmerdale Farm* was not networked. As a response to it going at 7.00, ITV for once got its act together and networked *Emmerdale Farm.* That was a blow,

but I knew—from my knowledge of ITV—that *Emmerdale Farm* went off the air in the summer for a number of weeks, and I only had to wait for that window, and then I would be away. What they did was that they somehow squeezed extra episodes and repeats, so there was no break in the clouds. So I thought, this is crazy, this is silly now, I'm going to have to move it. And because of the sort of press we have in this country, I didn't want them rubbishing the show—'panic move'—they'd have written that as a failure story. I had to dress up the presentation of that move in such a way as to protect the show, so I gave all kinds of reasons for the move, trying to disguise the fact that I was having to move it because it had reached a plateau and wasn't moving off.

It was at about this point—in September 1985—that Mary Whitehouse began her public attacks on the programme, and this provided Grade with a further explanation for the shift from 7.00 to 7.30. His claim that the move was made in order to protect 'family viewing time' was, not surprisingly, received with some scepticism by the press.

In addition to the two weekday episodes, Grade also decided to schedule an omnibus repeat edition at 2 p.m. on Sundays, a move which was primarily intended as a means of keeping the programme in the BBC's top ten. Adding the omnibus figures to those for the weekday broadcasts—which had long been standard practice on the part of the Broadcasting Audience Research Bureau—would, he felt, keep the ratings up for the first year and thus stave off press criticism. His original intention had been to drop the omnibus edition once the programme had established itself in its weekday slots, but it too eventually acquired a large constituency, not least because it was cleverly scheduled opposite ITV's statutory half-hour of religion.

Following the shift to 7.30 in September 1985, *EastEnders'* ratings began a meteoric rise, which eventually peaked at around 23 million in February and March of 1986. This rise coincided with the regular seasonal upturn in the ratings, and also with the ending of the latest series of *Dallas*, but *EastEnders'* climb to the top of the ratings charts was both faster and earlier than even its most enthusiastic advocates could have expected. The appreciation indices also continued to rise, averaging a phenomenal 85 in the early months of the new year. Studies of the demographic profile of the audience showed that the programme was successfully reaching a genuine cross-section of the population in a way that no British soap opera had previously managed to do, and that it was particularly popular with teenagers, traditionally the least captive section of the television audience. Ironically, qualitative research suggested that it was precisely those features which had initially been found alienating—and in particular its abrasive treatment of 'social issues'—which viewers were now ready to praise.

<table>
<tr><td>

The Broadcasters and their Audience

</td><td>

Ideas about the audience thus entered into every stage of the devising of *EastEnders*. The programme ultimately owes its existence to the BBC's need to reach a new early evening audience; many of the specific production decisions—about the location and setting of the serial, about the balance of characters, about publicity and scheduling, and about the themes and storylines—were to a certain extent informed by ideas about the type of audience the programme was aiming to reach, and by assumptions about what would interest and entertain it, and thereby keep it watching. Yet what is most remarkable is that these ideas and assumptions were based on comparatively little direct evidence about the audience itself.

</td></tr>
</table>

In a paper delivered to the Market Research Society in 1986 Vivien Marles and Nadine Nohr, of the BBC's broadcasting research department, described the launch of *EastEnders* as 'the launch of a new brand into a difficult market'.[13] The marketing metaphor is in many respects appropriate, yet what distinguishes the launch of *EastEnders* from, say, the launch of a new chocolate bar is how little market research was actually undertaken. Compared, for example, with US television, where the findings of audience research can effectively seal the fate, not merely of particular series, but also of individual characters within them, audience research in British television remains a relatively small-scale, marginal operation. In the case of fictional programmes it is unusual to undertake research prior to going on air, as was the case with *EastEnders*, although the limited scope of even this research remains surprising when one considers the substantial investment which was at stake.

Furthermore, at least according to the programme-makers, the evidence which was available was largely ignored. Julia Smith and Tony Holland were certainly adamant that they had not deviated from their initial conception, despite the considerable pressures upon them:

> TONY HOLLAND: All the time we're saying, 'Think of the number you first thought of.' That's what we're doing. 'What did you set out to do in the first place?' . . . Apart from one

13 Vivien Marles and Nadine Nohr, *EastEnders: The Role of Research in the Launch of a New Brand into a Difficult Market*, Paper Delivered to the Market Research Society Conference, 1986.

story, we've done everything we intended to do two years ago, and we're still on course. We've stuck to what our original intention was.

Of course, this is not to suggest that they remain indifferent to audience response, although their ways of assessing that response appear rather impressionistic. They regard ratings as an unhelpful indicator, not least because the production of new programmes takes place several weeks ahead of the figures appearing. Instead, they prefer to rely on more personal and subjective methods:

> TONY HOLLAND: To be quite honest, we're terribly thrilled by the ratings. It is very thrilling to think that for one episode, half the population was watching . . . It's terrifying, but it thrills you. Although we're thrilled, and rush for the figures each week to see what they are—at least I do—it's a straw poll, a feeling in the air that we pick up on. I buy the tabloids every day because my punters read them. I want to know what they're reading about. I want to know what they're calling Sarah Ferguson. I need that information so it sounds as though it's off the street. But I'm more inclined to do my own audience research, and Julia does the same in her world. What I pick up off the street reaction is my judge of the ratings. . . . It's better for me to hear somebody in a bar saying, 'When's Angie going to get her revenge, Tone?' I can pick it up from the tea ladies, I pick it up from somebody in the corridor, whatever.

This lack of information made it extremely difficult for them to explain the reasons for *EastEnders*' success. Indeed, in the case of Smith and Holland, this was a question which they were steadfastly unwilling to address, arguing that to analyse their success would interfere with their creative work.

> JULIA SMITH: There's nothing to say about it. What is there to say? It's a humble little twice-weekly serial churned out with a lot of hard work. An hour's worth of television, to entertain the public, that's all it is. . . . What is there for scholars to write about? In our minds, it's totally simple. We follow our noses, we don't do anything else. We had an instinct, we followed it. We follow our noses, we work on instinct, and that's that. There's no intellectualism.

While Tony Holland acknowledged that there was 'a certain built-in craft' to scriptwriting and production, it was this spontaneous creative intuition which was all-important:

> We just go by our noses. That's why we try to do the show hand-to-mouth, with as little planning as possible.

Analysing television, they argued, would destroy the 'magic and illusion and thrill of entertainment'. It was at least partly for this reason that they claimed not to watch other soap operas—with the notable exception of *Brookside*: not only would this influence them, or give them 'second-hand' ideas, it might also make them self-conscious about their own programme.

Others were more forthcoming, however. Michael Grade felt that the story of Den and Angie Watts was 'the spark that set off the fire': characters with weaknesses or with 'a hint of villainy about them' were a perpetual source of fascination for audiences. Jonathan Powell, on the other hand, argued that the story of Michelle's baby had been the winning factor: it was a 'human story' which had 'touched a public nerve'. Yet he, too, argued that the ratings did not tell the whole story:

> It was a question of *response*. Once it *responded* then you began to be able to play the tune, you began to be able to sense what your programme was. It was the response that was important, I think, the sense of response rather than the sense of audience. . . .

Discussing the controversy following Mary Whitehouse's public criticisms of the programme, he described this phenomenon at greater length, and in almost mystical terms:

> It was a good reminder of what you're playing with when you have something that's at that fever pitch, which the programme was—where somehow you're not just dealing with an audience any more. It's like a family row, and you're right in the middle of it: the programme is right in the middle of the culture and has almost gone beyond the screen. It's almost living out there. I don't claim anything special about the programme, except to note that at times the programme, as others do, went beyond the screen and almost lived—did live, actually—in the street. Somehow the barriers between the television screen and people's hearts and emotions were broken down.

For Smith and Holland, however, 'response' was more of a distraction, even a source of irritation. The public interest, reflected—and, admittedly, stirred up—in the tabloid press, made it more difficult, they argued, for them to get on with the job of producing the programme itself. Tony Holland even reported that there was a strict rule in his local pub that nobody was allowed to discuss *EastEnders*. They were particularly exasperated by the volume of letters from 'pressure groups' arguing for their pet 'issues' to be covered. They felt that the programme had become 'public property', and that others were attempting to take control of it away from them:

JULIA SMITH: It does seem that now almost the one thing we're not being given time for is to make the programme or to care about the programme, because we're being pulled more and more by various people who think it is their right to have access to us. It's taking a lot of time and effort to cling on. We're there to make a programme, we're not there for all these other reasons.

Both Smith and Holland claimed to be strongly anti-élitist, and committed to popular drama: in this sense, they argued, *EastEnders* was merely an extension of their previous work on *Z Cars* and *Angels*. They were not interested in making 'serious' or 'esoteric' drama for small audiences, and did not want to be seen to be 'effete' about their own work. Holland contrasted their approach with that of writers in 'fringe' theatre, who, he claimed, 'have absolutely no experience of life whatsoever':

They haven't gone through all the struggles we went through. . . . We actually know what's going on out there in the street. That's why we've got an instinct for it. . . . If you're in the business of communication, which is what television is all about, where you want people to relate to what you're doing, you actually want someone to watch the damned thing, you're devoted to that loyal and in our case huge audience. I don't want to do the programme for me. Julia doesn't want to do it for her. We're doing it for them.

Yet at the same time, it is significant that they did not regard themselves as part of their own potential audience:

JULIA SMITH: I wouldn't watch the programme if I wasn't making it. I've never watched a soap opera in my life, I wouldn't start now. I don't watch television. I'm a professional. I make it. I'm like a manufacturer. . . . If I watch television, I'll watch the news. I watch the odd opera. I enjoyed Huw Wheldon last night. I'm a horribly middle-class esoteric viewer.

As these quotations suggest, the programme-makers' conception of their relationship with their audience was confused and even contradictory. On the one hand, they felt able to claim privileged knowledge of 'what's going on out there in the street', and to value 'street reaction'. Yet, on the other hand, the tangible manifestations of this reaction in audience research, in the popular press, and in viewers' letters were ignored or regarded with suspicion. In each of these cases, there are certainly good reasons to doubt whether the data is in fact representative; yet to rely instead on 'intuition', or on even more impressionistic evidence, can scarcely be regarded as any more adequate.

As Philip Elliott has observed, one of the key skills in producing popular television is the ability to empathize with audience groups of which one is not oneself a member.[14] In the absence of any sustained, direct contact with their potential viewers, broadcasters typically put themselves and their colleagues into the role of audience. Producers may have favoured target audience groups, and may use their imagined reactions as a means of judging their own work. Yet these assumptions about the audience are fundamentally based on speculation, since there is very little hard evidence which broadcasters are prepared to trust—apart, of course, from the ratings, which are ultimately the crudest possible form of data.

This is not to suggest that broadcasters' attitudes towards their audience are merely arrogant or indifferent. The existing structures of broadcasting institutions place an extraordinary pressure on programme-makers: producing a programme as expensive and as popular as *EastEnders* requires a very high degree of 'nerve', because there is very little margin for error. Even when the ratings are high, there remains a perpetual fear that they might start to fall away and that one will be unable to discover the reasons why. Keeping one's nerve thus inevitably means insulating oneself from the variety of demands on one's attention—of which the audience is merely one among many.[15]

At the same time it is clear that this arrangement leaves broadcasters with a considerable degree of freedom to determine the kinds of programme they feel should be made, and this is—perhaps paradoxically—even more true in 'public service' broadcasting than in the commercial companies. As Julia Smith argued:

> I'm absolutely convinced that this programme could not have been made anywhere but the BBC. Because only in the BBC could two programme-makers be allowed to do their own thing, and fail if they were going to fail. . . . Nobody but the BBC could be as immune, could have sheltered us in that way.

Serving the Public   *EastEnders'* extraordinary popularity nevertheless means that it enjoys a rather ambiguous relationship with the 'official' Reithian definition of 'public service broadcasting'. The charge of 'catering to the lowest common denominator' could be made not only by the

14 Philip Elliott, *The Making of a Television Series: A Case Study in the Sociology of Culture* (London: Constable, 1972), ch. 8.

15 See Tom Burns, *The BBC: Public Institution and Private World* (London: Macmillan, 1977).

BBC's enemies, but also by those within the corporation who believe in broadcasting as a means of uplifting public taste. While Tony Holland agreed that the BBC had allowed Julia Smith and himself a considerable degree of autonomy, he also acknowledged that their work was 'very commercial', and in some respects had more in common with the ethos of independent television than with that of the BBC. For example, part of the 'craft of script-making', as he defined it, lay in knowing the correct time of year to 'blow the big story': getting in a good story at Christmas meant that you might stand some chance of keeping your audience until Easter, despite the seasonal drop in the ratings.

> We are, in that sense, not typical of the BBC. It has been considered for some years, although I think it's changing, that to actually promote a product—and we're the only people in the BBC that I know of who call our show a product—a lot of people in the corridors of power think it's terribly vulgar. But we like the packaging, we like the promotion, we like the hype.

As Holland indicated, this Reithian view of public service broadcasting is gradually changing, although it remains influential. Michael Grade and Jonathan Powell both contested the view that popularity was incompatible with the principle of public service—a view which they described as both outdated and condescending:

> MICHAEL GRADE: That's a patronizing argument by people who believe that the BBC should be an élitist ghetto of cultural high ground, inaccessible to the working classes, or inaccessible to people who aren't highly educated, appreciative of the finer things of life.

At the same time they rejected the suggestion that *EastEnders* was primarily about 'grabbing the ratings', or about popularity at any price. The idea that it was 'a lowest common denominator show' was incorrect, both on the basis of its broad demographic appeal, and on the grounds of its 'quality':

> JONATHAN POWELL: If we really wanted to grab the ratings, we wouldn't make *EastEnders* like we make *EastEnders*. I think *EastEnders* has attracted a large audience because it's good, it's mature, it's grown-up, and it talks to people on their level. It talks to them on a mature level. It's an entertainment programme, fine: but entertainment is not a dirty word. It addresses, within a quite wide interpretation of an entertainment format, quite significant and human problems. There are good episodes and there are bad episodes, sure, but there are 104 a year, so there are bound to be. But there are

episodes of *EastEnders* which I would frankly be very happy to put up as a one-off play.

Significantly, although popularity is clearly valued, 'quality' is still defined here by standards which derive from the 'cultural high ground' of the single play.

While Grade and Powell were therefore keen to argue the case for *EastEnders* as 'quality' television, they were also aware of its strategic role within the broader range of BBC programming, and within the context of public criticism of the corporation. There was a sense in which the popularity of *EastEnders* enabled other, less popular, programmes to exist:

> JONATHAN POWELL: I'm sure it helps our image to have programmes like this. I'm sure it helps to attract people to other programmes. And it creates space, too. . . . You have to create your space, allow yourself the space for specialized programming. It works when the balance is right. I don't think this department works with just *EastEnders* and *Bergerac*, but equally I don't think it just works with *Bleak House* and *Edge of Darkness*. They all complement each other.

Michael Grade argued that the BBC had always been in the business of producing popular programmes, although in the current context a major success like *EastEnders* could perform a particularly important function for the corporation as a whole:

> It's a problem for our enemies, because they don't want us to be popular. If we weren't popular, then there is a case for breaking up the BBC and selling it off to private enterprise. We do stand in the way of a lot of people making a lot of money. My belief is that we need to be popular, but we don't need to be popular all the time, every day, every week of the year. We need to *prove* that we can be as popular as the other side with quality programmes when we want to be.

In many ways these comments reflect the broader dilemma which has faced public service broadcasting in this country since the introduction of commercial television, and which was brought to a head in the period immediately preceding the launch of *East-Enders*. On the one hand, the BBC is obliged to justify its monopoly over the licence fee by producing programmes of artistic 'quality' and 'responsibility'. Yet, on the other hand, that monopoly can only be sustained if the BBC is seen to speak to the nation as a whole, rather than to a privileged minority, and it is therefore obliged to compete with ITV for a reasonable share of the mass audience. As Michael Grade argued, the BBC has always resisted the idea of catering merely to the educated middle class, yet in the context of a dwindling audience share, and a government committed to 'free market' economics, its delicate attempts to retain a balance between popular and minority tastes have inevitably been fraught with uncertainty.[16]

In this sense, the attempt to reconcile the popularity of *EastEnders* with the ethos of 'public service' represents a further shift away from the Reithian tradition. Although many of the basic Reithian tenets remain—the definition of 'quality', for example, or the idea that a popular programme might serve as 'groundbait', to lead viewers on to less popular, more 'specialized' programmes— there is a strong sense in which the agenda is being set from outside the BBC itself. Thus, the BBC has to 'prove things' in order to silence its 'enemies'; it has to produce programmes which will be 'good for its image' and thus 'create space' for 'specialized programming' (that is, for 'high culture'). What is perhaps most significant here is that these pressures on the BBC derive, not primarily from viewers, but from its critics in the press and in government, who for both economic and political reasons wish to see it privatized: in this sense, the BBC is becoming more accountable, not so much to the public, as to its powerful enemies on the political right.

| Educating the Audience | If 'quality' is one key term in the definition of public service broadcasting, 'responsibility' is certainly another; and it is around *EastEnders'* responsibility in dealing with 'social issues' that further controversy has been generated. I shall confine myself here to considering some of the ways in which the producers themselves perceived it. Julia Smith and Tony Holland were very concerned to refute the idea that *EastEnders* was an 'issue-based' programme. Although it did cover social issues, they argued that this was merely an inevitable consequence of its commitment to realism, rather than something which they self-consciously set out to do. The programme did have an educational function, but it was one which they saw as, by and large, incidental to its main purpose of providing 'entertainment' and exploring 'dramatic conflict'. Such issues 'grew naturally' out of the characters and the storyline, rather than the other way round. Simply by 'showing people in the real world', the writers would inevitably 'fall over' issues that lay in their path. |

JULIA SMITH: You can't live in this life and notice what goes on around you and not learn something. So hopefully you can't

16 For a useful account of contemporary developments, see Michael Leapman, *The Last Days of the Beeb* (London: Allen & Unwin, 1986).

watch *EastEnders* and not learn something. Mary Whitehouse might prefer that 15-year-old children didn't learn about the pill. Some other mother, who's got a 15-year-old daughter she's rather worried about, might be very grateful that she learnt about the pill.

TONY HOLLAND: . . . and because of the programme, be able to talk to her daughter about it, which she hadn't been able to do before. It is a focus. People do get information.

JULIA SMITH: But this is nothing new. *The Archers* did it. We don't sit down and say, 'This week we're going to do this, or this week we're going to do that.' Out of the characters we invented, out of their predicaments in life, out of the situation of low welfare state, out of whatever, things are going to happen. Arthur's going to have to learn about unemployment. Maybe other people who are also finding out about it will learn about it. . . . If anyone feels we are ever sticking anything on top, imposing a subject which wouldn't naturally come up, that doesn't come out of the characters we invented in Lanzarote three years ago, then we would be wrong, we would be imposing subjects on them.

In this respect, they sought to distinguish their own work from *Brookside*, which they felt 'went out of its way' to deal with social issues, and therefore tended to do so in an artificial and self-conscious way—what Tony Holland referred to as 'stick-on drama'. By contrast, *EastEnders* almost appeared to write itself:

TONY HOLLAND: Things do get raised, but only if the characters tell us to. We let the characters take us for a walk, we don't take them for a walk. I put a piece of paper in the typewriter and say, 'Talk to me!', and they do. So we are going to run into things, we are going to fall over what will eventually be called an issue.

On one level, these arguments might be regarded as an attempt to disclaim responsibility, at least for the kinds of issue which are raised, if not for the way in which they are dealt with. Yet on another level, they represent a strained response to the pressures which the programme-makers felt were being brought to bear upon them. The problem with being seen to be an 'issue-based' programme was that it made them more open to the demands of pressure groups and others who, they felt, wanted to influence their work.

In responding to Mary Whitehouse's criticisms, however, they used a very different argument, claiming that, on the contrary, their approach to 'social issues' was highly 'moral' and 'responsible' and that they 'cared dreadfully' about their audience. In the case of the attempted suicide of Angie Watts, for example—which had been followed by a series of 'copycat' stories in the press—Smith and Holland argued that the programme had been falsely accused, and was merely being used to sell newspapers. They expressed considerable concern at the possibility that viewers might confuse fact and fiction:

> TONY HOLLAND: We're make-believe. People can get involved, and terribly into *EastEnders*, and can sit there saying, 'I'm terribly into that, but thank God I don't have those problems!' They can switch it off and forget about it. They're not living in Albert Square. That's why we don't have guided tours around Albert Square. We don't want anyone to think it's real, because it isn't.

Conclusion   The very popularity of *EastEnders* thus highlights a number of tensions and contradictions in the relationships between the broadcasting institution, the programme-makers, and the audience.

On the one hand, the programme has clearly served a very useful function for the BBC, in a period of increasing uncertainty. As a significant element within its early evening schedule, it has managed to maximise ratings, and to reverse the downturn in its audience share, thereby staving off a certain amount of public criticism. Yet, on the other hand, its success has also provoked further attacks on the corporation from those on the political right. *EastEnders* has been seen as a symptom of the BBC's abandonment of its 'public service' obligations, whereby 'quality' and 'responsibility' have simply been sacrificed in a cynical drive for ratings.

In this context, the degree of autonomy which appears to have been granted to the programme-makers is quite remarkable. A considerable investment, both of money and of reputation, was at stake, yet there seems to have been very little overt management interference in their work. As experienced programme-makers, Julia Smith and Tony Holland are used to working within extremely rigid industrial and institutional constraints. They are required to devise a product which can be manufactured regularly and consistently within a given budget and with fixed plant and resources, and which will attract a large and diverse market. Over and above this, they have to negotiate the broader institutional tensions, and to balance the requirement to be popular with the historical commitment to serve and to educate the public. Yet, at the same time, they have their own very definite ideas about what the programme should contain and the form it should take.

Although assumptions about the audience are a crucial element within this process, they are based largely on professional 'intuition' rather than on hard evidence. Broadcasters' knowledge of their audience remains at best impressionistic. To a certain extent, this is symptomatic of their relative insulation from the public they claim to serve. The extraordinary pressures which are placed upon them mean that the audience itself tends to be perceived as yet another distraction from the intensely demanding and difficult business of making programmes.

EastEnders was clearly designed to create, and to retain, a large audience. In this sense, it was the product of a series of quite specific calculations. Yet these calculations were based on an extremely limited amount of data about the audience itself—and it is for this reason that its eventual success was far from guaranteed. In order to explain its popularity, we therefore need to look beyond the intentions of the programme-makers, and to investigate the complex and ambiguous relationship between the programme and its audience.

7

The Construction of a Community

Christine Geraghty

I thank God every night I'm not alone in a flat or stuck in the country.

> (Ivy, *Coronation Street*)

We haven't got much round here but we try and help each other out.

> (Arthur, *EastEnders*)

If they'd have been my own family, I couldn't have asked them for more.

> (Hilda of Sally and Kevin, *Coronation Street*)

I feel a slag.

> (Pat, *EastEnders*)

THE EXTENSION OF THE FAMILY into the community does not occur in all the soaps I am discussing. Neither *Dallas* nor *Dynasty* are concerned with notions of community; in their worlds, the family is so central that anyone outside it is liable to be a threat, not a friend or neighbour who shares the same concerns. But for the British soaps, especially *EastEnders* and *Coronation Street*, the extension of familial relationships into the community is very important, enabling a group to be brought together which might otherwise be split by the conflicting interests of age, gender, and class. A sense of community has been associated with British serials, and in particular with *Coronation Street*, in both theoretical and popular writing on soaps. As Richard Dyer puts it, 'life in *Coronation Street* . . . is defined as community, interpersonal activity on a day-to-day basis',[1] while Suzi Hush, ex-producer of *Coronation*

First published in Christine Geraghty, *Women and Soap Opera: A Study of Prime Time Soaps* (Cambridge: Polity Press, 1991), 84–106.

1 Richard Dyer (ed.), *Coronation Street* (London: BFI, 1981), 4.

Street, is quoted in a women's magazine as saying, 'the sense of community is a basic human requirement. It feeds our need for gossip, curiosity, belonging.'[2] *Coronation Street* is, as we shall see, exemplary in this respect, but its appeal to a notion of community was reworked in a quite conscious way for the 80s by *EastEnders*. The notion that the life of soaps 'is defined as community' seems a common-sense evaluation of the British soaps' appeal, something of which the viewers themselves are as conscious as the critic. Less attention has been paid to how that togetherness, that sense of belonging, is established, and the various factors in the process repay investigation. This chapter therefore looks at the value placed on the community in British soaps, in particular in *Coronation Street* and *EastEnders* and at the way in which a sense of community is constructed.

The Community Ideal

First of all, we need to define what is represented by the term 'community' and the values which are ascribed to it. For although community is an important unifying factor, it often proves elusive. British soaps offer the notion of a harmonious community, but the chimera is rarely pinned down. The soap opera format denies a final ending and the community can never therefore be finally and securely established. To do so would indeed be both implausible (and thus threaten the soap's commitment to realism) and dull in narrative terms since so many soap stories have personal disagreements and quarrels as their basis for action. Because of this, a sense of community cannot simply be assumed. It becomes an ideal which has to be worked for and which is, particularly in *EastEnders*, only occasionally achieved.

Nevertheless, the ideals of the community are clearly established as an aspiration. They are based on an ethos of sharing, an acceptance of each other's individual characteristics, and a recognition that everyone has a role to play if the community is to continue. The ideal of community which is presented depends on shared values of support for each other and stresses the importance of acting with the interests of the community at heart. As Albert Tatlock put it in a 1961 episode of *Coronation Street*, 'more sharing and less grabbing ... that's what happens when you bring folks together', or, as Arthur Fowler remarked, over twenty years later, in *EastEnders*, 'We haven't got much round here but we try and help each other.'

But this ideal of shared concern does not demand an impossible

2 Helen Franks, 'Why they're Cleaning up with Soaps', *Woman's Own*, 12 Feb. 1982.

perfection from the characters concerned. What is acknowledged, or indeed required, by the soap community is that individuals should be essentially themselves. While for some characters—Emily Bishop, Ken Barlow, Kathy Beale—work on behalf of the community comes naturally, for others it requires considerably more effort. Jack Duckworth, Albert Tatlock, Den Watts have to be encouraged to make their contribution, which is worth all the more because it requires them to reveal sides of their nature not normally on show. On certain ritual occasions, indeed, their reluctant presence is all that is required. It is in the nature of the soaps' ideal community that it can draw into itself all sorts of characters—the grumpy, the cantankerous, the complaining, the eccentric—and that they do not need to be transformed into ideal types for the community itself to be celebrated. The community needs the variety of their personalities and would not be complete without them. As Hilda Ogden said to her husband, Stan, in different ways on many occasions, 'you know what we are to folks round here—a couple of comedians', but no special occasion in *Coronation Street* was complete without them.

The notion of a shared responsibility to the community through a concern for and an acceptance of the individuals within it sounds considerably more priggish than the programmes themselves. Some concrete examples may help to show how the notion of a common viewpoint shared by those in the community saturates *Coronation Street* and *EastEnders*, for the ideal is often expressed in quite mundane ways. Neighbours regularly drop in on each other to ask a favour or share a problem. On a more organized level, help is offered when a specific difficulty arises. Thus when the curmudgeonly Ena Sharples is ill with back pain, the street grapevine finds out the cause of the problem and gets together to collect money for a new bed. When Arthur Fowler in *EastEnders*, who had been a victim of long-term unemployment, has his first wage packet stolen, his neighbours organize a collection to replace the money he has lost. On an individual basis, unlikely characters offer support to each other. In *Coronation Street* Curly, thrown out by Alf Roberts for not paying his rent, is offered a bed by the normally selfish Vera Duckworth; the tough, working-class Pat has a soft spot for middle-class Colin, the gay character in *EastEnders*, and offers him her monumental shoulder to cry on; Arthur Fowler, himself the object of the community's help, in turn befriends the teenage punk Mary Smith and tries to encourage her to better herself.

Such examples illustrate a number of important features of the community. They depend, first, on knowledge of particular individuals and of the specific problems which are being experienced. Community solutions can only be found through the intimate knowledge which the characters have about each other. Secondly, those examples which involve financial giving demonstrate a practical response in which the money itself is less important than the communal support which it represents. Such gifts are not perceived by the donors or the recipients as charity. They are based not on the notion of those who are comfortably off helping those in trouble; they demonstrate instead the concept that members of the community who are all more or less in the same position, all struggling financially one way or another, can help the person who is temporarily most in trouble in the expectation that the support will be reciprocated should the need arise. As Pauline Fowler remarked when she invited the financially stretched Cottons to Christmas dinner, 'It's just from one family to another. It's not pity or charity. It's just what you'd do if things were different.' And finally the examples show that the practical application of concern and support within the community need not be hindered by differences in generation, personality, or other factors. The old can help the young; the tarty Pat can commiserate with the fastidious Colin; the Cottons may lack charm and gratitude, but they can still share the Fowlers' Christmas dinner.

The community defines its existence particularly in moments of celebration. Again these moments can be quite mundane. The special evenings in the pub—the Lancashire hotpot supper night at the Rover's, for instance, or the country and western night at the Queen Vic—are arranged by the landlords as commercial ventures but serve to demonstrate the way in which all generations and types within the community are drawn into its social pleasures. Other gatherings can be equally casual. An underwear party held just before Michelle's wedding provides the women in *EastEnders* with the opportunity to have some fun together, to reminisce about their own weddings, and to try and offer some reassurance to Michelle about her doubts over the marriage. Because of the all-embracing nature of the ideal community, most parties in British soaps are intergenerational affairs. Although in *EastEnders* parties are sometimes attended only by young people, such events are normally a sign of trouble, and the successful social occasions cross generations and include a range of characters. Thus Sally Webster in *Coronation Street*, who specifically wanted her house-warming party to be confined to the younger generation, found herself entertaining a number of the older Street residents. Significantly, her determination to be exclusive was first breached by the clear signs that Hilda Ogden, with whom she had been lodging before her marriage, expected an invitation. Sally could not resist her mother by proxy and followed up the invitation with the explanation, 'You're practically family.'

The high points of the soap community's celebrations, indeed, occur on traditional family occasions. The community does come together for particular public occasions, most frequently those with a royal flavour—*Coronation Street*, for example, celebrated the Queen's silver jubilee with an elaborate historical parade. But the communities are at their most united at births, weddings, and funerals—all occasions when the extension of the family into the community is most clearly demonstrated and the community is deemed to share family feelings and participate in family rituals.

In *Coronation Street*, for instance, the weddings have taken on an almost ritual quality in which the elements are repeated and reworked so that, whichever couple is involved, the wedding story itself has a familiar pattern and the community acts as the family, providing the support (and the ritual disasters) necessary for such an occasion. It is striking, for instance, how rarely there is a father to give away the bride so the task falls to a member of the community (Alf Roberts, Ken Barlow) rather than the family. Preparations are often handled by women friends of the bride rather than the immediate family. Deirdre, on her marriage to Ken, looked as much to Emily Bishop as to her own mother for help and got married from Emily's home; Gail's mother was a positive liability, her inadequacy indeed being part of the plot. The wedding itself is preceded by separate celebrations on a gender basis—the traditional hen-night for the women and stag-night for the men. The stag-night is full of opportunities for stories which threaten the event itself. Hangovers, physical injury, and arrests for drunk and disorderly behaviour are all hazards which threaten the appearance of the groom and the best man at the ceremony itself. The women, as is generally the case in British soaps, behave more sensibly and usually manage to avoid falling downstairs on their wedding eve. They are not, however, immune to the practical disasters—flat tyres, lost items—which can delay either party and leave the guests waiting in suspense, although the audience will of course generally know that this is a tease.

The wedding ceremony itself brings together disparate members of the community, and different reactions are used to point up the individuality of the characters who have been brought together by the event. In the congregation waiting for Ken and Deirdre to arrive, Stan Ogden comments lugubriously to Hilda that 'churches depress me', while Mavis confides to Rita, 'I know what I'd be thinking [if I were Deirdre]. Another ten minutes and I've got him.' The service itself focuses on the romance of the couple, but there is time also to observe other reactions to the familiar words. At Rita and Len's wedding a close-up of Bet's face hints at her previous relationship with Len, while at Deirdre and Ken's the words 'all my worldly goods' are matched by a close-up of the elderly and congenitally grumpy Uncle Albert with whom the couple will be living.

The ritual of the wedding is also used to demonstrate the way in which difficulties within the community can be overcome. The initial stages of the event are often marred by some disagreement or resentment, usually on the part of those members of the community who feel themselves to have been slighted in some way. Hilda and Stan Ogden, for instance, feel hurt at not being invited to the ceremony when Rita and Len get married and decide to boycott the reception as well, loudly proclaiming their grievance to the empty bar of the Rover's. Gail and Suzie are not invited to Ken and Deirdre's wedding despite living in the street. Such problems are usually resolved by the end of the event and these narrative devices serve to point up the way in which the celebrations themselves bring together the community despite the disagreements and grievances that exist. Again the emphasis on unity is not at the expense of individual characters. The reconciliation is achieved by accommodating the sources of disagreement, not obliterating them. Gail and Suzie blithely gatecrash Ken and Deirdre's wedding, flirting with the official photographer and providing a reminder of the youthful pleasures which Deirdre Barlow has long left behind her. Hilda and Stan go to Rita and Len's reception in the end only to find that the free drink has run out. In both cases, characters initially outside the occasion are brought into it almost as it were on their own terms. The community has its inappropriate or awkward characters, but their presence is necessary for the assertion of the all-embracing ideal. The strategy is neatly summed up in a moment at Ken and Deirdre's wedding when Uncle Albert, despite the festive atmosphere, is being his usual awkward self. Deirdre kisses him resoundingly on the cheek: 'That's for being you,' she says.

The facility with which *Coronation Street* deploys the wedding both to create and to display community feeling is deceptive. Such celebrations need not automatically be presented in this way. At Glenda and Kevin's wedding in *Crossroads* staff from the motel attend the ceremony and reception but Meg and Jill leave early and Meg complains, good-humouredly but pointedly, that the motel has been left understaffed by the event. *Brookside* has apparently deliberately shown that it is possible to have a wedding that does not turn into a demonstration of community solidarity. The wedding reception of Laura and Jonathan took place in a marquee in Brookside Close, but close neighbours, such as the Grants and the Collinses, were not invited. Instead, the emphasis was on the rowdy behaviour of the yuppie outsiders who took over the Close and on an ongoing story dealing with the Corkhills' financial problems. There was no equivalent here of *Coronation Street*'s confident assertion of a community celebrating its own continuance, and the individual families in the Close were not drawn closer together by the event.

The Construction of the Community

It is wrong to think, therefore, that because community is given such high value in British soaps it is easily achieved. The moments of harmony in which all are temporarily included have to be worked for, and the sense of acceptance of each other on which the community at its best is based is easily threatened. Soaps like *Coronation Street* and *EastEnders* which offer the community as an ideal have to construct the ethos by which it is characterized and in doing so deploy in distinctive ways both the soap's setting and its references to the past. Geography and history thus become important strategies in establishing a notion of community.

The setting of a soap is an important way of creating a minimum of homogeneity among disparate characters. Whether it be a work-place or a region, the setting gives a sense of unified experience which draws on notions of the particular characteristics or attitudes generated by a common work experience or sense of place. The creation of a recognizable geographic space is one of the ways in which a soap opera engages its audience in the narrative, and regional references are used to authenticate the realism to which British serials often aspire. We can also see how these two aspects work together to create a sense of community which is a powerful source of the programmes' pleasure.

Both *Coronation Street* and *EastEnders* have successfully estab-lished a unifying sense of place in which the permutations of com-munity relationships can be worked out. Both soaps have at their heart a particular fictional space. The Street and the Square are public spaces; these serials, unlike, for instance, many situation comedies, are not locked into the four walls of the family home. Their geography allows for a large number of characters with a variety of reasons for living in the area and different ways of relating to the community. The setting also provides the boundaries which are necessary if the community is to have a sense of its own sepa-rateness, its means of asserting its own identity against outsiders. The Street, the Square provide a geographical identity for characters and a location in which outsiders can be recognized by the fact that they are neither literally nor metaphorically at home. The fictional geography of *Coronation Street* and *EastEnders* is indeed remarkably similar. Both communities are presented as working-class in speech and behaviour; both are part of but not economically central to a major British city (Manchester and London); in both soaps the characters live mainly in nineteenth-century housing rather than high-rise flats or new housing estates; in both the pub (the Rover's Return, the Queen Vic) holds a key place as the site for formal celebrations as well as for more casual meetings. Both *Coronation Street* and *EastEnders* use their settings, in other words, to invoke a particular kind of community, one which is urban, self-enclosed, and on a human scale.

The particularity of this setting is backed up by references to British regional characteristics which mark out the differences in attitude between the community and the outside world. Again, regional references for both programmes are similar. The north invokes, partly of course because of *Coronation Street* itself, an ethos of down-to-earth good humour and a stoical acceptance of disappointment and tragedy. Marion Jordan describes *Coronation Street*'s view of northern working-class life as one in which 'somewhere out there, remote from the metropolis . . . blunt common sense and unsentimental affection raise people above the concerns of industrialisation, or unions or politics or consumerism'.[3] In *EastEnders* a similarly mythical regional construction works to present an updated version of the London cockney with a sharp tongue and fierce local loyalty as its main characteristics.[4] These regional particularities were greatly played up in the publicity which preceded the launch of *EastEnders*, making it clear that regional characteristics underpinned the notion of community which was to be established. The British newspapers quickly latched on to the theme; the *Daily Express* talked of 'swarms of cockney characters' and described Lou Beale as 'the head of the cockney clan', while the *Standard* claimed that the inspiration for the programme came from a real street market and quoted a café owner from there: 'there are good and bad characters, they all mix together and it's typical of the East End'.[5] In addition, in both *Coronation Street* and *EastEnders* regional generalizations about character and behaviour are reinforced by a self-conscious use of a regional dialect which is both idiomatic and forceful.

What is important to the argument is not the accuracy of such regional stereotyping or the way in which the programmes themselves are part of the process by which more general regional stereotypes are established and maintained. The point at issue is not whether northerners are more good-humoured or East Enders more quick-witted than those living in other parts of Britain. What is significant is that the soaps have used such assumptions as a means of presenting the viewer with a community in which difference from outsiders is asserted not by money or ambition or power but by qualities which can be shared by virtue of living in the same place. The community, while it has its boundaries and is marked as

3 Marion Jordan, 'Realism and Convention', in Dyer (ed.), *Coronation Street*, 29.

4 David Buckingham, *Public Secrets: 'EastEnders' and its Audience* (London: BFI, 1987), 94–6, describes the well-established image of the cockney and gives some detail of the literary and televisual tradition on which *EastEnders* draws.

5 *Daily Express*, 11 Oct. 1984; *London Evening Standard*, 10 Oct. 1984.

hostile, as we shall see, to the outsiders who breach them, is still relatively open, available by an accident of geography to those born there and by patient study to those who move there. The ethos 'comes with the territory' and the setting is a physical expression of a particular set of attitudes which mark a common sensibility. To live in the Street or the Square for long enough is to become part not just of the place but of the way of life.

Tied up with the setting is the use of the past as a strategy for defining the community, the sense that it exists not merely in a particular geographical space but in its own time as well. It is this history which the young members of the community have to learn and which is used to whip into line the more recalcitrant members should it become necessary. The past is built up in both serials by the connotations of a particular setting, the accretion of the programme's own history over the years, and the reference to historical moments which have an existence outside the programmes.

I have noted that the geographical setting of both *Coronation Street* and *EastEnders* is old-fashioned. Although the programmes are set in the continuous present, the houses and flats in which the characters live are not twentieth-century tower blocks or stream-lined modern houses. Shopping is done in corner shops run by one of the locals, not in a large supermarket. The two key pubs are relentlessly down-market and Den's attempt to bring the Queen Vic up to date with modern music and videos was a disaster. Only The Dagmar, run by Den's rival, the upper-class Wilmot-Brown, had pretensions to a 1980s atmosphere. Its pink and green decor, umbrella-spiked cocktails, and designer lighting made the East End regulars look uncomfortable and, despite Angie's traditionally all-embracing welcome, Wilmot-Brown made it clear that he was expecting to attract a more discerning clientele from outside the Square. Significantly, neither The Dagmar nor its successor, the even more yuppie wine bar, became a permanent feature and, in the main, the settings of *Coronation Street* and *EastEnders* refer to an architecture of the past which, because of its smaller scale and layout, has connotations of a lost neighbourliness and community of interest. Richard Dyer has described this setting as one of the causes of *Coronation Street*'s nostalgic cast: 'this was most explicit in the period when the credit sequence was based on a camera zoom from a long shot of a high-rise block of flats to a close-up of a back-to-back street, from the impersonality of modern planned architecture to the human scale of the old working-class street'.[6]

The fictional history of the setting is used to give resonance to the community and to establish a sense of tradition which provides a

6 Dyer (ed.), *Coronation Street*, 5.

model for the present. Sometimes such references are used quite casually to conjure up a colourful past which, for the older members of the community, still adds pungency to the present. Sitting in the Queen Vic, Ethel and Lou Beale reminisce about the previous landlord, who on his wedding anniversary 'had a barrel of beer on the counter all day. The whole street was legless.' At other times the past is more deliberately recalled. Arthur Fowler, suffering from a mental breakdown caused by unemployment, takes his wife, Pauline, on a tour of his personal landmarks in the area and finds them closed down and derelict—the church they were married in; Cato Street, where the yearly fair was held, now 'acquired for redevelopment'; the factory where he worked now closed down. The scene demonstrated how Arthur's attempt to hold on to his place in the community was threatened by the way in which its fabric was crumbling around him.

More commonly, though, reference to the past does fulfil the function of making the present more manageable, of providing an example of how an order can be created which will enable the community to continue to survive. One striking example of this, though not of course unique in British television to soaps, is the way in which the experience of the Second World War is used to provide a model for how to behave. Much has been written on how the war provides British culture with images and references which are drawn upon and reworked in different contexts.[7] The process has a particular resonance in British soaps since the notion of the community which is at the heart of the representation of the war is also so central to the experience offered by soaps. The Blitz in particular is referred to as an example of how the community could and should respond in times of trouble. In July 1961, when a gas explosion forced the Coronation Street residents to bed down in the church mission hall, there was a good deal of grumbling, arguments, and confusion. But Albert Tatlock reminds the Barlow boys (and the audience) about how such moments should be handled: '[there was] more kindness done to me during the Blitz . . . more sharing and less grabbing'. When the train crashed off the viaduct into the Street in 1967, the rubble and searchlights provided the audience with a visual reference to the wartime searches through bombed houses and, with pointed irony, it is an American character, Alan Howard ('not one of us', as Hilda tells him), who draws the comparison to the Blitz as if to prove that he knows how to handle the situation and can therefore join the community in searching for the injured. A reference to the Blitz is not always

---

7 Geoffery Hurd (ed.), *National Fictions* (London: BFI, 1984), provides a wealth of examples of this practice and offers an account of the reasons for the tenacity of this source.

triggered by such dramatic incidents though; any occasion when the community buries its differences can be marked by such a reference. As late as 1987 a Street fête held to raise money for a local charity caused Vera Duckworth to remark, 'there we all were, all pulling together. Just like the Blitz.' Vera's somewhat marginal position as a troublemaker in the community gave the comment an ironic edge but did not reduce its force.

The Second World War has a particular effectiveness in bringing the past into the present in this way because of its historical status and its connotative power. More commonly, the serial's own past is linked to a general sense of the 'good old days' to provide a perspective on the present. It is in the past that the most perfect expression of the community's values is to be found and, at times, characters mourn this lost past of prosperity and safety when values were more secure and when, in a refrain which is repeated in *Coronation Street* and *EastEnders* with the regularity of a motif, 'We used to look after our own'. In the present, characters fitfully grope to reproduce these values, but the sheer difficulty of the task makes the achieved moments more fleeting. Nevertheless, there are such moments when the bridge between the present and the past is achieved. When Pauline Fowler in *EastEnders*, desperate for money, decides to pawn her wedding-ring and other small pieces of jewellery, the pawnbroker comes to see her. During the conversation it is established that he has known her family well and has been aware of their struggles over the years. Because of this history, he gives her more money than the trinkets are worth and trusts her to pay it back when she can. Hilda Ogden, contemplating a move from Coronation Street and a new marriage, deliberately recalls the early days of her marriage to Stan and the years of struggle together; she gains strength from her memories of this past and reconstructs her future in its light.

Both *Coronation Street* and *EastEnders* thus refer to a lost past of security and order. Nevertheless, it would be wrong to think that this use of the past as something positive in the present is always unproblematic or unambiguous. *EastEnders*, in particular, tries to hold off from an automatic espousal of past values by setting up 'the good old days' as a matter of dispute. The ambiguity of the meaning given to the community's past was clearly laid out in the astonishing first episode of *EastEnders*, which not only moved swiftly between a number of different plots but also established the existence of the community itself. The death of Reg, a long-term resident of the Square but one who is generally agreed to have been 'a nasty old man', provokes a running debate on what constitutes the community and where its roots lie. Lou Beale draws a tight line—'It's all strangers now'—and specifically excludes the Bengali couple, Saeed and Naima, who actually raised the alarm over Reg. But Lou's attitude is criticized by her daughter Pauline, who praises Saeed and Naima—'It's nice to know there's a bit of community feeling left'—and includes them in the community of the Square. At the same time a semi-philosophical debate is being conducted on the reasons for the decline in fellow feeling. Pete Beale, half-jokingly, ascribes it to political change—'Community spirit went out the window when the Tories came in. It's uneconomic'—while the older residents Lou and Ethel, with gloomy relish, blame changes in human nature and the newcomers to the Square. There is even a debate on how good 'the good old days' really were, dangerous stuff for a programme which is basing its appeal on the establishment of a traditional community:

ETHEL: We might have had a few fleas in the old days but at least we knew our neighbours.

DEN: The old days are gone for good, thank God. You don't see kids running around with snotty noses, rickets, or ringworms.

ETHEL: Not them old days. Not the bad old days. They're coming back. I'm talking about the good old days when everyone cared for each other. They're not coming back.

DEN: They're both the same. Now is where we are.

The first episode of *EastEnders*, then, established both the community and its past as an area of dispute, not a fixed concept, and that ambiguity has remained. It is always easy for the programme to slip into the notion of 'the good old days when everyone cared for each other' and, as we have seen, this is an important source of strength. But *EastEnders* has also consistently provided moments when the old days are criticized, as when Dr Legge reminds the Square of racism in the 1930s or when an attachment to the past prevents characters from dealing with the present. There have been times, for instance, when Lou Beale's use of the past as a source of support is criticized as blocking her off from understanding the real problems in her family. When her son Pete tries to discuss changes in the running of the market stall, he reports that Lou 'just carried on about the old days'. More seriously, Lou is so determined to observe the family's ritual visit to her Albert's grave that she fails to notice how ill her son-in-law Arthur is, and indeed makes matters worse by berating him for failing to pay due respect to the dead. Even the Second World War is in *EastEnders* an unreliable guide to behaviour. When Den offers Pauline Fowler a deal on cheap meat (dubiously acquired, as so many of Den's goods are), Lou encourages her daughter to accept. Smacking her lips over the shepherd's pie, she draws an analogy with the black market for rationed goods during the war and asserts blithely that everyone was involved. This model of a community based on anti-social behaviour is soon denounced by her granddaughter Michelle, who points out the risks of getting involved in Den's dealings. In a characteristically neat way the episode thus turned upside-down British soaps' sanitized recollection of the war as the model of community behaviour, while, in the process, dealing a glancing blow at easy assumptions about the attitudes of different generations to law and order issues.

The Community as Family

The setting and the past therefore provide important ways of identifying the community and bringing it together. But the task of transmitting the community's values and ensuring their survival remains a difficult one which ultimately relies, as does so much in soaps, on the quality of personal relationships. In his account of the affinities between *Coronation Street* and the working-class world conjured up by Richard Hoggart in *The Uses of Literacy* Richard Dyer parallels Hoggart's 'glowing portrait of the warmth of the working-class mother' with *Coronation Street*'s 'plethora of splendid mums'.[8] This stress on familial relationships in a discussion of the representation of the community is no accident, for *Coronation Street*'s strategy from the beginning has been to equate one set of relationships (the familial) with another (those within a community) and to present a world in which the two could be conflated. The effect is to make stricter the rules by which soaps' complexities can be understood. Not only are all crucial relationships, including those of the public sphere, expressed in personal terms, but all personal relationships within a group of people are framed within the terms of reference of the family. The family provides the model by which community relationships in *EastEnders* and *Coronation Street* can be understood and expressed.

The most obvious example is that which Dyer uses, that of the matriarch. We have seen how, in British soaps, the role of the mother is crucial and that one of the central questions of their narratives is the women's ability and willingness to undertake that role. In British soaps the grandmother figure is used as a sign of the relative openness of the family. Her role in transmitting the values of the community extends well beyond the boundary of her own family and the firm guidance she offers is backed up by genuine concern for those whom she adopts. But this role is not undertaken only by the formidable 'grandmother' characters such as Lou Beale,

---

8 Dyer (ed.), *Coronation Street* 3, 4.

Annie Walker, or Ena Sharples, who are specifically marked as matriarchial. It is a model also available to older women even if, in the past, they have lacked moral authority and status in the community. Many of the mature women in *Coronation Street* have, one way or another, adopted younger characters in the programme and a number of long-running stories have developed in which the older women try to encourage the younger and more rebellious members of the community to accept traditional standards and patterns of behaviour.

This mothering structure can be discerned in a number of relationships in *Coronation Street*. Rita Fairclough took the more formal route when she became a foster-mother and with sympathy and tact tried to adjust the expectations of Sharon and then Jenny to the setting of the Street. The less formal route has been through the device of lodgers, whereby the single women of *Coronation Street* provide board, lodging (and moral education) for the younger characters. Thus Elsie Tanner, towards the end of her long *Coronation Street* life, was placed in a number of 'open' family situations in which others turned to her for advice which she felt ill equipped to give. Nevertheless, she did try to guide her lodger Suzie Birchall through the vicissitudes of her love life and to restrain the headstrong impulses which Elsie recognized had been the source of her own problems in the community. Emily Bishop is presented as a very different character from Elsie Tanner; shy, frightened of speaking out until roused, a spinster type whose complex marital history is seldom referred to. But she too has mothered a lodger, Curly, trying to encourage his more respectable ambitions and to diminish the 'Jack-the-lad' influence of the disreputable Terry Duckworth. Curly moved out of Emily's care but after a short time found himself lodging once again, this time being knocked into shape by the rather less tender Vera. Hilda Ogden could not be more different again from Elsie and Emily—a widow whose own children have long disappeared and whose love of gossip and intrigue gave her a key role in the Street's Greek chorus. But Hilda, too, has been part of the mothering structure; first, in leading her lodger Eddie away from a life of petty crime, and subsequently in ensuring that Kevin, whose own family had moved out of the community, continued to have a family environment of clean sheets, hot food, and firm standards. Hilda's role indeed provides an interesting example of the way in which values which are acknowledged to be somewhat old-fashioned are nevertheless maintained by the mother figure. When Sally, Kevin's fiancée, was rejected by her own family and also came to live in the house, Hilda's attempts to ensure that there was no illicit sex under her roof were presented as both comical and rather pointless, a refusal to recognize that times have changed.

However, Kevin and Sally's marriage, from Hilda's home and with her practical support, vindicated her stance and ensured that another couple were establishing the kind of family on which *Coronation Street*'s community is based.

This mothering structure which is clear in so many of the *Coronation Street* stories and which plays an important part in the transmission of the community's values has a number of effects on how the community is presented in the serial. It confirms the way in which women dominate the narrative. It gives a value to the older women who do not have a role in their own families but who exercise an influence and a control within the community. The lodger device is indeed convenient in this respect, for it allows for a large number of independent women who are therefore themselves available for stories about love and potential marriage but who also perform a matriarchial function in passing on values within the community. The structure may also explain why *Coronation Street* has found the introduction of forceful and fashionable young characters so difficult. If the model for bringing youngsters into the community is that of a taming process by the older women, it becomes much more difficult to represent vividly stories of adolescent rebellion and escape.

EastEnders and *Brookside* are deemed to have changed the way in which teenagers have been addressed in soaps, but *EastEnders* also presents the community in terms of family relationships, if not quite in the same way as *Coronation Street*. Of course, the Beale–Fowler family is itself much more dominant in terms of size and influence than any one family in *Coronation Street*. Spanning four generations, it provides a model for intergenerational behaviour which applies to those technically outside it. Thus, Lou Beale was a source of advice to her grandchild Michelle, certainly, but also to Lofty even before he joined the family by marriage, and to Sharon, who qualified as Michelle's friend. Lou's role as a fount of wisdom is then parodied by Ethel, who, with malapropisms flying, tries to draw on the community's past as a source of advice to the young, and by Dot, who dispenses unheeded words of wisdom, mainly drawn from the Bible. Nevertheless, both Ethel and Dot do provide assistance to others in the Square even if it is in a more sporadic and eccentric manner than their counterparts in *Coronation Street*. Ethel, in particular, kept an anxious eye on Mary and offered soothing words to Sue and Ali in the middle of their public quarrels, while Dot took Michelle's part in the abortion debate and tried to give Donna a home during the downward spiral of drug-taking and the alienation from the community which ended in her death. It was significant that when Donna died both her natural mother, Kathy, and her adoptive mother acknowledged Dot's role in offering their daughter the home, however makeshift, which they could not provide. As the serial has developed, Dot's role in the mothering structure has been confirmed; she took under her roof Rod, whose aimless way of life could not be more different from her own but who responded with an irritated and amused affection, and she gave a home to Hazel despite her doubts about the legitimacy of having such a pair under the same roof. In a parallel action, the matriarchial Mo, who took up Lou's role on her death, provided lodgings for the hapless Trevor and attempted to fit him for life in the Square.

Other types of familial relationship can be perceived in the community of the Square. The fierce loyalty between Den Watts and Pete Beale had its roots in their teenage past, a fraternal code which, for instance, demanded that Den unquestioningly came to Pete's assistance when the latter was arrested by the police. The friendship between the women, in particular Pauline Fowler and Angie Watts, was similarly grounded in the past, enabling them to recognize that their lives were as intertwined as if they were related. A more stressful sibling rivalry was presented in the relationship between Angie and Pat in which they got drunk together, reminisced about past escapades, and fell out, as always, over Den. In the younger generation Michelle and Sharon describe their relationship in terms of being sisters. Even the gay Colin used family analogies to express his feelings for Barry as the latter tried to deal with his own emotions about his family. 'Look upon me as your Mum and Dad,' he offers, only half-jokingly, and later, after the pair have split up because of Barry's decision to go straight, Colin tells him that whatever happens, 'I'll be your mate, your friend, even your Dad.'

The transmission of community values is more fraught in *East-Enders* than in *Coronation Street*. Lou Beale's determination to mould the community to her model was criticized betore her death, and Dot's attempts to help are potentially undermined by her reputation for nosiness and self-delusion. Nevertheless, the notion of the community as a family with loyalties and traditions which do not depend on everyone liking each other is an important factor in understanding how soap communities pass on their values. Family relationships provide the model and the mothering structure the most important vehicle for the transmission of the ideals, however imperfectly expressed, of the community.

Marking the Boundaries

The community in soaps, then, is a structure in which the setting and the past provide the framework and the family provides the model for relationships. It depends on notions of mutual support and acceptance and defines itself in terms of its differences from the rest of the world. But the boundaries between 'us' and 'them' are not always clear, and many soap stories are concerned with the difficulties of marking them out. One further strategy in creating a sense of community is to exclude those who do not belong and to clarify the difference between those inside the community and those outside it.

On the one hand, the opposition seems clear and differentiates between those who live in the Street or the Square and those who do not, thus employing geographic setting as a key factor. This functions most clearly when the community is threatened from the outside—by developers wanting to pull down houses, for instance—or is subject to the scrutiny of officialdom. Outside agencies—the police, social security officers, social workers—are given a hard time in soaps even when the programmes' treatment of them attempts to be sympathetic, because they are inevitably subjecting the community to an outsider's objective gaze. Even when they are well-meaning, such agencies are problematic to the community because they try to rearrange the pattern of life in a way that may be tidier but is different from that agreed by the residents. Moreover, as we have seen, it is the sharing of problems which often provides the gesture of support within the community and the crucial means of sorting out what is wrong; such mutual support can only take place when all parties are directly involved in the problem. Over-friendliness on the part of officialdom is thus viewed as suspiciously as overt hostility since it cannot be based on genuine communal experience. Michelle's abortion was handled by the clinic staff with just such sympathetic friendliness, and she responded with an angry rejection of their claim to understand—'You act like we're friends. I don't know you. Why all this pretence?'

But the division between the inside and the outside is not always so clear. As David Buckingham has pointed out in writing about *EastEnders*, 'the forces of disruption are as likely to be found within the community as outside it.'[9] Many characters hover on the boundaries, moving between acceptance and rejection as the situation demands. At times these insider–outsiders are brought into the community; at others, their presence is marked by an unease as other characters attempt to re-establish the boundaries to exclude them. In examining these characters, however, it becomes clear that they reflect the internal tensions of a community that is not as stable as it first appears. The most prominent of such figures in British soaps can be described as the 'gossip', the 'bastard', and the 'tart'.

9 Buckingham, *Public Secrets*, 91.

The role of the 'gossip' is, as we have seen, crucial to the audience's engagement with a serial and provides both a source of information and a means of speculation for the viewer. In addition, as this chapter has demonstrated, the notion of support for each other based on intimate knowledge of likely problems is fundamental to the British soaps' representation of an ideal community in which practical and emotional needs can be met within the enclosed group. Nevertheless, there is an unease about the price paid for such support and an acknowledgement of the fine line between neighbourliness and nosiness. The 'gossip' personifies this unease, and though her task of passing on information and ferreting out problems is crucial to the community, she (and it is nearly always a woman) is frequently the butt of mockery and criticism. Although the information she offers is taken up and used, her role is rejected almost as if it draws too much attention to the web of gossip which holds the community together. Thus, Hilda Ogden began her *Coronation Street* life as a nosy informant on everyone's doings and, despite mellowing with the years, her capacity to overhear and pass on information was still the subject of critical comment. Her last act on leaving the Street was to pass on to the newly married Alec a piece of old scandal about his wife, Bet's, previous affair with Mike Baldwin. The crudeness of Hilda's original role has been picked up by Vera Duckworth, whose 'big mouth' frequently gets her into trouble and whose eagerness to pick up information on other people's troubles is frequently criticized.

In the same way, in *EastEnders* the avidity with which Dot Cotton seeks out news is the subject of some embarrassment to her more restrained neighbours, but the exchange of information which she provides is essential if the community is to give support to its members. The blurred boundaries on which the characters of the 'gossip' operate were clearly seen when Sue left her husband, Ali. Dot both notices her absence and speculates with her friend Ethel on its cause, running the gamut of violence on Ali's part and infidelity on Sue's. When Pauline protests, Dot declares that she is just showing a 'neighbourly concern'. Pauline points out that 'you don't know any of the facts', but Dot and Ethel reassert their commitment to the community values of support and acceptance: 'We only wanted to help . . . We've got to find out what happened otherwise we can't help.'

This is on the face of it true; the community's capacity to respond to problems depends on its ability to find out that something is wrong. The very relish with which Dot and Ethel discuss Sue's disappearance is a sign of their active engagement with the life of their own community. But there is clearly an underside to this neighbourliness which is personified in the 'gossip'. The very transparency of lives within the community, their openness to each other, makes individual members vulnerable. The 'gossip' draws attention to that vulnerability, which is an inevitable part of being in the community, and her participation in the very process of exchanging information makes her an essential but mistrusted figure.

Other tensions in the community are expressed through another insider–outsider figure, the 'bastard'. We have seen how British soaps are dominated by women, and particularly by the mother, and that men rarely challenge the women's control of the personal sphere. Nevertheless, this weakness of the men remains a source of some unease, and the 'bastard' figure represents an attempt, albeit unsuccessful, to wrest back some power for the male. The archetypal figures are Den Watts in *EastEnders* and Mike Baldwin in *Coronation Street*, both of whom transgress the codes of the community by refusing to espouse its female-centred values. Den liked to think of himself as a bit of a bastard, attractive to women, whom he prided himself on giving the run-around. He was accused by both his wife and his mistress of being unfeeling and selfish. He dispensed advice to the men of the Square which ran counter to the community's official ethos of care and acceptance. Thus he advised Ali not to make the first move after a quarrel with Sue since it would be 'a sign of weakness'; give presents when 'you're on top' he concluded, 'not under the cosh'. Similarly, Den continually told Lofty to be more assertive with Michelle and criticized other men in the Square for giving in to their wives. This attitude to women was reinforced by other aspects of the characterization: Den was caught up in a series of shady deals: he cheated the brewery; he sold stolen goods on the side; and he had connections with the local criminal underworld. He trusted no one and did not expect to be trusted himself. He mocked those like Ethel or Pauline who asserted a notion of community centred on the Square, and indeed his character was constructed around a series of rejections of the demands the Square made of him for friendship, loyalty, and support.

A similar description could apply to Mike Baldwin in *Coronation Street*. Paterson and Stewart describe him 'as an insider of sorts, but still suspect because of his London background, and marked by his exploitation of women'.[10] His character, as is common in soaps, has mellowed over the years and he sometimes joins in the Street's community life as unproblematically as Alf Roberts. Nevertheless, his potential as the 'bastard' figure still remains. His history of casual relationships with women marks him as unfeeling and manipulative. During his marriage to Susan Barlow he behaved as if

10 Richard Paterson and John Stewart, 'Street Life', in Dyer (ed.), *Coronation Street*, 85.

he were the boss in his own home as well as in the factory, laying down the law and undermining her attempts to establish her own career. His emphasis on making money as an end in itself and his flashy lifestyle are a marked contrast to the values of the community. Like Den, he gets involved in dubious deals with shady characters, and the source of his money is not always entirely clear. Like Den, he too asserts the importance of being free of ties or responsibilities to others in the Street.

The 'bastard' figures thus represent in British soaps an attempt to establish a strong male figure in the face of female dominance. They express an unease about the weakness of most of the male characters and a challenge to the values of the community so strongly held by the women. Nevertheless, although they provide an opposing voice, their challenge is rarely successful. The ethos of the serials is so strong that it seems impossible for the 'bastard' to be fully developed as in *Dallas* and *Dynasty*, where they are structured at the heart of the family. Both Den Watts and Mike Baldwin are basically soft-hearted. When pressed, they do join in with the community even if they sometimes prefer to do so unobserved. Mike Baldwin participated in the Street celebrations such as the party for the Queen's silver jubilee and indeed helped to organize the farewell party in the Rover's when Hilda Ogden left. Den was the harder of the two, but he presided with sardonic relish over the locals' celebratory get-togethers in the Queen Vic and could be generous with his money when no one was looking.

In addition, the 'bastard' figure's attempts to assert masculine control are singularly unsuccessful. Den's marriage to Angie was marked by his inability to control her drinking, her moods, or her behaviour; when she left, giving him the freedom he apparently wanted, she succeeded in wrecking his finances and his relationship with his mistress, Jan, who refused to join him in serving behind the bar at the Queen Vic. Similarly, Mike Baldwin, though financially more successful than Den, has failed to establish a relationship with a woman on the terms he wants. His affair with Deirdre collapsed when she decided it was time to end it. He has a son whom he was not allowed to see, and later his wife, Susan, left him after she had had an abortion. His attempt to have a subsequent fling with Gloria was foiled by her dignity and common sense. Despite a lot of noise, neither Den nor Mike succeeds in asserting a different set of values from those of the female-centred community in which they live.

If the insider–outsider figure of the 'bastard' marks the boundary of unacceptable male behaviour, the figure of the 'tart' represented unease about how far female characters should assert their autonomy, particularly in the sphere of sexuality. Soaps give a strong presence and endorsement to their women characters, but it is important to note that at some points the reins are pulled in. As we have seen, soaps are centrally concerned with personal relationships and sexuality is clearly at the heart of many of these liaisons. It is not surprising, then, that the community seeks to mark what is acceptable behaviour, since those who go too far threaten the community's own stability. The boundaries to be established are not, however, between those who are chaste and those who are not, since 'respectable' women like Deirdre and Michelle can just as easily be caught up in a love affair. The distinction which the 'tart' figure marks is between those who are taken unawares and those who make themselves available, who are aware of sexual possibilities.

The 'tart' thus marks the boundary for the women characters, a warning for those who are tempted to go too far. Pat in *EastEnders* is clearly such a figure. Her appearance, the dyed blonde hair and solid stature, identify her as suspect. Her vindictiveness towards her ex-husband, Pete, and particularly to the sympathetically presented Kathy, his second wife, combined with her crude language and bad temper to reinforce the first impression, and it was no surprise to find that she was flirting with prostitution. Pat was clearly marked as an outsider, and her subsequent move into the community through taking on Angie's role as the landlady of the Queen Vic had to be accompanied by a parallel move into more respectable monogamy with Frank. The 'tart' is not always clearly identifiable as an outsider. Mary Smith was an insider–outsider from the beginning of *EastEnders*, her appearance as a punk marking her as different. But the real ambiguity about her position was expressed when she tried to earn a living for herself and her baby through exploiting her sexuality—first through stripping and then, at Pat's instigation, through prostitution. Both Pat and Mary were brought back into the community at the point when their involvement with prostitution forced the issue. This was done through a *deus ex machina* of plotting—both were assaulted in the street—and by the reaction of the other women, which, through friendly and not so friendly support (neighbourliness and nosiness once more combining), brought them back into line. Donna was not so 'lucky'; her act of sleeping with Ali, for money, for a drink, for companionship, back-fired badly when he rejected her, and she was blamed for breaking up his marriage to Sue.

Coronation Street has not dealt with the issue of sexuality so directly, but the same pattern can still be seen. Elsie Tanner was perhaps the most ambiguous 'tart' figure, clearly an insider at the centre of the community but for many years an outsider whose sexuality challenged the mores of the Street. Like Pat and Mary, her appearance marked her out. Often slovenly and untidy, she dressed to draw attention to her figure, and the history of her love affairs and marriages provided a basis for much talk. Elsie's demand to have her own private life challenged both the community's unspoken views on sex and the assumption that whatever happens is fair game for gossip. Many stories centred on Elsie's affairs, stressing their impact not only on her but on the rest of the community. Unlike Pat, Elsie's adventures were treated understandingly, and the viewer was invited to sympathize with her weakness rather than condemn her waywardness. Nevertheless, the tensions caused by Elsie's behaviour, particularly in the early years, were clearly marked as divisive in the community. Thus, in one typical story Elsie receives an anonymous letter warning her about messing about with men. Elsie's violent reaction draws further attention to her capacity for a passionate response, which the letter criticizes. Her alienation from the community—the pub falls silent as she enters it—is increased by her accusations about the letter's author and by her wrong identification of Annie Walker. The episode ends with a fight in the Street as Elsie discovers the letter's true source in Ena Sharples and physically attacks her. While Ena is clearly in the wrong (she is fulfilling the figure of the 'gossip' in this episode), it is Elsie's sexuality which has opened her up for criticism and caused dissension in the community. Throughout *Coronation Street*, Elsie Tanner's pursuit of her own pleasure, at the cost sometimes of her own happiness, invited the strictures of other Street residents. Her behaviour indicated that the strong woman of British soaps could only go so far before she became a problem to the community rather than its prop.

Too often it is assumed that a sense of community is easily achieved in soaps. This chapter has shown that this is far from the case and that the moments of acceptance and sharing on which the communities of *Coronation Street* and *EastEnders* depend have to be worked for. The establishment of boundaries between the community and the rest of the world, the distinctions based on ethos, setting, and the past are not always clear and can be challenged from within the community itself as well as from the outside. The strategies used to create a sense of community are not themselves free of ambiguity: neighbourliness turns into nosiness; the past becomes an escape route rather than a source of strength; insiders become outsiders. Nevertheless, soaps have successfully presented to the viewer a community which, if not perfect, at least seemed indestructible. It took more than Elsie Tanner's wandering eye to break up the world of *Coronation Street*. But the pressures of gender, class, and race were beginning to build up, and in their very different ways *Brookside* and *Dynasty* were to take them on in the 1980s.

8

The Structure of Anxiety: Recent British Television Crime Fiction

Charlotte Brunsdon

IT IS A COMMON COMPLAINT amongst television previewers and critics that the British television schedules are dominated by crime fiction. A. A. Gill once characterized the essential quality of a television reviewer as having 'a bottomless bucket of facile things to say about policemen. Review television and you will meet more policemen than the Krays.'[1] In May 1997 James Rampton, previewing the new Caroline Quentin vehicle *Jonathan Creek*, asked, 'But haven't we had it up to here with detective series: aren't there already more tv whodunnits than suspects in an Agatha Christie novel?'[2] In April 1996 the Independent Television Commission censured independent television for depending on an excessive number of programmes based on the police, violent crime, and the underworld.[3] And in response, Peter Ansorge, head of drama at Channel Four, has agreed that 'There are too many cop shows and they are becoming all the same. The same stories, the same lighting, same camerawork, same dead bodies.'[4] Whilst I have considerable sympathy with Ansorge's position now, in the late 1990s, I want here to look at the proliferation of crime-based fiction in the 1980s and early 1990s, and to argue that far from showing a lack of imagination on the part of television producers, crime fiction in this period speaks very directly to the concerns of a Great Britain in decline under a radical Conservative government with a strong rhetoric of law and order. Television crime fiction, I will suggest—

First published in *Screen*, 39/3 (1998), 223–43.

1 A. A. Gill, 'They've Dunnit to Death', *Sunday Times*, 27 Oct. 1996, 16.

2 James Rampton, 'Balls to the Lot of Them', *Independent Tabloid*, 6 May 1997, 6.

3 Independent Television Commission, *Annual Performance Review*, Apr. 1996.

4 Peter Ansorge, quoted by Maggie Brown, in 'The Thick Blue Line', *Guardian*, 29 Apr. 1996, 16.

and particularly the police series in its various mutations—has been a privileged site for the staging of the trauma of the break-up of the post-war settlement.

Seen from the point of view of the generic concerns of the crime series, the 1980s could be characterized as a period in which issues of policing and government of civil society, which provide the referential terrain of the genre, recur relentlessly in the news media. The well-documented widening gap between rich and poor since 1979, with the discursive creation of the new 'underclass'; the decline of skilled working-class male employment; civil disorders both unambiguously political (following the death of Cherry Groce, or the poll-tax protests) and less clearly motivated (for example, the 1991 disorders in Meadowell); the policing of the miners' strike in the mid-1980s; a series of challenges to the integrity of the police force and the system of British justice (the disbanding of the West Midlands Regional Crime Squad, the release of a series of prisoners); and major scandals of sexual abuse—all these speak, and have been made to speak, to generic concerns with justice, truth, agency, and accountability. Indeed, I think it arguable that the crime genre in the 1980s developed new tropes comparable to, but superseding, the iconographic repertoire of the 1970s: squealing tyres, unmarked squad cars, East End armed robbers. In the 1980s, I would suggest, the figure 'riot' begins to appear, deployed across a range of locations, while two younger criminal personae—the drug-abuser (black, white, male, and female) and the joyrider (usually white male)—are also produced.

However, the very proliferation of series and the considerable variation between the different manifestations of the genre caution us against too simple a correspondence between crime and unrest on the streets, and crime on television. My proposition is not this literal, although I do think that the history of generic realist innovation associated with some branches of crime fiction is germane here—for example, the decision, in the 1960s, to set *Z Cars* (1962–6, 1967–8) in a 'new town', or the increased gender and ethnic diversity of television police forces. Similarly, the acknowledged use of news stories as plot stimulants, and the reporting and re-enactment of news stories using fictional generic conventions, as well as the increasing use of documentary footage of the emergency services for entertainment programming, clearly offer very complex imbrications of street crime and television crime. Limiting ourselves only to drama, there is no simple story to tell when the successes of the period range from, for example, the Sunhill police station-based, thrice-weekly, thirty-minute *The Bill* (1984–) to the widely exported two-hour films of *Inspector Morse* (1987–93), from the differently dour, explicitly regional *Spender* (1991–3) and *The*

Chief (1990–4) to the finally paranoid *Between the Lines* (1991–3); or when *Miss Marple* (1984–92), Jane Tennison (*Prime Suspect*, first series 1991), Pearl and Finn (*South of the Border*, 1988–9) and *Chandler and Co.* (1994–5) have picked up the walkie talkie from *Juliet Bravo* (1980–5) and Maggie Forbes (*The Gentle Touch*, 1980–4). I am not suggesting that we find a literal representation of the last fifteen years in the crime series on television. However, I am suggesting that this genre, in its many variants, works over and worries at the anxieties and exclusions of contemporary citizenship, of being British and living here, now. This genre, I would argue, has proved so resonant with both producers and audiences because it repeatedly, even obsessively, stages the drama of the responsible citizen caught in the embrace of what increasingly seems an irresponsible state.

I wish here to sketch out some of the stories we might tell when we attempt to account for the millions of people in Britain—of whom I am one—watching the detectives in the late twentieth century. To do this I will point initially to three relevant discursive contexts for the production and consumption of these programmes. The first of these is the significance, throughout the 1980s and 1990s, of an increasingly punitive law and order rhetoric: an invocation of 'short sharp shocks' and 'life means life'; of political parties 'tough on crime, tough on the causes of crime'. Despite the intransigent humanitarian stance of public figures such as the former HM inspector of prisons Judge Stephen Tumim, in matters of crime and punishment the do-gooders have been resoundingly defeated. Schlesinger and Tumber quote the producer of *Crimewatch*, Peter Chafer, commenting on the origins of the programme in the mid-1980s in the context of the Thatcherite emphasis on law and order politics: 'Ten or fifteen years ago I don't think it would have worked because . . . then we were very concerned as a society about what it was we were doing to people to make them criminal. . . . In the last three or four years we've suddenly said to ourselves, "To hell with the criminal, what about the poor bloody victim?" '[5] The humanity of offenders is increasingly denied in a penal system which, assailed by financial pressures, has increasingly cut education, exercise, and a range of special programmes. 'Prison works' is the astonishing slogan with which the last Conservative home secretary presided over the ever growing prison population and the building of yet more prisons.

At the same time (and we have relevant examples in the building of private prisons and the involvement of security firms in the transport of prisoners) the 1980s saw the systematic privatization of

---

5 Philip Schlesinger and Howard Tumber, 'Fighting the War against Crime: Television, Police and Audience', *British Journal of Criminology*, 33 1 (1993), 19–32: 22.

a range of bodies, from public utilities to schools inspectors. Accompanying this privatization, indeed legitimizing both privatization and deregulation, has been the aggressive abandonment of ideals of public service in favour of notions of market-governed choice. Thus the second relevant discursive context is one of privatization and private enterprise. It is this deregulatory project which allows a periodization which separates the mid-1980s, in terms of the police series, from the 1970s. For, as commentators on the genre in the 1970s such as Alan Clarke have shown, the 'law and order' debate, which informs my first discursive context, was a key component of 1970s approaches to policing in the perceived crisis of government of the Heath years.[6] It is only after the election of the 1979 Thatcher government that the radical project of dismantling the post-war settlement becomes articulated through the legitimization of 'heritage and enterprise'.[7]

The privileging of entrepreneurial practices, the validation of 'each man for himself', and the abhorrence of state interference (and support) that we find in the 1980s discourses of privatization are, potentially, directly in conflict with elements of police professional ideologies in a way which is rather different to 'law and order' discourse. For law and order discourse occupies, and contributes to, a Manichaean universe in which guilt, innocence, and blame can be clearly attributed. Wrong is wrong, and should be recognized as such and punished. The discourses of private enterprise, in contrast, pose both structural and moral challenges to aspects of police practice and world-view. For the attack on state intervention undermines the traditional function of the police as part of the executive, while ideologies of 'getting ahead', 'making the best of opportunities', and so on offer space for a moral entrepreneurship which is far removed from the 'old-fashioned' certainties of the law and order discourse. Particularly problematic is the way in which this discursive context opens up the possibility for actions which would previously have been perceived as immoral to be recast as merely enterprising. Most significant for the genre in this context are freemasonry, with its whiff of mutual aid, and what has now become an established iconographic element of the genre, but was unknown in the 1970s, the police computer. Access to the computer,

6 Alan Clarke, ' "This is not the Boy Scouts": Television Police Series and Definitions of Law and Order', in T. Bennett, C. Mercer, and J. Woollacott (eds), *Popular Culture and Social Relations* (Milton Keynes: Open University Press, 1986); ' "You're Nicked": Television Police Services and the Fictional Representation of Law and Order', in D. Strinati and S. Wagg (eds.), *Popular Media Culture* (London: Routledge, 1992); James Donald, 'Anxious Moments: *The Sweeney* in 1975', in M. Alvarado and J. Stewart (eds.), *Made for Television: Euston Films Limited* (London: BFI, 1985).

7 John Corner and Sylvia Harvey (eds.), *Enterprise and Heritage* (London: Routledge, 1991).

and the distinction between legitimate perks of the job (such as discovering whether you are about to buy a dodgy motor) and corrupt usage (for example, altering records, or selling on or blackmailing with data), is one of the sites on which the genre in the 1980s and 1990s explores the relationship between policing and private enterprise.

The final discursive context I want to propose as relevant is that of 'equal opportunities', which has been shown to have had very particular inflexions in the context of the police force and the justice system in the 1980s. The nodal point here is clearly the Alison Halford case (lodged in 1990, heard in 1992). Halford, the highest-ranking British policewoman, filed a case of sexual discrimination against the Merseyside police authority with the support of the Equal Opportunities Commission after she had been refused promotion nine times while less qualified men were successful. The case received considerable publicity in Britain, with extensive tabloid coverage of the drunken culture of the police force that was revealed. Beatrix Campbell, who reported on the industrial tribunal, quotes from the *Independent* newspaper's commentary on the Halford settlement:

> The Alison Halford affair could not have exploded at a worse time for a police service already on its knees from a succession of miscarriages of justice, shattered public confidence and rising crime rates. . . . Accusations of drunkenness [and] misogyny . . . appeared to confirm the worst public suspicions that sections of the service are brutish and sexist.[8]

This comment brings out the double-faceted nature of equal opportunities discourse in relation to the police. For if on the one hand, with its commitment to recruiting the different—those gendered and ethnicized by the hegemonic culture—the discourse of equal opportunities has its own clearly delineated debate zone of affirmative action and positive discrimination, on the other, it threatens to characterize the existing culture and practices of the police service as equally specific in terms of gender and ethnicity. Accusations of 'special treatment' always threaten to unveil what normal treatment is. What was most revealing about the Halford case was not the discrimination, but the revelation of what passed for normal and acceptable behaviour and opinion in the higher ranks of the police force.

The impact of the discourse of equal opportunities has registered on all manifestations of the police genre in the 1980s and 1990s. I discuss the most obvious case, *Prime Suspect*, at more length below.

8 Beatrix Campbell, *Goliath* (London: Methuen, 1993), 136.

But even the most laddish and formulaic vehicles have token women, and, as Diran Adebayo has commented, 'TV land is full of black people turning up in the unlikeliest of places.'[9] It is particularly noticeable that team cop shows, such as *Rockcliffe's Babies* (1987–8), or indeed *The Bill*, have casting policies marked by some notion of equal opportunities representation. Not only does the equal opportunities discourse structure the texts at the level of casting (even grumpy old Morse has to learn to be civil to female pathologists) and, as in the case of *Prime Suspect* and single episodes of other series, provide a secondary plot line, but it is also inscribed as a discourse within the generic conventions of the series. Thus the initial response by a senior officer of the investigating team in *Between the Lines* to a sexual harassment case brought by a white female officer against a black male officer is: 'Since the commissioner's been parading his equal opportunities policy all over the Met., I'd appreciate a fairly sensitive handling of the case' (Huxtable in 'Words of Advice', 18 September 1992). This public line is shown to contrast strongly with private opinion in the pub, but even there, change is recognized: '[Drake] should've been sweet to her, promised her everything, do her legs later.' 'Those days are gone, Harry.' 'Yeah, nowadays we throw away the parachute and land on our arses' (Deakin and Harry, ibid.).

It is in these contexts that I want to locate an analysis of three important programmes from the period: *Inspector Morse*, *Prime Suspect*, and *Between the Lines*. The key term in my analysis, the term which I will argue elusively governs both narrative structures repeated over many different shows, and is the personal attribute of any character offered as admirable, is that of 'responsibility'. If the slang generic term for the crime novel, the 'whodunnit', could hardly make this clearer, the issue in the crime series of the late 1980s and 1990s could hardly be more obscure. Whodunnit indeed, and who can be trusted to find out? We can usefully approach this investigation through two questions: 'Who can police?' and 'Who is accountable?'

Inspector Morse and Heritage Television

Inspector Morse (Zenith for Central Television, 1987–93, with subsequent single films) was the most popular television crime series of the late 1980s, regularly attracting audiences of about 15 million. Set in contemporary Oxford, the twenty-eight broadcast films were based on the novels of Colin Dexter, with additional scripts by, among others, Julian Mitchell, Alma Cullen, Daniel Boyle, and Peter

9 Diran Adebayo, 'TV Cops Show a False Harmony', *New Nation*, 17 Feb. 1997, 17.

Buckman, and starred John Thaw (Inspector Morse) and Kevin Whately (Sergeant Lewis).

There are two substantial existing accounts of the series. Richard Sparks, developing the concerns of his book *Television and the Drama of Crime*, analyses the series in the context of the history of the television representation of the police, in an article which concentrates on a Peter Buckman episode, 'The Last Enemy'.[10] Sparks's analysis draws on the work of criminologists and critics such as Alan Clarke to offer a nuanced account of the pleasures and possible social comment of the series, to which I shall return. Lyn Thomas, with very different interests, investigates the appeal of the programme in general, but Morse in particular, in discussion with self-proclaimed Morse fans.[11] Comparing the films with the Dexter books, she also shows how very much less misogynistic the films are, with Morse's predatory attitudes towards women replaced with a romantic yearning which makes him particularly attractive to the feminist women she interviews. This contrast between Dexter's rather leering detective and the more melancholy figure we find on television can be read as an instance of the way in which what I have called the discursive context of equal opportunities has specific consequences in the production of a television text. At some point in the production process decisions were made to modernize gendered elements of characterization. As Thomas puts it, 'The principal difference . . . is the relative absence of sexual objectification in the portrayal of the women characters in the TV version. The requirement of quality television in the late 1980s clearly demanded a more subtle approach.'[12]

For our purposes, the other interesting quality of *Inspector Morse* is the way in which, although it is clearly and firmly located in a present, in which there are heroin addicts ('The Dead of Jericho', 1987), American tourists ('The Wolvercote Tongue', 1988), female pathologists (third season, 1989), and too much fizzy beer, it also seems to be set in the past. Here, I think, two different taxonomies are useful. On the one hand, the high production values and the focus on the single investigator (with sidekick) link the series with other 'retro-crime' series such as *The Adventures of Sherlock Holmes* (Granada TV, 1984–5), *Agatha Christie's Poirot* (LWT–Carnival Films, 1989–), *Campion* (BBC1, 1989), and *Miss Marple* (BBC1–A & E–Network 7, 1984–92), many of which were also extremely

10 Richard Sparks, *Television and the Drama of Crime* (Buckingham: Open University Press, 1992); Richard Sparks, 'Inspector Morse: "The Last Enemy " ', in George Brandt (ed.), *British Television Drama in the 1980s* (Cambridge: Cambridge University Press, 1993).

11 Lyn Thomas, 'In Love with Inspector Morse', *Feminist Review*, 51 (1995), 1–25.

12 Ibid. 6.

successful, particularly in terms of overseas sales. This is the terrain of the private investigator and the English country-house murder. *Morse* is the only one of these series set in the present, but it shares some of the iconographic elements of an England of village greens, country pubs, and yokel locals. However—and this contributes a pleasing tension to the series—the casting of John Thaw as Morse repeatedly returns us to the history of the police series on television, for Thaw's previous success as Inspector Regan of *The Sweeney* (1975–8) underlies his stardom as Morse, providing, for the viewer familiar with this history, a *frisson* at every burst of bad temper and the memory of another type of crime story. Indeed, the very first *Morse*, 'The Dead of Jericho', appears to offer a self-conscious recognition of John Thaw's generic history, opening and closing with Morse's maroon classic Jaguar smashed up in two different, unavoidable (and successful) bids to stop escape attempts by villains.[13] It is as if we are being forcibly reminded that in the 1970s we watched a different kind of police series. Regan would not have given a second thought to the crashing of his car, Morse's pain is palpable, but the uncomfortable integrity of the two men is very similar. Jack Regan, dismissing the attractions of promotion in 1975, observed that there was 'nothing up there except ulcers and disappointment' ('Jackpot', 9 January 1975). Morse too is shown not to get promotion. The inference in each case is that it is their responsibility towards a higher morality rather than to their superiors which prevents their elevation. While *The Sweeney* was aggressively contemporary in a way which contrasts strongly with *Morse*, the two series share the invocation of what is presented as an old-fashioned integrity. The morality in both series suggests that individuals are responsible for their wrongdoing, even if only Jack Regan and Morse have the unerring gaze with which to detect this responsibility.

However, *Inspector Morse* also belongs to a bigger category, a category constructed not through a generic economy, but through what John Corner and Sylvia Harvey have identified as one of the key projects of the 1980s, that of the heritage industry.[14] Following the work of Tana Wollen, Andrew Higson, Richard Dyer, and Ginette Vincendeau on 'heritage cinema', we can perhaps most usefully place *Morse* within a category of 'heritage television'.[15] This is a

---

13 I must acknowledge the reading of this opening sequence by Sissel Vik to my 1994 MA class.

14 Corner and Harvey (eds.), *Enterprise and Heritage*.

15 Tana Wollen, 'Nostalgic Screen Fictions', in Corner and Harvey (eds.), *Enterprise and Heritage*: Andrew Higson, 'Re-presenting the National Past', in Lester Friedman (ed.), *British Cinema and Thatcherism* (London: UCL, 1993); Richard Dyer, 'Heritage Cinema in Europe', in Ginette Vincendeau (ed.), *Encyclopedia of European Cinema* (London: BFI–Cassell, 1995).

category delineated partly through its representational domain, a certain image of England, partly through its dominant structure of feeling, an elegiac nostalgia, and partly through its production values and export destiny, which offer the (tasteful) pleasures of money on the screen. This grouping—which in the main incorporates the detective fiction referred to above—also offers us the England of *Brideshead Revisited* (1981), of *Pride and Prejudice* (1996), but also of *The House of Elliott* (1991–4) and *Lovejoy* (1986–94). Lyn Thomas, who places *Morse* in the cognate grouping 'quality television', argues that while the programme does leave undisturbed this image of England, at the same time there is a resistance to the enterprise culture of the 1980s, and a certain interrogation of the virtues of heterosexuality.[16] Certainly, I think it can be argued that the heritage for which this programme is nostalgic is in some ways a pre-Thatcherite one, and that this nostalgia is articulated through Morse's constant grumpiness, his sense of being out of sorts with the times.

Richard Sparks addresses this issue by returning in the conclusion of his fine essay on Morse to his initial question about the ways in which 'detective fictions might be considered to be phenomena which bear the imprint of their times'.[17] At a methodological level he suggests there are two kinds of answer to this type of question: 'they concern what is included and what is left out'. Addressing what is included, he makes the case for reading the manifest corruption of the corridors of power in *Morse*—a corruption which perfectly matches Morse's own pessimism and recognition of human frailty—as metaphorical. This case is strengthened by Sparks's analysis of the self-conscious cleverness of *Morse*, its address to a literate audience, its consciousness of the game—the crossword puzzle—which is one of the pleasures of the genre. This address to a knowing audience—always mediated through Lewis (Kevin Whately), for those of us without the cultural capital—supports a reading of the series which also asks of its audience a reflection on a wider field. In the terms in which we have been working, trouble frequently comes in *Morse* from entrepreneurs, from those in a hurry to get riches or honours or fame; or from those who may have cut a few corners on their journey, and now have no qualms about defending their position. Thomas points out that possession of a swimming-pool is almost always a sign of bad faith.[18] Morse is not tempted by the things of this world—apart from beer, opera, and a certain type of woman—and is therefore, within the world of

---

16 Thomas, 'In Love with Inspector Morse', 7.
17 Sparks, 'Inspector Morse: "The Last Enemy" ', 99.
18 Thomas, 'In Love with Inspector Morse', 4.

these wrongdoers, absolutely incorruptible. But Morse's unerring moral sense is not recuperable to law and order rhetoric. His is not a world in which 'prison works', but instead a melancholy place in which often the death of the offender by their own hand is the best solution. Morse's is a world in which he at least believes in responsibility, but also one in which there is considerable scepticism about the apparatuses of the criminal justice system.

However, as Sparks also points out, 'Morse's Oxford has no Blackbird Leys estate. Neither do Morse's 1980s show any sign of having included a Miners' Strike, a Broadwater Farm, nor any of the consequent queries about the roles and powers of the police.'[19] These omissions can clearly be identified within the project of 1970s film studies as 'structuring absences'; absences inscribed, for example, in that most characteristic *Morse* shot, the spectacular, narratively unnecessary crane or helicopter shot over Oxford, showing colleges, spires, greens—a visual present of a fantasy past. Just as *Morse* in some ways denies the 1980s, so the series also, in these moments of visual splendour often matched by an operatic soundtrack, denies that it is television.

| *Prime Suspect:* | *Prime Suspect*, in contrast, embraces rather than disavows its place |

**Prime Suspect:
One of the Lads
at Last?**

Prime Suspect, in contrast, embraces rather than disavows its place as television. It is easy to imagine *Morse*, with its continual high-cultural references and use of operatic soundtrack, as a programme for which people who think of themselves as non-viewers might make an exception. Indeed, Morse himself does not watch television ('That's a technical television term'. Morse: 'I hardly ever watch'; 'Greeks Bearing Gifts', 1991), and the arrangement of his flat does not reveal a television set. *Morse* offers itself as television for those who neither arrange their living spaces around the television set nor watch violent and formulaic police series. *Prime Suspect* is full of people watching television. This is partly because of the self-referential device of having Jane Tennison (Helen Mirren) appear on a programme called *CrimeNight*. Clearly modelled on *Crimewatch*, this programme presents a reconstruction of the last hours of a murder victim, Karen Howard, and an appeal for witnesses from Tennison. This programme is then watched in a series of narrative sites in a way which echoes recent sociological research into the varied manner in which people watch television. Jane's family watch the programme, interrupting the celebration of her father's birthday. This watching is attended by anxiety about whether the video is correctly set and Jane's mother, the naïve

---

19 Sparks, 'Inspector Morse:"The Last Enemy"', 100.

viewer, failing to understand that the reconstruction is a reconstruction. Karen's parents watch, in a room too spacious to be cosy, hardly speaking but touching each other in grief. Sergeant Otley (Tom Bell) watches—drunk, furious, and hoping that Tennison will slip up—surrounded by the drunken male camaraderie of the police force at a boxing-match benefit for senior officer John Shefford's family. Marlow (John Bowe), the prime suspect, tries to watch; but his wife, Moyra (Zoë Wanamaker), turns the television off and starts aggressively cleaning the coffee-table wearing rubber gloves. Only Jane Tennison, initially so excited about her prospective appearance—'I'm going to be the first female DCI on *CrimeNight*'—is initially unable to watch, as her parents have indeed set the video wrongly, recording, wonderfully, the ice-skating instead.

When Jane does get to watch herself on television, at home in the bedroom with her lover Peter (Tom Wilkinson), the scene is used to reveal her absolute absorption in her job and her failure to recognize his claims on her attention—after an evening at which he had celebrated her father's birthday in her absence and correctly set their own video for her. Jane is centre-frame, with the television to her right, Peter's head to her left. The meaning of this relatively traditional set-up is completely transformed by the fact that it is the back of Jane's head we see. She looks away from Peter, away from us, to the magic image on the box. In this absorption in the television, herself, and her job, Jane is shown to take up too much space for even such a manifestly domesticated and decent man as Peter (he loves his son, is never shown outside their flat except at her parents') to tolerate. It is upsetting, but not surprising, when he later leaves without a word as the investigation hots up.

Despite its relatively unusual form for British television in 1991 (a two-hour episode on each of two consecutive nights), *Prime Suspect* is deeply embedded within the traditions of British commercial television, and particularly the relatively populist heritage of the crime series associated in the 1970s and 1980s with Euston Films.[20] While in some ways presenting itself as quite classy—in the casting of Helen Mirren and Zoë Wanamaker, for example—it at the same time eschews respectability (rape, torture, and serial killing with a graphic display of bodies). The interesting balancing act that the programme performs is to inscribe a story about sexual discrimination, with its implicit liberal–feminist address, into what we might call the smoking-and-drinking end of the television police genre, with its explicitly tabloid, masculinist address. Not only do characters in *Prime Suspect* watch television, but the series explicitly addresses fans of the crime genre through its condensation

---

20 Alvarado and Stewart (eds.), *Made for Television*.

of procedures and reworking of familiar tropes. Like Jane's lads, some large part of the audience is assumed to be drinking lager and smoking while watching.

It is this combination which contributed greatly to the success of *Prime Suspect*, and which I want to address here. For just as the (script) generosity shown to Marlow (the murderer), with scenes of real poignancy and intimacy between himself and Moyra, and, to a lesser extent, his mother, enormously strengthens the drama of pursuit and detection, so too does the affection for the masculine camaraderie of the police force strengthen the portrayal of Jane Tennison's position.

Prime Suspect (7–8 April 1991) tells the story of DCI Jane Tennison—a senior officer in the Metropolitan Police who has been kept on paperwork since she was promoted—demanding, and being given, the leadership of a rape–torture–murder case after the senior investigating male officer, John Shefford, dies on the case. No female officer has previously led a murder inquiry, and Tennison has to confront the prejudice of both her seniors and the team. Chief among her antagonists is Sergeant Otley (Tom Bell), who had been particularly close to Shefford, and who knows that Shefford had used prostitutes as informants—and for sexual services. Under Tennison's leadership the case expands to be a hunt for a serial killer, although the prime suspect, George Marlow, remains the man identified by Shefford before his death.

This brief outline reveals that there are at least two main narratives in *Prime Suspect*. The genre-traditional narrative is that of the interrogation, observation, and pursuit of the killer—Marlow. This narrative is organized through the increasing revelation of the extent and horribleness of the crimes, which is juxtaposed with the presentation of Marlow as a nice bloke who lives with a tough and loyal beautician–former prostitute and loves his mother. The genre-innovative narrative is that of Jane Tennison's progress from 'that bitch' to a well respected 'guv'nor', supported by her men when her removal is threatened by those upstairs, and finally successful in extracting a confession from Marlow.

Prime Suspect is clearly formed in the context of equal opportunities that I have described above. At the time of the first broadcast it was known that Lynda La Plante had been helped by DCI Jackie Malton in her research,[21] and for La Plante the series has clear continuities with her earlier role-reversal crime drama success *Widows* (1983–5). In each case a tired generic story is given new life through the substitution of women for men. There is in *Prime Suspect* a clear agenda about women in the police force, and

---

21 Yvonne Roberts, 'Tough Lady with the Blue Lamp', *Observer*, 14 Apr. 1991, 55.

discrimination against Tennison at a range of levels is shown throughout the programme. The programme explicitly addresses the question of who can police, particularly in a subplot in which DCI Shefford himself seems to be a possible suspect for the murders, given his connections with several of the prostitutes. This agenda is pursued further, although less successfully, in the following two films in which the racism of the police force (*Prime Suspect II*, 1992) and possible involvement in boy prostitution (*Prime Suspect III*, 1993) come under scrutiny.[22]

What is clever about the first *Prime Suspect* is the way in which the two different stories, the investigation and Jane's progress, are integrated and made to develop through specifically feminine skills and friendships. It is Maureen, Tennison's gofer, who puts to Tennison the question of the significance of investigations in Oldham, just as it is Maureen who makes the imaginative connection—Nu-Nails nail extensions—between the female victims. This crucial link is filmed in such a way as to make the shifting power relations in the incident room apparent. Maureen starts making her suggestion tentatively to Tennison alone in the busy room. The camera zooms out from Maureen and Tennison, encompassing the other officers gradually as Tennison's insistence on 'quiet' becomes louder. What started as a conversation between the two women becomes the focus of everyone's attention. Maureen's tentative idea about the nails—'It could be nothing'—an idea only accessible within feminine cultural competence, is both listened to and recognized by the squad room at large. Knowing about manicure is, like Tennison's earlier recognition of the quality of a victim's clothing, shown to make a critical contribution to a traditionally masculine game of detection. Similarly, it is Tennison's respect for the prostitute women she meets in Oldham that elicits crucial information from them in a scene which shows both female solidarity and the way in which class difference fractures this. She goes to the pub to drink with the women, and is there propositioned by a lorry driver, who tells her that he's got fifteen minutes and the cab's outside. To the subsequent hilarity of the women, Tennison does not disturb his assumptions about her, or distinguish herself from her company, merely saying that she is busy. However, the unity of their laughter is broken by her reference to her dinner party that evening, at which the two other women look at each other.

So Jane Tennison shows not only that she can police, but also that her policing brings new competencies to the job. The success of the show suggests that its complex audience address was successful. Put

---

22 The 'who can police?' agenda becomes less evident in the later series of two-hour *Prime Suspect* films with which La Plante had little to do. Detection dominates discrimination.

simply, inserting a senior female police officer into an investigation was shown to spoil neither investigation nor genre. The balancing act of the project, and the manner in which its dual address leads to real ambivalences, is shown most clearly in the repeated shots of Tennison in charge, but surrounded by images of mutilated female bodies. This *mise-en-scène* condenses the dual address of the show and represents the price of Tennison's success. Equally telling is the language in which the film's consummation, her acceptance by the lads, is expressed. They salute her by singing, 'Why was she born so beautiful, why was she born at all? She's no bloody use to anyone, she's no bloody use at all.' She responds, wiping away a tear: 'You bastards. I thought you'd all pissed off and gone home.' She is now fully integrated into the language of the lads, but unlike them she no longer really has a home to go to.

Between the Lines: 'No one's fireproof'

Prime Suspect addresses the issue of 'who can police' with a systematic roll-call of categories of people—other than white men—who might be considered capable and trustworthy, such as straight white women, straight black men, and gay white men, finding each more trustworthy than the white males who are shown to discriminate systematically against them. It also, implicitly, suggests that an uncorrupt policing is possible through an alliance of 'new forces' with the honest individuals of the old guard. Accountability is a possibility, crimes can be solved, villains can be locked away—even if, as I would argue, these narrative solutions are partly achieved through the displacement of the crime story by the corruption–discrimination story at certain key narrative moments.

Between the Lines (BBC–Island World, 1992–4) in contrast, is much less certain of who can police and, certainly, of whether effective policing can be achieved without a necessary blurring of boundaries between policing and criminality. Devised by J. C. Wilsher (who had written episodes for *The Bill*), with Tony Garnett as executive producer, the series is set in the complaints investigation bureau (CIB) of the London Metropolitan Police. The series is self-conscious in relation to both genre and issues of policing. This self-consciousness is immediately signalled by the location of the narrative in the CIB, a unit which is solely concerned with the conduct of the police. In generic terms, the referential world of the series has shrunk not just to the community figured as the police force, but to a group of three within the police force whose purpose is to investigate their own. The first episode of the first series, 'Private Enterprise' (written by Wilsher, 4 September 1992), dramatizes what is at stake here both for the genre and for the individual police characters.

The episode opens by introducing three elements, all of which are shot using a relatively high proportion of close-ups and low-key lighting effects, which, with a fast edit, contribute to an overall impression of grubby realism. The first, a standard generic narrative event in the crime programmes of our period, shows drug-dealing between young people on a run-down London council estate. The dealer, Andy, is then jumped by two men, who are revealed to be police officers Flynn and Tanner. Andy, it turns out, is an informant working under considerable police pressure, as well as a dealer. This too is familiar; there is a long film and television history to the 'nark' and 'snout', while the police themselves are clearly represented within the British macho heritage of *The Sweeney*. The second element, which introduces two of the three key characters of the series, Harry Naylor (Tom Georgeson) and Maureen (Mo) Connell (Siobhan Redmond), shows a meeting between Andy and these two in an underground car park. While the setting is generically familiar, as is the brief flash of headlights with which the police announce their location, their role and narrative significance is more obscure and is not explained. Maureen introduces herself and Harry as 'the people you want to see if you want to complain'. Andy then informs Harry and Mo that 'if you want bent coppers, you should try Mulberry Street'. The final scene of the introduction is a party for what turns out to be Mulberry Street officers to celebrate the promotion of their head of CID, Tony Clark (Neil Pearson), to the rank of detective superintendent. It becomes clear at this party— a familiar generic trope for displaying the camaraderie of the job— that Clark's promotion will mean a move to a post as yet undecided. Clark's own ambitions are made clear by his smirk when a senior officer hints at one of the more glamorous postings in the hierarchy of the police service: 'It may be that Mulberry Street's loss is the Flying Squad's gain.'

The burden of the episode is the recruitment of Clark to investigate his own comrades at Mulberry Street as the only way of answering the question posed to him at an interview in which he expects to hear about a posting to the Flying Squad: 'We have information that there's a bit of private enterprise going on at Mulberry Street. What takes you out of the frame?' For Clark the character, this investigation demands duplicity and manipulation as he recruits his wife and his lover to investigate both team members and superiors. It also involves generic bad faith, for, as he says, 'my cover's fireproof at Mulberry Street. No one's going to think that I'm a grass in my own nick.' The criminologist Mary Eaton, writing about the representation of police canteen culture in this series, argues that 'The CIB works against two prevailing values within the Met. and other police forces. The first is the widespread belief that it is acceptable to break the rules to bring villains to justice, the second that it is not acceptable to betray a colleague.'[23] In this episode we see Clark as an individual experience the shame of the betrayals he must commit. But in these betrayals (represented most vividly in Clark's denials: 'You can't be a policeman without knowing villains'; 'This is my firm, we look after each other') and in the failure of those no longer trusted to meet his eyes, we also see the series stake out a new generic terrain for itself, in which the ethics of police practices move into higher relief than the pursuit of villains. This first episode, which ends for Tony with the traumatic news that his promotional posting is to CIB, not the Flying Squad ('But I don't want to work in Complaints Investigation.' 'If you did, you wouldn't be suitable'), both catches Tony in a double bind through his own career ambitions and signals to the viewer that the object of investigation in this series will be slightly different. This is posed directly in the second episode, 'Out of the Game' (11 September 1992), when Tony detects what really happened among the perpetrators in an incident they are investigating, but has to be reminded by each of his new colleagues in turn that they are only interested in police behaviour. As Mo says, 'It's not down to us, it's not our brief,' and Deakin, sealing the episode with the reminder to both Tony and viewers: 'You're not CID any more, you're CIB.'

There were three series of *Between the Lines*, broadcast in 1992, 1993, and 1994. While each series used the same core characters, Clark, Naylor, and Connell, and their immediate boss, John Deakin (Tony Doyle), the emphases and locations of the series were different, and by the final series the police force was not the employer. It is the first series which is most interesting for our purposes: thirteen episodes first broadcast on a Friday night at 9.30 on BBC1 in autumn 1992, attracting between 6 and 8 million viewers. This series is centrally and repeatedly concerned with the dilemmas of the police investigating themselves, while the second series is more occupied with the power struggles between the police force and MI5. The third series, which has some overseas location shooting, moved into the terrain of international terrorism, and particularly the relationships between terrorism and private and state security bodies. Chris Dunkley, who had championed the first series as among the best on television in 1992, observed of the third series, 'How quickly things change.'[24] Although many series fail to maintain their quality through subsequent seasons, it seems arguable

---

23 Mary Eaton, 'A Fair Cop? Viewing the Effects of the Canteen Culture in *Prime Suspect* and *Between the Lines*', in David Kidd-Hewitt and Richard Osborne (eds.), *Crime and the Media* (London: Pluto Press, 1995).

24 Chris Dunkley, '*Between the Lines*', *Financial Times*, 16 Sep. 1992, 19; 'Reflections on the Sleaze Factor', *Financial Times*, 26 Oct. 1994, 21. Thanks to Tom Richmond for checking my reading of *Between the Lines*.

here that it was precisely the loosening of the generic ties which contributed to the problems of the third series. The rich texture of the first series, with its narrative and formal investigation of a key television genre, was dissipated by the rootless narrative premisses of the third.

The programme is a good example of the hybrid serialized series, offering both particular, episode-bound stories and a continuous developing narrative which focuses particularly on DS Tony Clark. At the same time the concentration on trouble within the police force reveals the clear recognition of the increased public concern with police conduct and accountability. Thus the very imaginative premiss of the series is 'news-responsive', as are many of the topics for individual episodes. In the first series stories included: a police killing in an incident with an imitation gun (episode 2); sexual harassment in the police service (episode 3); freemasonry (episode 4); death of a young black man in custody (episode 11); arrest of a senior police officer on a soliciting charge (episode 12). Both the format and particular stories, then, reveal an alertness to contemporary representations of policing in the news media, and offer a particular late 1980s–1990s British embodiment of the ancient question of policing, *quis custodiet ipsos custodies?* ('Who will guard the guardians?'). Garnett himself is on record as suggesting that the debate about policing within the service is of considerable sophistication:

> 'There is a very intelligent debate going on at senior levels in the country questioning this very matter [who should police the police]', says Garnett. 'The left is more at fault in this than the right. It is one of the fallacies of the left to think that the police are stupid. There are a number of extremely intelligent officers who are very concerned about the relationship between the police and the public. In some ways, there is a more intelligent discussion going on inside the police than outside.'[25]

This question is particularly figured not only through the issues of who can police, as we have seen in the other series, but also in a debate which runs through the series about effective strategies for policing. Deakin, the immediate boss of the CIB team which Tony heads, puts it like this in episode 13, the final episode of the first series: 'The Met. has never been cleaner. I can tell you that for a fact. It's also a fact that our clean-up rate is at an all-time low. What conclusion you draw . . . is entirely up to you.' This concern runs through the series, expressed usually in metaphor—'you hang around with dogs, you get fleas' (episode 9)—but also providing a

25 Jonathan Miller, 'Watching the Police', *Sunday Times*, 20 Sept. 1992, 25.

demotic history of policing within the series. For example, a senior officer observes of being picked up with a prostitute: 'When I first joined, it was one of the fringe benefits of the job' (episode 12); or (of the same officer), 'There've been stories about Urquhart since he was in the Vice Squad in the 1970s. It goes with the territory.' The simplest version of this history is given to Charlie McGregor, a charismatic retiring officer who, in his farewell speech, mourns the days when 'we banged up villains if they broke the law', and evokes in contrast a world of sociology lecturers, counselling, and political correctness (episode 10). In this demotic history the series has very clear affiliations with 1970s programmes like *The Sweeney*, where, as Ed Buscombe has noted, the constant implication was that the police would be able to do their job better were 'the do-gooders and penpushers to get off their backs'.[26] Charlie's final question, 'Who wants a police force with real coppers in it these days?', looms over the series, and particularly over the fate of those who are shown to be 'real coppers', like DI Kendrick (Michael Angelis) (episode 6), who prove to have bent the rules a little too far. This is a question of both a 'who' and a 'how' of policing, and one on which the series shows real ambivalence. DI Kendrick is shown to be an honourable man, but Charlie McGregor himself, the source of the most eloquent version of this demotic history, turns out to be corrupt.

For our purposes, what is perhaps most significant about *Between the Lines* is the clarity with which it addressed key issues of policing in the 1980s and 1990s—civil disorder, drugs, corruption, freemasonry, secondary picketing, use of informants, racism and sexual discrimination within the service—and the ambivalence which it maintained about the strategies used to address these issues. If we examine the structure of the series with particular reference to the discursive contexts outlined at the beginning of this chapter and the governing questions of 'Who can police?' and 'Who is accountable?', the particular contours of this clarity and ambivalence can be traced. Each episode has two main components: the episode story, which is usually a policing issue, and Tony's progress, which is a continuing narrative involving his love life, where he lives, and his progress in the new job. However, from episode 5 a third element, the Carswell investigation, is introduced, and this continues right through, increasing in significance, implicating more and more people, and eventually containing all other stories. Each episode is filmed in the slickly edited but naturalistic style I have termed grubby realism, which clearly has resonances in Garnett's earlier projects, including both *Law and Order* and his Hollywood period.[27]

26 Ed Buscombe, 'The Sweeney—Better than Nothing?', *Screen Education*, 20 (1976), 66–9.

27 James Saynor, 'Imagined Communities', *Sight and Sound*, 3, 12 (1993), 11–13.

Just as the CIB team investigates the police, the series investigates the genre. This is done in a range of ways. One key sequence in episode 2 shows Tony taking statements from police officers involved in a shooting incident with a replica pistol. Tony patiently takes the men through their statements, all of which are given in television police argot, repeating the statements back to the men, translating back and forth between this strange generic language and everyday speech.

The show explicitly situates itself in relation to what I have called the 'law and order discourse' and that of privatization. In relation to the first, it asks how law and order is to be achieved. The second is the name given to corruption within the force, and offered explicitly, in a speech about Docklands by Charlie McGregor, as the legitimization for corrupt behaviour (episode 10: 'Nothing to Declare').

About equal opportunities discourse, the programme is knowing and displays an unusually light touch. This is signalled early on by Mo's response to Harry's purchase of a pornographic magazine for an informant they are protecting. Mo makes a face at Harry when he displays the purchase and then takes it from him, calling to the informant that Harry has brought him a copy of 'the gynaecologists' gazette'. As with *Prime Suspect,* there is a successful rendering of the embedded masculinism of police culture, most notably through Tony's signal failure to keep his pants on whenever he meets an attractive woman. His affair with PC Jenny Dean, introduced in the first episode, runs throughout the first series. The married Clark presents it as normal and when questioned by superior officers observes, 'She's a sensible kid, she knows the score' (episode 1). Dean's suicide in the penultimate episode suggests that 'the score' was unfairly weighted. Both Mary Eaton and Robin Nelson have commented on perhaps the most exceptional aspect of the series' sexual politics, the revelation in the second series that Mo is lesbian.[28]

The ambivalence of *Between the Lines* extends beyond this, however, to the representation of CIB itself. *Between the Lines* is strongly invested in the seedy glamour of a certain image of the heavy-drinking, chain-smoking, promiscuous plain-clothes man, with considerable commitment to the rendering of the pleasures of a defiantly laddish culture. When Tony first meets his new team he turns up with a bottle of whisky, and it is the command 'Let's open the bottle' which really signals the beginning of getting to know each other. Here, it is crucial that Mo is one of the lads, purposefully raising a tumbler full of Scotch to her mouth. This is the culture of

28 Eaton, 'A Fair Cop?'; Robin Nelson, *TV Drama in Transition: Forms, Values and Cultural Change* (Houndmills: Macmillan, 1997).

the police genre and indeed if we are to believe criminologists like Eaton or the revelations of the Halford case, of the police force itself. The question of the series is whether this culture, with its necessary commitment to the lads, is necessarily a corrupt and discriminatory one. For if the series is marked by a deep nostalgia for this culture (the demotic history referred to above), at the same time its very conception implies a modernizing project.

The series offers a very politicized image of the police, with explicit recognition of high-level political pressure, mention of the home secretary and other less clearly identified sources of power—as in the instruction to Tony in episode 4: 'Our elders and betters want a result, so get one.' On the one hand, the diegetic world of the series is well accommodated to an interventionist home secretary; on the other, this centralizing project is repeatedly confirmed through the episode-specific stories of the rooting out of 'local' corruption. CIB is a centrally controlled hit squad without a local base, with no community to answer to. Tony, Harry, and Mo repeatedly descend on different local manors—Beckett Park, Hamley Road, Oakwood, St Helen's—to purge the stations. The pursuit of a clean force is followed without any reference to the notions of the embeddedness within a community which has sustained many accounts of the police service.

At the end of the first series these contradictions come together in what Tony is expecting to be a celebratory evening. The modernizing project has been successful: corruption has been rooted out at the highest ranks, implicating the trio's own boss, Deakin. Tony, Maureen, and Harry sit drinking together. But they are not in a boozer, drinking beer and spirits. Instead, they are in a wine bar in Covent Garden with a bottle of champagne. Gone are the drinking haunts and habits of the old generic police force, gone is locality, and gone too is the camaraderie. Tony tries to order another bottle, but it turns out that neither Mo nor Harry can stay. Tony leaves alone, only to catch sight of his abandoned wife on an evening out with a new lover.

Conclusion: The Structure of Anxiety

While I have been writing this chapter the 1997 general election in Britain has been won by the Labour Party with an enormous majority. The extraordinary change of mood in the country suggests a rather neat periodization of eighteen years, making my concern, the British television crime series 1979 to 1997, the period of the Conservative government. Attractive as this tidiness is, I do not think that the argument I have been making about the peculiar vividness of the genre in the 1980s is adequately served by this periodization. It claims both too quick and easy a correspondence between changes in the political sphere and the production of cultural goods, and simultaneously promises to mislead us about the continuities between, for example, the 1970s and the 1980s, or the last Conservative government and the new Labour one.

Instead, I would want to suggest that my argument is most relevant for the period from 1983–4 to 1992–3. This permits us to recognize the continuities between the 1970s law and order debate and the dominance, within the 1980s, of a retributive, punitive version of this debate. The early equal opportunities crime series (*Juliet Bravo*; *The Gentle Touch*; *The Chinese Detective*, 1981–2; *Wolcott*, 1981) thus move out of main focus, and the period begins with *The Bill*, *Widows*, and *Miss Marple*. *Crimewatch* (1984–), although not ostensibly a fictional programme, offers a symptomatic origin in the shift of focus described above, just as *The Bill*, with its move back into straight policing (as opposed to *Sweeney*-type policing), is symptomatic in another way of the resurgent rhetoric of the virtues of 'the bobby on the beat'. *The Bill*, though, while offering what is in some ways a return to the police station iconography of *The Blue Lamp* (Basil Dearden, 1950) and *Dixon of Dock Green* (BBC, 1955–76), features a cast list clearly constituted in what I have called the discursive context of equal opportunities, particularly in the character of WPC Datta (Seeta Indrani). In the same way, the huge success of *Miss Marple*, with its elderly spinster heroine, offers a particular inflexion of heritage television. Whilst a strain of equal opportunities programmes continues throughout the decade (for example, *Widows II*, 1985; *South of the Border*, 1988; and *Bloodrights*, 1990), it is *Prime Suspect* that offers the most achieved version of this cycle. For a range of reasons, some discussed by Jim Pines in his essay on crime fiction, the discursive context of equal opportunities has proved more productive in relation to white women than any other category.[29] Colin Salmon as DS Oswalde in *Prime Suspect II*, subject to racial discrimination from, among others, Jane Tennison, has remained a character confined to that particular text, unlike Tennison herself. Amy Taubin has suggested that, to a US audience, the most astonishing feature of Tennison as played by Helen Mirren is how flawed the character is shown to be, while still, in Taubin's terms, 'the hero of our time'.[30] In contrast DS Oswalde, as Jim Pines points out, is still typical of the genre in Britain: as a 'good' black character he must also be noble.[31]

29 Jim Pines, 'Black Cops and Black Villains in Film and TV Crime Fiction', in Kidd-Hewitt and Osborne (eds.), *Crime and the Media*.

30 Amy Taubin, 'Sex and Race and Law and Order', *Village Voice*, 16 Feb. 1993, 44.

31 Pines, 'Black Cops and Black Villains', 74. Colin Salmon, who plays DS Oswalde, recently appeared in the much more traditional role of pimp and murderer in the generically cognate *Gold* (ITV, 1 Dec. 1997).

In terms of periodization, I would suggest that *Prime Suspect*, the first series of *Between the Lines*, and the end of *Inspector Morse* (except for the one-offs) conclude the grouping with which I have been concerned, with *Cracker* (1993–5) as a text of transition. The early 1990s, particularly through Jane Tennison, familiarize us with the figure of a senior (white) woman giving orders, even as her screen presence is juxtaposed with images of mutilated female bodies. *Cracker's* Jane Penhaligon is clearly a related, but later 1990s, figure. What I have attempted to show through detailed analysis of three quite different programmes from this period is the way in which they share a concern with the apparatuses and institutions of policing and criminal justice, as well as, in different ways, an engagement with the television police genre.

An obvious response would be to suggest that these are, in fact, the features of the genre. My argument would be that there is a historical specificity to the intensity of the engagement with these issues during the period 1984 to 1992, particularly articulated through questions of responsibility and accountability in policing. This 'age of anxiety' for the genre involves qualitatively different inflexions of the recurrent questions of policing than we find in either the 'law and order populism' of the 1970s or the 'equal opps–GLC' period of the early 1980s. These are programmes produced in, and responding to, what we might, to raid an idea from Raymond Williams, call a 'structure of anxiety', a structure of feeling that I have tried to show is clearly articulated within the programmes themselves—and the many others of the same period.

The later 1990s have brought a move away from an address to the social in the genre. Arguably, the dynamic genre of the mid-1990s is the medical drama. There is at the same time a move towards the medicalization of crime within the crime series, with the focus moving away from the police as the solvers of riddles to pathologists and criminal psychologists (*Cracker*, *Dangerfield*, 1995– ; *Silent Witness*, 1996– ; *McCallum*, 1997– ; *Bliss*, 1997). In the terms in which I have been working, I would suggest that the dynamism of the questions about policing—Who can police? Who is responsible?—has become diminished, and instead there is a detectable tendency towards a spectacularization of the body and site of crime. I am not sure that the structure of anxiety has gone, but the worrying seems to be less about policing and justice. Should this chapter end, then, with a more sustained address to the issue of what complex sets of causality lead to certain television genres being more dynamic, and perceived as more socially expressive, at particular periods? Why, to put crudely what I think has recently happened to British television, was it then cops and now docs? Why did the investigation of the police and the genre cede airtime to staring at bodies and speculating about the supernatural? I have offered an outline of the significant discursive contexts in which I would argue those cop shows were produced, and to which they in turn contributed, although I have not addressed the significant influence of the US entertainment industry—for example, *Prime Suspect* cannot really be fully addressed without attention to *The Silence of the Lambs* (Jonathan Demme, 1991). I do indeed think that further exploration of these arguments requires engagement both with theories of genre in television, and with empirical work on the production processes of television. But that would be another story.

9

Crime and Crisis: British Reality TV in Action

Annette Hill

Infotainment and
Reality Television

DURING THE EARLY 1990S in America so-called reality programming became one of the hottest genres on television. In a special report in *Variety* in 1991 John Dempsey (1991) wrote:

> Like a rockslide that snowballs into an avalanche, the volume of reality shows on television has multiplied exponentially over the last few years, to the point where the shows now saturate network prime-time, first-run syndication and cable TV schedules. There are now nearly two dozen reality-based shows on TV and over a dozen waiting in the wings.

According to *Variety*, the reason for the genre's success is that these programmes are cheap to make and appeal to a wide section of the general public, and, in the words of Phil Oldham, reality shows can be 'more compelling than fiction'.[1] In Britain reality TV has not yet come to dominate the schedules to quite the same extent, but with the arrival of a range of reality programming in the 1990s, from the BBC (*999 Lifesavers*, 1992– ; *Children's Hospital*, 1992–), ITV (*Police, Camera, Action*, Carlton, 1995– ; *Blues and Twos*, Carlton, 1993–), and Sky One (*Coppers*, 1994– ; *Speed*, 1996–8), reality TV certainly appears to be making its mark on the television public. In 1992 the BBC's *999* attracted an audience of over 12 million in its first run and began its eighth series in 1999.

Journalists and television critics were quick to deplore this new style of 'Ghoul TV' (Naughton 1994, p. 23) when it first began to appear. Jane Thynne (1992, p. 25) wrote a piece on reality programming in the *Daily Telegraph* with the headline 'Rescue of the Ratings', whilst Henry Porter (1992, p. 9) asked in the *Evening*

Published here for the first time by permission of the author, copyright © Annette Hill 2000. 'If . . .' cartoons by Steve Bell reprinted from *The Guardian*, May 1998, copyright © Steve Bell 1998, by permission of Steve Bell.

1 *Variety*, 9–15 Jan. 1995; Oldham is speaking on behalf of Genesis Entertainment, who produce reality TV shows.

Standard 'Should we indulge this lust for gore?' Most critics of reality TV feel that these programmes appeal to the voyeur in us all. 'When we watch *999*', Porter wrote, 'we are slowing down the car to gape at the squashed motorcyclist at the side of the road.' John Naughton agreed: 'These programmes are all about maximising ratings whilst minimising production costs. And they do so by pandering to the oldest and most disreputable traits in human nature—the desire to gawp at other people's misfortunes.'

The fear is that these programmes not only maximize our 'lust for gore' but do so in a half-hour format aimed at all the family. This is why they are seen as a cause of concern for parents. In 1992, when reality programming was beginning to make an impact on British TV, the *Daily Telegraph* invited one family of four to deliver a verdict on whether programmes such as *Crimewatch UK* (BBC, 1984–) or *Crime Monthly* (LWT, 1989–) were exploitative and unacceptable for family viewing. The Thomas family found only one programme acceptable (*Crimewatch UK*); the rest left them with a 'lingering sense of unease' (Rodwell 1992: 18).[2] *Crimewatch UK* was thought by the Thomas family to be professional, and to serve a useful purpose, whereas other types of reality programming were seen to be more sensational and exploitative in nature.

This distinction between good and bad types of reality TV is also used by programme-makers themselves. Nick Ross, one of the presenters of *Crimewatch*, made this claim about reality TV: '*Crimewatch* and its sister programmes are in the public interest. *True Crimes* by contrast, for all its skilful use of television arts, could only be of interest to the public.'[3] Indeed, Ross went as far as to say that *Michael Winner's True Crimes* (LWT, 1992–4) is 'something of a whore', and that 'the genre has been debased by crudely violent programmes on ITV'. Robin Paxton, controller of features and current affairs at London Weekend Television, also feels that the genre has been debased. In 1992, he said there is 'a genre of reality television that's extraordinarily sleazy [and] ITV won't venture down that track'.[4] It is important for programme-makers to dissociate themselves from 'other' types of reality TV, a type of TV that is metaphorically associated with sordid and venal sexual encounters. When series such as *999*, *Crimewatch*, *Blues and Twos*, or *Police, Camera, Action* attract family audiences of over 12 million, programme-makers cannot afford to alienate

2 The Broadcasting Standards Commission receives complaints from the public about reality programming; it upheld complaints about *Blues and Twos* and a trailer for *999* because it thought an episode of *Blues and Twos* was exploitative and considered the trailer for *999* too graphic for pre-watershed transmission (*BSC Monthly Bulletin* (June 1996), 8, (July 1996), 21).

3 See Nick Ross, 'When TV Helps Justice', *Daily Telegraph*, 2 Sept. 1994, 21.

4 John Dugdale, 'Not the "Nine o'Clock News" ', *Independent*, 29 July 1992, 13.

viewers or to be seen to be cashing in on the 'sleazy' side of reality programming.

One way of dismissing reality TV is by seeing it as the offspring of tabloid journalism. Traditionally, the news values of the tabloids have been subject to a great deal of criticism. John Langer, in *Tabloid Television: Popular Journalism and the 'Other News'*, cites a long list of criticisms of this 'other news', which is seen to be 'in the business of entertainment', 'traffics in trivialities and deals in dubious emotionalism' (Langer 1998: 1).[5] For Langer, reality TV owes its origins to this 'other news'. However, the issue is not only whether these programmes are examples of tabloid TV, but also the manner in which these programmes present a constructed version of reality which is aimed at a family audience. In the next section I want to take a look at three reality TV programmes which concentrate on British emergency services. Each of these programmes focuses on crime and crisis in the home and the local community and presents a message to the family audience which suggests that our safety and well-being depends upon the heroism and hard work of emergency service personnel (see Corner, 1995).

Crime and Crisis   In May 1998 the cartoonist Steve Bell ran a series of cartoons on reality programming.[6] His cartoon strip, about a programme called 'Police Vet Camera Hospital Action', showed a penguin coming to a hospital for emergency treatment, who is then chased by vets–police using helicopters, and who finally explodes. Once the penguin's spectacular death is caught on camera, the reality programme shrewdly changes its name to 'Police Vet Camera Hospital Death in Your Face Action'. During a daytime screening two children watch the 'important live coverage of a penguin actually exploding', shouting 'again, again' before beginning to deconstruct the image. This cartoon strip encapsulates in satirical form many of the arguments marshalled against reality TV. British emergency services such as hospitals, veterinary clinics, the police (Bell could also have included river patrols, customs officials, or coastguards), have all been the subject of fly-on-the-wall programmes which sensationalize ordinary events. Not only is the cartoon programme absurd and exploitative but it is also shown to be aimed at children, who take

---

5 This 'other news' is a means of presenting social events or human interest stories, but this type of reportage can oversimplify and sensationalize news stories to the detriment of more 'worthwhile' news events. There has been some very good research into the way in which the news is represented on television and in newspapers (see Brunsdon and Morley 1978; Schlesinger 1978; Hartley 1982; Dahlgren and Sparks 1992; Gunter 1997; amongst others).

6 *Guardian*, 18–22 May 1998.

Steve Bell's vision of
reality television

great delight in seeing a real 'exploding penguin'. On the one hand, these children are innocent victims of television companies and their desire for ratings—the TV channel interrupts *Teletubbies* to show this live-action event—but, on the other hand, the children are seen to be media-literate, perhaps too media-literate, in their response to the construction of real action as entertainment.

Actual reality TV programmes are not as surreal nor as funny as this one, but what programmes such as *999*, *Blues and Twos*, and *Coppers* have in common is an appeal to a family audience. I want to present a brief overview of each programme in order to illustrate this.

---

999 Lifesavers   *999 Lifesavers* is a BBC1 series based on reconstructions of real emergencies. The first series was shown in 1992, and attracted audience viewing figures of over 12 million.[7] *999* is scheduled after the 9 p.m. watershed, between 9.30 and 10.20 p.m. Michael Buerk presents the programme, which uses his reputation as a newsman and journalist to give *999* extra status as a serious and responsible reality programme. The series is loosely based on the American show *Rescue 911* (CBS, 1989–), but the BBC claim that there are few similarities between the two. According to Peter Salmon, then head of features at BBC Bristol, '*Rescue 911* doesn't contain any public service information. And it's presented by William Shatner (Captain Kirk in *Star Trek*), which I wouldn't dream of doing because this isn't make-believe. You can't have someone zapping aliens with a ray gun one minute, and dealing with genuine stories the next.'[8]

Clearly the BBC feel there is a distinction to be made between different types of reality TV programme. Although *999* does use a mixture of real footage and reconstructions to present 'true stories' to the audience, it also offers safety advice to the public in every episode. These public service announcements help to make the series 'different' from other reality programming, and the BBC can be seen to be borrowing certain conventions from *Crimewatch UK*, another BBC programme that deals with crime reconstructions, and which appeals to the public for information to help the police solve these crimes. Both of these programmes aim to convince an audience that the crime–emergency reconstructions which are part of the shows are firmly 'rooted in the detailed authentication of the

7 Viewing figures taken from Dugdale, 'Not the "Nine o'Clock News" '. For further discussion of *999* see John Corner, *Television Form and Public Address* (London: Edward Arnold, 1995).

8 Ibid.

events portrayed' (Schlesinger and Tumber 1993: 24). For the BBC, *999* is not another sensational 'tabloid TV' show, but rather a responsibly constructed programme that can teach the public how to save lives. As Salmon explains, 'If you have emerged from the BBC public service philosophy it's inconceivable that you would make something that wasn't careful and cautious. We agonise about what to leave in or take out, and we regularly curb the dramatic tendencies of our directors.'[9]

Two trailers for *999* show that this balance between information and entertainment is not so easy to achieve.[10] One previews stories that will appear in the new series of *999*—a girl struggles for air as she is trapped under water; a man attempts to stem the flow of blood from a large gash in his leg.[11] These are clips that emphasize drama, and they are presented to the public not as public service information but as teasers: will the young girl survive the boating accident, will the tree surgeon save his leg? Another advert for *999* shows the emergency services at work saving lives, juxtaposed with David Bowie singing, 'We can be heroes just for one day'.[12] This is not public service information, but an open attempt to glamorize, even sensationalize, Britain's emergency services.

If we take a look at the opening to *999* we can see this uneasy mixture of fact and fiction becomes part of the programme's identity as a whole.[13] *999* starts with a ticking clock. A high piano solo follows, with images of bright lights and long shadows to emphasize a sense of unease. The colour blue features strongly, an indication that the emergency services (the blue flashing light) are nearby. We see feet running, and then a high-angle shot of the emergency team climbing into a helicopter. Michael Buerk tells us: 'All of tonight's rescues are true stories. We've sometimes used actors or stuntmen, but everything you see is based on the account of the people involved. They've helped us to reconstruct the events as they happened.' On the one hand, *999* tells us that this is a highly stylized presentation of Britain's emergency services, and yet at the same time it is at pains to emphasize that this is 'real'.

999 uses a strange mixture of highly stylized reconstructions combined with conventions which we would associate with factual reporting. For example, Michael Buerk will often introduce a dramatic reconstruction by standing near the location where an

9 Ibid.

10 Kilborn and Izod (1994, 432) point out that reality TV programmes often follow modes employed in dramatic fiction, and this is certainly the case in these trailers for *999*.

11 Trailer for *999* (BBC1, 15 Apr. 1994, 6.30 p.m.).

12 Trailer for *999* (BBC1, 1 June 1998, 9.30 p.m.).

13 The credit sequence I describe has been changed for the latest series.

accident happened, talking to camera, as if he is reporting the news. And yet, when the reconstruction begins, we are in no doubt that this is an account of a crisis, not real footage of the crisis itself. A logo appears to tell us this is a reconstruction, and we are told that actors have been used alongside real rescuers and rescuees. If an actor has been used, we often see the real victim talking in a studio, recounting the events that occurred. If real footage has been used, then we are told that this is 'live action' not a reconstruction. 999 is very careful to give the viewer as much information as they need to ensure that they know what is real and what is reconstructed. However, the reconstructions them-selves use a variety of different film techniques. One, of a fire in a riding stables, used trained stunt horses to add dramatic effect, and we are shown horses running in every direction, nostrils flared for the camera.[14] Another reconstruction—of a stabbing in a night club—adopted MTV-type editing techniques, slowing the images down, using angled shots, and high-contrast colour.[15] At the end of the reconstructions a montage of 'best bits' is some-times shown as a means to highlight the drama and danger that occurred. This stylized representation of real events seems to work against the clear definitions of reality and reconstruction that accompany 999 stories.

999 places a great deal of emphasis on the 'what if . . .' scenario that is a common feature of reality programming. At all times we are left in no doubt that the people who were involved in these life-threatening situations could very easily have died. Certain conven-tions are used by the programme-makers to emphasize this. Friends and family say things like, 'If they hadn't found him, he wouldn't be alive today,' or 'We were very concerned about their chances of survival,' and the emergency services tell us, 'It was one of the most difficult rescue operations that we have been asked to perform,' or 'I knew it was getting very, very serious.' Although 999 never shows a rescue operation that was not successful, they certainly highlight the tension of these scenarios and play to the audience's feeling of 'There but for the grace of God go I'. The reconstructions serve as a reminder that, as Buerk tell us, 'accidents can happen any time, any place'.[16]

Nowhere is this more emphasized than in reconstructions of family crises. More often than not, the 999 Lifesavers stories are concerned with parents and children. The focus here is on unusual accidents, accidents that one cannot be prepared for. A 2-year-old opens a bean bag and suffocates from the small polystyrene beans

14 999 (26 May 1998, 9.30 p.m.).
15 Ibid.
16 Ibid.

inside the bag; a family are stranded on a cliff face as the tide comes in and threatens to engulf them; two teenagers are involved in a freak sailing accident whilst their father stands helpless on the shore.[17] Michael Buerk does his best to alert parents and children to the possibility that this may happen to them. The two teenagers' accident was extremely unusual, but, Buerk tells us, 'in 1991 twenty-one people were killed in UK waters alone'. Before showing the reconstruction of a young boy who wandered out of his house into a life-threatening situation, Buerk says: 'Young children are naturally curious, naturally adventurous, and despite all our best efforts as parents they can so easily get into trouble.'[18] Similarly, in a reconstruction about a child who nearly drowned by falling upside-down inside a dustbin with water inside, Buerk talks to camera, standing in a back garden, next to a small child playing near washing on the line, and tells us: 'Anyone with small children knows how difficult it is to keep a close eye on them all the time and how quickly and easily they can get into danger. Every year thousands of children in this country have accidents—around half of those accidents are in the home.'[19] In the same episode there is a feature about a young child who has convulsions, and Buerk, sitting in a crèche full of healthy, happy children, informs us that 'it must be a nightmare for every parent, babysitter or crèche leader' to have to deal with a sudden crisis such as this one.

These alarmist stories of family crises prey on fears in all parents and children that they will be unprepared and unable to help save the life of those they love. The stories focus on how lucky these victims were to have family or emergency service personnel who knew what they were doing. Will the grandparents be able to save their grandchild's life? They can if they know how to perform emergency resuscitation.[20] Will the young boy be able to help save his father's life after a barbecue fire? He can if he knows that he must keep his father in cold water until the paramedics arrive.[21] This is where the *999* safety information and videos come in. We are given a step-by-step guide to what to do if someone has been burned, and we are told about the *999 Family Safety Video*, which is 'packed full of tips for how to keep your family safe when you are out and about.'[22] The programme also runs a *999 Lifesaver*

---

17 *999* (8 Apr. 1994; 19 May 1998; 12 Apr. 1996; all at 9.30 p.m.).
18 *999* (8 Apr. 1994, 9.30 p.m.).
19 *999* (22 Apr. 1994, 9.30 p.m.).
20 Ibid.
21 *999* (19 May 1998, 9.30 p.m.).
22 The *999* safety videos and booklets are advertised in every programme; this reference is taken from *999* (19 May 1998, at the later time of 10.30 p.m. after *Crimewatch*).

Roadshow, and urges viewers to call and reserve a free place, so that they will also be able to help save lives when an emergency arises.

In this reality programme the British emergency services are shown to be both professional and brave. Those members of the public who are called upon to help save a life are shown to be inventive and brave—they are not trained professionals but they can remain calm in a crisis, and often, through a stroke of luck or ingenuity, they can ensure someone's survival against all odds. This message to the public is to be commended, but the use of reconstruction techniques derived from entertainment formats, together with the insistent playing on the fears of parents and children, raise questions about the balance that has been struck between the public service aspects of the programme's informational content and its evident desire for ratings.

Blues and Twos and Coppers

After *999* proved that British emergency services could attract large audiences, companies in the ITV network such as Carlton and LWT were quick to schedule new reality shows at peak family viewing times. Roger Bolton, head of factual programming for Thames TV, had this comment to make in 1992 about the success of *999*: 'The danger is that you get swamped by inferior imitations, and that other forms of factual programming will be sacrificed. . . . There is a risk of crime shows and programmes like *999* becoming the only factual prime-time series.'[23] Certainly, if we look at the amount of reality programming at the end of the 1990s, we can see that Bolton's comment is a prescient one. Even as early as 1993 *Blues and Twos*, made by Carlton, was categorized as an 'inferior imitation' of *999*. Victor Lewis-Smith (1993) called it a 'disaster in the making' and went on to say of the show 'this was voyeurism at its most despicable and, whatever excuse Carlton offers, it won't be good enough'.

In the promotional information for *Blues and Twos* it was claimed that the programme 'goes to the heart of the nation's emergency services—the men and women on the front line who respond to the nation's 999 calls'. Shown before the 9 p.m. watershed, at 8.30, *Blues and Twos* followed Carlton's earlier success in 1992 with a reality programme about London's helicopter emergency service, which attracted over 11 million viewers. This time Carlton used miniature cameras placed on the uniforms of emergency service personnel to give a 'real insight' into a range of Britain's emergency services—paramedics in Belfast, firefighters in Gerrard's Cross, the Solent Coastguard. The series producer, John

---

23 Dugdale, 'Not the "Nine o'Clock News" '.

Pettman, said: 'We've been on the front line with the professionals, men and women who have no doubts about putting other people's lives and livelihoods before their own. Watching them put their skills and training into practice proved not only very exhilarating, but on countless occasions, highly emotional.'[24]

We can see here the similarities and differences between this and *999*. Like *999*, *Blues and Twos* focuses on emergency services around Britain, and, like *999*, it highlights the drama and danger that these professional people experience every day. Unlike *999*, *Blues and Twos* emphasizes the 'real' footage that is used; watching this programme is like being on the 'front line', just as a war reporter might be, and this means that the depictions of real crises in this show are far more immediate than what we might see in the reconstructions that take place in *999*.

This 'real TV' is advertised as exhilarating and 'highly emotional'. Full-page features on *Blues and Twos* appeared in *TV Times*, with headlines such as 'The Flying Doctors: TV follows London's daring air ambulance service with exclusive film of the dramatic weekend when the IRA bombed the capital.' In this show we are not told beforehand what emergencies take place and so there is an element of suspense. For example, when a motorbike paramedic races to attend to an injured pedestrian, we do not know what to expect until the camera arrives at the scene. Is there substantial loss of blood? Will the pedestrian survive? It turns out that the pedestrian is a tourist who has been knocked over by a cyclist. She is bruised and in shock, but has suffered only minor injuries. The cyclist and passers-by show their relief as the paramedic helps lift the injured woman into an ambulance and she is taken to safety. This example reveals how little narration there is in *Blues and Twos*, the show relying upon actual footage to tell the story. This means that editing becomes very important to the identity of the programme. Part of its exhilarating feel comes from the build-up of suspense. For example, in an episode about rescue paramedics, there are forty-four shots of the motorbike paramedic on his way to an emergency in an underground station. There are shots of the street speeding by, close-ups of the paramedic, and long shots of the bike travelling through London traffic. Some of the shots that the miniature camera takes offer interesting perspectives; as the paramedic races to his destination, we see Pall Mall at an unusual angle, with two hands at the edge of the frame guiding us through the archway. This is high-powered film-making, and *Blues and Twos* makes it its business to use short, sharp editing and a succession of emergency events that keep the narrative moving forward.

24 Promotional information about *Blues and Twos* (London: Carlton, 1992).

What is striking about *Blues and Twos* is that it is open about its intention to entertain, and this is both one of the reasons for the criticism it receives and also a key to its success against rivals such as *999*. Large numbers of motorbikes, helicopters, ambulances, and police cars are involved in immediate response calls, where reaching a destination in a short space of time is a matter of life and death. These high-speed responses are filmed in such a way that they appear to imitate crime dramas. For example, a London motorbike paramedic is called to help the victims of a bomb attack on the Israeli embassy in Kensington; he must race to the scene to help the injured; we are told another bomb may have been found, and the motorbike paramedic arrives just as the police have cordoned off the street. The stylistic techniques used here, the fast editing, the build-up of suspense through the use of narration and the sequence of the images, combine to create a real-life drama that is as, if not more, entertaining than crime fiction.

When the Thames Valley Police are called to investigate a suspected death, they approach the house of an old-age pensioner with some trepidation. They open the window from the outside and immediately notice a smell. It turns out that the owner is alive, but has been unable to eat or use the bathroom for over three weeks. 'I'm 89,' he tells the officer, who gallantly responds, 'You don't look a day over 60.' The man is taken away in an ambulance. The camera pans the front room, and focuses on a bare electric light. An officer switches the light off, and we are told that the man 'never did return home'. This is poignant drama, but it is also disturbing because it is real. The Broadcasting Standards Commission upheld a complaint about this episode because it crossed the boundary between 'information, assistance and exploitation' in a 'film being shown on prime-time television as part of an entertainment programme'. Part of the concern over this episode of *Blues and Twos* is the way in which the programme depicts real events in such a way that they appear dramatic and 'entertaining'. The death of the 89-year-old man is a tragic event, and yet the programme-makers choose to highlight the drama of his life and death: his flat resembles the interior locations of the Hollywood serial-killer film *Se7en* (David Fincher 1996); the metaphor of the bare light bulb signifies his lonely existence, and when the light is extinguished, this also serves to symbolize his death, which occurred three weeks later in hospital. These stylistic devices are traditionally associated more with fictional drama than with serious documentary.

The fact that *Blues and Twos* followed ITV's *The Bill* (Thames Television, 1984–) on a Thursday night should tell us something about what kind of audience the programme-makers would like to attract. They are offering a reality-based show that is aimed at a family audience, an audience that may well have watched *The Bill* first. *Blues and Twos* clearly states that it is a factual programme; like *999*, it is anxious to ensure that audiences are in no doubt that what they are seeing is real. While the opening credits roll, we are told: 'Everything you are about to see in this programme is real, real events filmed as they happened.' But what *Blues and Twos* delivers is an exciting half-hour programme, with high-speed pursuits and life-and-death situations that are highly dramatic in nature and which also share some similarity with the type of fictional stories that take place at Sun Hill police station in *The Bill*.

Blues and Twos is not interested in family safety, but instead with entertaining the family. It achieves this by borrowing some of the techniques of the fictional programmes it is competing with. Though it avoids reconstructions, it uses its documentary footage to build up characters of the kind that audiences can relate to, as in drama programmes, so that the emergency service personnel become the stars of the show. We follow the same personnel throughout the half-hour slot, seeing what they see, and getting a glimpse at what they must do in order to protect lives and uphold the law. These personnel are the stars, but they are also real people. This mixture of the ordinary and the extraordinary is something that has been borrowed from the 'other news' of the tabloids (Langer 1998: 148–9), with their preference for the 'human interest' story, and from crime drama series such as *The Bill*. Paramedics and police officers are shown to be ordinary people, capable of feeling scared or saddened by what they see, and they are also shown to be exceptional in the way that they handle potentially life-threatening situations. When two police officers arrive at a road accident, they are visibly shaken—there is blood, badly smashed cars; as one officer says sorrowfully into his radio, it 'doesn't look good'.[25] And yet they must get on with the job, and it is the function of *Blues and Twos* that it depicts Britain's emergency services in a way that emphasizes the bravery and professionalism and the ordinariness of these people.

We can see this even more clearly with the show *Coppers*, which models itself on its American counterpart, *Cops* (Fox, 1989–). This programme is also shown before the 9 p.m. watershed, at 8.30 on Tuesday evening, Sky One's reality TV night. It is usually flanked by other reality programmes such as *Speed*, a British-made show, or *Cops*, or *When Animals Attack* (Fox 1996–), another American reality programme. Very little has been written about *Coppers*, perhaps because it is on Sky One and not deemed 'worthy' of the type

25 *Blues and Twos* (22 Feb. 1996, 8.30 p.m.).

of criticism that terrestrial reality shows are subject to.[26] *Coppers* follows different police units around the country, and because it is concerned with the police, there are fewer life-or-death situations, but instead a steady stream of criminal incidents, some of which are solved and some not. Thus, like *Blues and Twos*, it portrays real events as they happened, but *Coppers* appears to adopt a less intrusive approach to its subject. The camera records and we watch; there is very little high-speed editing or stylized camera technique. This is fly-on-the-wall documentary, convincing in the very humdrum nature of what it shows.

For example, one episode follows Southend-on-Sea police on an August bank holiday weekend.[27] We begin with two policemen running to their car—an exciting opening—but when they arrive at the scene of the crime, they find nothing but a group of drunken teenagers and their mother, who have been thrown out of a pub. The main priority of the two policemen is to establish what has happened, but the family are shouting and gesticulating, and in the end the police handcuff one of them and walk them to a police car. A teenager shouts, 'They're arresting mom,' before being taken down to the police station himself. Next, the policemen investigate credit card theft, and find the thief in a local bed and breakfast, partially clothed, with credit cards stuffed down his underpants. This is real life, and real life is not always exciting. The medium-paced editing, the fade to black when another incident is followed up, the way in which the policemen talk calmly to the camera, all add to the overall effect. Sometimes a drama occurs; one man threatens to jump off a building because his girlfriend has left him, and we see the officer successfully talk him down, but it isn't long before the same officer is arresting another drunken man on this bank holiday weekend.

Coppers can be seen to be more 'accurate' in its depiction of the work of Britain's policemen and women than *999* or *Blues and Twos*. When *Coppers* spends a week with Thames Water Patrol, we see them find a dead body. We see how long it takes the divers to search for the body in the River Thames, how awkward it is to lift the body out of the water, and how cold everyone gets waiting for the procedure to be over.[28] What this means in terms of family entertainment is an interesting question. Here, people are shown to die, and there is nothing the emergency services can do about it. When someone throws themselves into the Thames and there is no one to jump in and save them, they die. Similarly, when someone gets drunk and is thrown out of a pub, they are arrested. Indeed,

26 See Nichols (1994) for a detailed discussion of *Cops*.
27 *Coppers* (26 May 1998, 8.30 p.m.).
28 *Coppers* (2 June 1998, 8.30 p.m.).

when a member of the public is caught on camera under the influence of alcohol, they are invariably presented as foolish.

The 'Real' Story These reality shows are aimed at a family audience, and the message is that life is short and we must appreciate it while we can. *999* encourages viewers to be ever vigilant in protecting their family and to be prepared at all times. It shows that accidents can happen at any time, especially to children. *Blues and Twos*, on the other hand, encourages viewers to experience vicarious pleasure in the bravery of emergency service personnel. The family is made to feel safe in the knowledge that there are skilled professionals who care for the community. *Coppers* encourages viewers to witness the day-to-day activities of the police. Here the ordinariness of crime serves as a reminder to the family audience that criminals are not heroes and that there is little reward in breaking the law.

However, what is absent from these reality programmes is the 'real' story of Britain's emergency services. The economic and recruitment problems of the National Health Service, or the evidence of racism and corruption in the Metropolitan Police, are not part of the agenda of reality programmes. High-profile coverage of cases such as the Stephen Lawrence murder investigation, or events at Bristol Hospital's children's unit, has made the public aware of serious problems in health care and law and order.[29] In February 1999 the Stephen Lawrence case was dramatized on both ITV and BBC in the same week.[30] The fact that such high-profile cases have been dramatized on TV suggests that the 'reality' of Britain's police force is thought to be a good subject for television entertainment. *The Murder of Stephen Lawrence* (Vanson Productions/Granada, 18 February 1999), adopted a subdued documentary style and chose to emphasize the reconstruction, rather than drama, of the case. For example, the depiction of the attack lasts only a few seconds, and no details are shown. Much of the reconstruction takes

29 Stephen Lawrence was murdered in a racist attack on 22 Apr. 1993, and the subsequent murder investigation failed to apprehend the murderers, even though there was strong evidence to arrest five white youths. Two doctors at Bristol Hospital's children's unit were found to have undertaken high-risk operations; an unusually high percentage of the children died in open-heart surgery. For coverage of the Lawrence investigation, see *Guardian*, 11 June 1998, 2, 3, 7. For coverage of the Bristol Hospital's children's unit story, see newspapers on 30 May 1998—the story made headlines in most national newspapers. Reality shows such as *Jimmy's* (Yorkshire, 1987–) and *Children's Hospital* (BBC, 1984–) are concerned with high-risk operations on young children.

30 When ITV transmitted the drama-documentary *The Murder of Stephen Lawrence* an NHS commercial was shown in the advertising breaks. It depicted a young girl's traumatized face, and informed the public that the NHS has improved pay and working conditions but is still short of nurses to care for people like 'Rachel'.

place in the Lawrences' home, as they come to terms with their grief and anger at the Metropolitan Police, and title cards tell us the exact time-frame, as the weeks, months, and years go by in the police investigation. Similarly, *The Colour of Justice* (BBC2, 21 February 1999) is a reconstruction of the Lawrence inquiry and takes place in a courtroom, and yet, as Jane Edwards points out, 'the subdued atmosphere of the inquiry bears little resemblance to the average courtroom drama. No tears, no breakthroughs, just conflicting evidence that the viewer has to sort out for themselves.'[31]

Very little research has been done into what audiences have to say about drama-documentaries or reality programming, but the British Film Institute's Audience Tracking Study does contain empirical research on reality programming in Britain.[32] Briefly, the impression that people have of British emergency services is that they are dedicated and efficient. Viewers talk about how they find reality TV shows like *999* both exciting and informative. They praise the factual information offered to families who may be able to cope better in hazardous situations because of seeing emergency personnel in action. And they talk about the fact that watching reality programmes can make them appreciate life. Indeed, there is evidence to suggest that when viewers tune in to watch programmes such as *999*, they expect an edited version of reality that guarantees a message of hope. Viewers know that the real world is not necessarily like this: they are aware of NHS cuts and corruption in the police force, but they wish to see a positive depiction of emergency services, who are shown to care for the community.

Thus, viewers can see the 'real' story of Britain's emergency services in fictional drama, but reality programmes such as *999* or *Blues and Twos* present an unproblematic picture of health care and law and order. This may seem a contradiction. The documentary tradition has always been praised for its 'realist' credentials, and yet here it is the drama-doc which can be seen to be tackling social problems in a realistic manner. For many critics of reality programming, its sensational format has blurred the boundaries between information and entertainment to such an extent that it can no longer be associated with the aims of the traditional documentary. However, pioneer documentary-maker John Grierson's commitment to the British documentary as a national educational tool does not seem so far removed from the agenda of reality programmes such as *999*. Grierson's contribution to the public

31 'Inquire Within', *Time Out*, 17–24 Feb. 1999, 183. *The Colour of Justice*, an edited version of the actual inquiry into the death of Stephen Lawrence, is a television play, first produced at the Tricycle Theatre in London.
32 The BFI Audience Tracking Study is a longitudinal ethnographic study on television audiences and everyday life. See also David Gauntlett and Annette Hill, *TV Living: Television, Culture and Everyday Life* (London: Routledge, 1999).

relations industry in pre- and post-war Britain showed that, for him, the documentary could be used as a way to promote citizenship and social responsibility.[33] Reality programmes about emergency services also have a clear public relations agenda. These programmes are committed to educating families and promoting a positive message of health care and law and order in Britain.

Conclusion

British reality programmes appear to be both popular and successful in their treatment of crime and crisis. They use different techniques to portray 'reality', but the message 'There but for the grace of God go I' seems to be a universal one that the viewing public understand. Critics of reality programming are dismissive of the sensational and 'tabloid TV' format that many of these programmes adopt, but the fact that such programmes regularly attract 12 million viewers should alert us to the possibility that something other than 'ghoul TV' is taking place here. We have seen that a great deal of care and attention is devoted to the making of these programmes, and the construction of Britain's emergency services as caring and professional sends a particular message to the general public. *These* emergency services do not suffer from lack of morale, or cuts to their annual budget. *They* are not subject to criticism, nor accusations of racial discrimination, but are praised by the programme-makers and by the real people who agree to take part. The general public, and in particular the family audience, are encouraged to see that they are always at risk, that they always need protection, and that without the dedication and bravery of emergency service personnel, many children and adults would not be alive and well today. The message is, our taxpayers' money has been well spent.

References

Brunsdon, C., and Morley, D. (1978), *Everyday Television: 'Nationwide'* (London: BFI).

Corner, J. (1995), *Television Form and Public Address* (London: Edward Arnold).

Dahlgren, P., and Sparks, C. (1992), *Journalism and Popular Culture* (London: Sage).

Dempsey, J. (1991), 'Hot Genre Gluts TV Market', *Variety*, 3 June 1991, 32.

Gunter, B. (1997), *Measuring Bias on Television* (Luton: John Libbey).

Hartley, J. (1982), *Understanding News* (London: Methuen).

33 See Jacquie L'Etang, 'Grierson's Influence on the Formation of Emergent Values of the Public Relations Industry in Britain', paper delivered at the conference 'Breaking the Boundaries', University of Stirling, 28–31 Jan. 1999.

Kilborn, R., and Izod, J. (1997), *An Introduction to TV Documentary: Confronting Reality* (Manchester: Manchester University Press).

Langer, J. (1998), *Tabloid Television: Popular Journalism and the 'Other News'* (London: Routledge).

Lewis-Smith, V. (1993), 'A Disaster in the Making', *Evening Standard*, 23 Nov. 1993, 53.

Naughton, J. (1994), 'The Rise of Ghoul-on-the-Wall TV', *Daily Telegraph*, 16 Sept. 1994, 23.

Nichols, B. (1994), *Blurred Boundaries: Questions of Meaning in Contemporary Culture* (Bloomington: Indiana University Press).

Porter, H. (1992), 'Should we Indulge this Lust for Gore?', *Evening Standard*, 2 July 1992, 9.

Rodwell, L. (1992), 'TV Crime Shows on Trial', *Daily Telegraph*, 24 Oct. 1992, 18–19.

Schlesinger, P. (1978). *Putting 'Reality' Together: BBC News* (London: Constable).

—— and Tumber, H. (1993), 'Fighting the War against Crime', *British Journal of Criminology*, 33/1: 19–32.

Thynne, J. (1992), 'Rescue of the Ratings', *Daily Telegraph*, 6 Aug. 1992, 25.

10

'Ill news comes often on the back of worse'

John Eldridge

> Living by proxy in the half light,
> Items of news slip by like flakes of food in a fish tank.
> Between the un-seating of a royal jockey
> And the bland insincerities of talking heads
> We see, for an instant, the awkward dead
> Heaped carelessly at the corner of a street
> Like brushwood piled for burning.
> This wood is green, unsuitable for firing.
> Sap still comes from the stricken limbs of striplings,
> Broken boys and girls
> With faces made anonymous by death.
> Only a tear in the knee of a pair of jeans,
> A shoeless foot unnaturally bent,
> A rucked up sweat shirt revealing pitiful flesh,
> Reminds us that they once possessed a singularity
> Beyond the comprehension of the killers
> Who stare at the camera lens with eyes
> As blank as bottle tops.
>
> ('An Item of News', Ewan MacColl)

WHEN WE in the Glasgow University Media Group (GUMG) called our first three books on television news *Bad News* (1976), *More Bad News* (1980), and *Really Bad News* (1982), we were, of course, being a touch mischievous. The binary contrast good news–bad news is deeply embedded in our history and culture. We are all familiar with the injunction not to blame the messenger for the bad news. But in an age of mass media the messengers are typically contracted to powerful institutions in press and broadcasting. The stories they tell and the how, when, where,

First published in C. Arthur (ed.), *Religion and the Media* (Cardiff: University of Wales Press, 1993), 146–61.

and why of the telling are an important part of our media culture. In scrutinizing those stories, which are communicated to us day by day, we begin to learn about news values. The processes of creating, transmitting, and receiving messages are not just a secondary feature in modern society, they are part of the warp and woof of it. What takes place in and through these processes is, therefore, not simply a comment on social reality but part of it.

The case of television news—a specific form of mass communication—was and remains an important site of study. The reason for this is that one particular value is formally required from news broadcasts: impartiality. Clearly, this is different from the press, where editorializing is built into the activity. Impartiality, by contrast, is typically seen as the cornerstone of good public service broadcasting, so far as news is concerned. The rationale for this is to resist the capture of this news medium by a particular interest group, so that it will not be regarded as partisan or propagandist. This, indeed, is seen both as the guarantee of its reliability and trustworthiness and also as the source of its authority and objectivity.

However, I want to argue that the concept of impartiality is inherently problematic. Indeed, however worthy their motives, those who seek to base their claim to credibility by appeal to the concept of impartiality will constantly find themselves immersed in challenges and attacks. Seasoned broadcasters know standard ripostes to some of this: we know our own business and should be left to get on with it; or, since we are attacked from all sides, we have got it just about right. Moreover, to replace impartial, objective news with partial and subjective news would surely be to lose one's credibility at a stroke. I want to suggest that there is another way of coming at this which dissolves a spurious dichotomy.

What does adherence to the concept of impartiality mean in practice? Let us recall the way this impinged on John Reith (later Lord Reith) in the early pre-television days of the BBC. In his capacity as first director-general of the BBC, he promoted the view that broadcasting could help to develop an informed and enlightened opinion on the issues of the day. His position, while clearly paternalist, was one which explicitly resisted the idea that the BBC was there simply to relay the instructions and views of the government of the day. That was precisely why he favoured the setting up of a public corporation rather than have it working under the aegis of a government department. He wanted the BBC to be free from state interference and political interference. But he also wanted it not to be subject to the normal commercial pressures. Within such a space and within these institutional arrangements, public service broadcasting could, he believed, flourish. So it was, he thought, that a public corporation could serve the public interest with the state's role being confined to the operation of the licensing system. In this regard the public interest was seen as the guiding consideration in contradistinction to private interests.

But from the beginning the worm was in the apple. The BBC was not immune from political pressure as the Reith diaries make clear. In time of controversy and political conflict this is particularly so. At the time of the 1926 General Strike Reith records that the government was going to set up its own newspaper, the *British Gazette*, edited from the war office. According to Reith, the editor expected to see the BBC news as an offshoot of that, which Reith characteristically refused to accept. An argument developed within the Cabinet, with Winston Churchill insisting that the instrument of radio should be used to the best possible advantage by the government. This view did not prevail in straightforward propagandist terms. Reith's diary entry for 11 May shows a more subtle policy:

> The Cabinet were to make a decision at long last about the BBC. Davidson was going to it. I primed him up with all the arguments and he came to see me at 7 15. As he was smiling broadly I knew it was all right. The decision was not a definite one, but at any rate we are not going to be commandeered. The Cabinet decision is really a negative one. They want to be able to say that they did not commandeer us, but they know that they can trust us not to be really impartial. Davidson came around again at 9.15 and we were supposed to draft a notice defining the BBC position. I wanted the inconsistencies in our acts so far squared up, setting us right with the other side. Davidson, however, thought the Cabinet would only agree to a statement that we could do nothing to help the Strike since it had been declared illegal. This does not seem to me to be straight.[1]

As Reith pointed out, the BBC was in a very awkward position. He was clear that to turn the BBC into a propaganda arm of the government would have destroyed its credibility, and even more so if it had been commandeered. In seeking to resist that, he tried in vain to square the circle. His declared sense of loyalty to the prime minister cut across his uneasiness that impartiality was a cloak for supporting the government's position—at the very least by keeping other views off the air. What Reith had to come to terms with, albeit with a bad conscience, were the interests of the state in a moment of crisis. The decision on the part of the government as to how to play it was a matter of strategy and tactics.

What does happen when events that take place in the world are conflict-riven and controversial as so many are? We are given in the

---

1 Lord Reith, *The Reith Diaries*, ed. C. Stuart (London: Collins, 1975), 96.

press and broadcasting news stories about them. Let us remember that the journalists telling these stories on television share an occupational background with press journalists: they may even move from one medium to another. They attend the same press conferences and relate to one another's output. What emerges to count as the news of the day is itself a cultural construct. In the case of television news, a whole range of professional conventions in the presentation operate. These are not unchangeable, as archive film of old news programmes show, but there are established continuities. Let us recall some: the use of music and established iconic forms at the beginning and end of bulletins; the newscaster(s) as providing continuity (sometimes bringing to the programme their own celebrity status); the use of film to delineate the event or graphics to reference it; the use of correspondents to report, describe, interview, and interpret what is going on; the use of experts to comment (which nowadays may incorporate the reporter: 'our economics–political editor, Peter Jay–John Cole'); the boundary markers—headlines and devices for turning from one item to the next; and the overall 'ordered' structure of the news bulletin.

These activities, complex though they are in terms of organization and technology and often taking place with considerable time constraints, are grounded in professional routines and practices. Indeed, without such constitutive rules by which news of the world can be made meaningful to us—organized, encoded, framed—the daily production of news would be impossible. This output, its nature and significance, not least in relation to the values of impartiality and objectivity, is what we have attempted to examine in the *Bad News* and later studies. An important part of the research strategy was to consider, through quantitative and qualitative analysis, what these routines and practices produced to make up the product we know as television news and, more particularly, to look at the treatment of issues which were socially or politically divisive such as the state of the economy, industrial conflict, or questions of defence and disarmament.

In 1975, with a Labour government in power, we showed how television newsrooms adopted a number of strategies for concretizing and dealing with economic affairs. Central to this was a constant and ongoing assessment of the government's agreements with the trade union movement, known, in the parlance of the time, as the social contract. This was an attempt by the government to set out guidelines for collective bargaining in the period following the previous Conservative administration's attempts to impose an incomes policy. Not only did this concept provide the thematic frame within which stories about the economy were covered, but the containment of wages was presented as the main instrument for the control of inflation. Thus many of the industry wage agreements signed during the first half of 1975 were reported on the news in terms of whether they were within or outside the terms of the social contract. In 1992 we do not routinely hear about wage settlements but in 1975 all the major settlements were reported within this frame. The identification of these matters as newsworthy is an interesting indicator of a particular social and political climate but it also tended to be from a definite perspective. Whether one agreed with that perspective or not, it was not value-free.

Take, for example, the case of a wage negotiation between the miners and the National Coal Board. As the reports of the negotiations developed, we had the BBC's industrial news reporter telling us that the deal was outside the social contract, even though the parties concerned said it was within the terms. And, at the end, the BBC newscaster summed up the position: 'The miners through their negotiators put the Coal Board out of its misery this week by accepting a large pay offer. After some haggling the offer crept pound by pound to the miners' own demands' (BBC2, 15 March 1975, 6:50 p.m.). Employers offered, workers demanded. The employers were put out of their *misery*. The pay offer was a *large* one. The story was told in a particular way. The pay negotiations were presented in the language of battle and as an 'acid test' for the social contract. Through the narrative we learn more about the journalists' assumptions regarding an agreement which saw the advent of a £3,000-a-year basic rate for some miners and £41 a week for surface workers. Analysis of the narrative showed that while some of the participants in the negotiations were able to comment, explain, and justify, this was typically within highly structured conventions of interviewing. There were, moreover, more general assumptions about the role of trade unions and the nature of the economic crisis. Thus within the overall frame of the social contract was a series of strike stories. The connecting links were about workers and trade unions who were causing inflation, whose disruptive activities were the cause of our economic ills and therefore against the national interest.

The point to be made about this is that news is from a distinct perspective. In so far as this was the dominant tendency in the coverage of industrial and economic questions, not only did it represent a particular ideological view, but it also effectively excluded other kinds of explanation—those which had to do with concerns about investment, the role of management, education, training, and the structural problems of the economy in a world context, after the oil crisis of the early 1970s. Whatever our opinions of these stories, they are restricted accounts, given that other accounts were publicly available. In other words, our analysis concluded that news accounts were limited and narrow. Such restricted news was, we said, bad news. Not only did it present stories within a dominant interpretative framework, but it did so from a position that laid claim to impartiality.

In his review of *More Bad News* Raymond Williams commented:

> Let us face it then: the news has been very bad lately. But it is very difficult to be sure how much of this badness has been in the events themselves, and how much in their intense and relentless interpretation by the authorities: a one-sided polemic which I cannot remember being at this pitch since the late Forties. . . . To be sure, we cannot draw any firm line between events and their presentation. A very large number of the events now presented are in fact interpretations, by a small group of highly privileged voices, directly transmitted or read out by hired celebrities. The privilege of such voices would matter less if it were not also in the leading cases, the privilege of command of men and resources.[2]

He goes on to point out that as events become the subject of news reports, even when the evidence for their occurrence has been reliably tested, long-standing problems of narration remain, including the identity of the narrator, his/her authority, point of view, assumed relationship to audience, and the possible wider purposes in selecting and narrating the events in the way chosen. In everyday encounters when we hear stories we learn to ask such questions.

> Yet it seems that we have only to ask them about a broadcasting service or a newspaper to produce outraged cries about an assault on professional competence and independence, or to provoke dark hints, which at least sometimes are surely projections, about a conspiracy to interfere with freedom of news and indeed to manipulate or censor it.[3]

There are, I think, a number of ways in which the media critic can respond to the media professionals who manifest such concerns. What can we reasonably expect from a television news service in a society that embraces democratic ideas? We expect the information to be reliable and accurate. This, after all, is the *sine qua non* of professional journalism and the touchstone of its integrity. At the simplest level, when the football results are given, we expect them to be accurate and have good reason to think that they are. They can be corroborated by many witnesses, whatever their view of the outcome. Any mistake in conveying the results can be quickly corrected. It is helpful to take a simple example since it reminds us that

2 Raymond Williams, 'Isn't the News Terrible?', in Raymond Williams, *What I Came to Say* (London: Hutchinson, 1980) 114.

3 Ibid 115.

issues of truth are involved. So while, for reasons already touched upon, objectivity in news narratives is problematic, the alternative is not an undisciplined subjectivity where anything goes and one account is as good or as bad as another. Why these facts should be reported raises quite other questions of their presumed significance to the audience. And once these facts become embedded in accounts of matches, then we are into a narrative which character-istically will have its judgements, interpretations, and sometimes speculation.

If, as the adage has it, journalism is the first draft of history, we can appreciate that, as with historical study itself, selection and interpretation of facts will take place and we are dealing not with unassailable facts marshalled incontrovertibly together but with provisional accounts. Indeed, the epistemological basis on which these accounts rest can vary. We, as readers, hearers, or viewers, will not necessarily be aware of this.

In their paper, 'Accidental News: The Great Oil Spill'[4] Molotch and Lester describe how President Nixon visited the beach at Santa Barbara in January 1969 and stated that it had recovered from a massive oil spill. This was duly reported in the national media of the United States despite the fact that there was plenty of evidence, which the journalists could see and smell, that it was not so. In their view this was an example of professional news services being sub-ordinate to political interests. If they are correct, then this has the character of cover-up. Unless we are there and have direct experi-ence of that situation—we can see and smell the oil slick—or unless someone, as it were, breaks cover or leaks an alternative version, we have no independent way of evaluating that story.

The above example, if typical, would fit in with a conspiracy view of the media—that they operate as servants of the powerful. As a general theory of the role of the media, I think this is unconvincing. But it does draw our attention to the issue of verifi-cation. For example, in the Falklands War ITN lunchtime news showed some film taken by an Argentinian amateur cameraman. The defence correspondent worked on the assumption that all the film was taken on 1 May, when, according to the ministry of defence, no British planes were lost. This is what he said:

> But the attack had been concentrated on the airfield [i.e. Port Stanley] where it is assumed these pictures of wreckage were taken. This roundel is not in the colours carried by the British Harriers and may have come from an Argentine plane destroyed on the ground. The variety and totality of wreckage scattered

---

4 Harvey L. Molotch and Marilyn Lester, 'Accidental News: The Great Oil Spill', *American Journal of Sociology*, 81 (1975), 235–60.

around the airfield suggest British reports of inflicting severe damage to aircraft and military equipment were true. One piece of wreckage which had the word 'Harrier' on it was unidentifiable. Britain says she lost no aircraft during this raid though one Harrier was shot down three days later near the other airport at Goose Green. These would seem to be aircraft wheels, although it's not yet clear what type of plane they came from.[5]

The film actually showed the colours of the roundel, which were unmistakably British, the unique undercarriage design of the Harrier, its name—Harrier—and its serial number. Because the correspondent believed it was Port Stanley and not Goose Green, he was unable to accept this evidence and actually used British wreckage to stress the success of British bombing! Now this was not a cover-up. It was a mistake. Indeed, although there was no apology for it, the evening news used the same film with the following commentary: 'The cameraman was also taken to the Goose Green airstrip, where a British Harrier jet was shot down last Tuesday. The Royal Navy roundel showed through the film of paint.'[6]

What was happening? It was difficult to get news, let alone film, out of the Falklands, and there was in practice heavy reliance on ministry of defence briefings. They had been stressing the success of the bombing raids on Port Stanley airport. Part of the film ITN received was of Port Stanley and part of Goose Green. Given the success theme, the correspondent could not believe the evidence before him and actually turned a failure into a success. Ironically, the success theme about the bombing of Port Stanley was to bring other news reporting problems to the surface. The ministry of defence stated that the bombing on 1 May had severely cratered the runway at the airport. BBC and ITN news embraced this account. ITN reported: 'The Vulcan's task was to pockmark the runway and it did it with 1000 lb bombs, ten tons of explosives.'[7] This was accompanied by a graphic of the runway with the pockmarks circled along the length of it. Yet eventually this was shown to be inaccurate. Gradually another story emerged that the airport was still operational. It is not a simple matter of cover-up news. In *War and Peace News* we came to the following conclusion:

Once having established a view of the Port Stanley raids—a destroyed runway and cut-off garrison—the news found it difficult to go beyond it. New facts and information were fitted into this framework. The constraint seemed to emanate from the

5 ITN Lunchtime News, 9 May 1982, 12 noon.
6 ITN News, 9 May 1982, 6.50 p.m.
7 ITN News, 1 May 1982, 9.55 p.m.

need for broadcasters to maintain their image as purveyors of reliable, balanced and objective information. Journalists found it difficult to admit they had made mistakes. Following the ceasefire, TV news expressed surprise concerning the condition of the airfield. The subject was not considered in any detail. In *Task Force South*, a BBC production in August, viewers were finally told what British troops had heard before the final push on Port Stanley. In it we see shots of a briefing for troops. A soldier comments: 'The RAF missed the fucking runway . . . bombs all around it but there are thirteen aircraft, some of which are definitely Pucara, parked on the aprons around Stanley airfield. There's also another report that they have managed to reinforce themselves from the mainland' (BBC1, 12 August 1982). This piece of film was absent from the pictures of the advances on Stanley which were first shown on British TV on 25 June.[8]

Our general conclusion about television news coverage of the Falklands War was that both BBC and ITN kept close to official sources. Where, we may ask, does impartiality figure in this? In some respects we get a rerun of the Reith difficulty, discussed earlier. So, the director-general of the BBC told an internal meeting of the news and current affairs committee that he anticipated the BBC would come under pressure, as it had during the Suez Crisis to 'conform to the national interest'. He accepted that there was a legitimate point in this but the difficulty was to define precisely what 'the national interest' was. Clearly, he argued, the BBC should be careful not to do anything to imperil military operations or diplomatic negotiations, but it should report accurately and faithfully the arguments arising within British society at all levels. This in practice didn't happen. The director-general's remarks were made at the beginning of April; by 11 May the BBC's political editor was telling the committee that 'the BBC was most vulnerable to criticism over its limited coverage of the internal debate in the country, though many Tories would regard any coverage of this as pure speculation because the dissenting views were being kept so private'. Meanwhile another senior broadcaster 'reminded the meeting that the BBC was the *British* Broadcasting Corporation. It was now clear that a larger section of the public shared this view and he believed it was an unnecessary irritation to stick to the detached style.'

Nevertheless, as has been well documented, the Tory government was very critical of the BBC's coverage of the war.[9] BBC's *Newsnight*

8 Glasgow University Media Group, *War and Peace News* (Milton Keynes: Open University Press, 1985), 91.

9 See e.g. Ibid; Robert Harris, *Gotcha! The Media, the Government and the Falklands Crisis* (London: Faber, 1983); Derrik Mercer, Geoff Mungham and Kevin Williams, *The Fog of War* (London: Heinemann, 1987).

programme was criticized for giving the appearance of being too detached, and an episode of the BBC's flagship current affairs programme *Panorama* was the subject of heavy criticism from sections of the Conservative Party. This particular programme, broadcast on 10 May 1982, included some dissenting views on government policy, alongside those of Cecil Parkinson, a member of the war Cabinet. Conservative MPs complained that some of the programmes on the BBC appeared to give the impression of being pro-Argentinian and anti-British, while others appeared to suggest that this was an issue over which the BBC could remain loftily neutral. A senior Conservative, Sally Oppenheimer, referred next day at prime minister's question time in the House of Commons to the *Panorama* programme as 'an odious, subversive travesty in which Michael Cockrell and other BBC reporters dishonoured the right to freedom of speech in this country'. In her reply the prime minister indicated that she shared the concern that had been expressed. She continued:

I know how strongly many people feel that the case for our country is not being put with sufficient vigour on certain—I do not say all—BBC programmes. The Chairman of the BBC has assured us, and has said in vigorous terms, that the BBC is not neutral on this point, and I hope his words will be heeded by the many who have responsibilities for standing up for our task force, our boys, our people and the cause of democracy.

The difference between this situation and the Reith episode over the General Strike was that it was much more exposed to public view. The *Panorama* programme was called 'Traitorama' by the *Sun* newspaper (echoing some of the comments in the House of Commons). After a stormy meeting between the chairman and director-general of the BBC and the backbench media committee of the BBC, Alasdair Milne (then director-general) told the *London Evening Standard* in an interview on 12 May 1982:

The notion that we are traitors is outrageous. There is no one in the BBC who does not agree that the Argentinians committed aggression. But this is not total war. One day we will be negotiating with the enemy so we must try to understand them. We at the BBC have re-examined our broad policy and will not change it. We have no sense of guilt or failure.

What was also significant about this episode was the strength of feeling that was generated and how specifically government hostility was directed at the BBC. In *The Fog of War* Derrik Mercer, Geoff

Mungham, and Kevin Williams cite a member of the war Cabinet who told them:

> At a war cabinet meeting there was a general hate of the BBC whom we reckoned to be biased, and pro-ITN whom we reckoned were doing much better. One minister said: 'Well, you know we give all this information to the bloody BBC and what do they do with it? We don't help ITN enough and we ought to help ITN more.'[10]

What emerges from all this is not a conspiracy theory of the media but rather the consequences of a professional set of practices which, while valuing the principle of independence, relies heavily upon official sources for its news. In some respects the very mark of its professionalism is that it has access to these sources. The controversy over the *Panorama* was a sharp reminder of the tight limits on dissent that were regarded as permissible in time of crisis, which the Falklands conflict undoubtedly was. It was, after all, the government that had left the Falklands undefended in the first place and it was in jeopardy of falling as a result.

The government's hostility to the BBC was to have further ramifications. When the United States bombed Libya in April 1986, Norman Tebbit, then chairman of the Conservative Party, produced a report of the coverage comparing the BBC unfavourably with ITN.[11] He accused the BBC of carrying Libyan propaganda uncritically. In his letter to the BBC accompanying the report he questioned 'whether an increasingly confrontational style of BBC news coverage is appropriate for a public-service broadcasting system, funded by the taxpayer, required to emphasise impartiality, objectivity and factual reporting'. The BBC offered its own detailed reply. Nevertheless, Alasdair Milne had been forced to resign as director-general by the end of 1987 by a board of governors that had become increasingly politicized. Before his successor was appointed, the offices of BBC Glasgow were subjected to a police raid. The government was unhappy with two programmes prepared by the journalist Duncan Campbell in a six-part series entitled *Secret Society*. One of these was on the procedures surrounding the financing of the Zircon satellite, which Campbell argued had been irregular; the other was on the operation of secret Cabinet committees, which, among other things, produced evidence of the government's campaign against the peace movement in 1982–3. No

---

10 Mercer et al., *The Fog of War*, 134.

11 Conservative Party Central Office, *The American Raid on Libya: A Comparative Analysis of its Treatment on the BBC 9.00 O'Clock News and ITN News at Ten* (London: Conservative Party, 1986).

charges or arrests were made but the pressure on programme producers and journalists was clear enough. The Zircon programme was eventually screened and the Cabinet programme remade for Channel 4. This is a sharp reminder that those in positions of power will certainly make attempts to control the media, but the concern for independence is a journalistic value that is genuinely striven for and embraced by many journalists, even while they are aware that they can sometimes be restricted, censored, and constrained by the powerful.

But impartiality as a journalistic value becomes almost a will-o'-the-wisp phenomenon: now you see it, now you don't. In time of war or national crisis the governmental concern with broadcast (and other) news is not 'Are you impartial?' but 'Which side are you on?' If, in other instances, the broadcasters say we cannot be impartial about apartheid, they will find themselves criticized from the right. Norman Tebbit, for example, in the report on the Libyan coverage, took a sideswipe at the BBC, because its assistant director-general had said that they could not be impartial over apartheid. The report stated that this was in breach of the BBC's constitutional duty.[12] This from the same Norman Tebbit who, in an Open University programme on the media, was to state that impartiality was very difficult and that the problem was of balance rather than impartiality. This, he pointed out, was a matter of judgement in practice.[13]

In the end, if we take account of the conditions under which news is gathered, it is difficult to apply concepts of objectivity or impartiality to it. The question of accuracy is and will remain a bedrock of credibility and trustworthiness. However, where there are grounds for doubt or uncertainty on factual accuracy, this needs to be indicated. In the Gulf War Martin Fletcher of NBC spoke from Israel on the second night. Wearing a gasmask, he reported that Israel had been hit with a chemical weapon. This was relayed on BBC news, where the source for the story was claimed to be NBC's monitoring of police radios in Tel Aviv. However, the BBC's veteran reporter in Washington Charles Wheeler urged caution: 'Everybody here's getting in a dreadful panic.' As the programme went on, more uncertainty about the missile attack seeped through. Towards the end of the bulletin we heard this exchange:

MARTYN LEWIS: So that report from NBC could well be wrong?

CHARLES WHEELER: A lot of reports could well be wrong.

12 *The American Raid on Libya*, 12.
13 Open University programme D103, *Society and the Social Sciences*.

It is precisely that kind of scepticism that is important and in my view is a more effective way to judge the quality of news reports than an appeal to impartiality. After that we can ask questions about the framework within which the facts are presented. To understand that these frameworks are not determined by the events themselves is the beginning of wisdom and incidentally provides a solid reason for media studies. The general point has been nicely made by Robert Manoff:

> Narratives are organizations of experience. They bring order to events by making them something that can be told about; they have power because they make the world make sense. The sense they make, however, is conventional. No story is the inevitable product of the event it reports; no event dictates its own narrative form. News occurs at the conjunction of events and texts, and while events create the story, the story also creates the event. The narrative choice made by the journalist is therefore not a free choice. It is guided by the appearance which reality has assumed for him, by institutions and routines, by conventions that shape his perceptions and that provide the formal repertory for presenting them. It is the interaction of these forces that produces the news, and it is their relationship that determines its diversity or uniformity.[14]

So I want to suggest that television news, like other journalism, occupies a space that is constantly contested, which is subject to organizational and technological restructuring, to economic, cultural, and political constraints, to commercial pressures, and to changing professional practices. The changing contours of this space can lead to different patterns of domination and agenda-setting and to different degrees of openness and closure, in terms of access, patterns of ownership, available genres, types of disclosure, and range of opinions represented. Although it is intrinsically difficult to theorize about the complexities which are implied in this formulation, the implications of the empirical outcomes of the struggle over this terrain are crucial for the ways in which they help or hinder the democratic process. For this reason journalists and their audiences when they first hear news should always ask the irreverent question: 'Says who?' This may be bad news for the official managers of society, but it will be good news for democracy.

---

14 Robert Carl Manoff, 'Writing the News (by Telling the "Story")', in Robert Carl Manoff and Michael Schudson (eds.), *Reading the News* (New York: Pantheon, 1986), 228–9.

11

Every Wart and Pustule: Gilbert Harding and Television Stardom

Andy Medhurst

I just behave as I am and talk as I think, which for some reason appears to be remarkably novel.

Gilbert Harding

HE **WAS FAT**, he was ugly, and he was headline news. GILBERT HARDING HAS BRONCHITIS. GILBERT HARDING ORDERED OUT. CLASH OVER SAUCE A LA HARDING. GILBERT HARDING IN GREAT RAIL DELAY. ANOTHER HARDING RUMPUS. HARDING APOLOGISES AS 3,000,000 WATCH. STOP HARDING'S RUDENESS: THE JOKE IS OVER. He turned on the Blackpool illuminations, he made a record the BBC banned as obscene, he was offered stage roles as both Toad of Toad Hall and Hamlet, he advertised cigarettes and indigestion remedies, he tried his hand at being an investigative journalist and a disc jockey, he cooked with Fanny Craddock, and he acted with Cliff Richard. For nine years he was one of the most famous people in Britain, but who exactly was he and why did he matter so much to so many people?

Today we suffer from a surfeit of stars. It doesn't take much to earn a back-page pin-up in *Smash Hits* or to have your favourite recipes outlined in TV *Times*, but there was a time when television was a novelty and when the television star was a new and unfamiliar phenomenon. Gilbert Harding was the single most emblematic figure of that era—in the popular imagination he *was* television. For in the first half of the 1950s television meant, above all, *What's My Line*, and *What's My Line* meant Gilbert Harding.

First published in John Corner (ed.), *Popular Television in Britain: Studies in Cultural History* (London. BFI, 1991), 60–74.

It has to be one of the unlikeliest success stories in the history of British popular culture, but it's also an exemplary narrative, a cautionary tale that reveals a lot about how television was constructed, perceived, and understood in the 1950s. I want to try to use the career of Gilbert Harding as a way of unravelling some of those discourses, because it fell to poor Gilbert to be Britain's first major television personality. He was the test-case for definitions of televisual stardom, for the placing of the dividing-line between 'star' and 'personality', for the working out of the acceptable limits of public curiosity and press intrusion. Before him there was no yardstick, so the particular and tragic fascination of his career is that it enables us to see what has become an archetypal trajectory acted out for the very first time.

Gilbert Harding: A Career Outline

Although this chapter is concerned with a far wider area than the merely biographical, clearly it's necessary to have some sense of the man at the centre of it all. He was born in 1907, in Hereford, in a workhouse. Not as a child of one of its inmates, however, but the child of its master and matron. His father died while Gilbert was very young. He went to school in Wolverhampton and studied history and modern languages at Queens' College Cambridge. He became a Catholic and in the 1930s worked as a teacher, a police constable, and a journalist. His ambition to become a lawyer was thwarted by the outbreak of the Second World War, and in December 1939, being found medically unfit for the armed forces, Harding joined the BBC's monitoring service as a sub-editor. He subsequently moved to the outside broadcasting department and here made his first radio broadcasts. In 1944 he went to Canada for three years, working at the BBC's Toronto office. On returning to London, he became question master in a new radio panel game called *Round Britain Quiz*, though in doing so he left the BBC staff (at whose insistence, his or theirs, remains unclear) and worked on a freelance basis. This programme was his first bite at a regular broadcast slot, though his function was limited to introducing the panellists and asking the questions. There was little scope for individuality.

Panel games and quizzes were a central part of BBC output at that time, both on radio and television. They were relatively cheap to produce, had the appeal of regularity and familiarity within tightly circumscribed guidelines, and blended entertainment with education in a way that adhered securely to the prevailing Reithian ideology of broadcasting. Harding also introduced *The Brains Trust* and *Twenty Questions*, though his pretensions to intellectual seriousness ensured that he greatly preferred the former, in which academics and philosophers chewed over weighty metaphysical issues, to the latter, in which variety performers and radio comedians strove to identify a mystery object. This tension between intellectual capability and the supposed soft option of light entertainment is one that runs throughout his career.

Television, at this stage, was still very much the junior partner to radio. It could only be received in a small area around London, and transmissions only lasted for a few hours per day. The BBC *Yearbooks* of this period clearly indicate, by the number of pages and detail of information allotted, the relative standing of the two media. Television was a tricksy upstart, radio was where the serious broadcasting went on. Harding's early ventures into TV, then, were seen by him as an adjunct to his proper work. None the less, it was on television that he first achieved some public impact, when, on a panel game called *We Beg to Differ*, in which a male and a female team debated whether men and women viewed issues differently (a touching indication of the innocence of early post-war television), he told one of the opposing side to 'mind your own business'. This incident was the first sighting of the quality on which Harding's stardom was based—his legendary rudeness.

Early 1950s Television and *What's My Line*

What's My Line, which originated on American television, was a simple game in which four panellists sought to guess the occupations of members of the public. There is no indication at all that anyone in the BBC saw it as substantially different from the other panel games then being broadcast. It was cheap, inoffensive entertainment; nothing as brash as large prizes were on offer—if a contestant succeeded in baffling the panel she or he went away with nothing more than a commemorative scroll. That was the official prize, perhaps, but like any game or quiz show the real trophy on offer was a brief taste of fame, a few minutes *on television*. And, as the series progressed, a few minutes on television *with Gilbert Harding*.

Harding at first thought he would be suitable as the question master, but, after his one attempt was wrecked thanks to backstage mistakes, that job went to Eamonn Andrews. Harding reappeared as a panellist on the fifth programme, broadcast on 13 August 1951. The series rolled along on its mild, bland, early 1950s way for another few weeks, but then something happened. Harding took a vehement dislike to a particularly evasive contestant and, losing all patience, snapped at him, 'I am tired of looking at you.' Now it was, perhaps, not one of the great savage put-downs of all time, but this was 1952, the era of Sylvia Peters and Muffin the Mule, when the world of BBC television was a world of almost inconceivable niceness. Everyone on screen behaved with deep-frozen cocktail party politeness, in the midst of which Harding's offhand sourness came across like Kenneth Tynan saying 'fuck' some years later.

Complaints poured in ('I felt like walking out of my own drawing room,' wrote one viewer[1]) and the incident was widely reported in the national press—and this, remember, at a time when most of the country could not yet receive television. What had happened was that Harding had become a talking-point, last night's TV became what you discussed next morning on the train, or at school, or over the garden fence. If, that is, you owned a television set. Harding and *What's My Line* became central to the process whereby those without television increasingly perceived themselves as socially disadvantaged, left behind. That first outburst should not be given unique credit for any of this; Harding's manner on the programme had always been somewhat tougher than his colleagues', since to be the 'hard man' was his function in the text, but his impatient attacks now increased in frequency and punctured the balloon of blandness in which the BBC had hitherto cocooned itself.

Rudeness-by-Harding became *What's My Line's* secret weapon, the Ingredient X that marked it out from other panel games, and here we reach another of the key tensions in the Harding persona. The 'rudeness' began to be seen by an enthralled public as Harding's 'act': it was what he *did*. But for Harding it was not an adopted device, a behavioural catchphrase, but his genuine personality—it was what he *was*. This tension between role and real is crucial, and I'll come back to it when discussing the precise contours of the notion of the 'personality' on television.

Harding's inherent tendency towards short-temperedness was only increased by his fondness for alcohol. He often appeared on *What's My Line* mildly (or less mildly) drunk. The looser his tongue became, the more the audience approved—frequently, of course, concealing that approval behind a thin cloak of affronted outrage. He told one contestant she was 'too elegant to come from Rugby', and in response to Eamonn Andrews' attempt to defend that town added, 'Have you ever been there?' When the mystery celebrity contestant was the hairdresser 'Teasy-Weasy' Raymonde, Harding spat, 'you call yourself some peculiar name which I am determined not to remember'. Television viewers were not used to

---

1 Quoted in Dicky Leeman, *'What's My Line': The Story of a Phenomenon* (London: Allan Wingate, 1955), 127. The sheer existence of this book, with its detailed account of the minutiae of every programme in the series, testifies to how central to 1950s television *What's My Line* was.

this bitchy abuse, and Harding's elevation to stardom rocketed on the back of his crushing one-liners.

Better yet, his behaviour off-screen was scarcely different—in fact Harding's whole argument, repeated *ad infinitum* in interview after interview, was that there was no difference at all. He was the way he was, on television or off, and if people were shocked by his actions and outbursts then they had no reason to be. They had seen him on TV—they ought to know what he was like. On what was probably the most celebrated occasion he arrived rather drunk at an annual dinner for Hounslow magistrates and denounced it as 'third-rate . . . just another suburban do'. The headlines screamed, the public clucked, Hounslow never recovered.

This was not, after all, the way BBC employees were expected to behave. Harding's only possible rival for the title of television personified was Richard Dimbleby, and the contrast between the two men is stark enough to bring out the full flavour and significance of Harding's transgressive appeal. Dimbleby was measured, calm, solemn, reliable, authoritative, a man of sonorous marble—Harding inverted all those adjectives: he was a bluff, reckless bottle of scotch on the loose.

This is not to say he relished his notoriety. On the contrary, he was frequently and publicly contrite (remember HARDING APOLOGISES AS 3,000,000 WATCH?—which may well have been the first newspaper headline to cite an audience figure for television), pleading in mitigation that the rudeness was not affectation but simply the way he was made. What he failed to appreciate, though, was how much the rudeness was central to his popularity. This persona (which he always denied was anything other than his true self) was far too adored to allow any modifications—the circus audience had acquired its very own dancing bear, and all he was permitted to do was dance.

The Harding Industry

The real Harding boom occupied the first half of the 1950s, the period before the arrival of commercial television. Harding was front-page news because if he was on TV, nothing else was—literally. There was only one channel, and *What's My Line* epitomized that era of BBC monopoly, with its Festival of Britain graphics and its fuss over necklines. ITV introduced big-money quizzes like *Double Your Money* and *Take Your Pick*, which offered far more than scrolls. *What's My Line* maintained its success, but increasingly it couldn't help looking dated. No longer did it encapsulate the televisual *Zeitgeist*. So where could Harding, its unquestioned star, go next? The problem was that he was so overwhelmingly associated with that one programme that it was difficult to find convincing alternative slots. His popularity was so huge that the sheer force of his personality carried some limp programme ideas like *Harding Finds Out*, a stab at investigative reporting, and *I Know What I Like*, in which audiences were treated to Gilbert's defiantly middlebrow tastes in poetry, music, and painting. There was even a fifteen-minute slot shown late at night (or what passed for late in those days of early bedtimes), in which he simply sat and pontificated on issues of the day.

This role as national oracle seems hard to imagine from today's perspective. Why did people take so seriously the views of a quiz panellist? It's as if, in terms of 1990s division of televisual labour, there was no difference between Jeremy Beadle and Michael Ignatieff. What seems to have been behind Harding's elevation into guru status was his reputation for 'speaking his mind'. He wrote various newspaper columns, most prominently in the *People*, where he took on cases of bureaucratic injustice rather in the way later adopted by *That's Life*. Perhaps it was the crusty schoolteacher exterior, perhaps it was a naïve belief that he 'wouldn't take any nonsense', but readers trusted him with all manner of problems. He was seen as a superhuman ombudsman.

Then there were the books. His autobiography (ghost-written, like all the publications that came out under his name) was serial-ized in magazines and on radio, bought by a major book club, and reprinted a number of times. This was followed by, among others, *Gilbert Harding's Book of Manners*, the gag–tag being, fairly obviously, that here was the man dubbed 'Britain's rudest' giving his version of correct societal interaction (a phrase he would have loathed). *Master of None* was a collection of anecdotes loosely related to work and occupations, the association with *What's My Line* thus still strongly maintained. Harding even formed a com-pany to take care of this burgeoning industry. It was called, with touching self-deprecation, Gilbert Harding (Exploitation) Ltd. The array of media outings and opportunities I list in this chapter's first paragraph were only some of the more notable of his high-earning achievements. He had become this country's first unequivocal media personality. He was famous for being famous.[2]

2 See Gilbert Harding, *Along My Line* (London: Putnam, 1956), *Gilbert Harding's Book of Manners* (London: Putnam, 1956), *Master of None* (London: Putnam, 1958). Also, there are two biographies of Harding that I have used in researching this account: Roger Storey's *Gilbert Harding* (London: Barrie & Rockcliff, 1961), a memoir written by Harding's private secretary; and Wallace Reyburn's *Gilbert Harding: A Candid Portrayal* (London: Angus & Robertson, 1978). This latter, as its subtitle suggests, is a muckraking, warts-and-all biography, the prurient tone of which is especially gratuitous in its offensive, misinformed chapter about Harding's homosexuality. At one point, for example, Reyburn uses the phrase 'alcoholics, neurotics, murderers, homosexuals and so on' (p.104).

The underlying paradox of all this success was that Harding the man was lonely and dreadfully unhappy. There's a way of reading this which slips it neatly into the 'tragic star' stereotype, particularly as his personal unhappiness was directly linked to his homosexuality (the register shifts slightly to 'tragic queer' in this case[3]). The fact of his sexuality *is* relevant, and I'll return to it later. But it's relevant in a way that most accounts of Harding seem either blind to or unwilling to grasp. First, though, it's important to look at the exact moment when the rude-Harding paradigm is overtaken by the unhappy-Harding persona.

The 'Face to Face' Interview

Face to Face was a series of interviews with prominent people in which John Freeman attempted to penetrate more deeply than the standard conventions of televisual conversation allowed. The studio was dark, the camera kept fixed on the person being interviewed (either in painfully tight close-up for the especially tortured moments, or a more reticent medium shot), while Freeman was only seen from behind. Its ambience now reminds one inevitably of *Mastermind*, but the victims' specialized subject was always the same: themselves. According to at least one of Harding's biographers,[4] Freeman had had Gilbert in his sights for some time. The reason was not made clear at the time but when in 1988 a batch of *Face to Face*s were shown again, a letter to the *Listener* from a former executive involved with the series let this fascinating and rather chilling cat out of the bag:

> In the Harding interview, John Freeman had been intending to bring the conversation around to the fact that Gilbert was homosexual—then a virtually unmentionable subject.[5]

The Harding *Face to Face* has always had a legendary status as an exceptionally tough, relentless piece of interviewing. Armed with the above information, it takes on another, more sinister, connotation entirely.

It is an extraordinary piece of television, even today. There is nowhere to look except at the great mournful landscape of Harding's face as Freeman drills away, almost all his questions being

---

3 I ought to say that, being gay myself, I'm using the term 'queer' not to endorse it, but because it is the term most in use at the time concerned. As Simon Shepherd suggests in *Because We're Queers: The Life and Crimes of Kenneth Halliwell and Joe Orton* (London: GMP, 1989), 9, the word 'queer' can be used to 'denote, historically, a pre-gay homosexual identity and culture'.

4 See the final chapter of Storey, *Gilbert Harding*.

5 Leonard Miall, letter to the *Listener*, 3 Nov. 1988.

variations on a theme of pain and discipline. The interview has inescapably taken on an obituary flavour, since it was broadcast only a few weeks before Harding's sudden death in December 1960. What makes it grisly and gripping is the victim's complicity in carving his own headstone—it's an *autobiographical* obituary, and as such it serves as a convenient summary of all the conflicts and tensions created by the success of this most unlikely of stars.

Thus we get the idea that Harding has sold short his intelligence (his 'first-class mind', as Freeman puts it) by participating in light entertainment. Then there is the pivotal issue of the role of 'Harding' versus the real Harding. The exchange runs like this:

FREEMAN: Are you ever conscious of cultivating the mannerisms of Harding the public figure?

HARDING: I've never had any mannerisms.

FREEMAN: Well, you know, you have, but you're not conscious of them.

HARDING: I've never cultivated my mannerisms. I have never pretended. If I knew how to pretend, I would. But I don't know how—so I don't.

This, encapsulated with a kind of tragic inarticulacy, is the absolute core of the Harding dilemma, a dilemma which has been played out so many times since by later personalities—when you are only known and liked for certain characteristics, do you risk alienating the public by changing, or do you suppress your own need for change and conform by playing out the same, tired tropes?

Freeman strides on, and Harding admits to profound unhappiness with almost every response—'Nothing has ever happened that's given me any sort of a sense of achievement or satisfaction'—until the (in)famous moment when Harding's reserve cracks and he cries on recalling the death of his mother. This is the incident that burned itself into the memories of those watching, precisely because it is a rare moment of unmediated emotion, a glimpse of profound and untreated grief that has no place on a medium as committed to sparkling insincerity as television. It is, in many ways, the logical conclusion of the whole Harding trajectory; the man who made his name by rejecting the toning-downs, the evasive gloss of television, achieves here the most direct, naked communication possible.

Freeman clearly subscribed to that school of thought which traced male homosexuality back to a 'dominant mother', so he seized on Harding's grief as another way of trying to get at his sexuality. The question is painstakingly, exquisitely polite:

Is there any truth in the notion I have in the back of my mind that it is this particularly deep relation you obviously had with your mother which has made it impossible so far for you to marry?

(Note, especially, the feline inclusion of 'so far'), but its meaning is plain enough. Harding was being invited to declare his queerness, but he refused to deliver the 'confession' that Freeman was so assiduously pursuing; instead he does something even more remarkable: he sketches the sexual predicament of an entire culture:

> My sister didn't marry, and I didn't marry and my mother was a widow when she was just thirty, and so when we came to live together we put up a sort of cloud of sexual frustration that was enough to blot out the sun.

There's a terrible eloquence in this, a revelation of the pain and fear engendered by living in a society committed to the repression of all but the most conventional sexual options. It's the kind of statement, I'd argue, that has a particular relevance and poignancy coming from a homosexual man on the brink of the 1960s.

Harding and Homosexuality

The importance of Harding's sexuality has a far wider relevance than as the subtext of the Freeman crucifixion. His anxiety about maintaining privacy was particularly acute given the possibilities of blackmail at a time when homosexual acts between men were still illegal. The 1950s had seen an unprecedented level of public debate around this subject (a fact that makes nonsense of Leonard Miall's claim, in his letter about *Face to Face*, that it was 'virtually unmentionable').

Whether in vindictive tabloid articles called 'Evil Men' or purportedly balanced analyses called *They Stand Apart*,[6] that debate was invariably couched in terms of homosexuality as otherness, and was undertaken primarily by heterosexuals, but at least the subject was being aired. Harding is an intriguing figure in this context, since, if he embodied television in the history of the 1950s, he also embodies the 1950s in the history of television—that is to say he was a key cultural figure of the decade in which, thanks to the Burgess–Maclean scandal, the Lord Montagu trial, and the Wolfenden Report, homosexuality was centrally on the social agenda.

Some of the images of Harding, seen today, are almost comic in their conformity to known stereotypes of homosexuality. He lived in *Brighton*, doting on a *Pekinese*, a big fan of *Marlene Dietrich*, and

---

6 'Evil Men' was published in the *Sunday Pictorial* in 1952. *They Stand Apart* was published by Heinemann in 1955. For the best overview of this period, see Jeffrey Weeks, *Coming Out* (London: Quartet, 1979).

so on. Clearly such signals were available for interpretation to the homosexual *cognoscenti* at the time, but it's interesting to speculate what the mass heterosexual audience made of them. Alison Hennegan, recalling her 1950s childhood with lesbian hindsight, comments on Harding's much-publicized relationship with another gay television personality:

> At twelve . . . I wasn't clear who I was yet, but I had inklings. I knew that the figure of Nancy Spain, with her uncoiffeured hair, well-cut hacking jacket, open-necked shirt and rakish cravat, gave me a warm glow . . . And I knew that . . . her . . . cross-talk act with Gilbert Harding . . . gave me the same comforted pleasure, but I couldn't explain it. Now, of course, I know that they were having a whale of a time playing at being a flirtatious heterosexual couple, enacting an outrageously camp open secret. It was fun, it was flagrant, and utterly unperceived by the bulk of their audience.[7]

The Spain–Harding relationship was one of the odder gossip column items from the mid-1950s, and what is attractive about Hennegan's reading of it is how enjoyable she makes it sound. The prevailing construction of Harding as a poor, unhappy homosexual would clearly have to be modified to accommodate the idea of Gilbert playing an extended camp trick on the great British public.

That, though, does seem to have been the case, particularly with reference to press speculations about a Spain–Harding marriage. Nancy Spain's contribution to *Gilbert Harding by his Friends* (a collection of reminiscences published the year after his death, the very existence of which amply demonstrates the level of public interest in the man), declares that:

> we talked it over one lunchtime at Antoine's in Charlotte Street. 'It would be a very good idea,' Gilbert finally summed it all up, large myopic eyes glazing over like two lightly-boiled plovers' eggs. 'But I should want *all* the serial rights!'[8]

This is the kind of camp one-liner that would have a special reson-ance to those in the know. Other contributions to this tribute vol-ume hint at Harding's sexuality, though they tend to shore up the tragic-and-unhappy side. Robin Maugham, another resident of Brighton's 1950s gay community, recalls an evening when Harding confided his entire life story:

7 Alison Hennegan, 'On Becoming a Lesbian Reader', in Susannah Radstone (ed.), *Sweet Dreams: Sexuality, Gender and Popular Fiction* (London: Lawrence & Wishart, 1988), 167–8.

8 Nancy Spain, 'Gilbert and Women', in Stephen Grenfall (ed.), *Gilbert Harding by his Friends* (London: André Deutsch, 1961), 162.

Even now, I cannot bear to think of the story he told me that night . . . without going into any details by revealing anything I shouldn't, I think I can say this. If ever a man had difficulties of character and temperament to contend with, it was Gilbert. The trouble was that he was fastidiously honest with himself and his standards were extremely high. The result was that he disliked various aspects of his own nature . . .[9]

These 'difficulties' could be taken to mean the irascibility, the fondness for drink, the standard Harding complaints, and no doubt they're relevant up to a point, but I trust my own gay judgement to decode this as a comment about sexuality, more specifically about homosexual self-oppression.

Self-oppression sounds like a loaded term, perhaps, but what I mean by it here is the variety of ways in which homosexuals were persuaded to collude in the negative constructions of homosexuality circulated by certain strands of heterosexual opinion. The comparatively widespread and public discussion of homosexuality in the 1950s included all manner of proposed 'solutions' to the 'problem'. The idea that it was possible to be happy and homosexual was strenuously discouraged, one psychiatrist going so far as to state:

Possibly the greatest importance of homosexuality is that it causes so much unhappiness. If happiness is of any value . . . then homosexuality should be eliminated by every means in our power.[10]

It was that kind of breathtakingly arrogant illogicality (if homosexuals are 'unhappy', it is because of the heterosexual misrepresentation and bigotry that surrounds them), which led otherwise intelligent men like Gilbert Harding to seek a way out of their 'condition'. He affixed himself to two of the more tenacious heterosexual disciplines, Roman Catholicism and Freudian psychoanalysis, as part of this saddening search.[11]

It's a relatively unbroken line from Harding to Russell Harty, in terms of press treatment of homosexual celebrities. After Harding's death a pack of journalists descended on Brighton trying to unearth some scandal, much as the ghoulish hacks of the late 1980s flocked to the dying Harty's hospital in an attempt to generate some seedy copy. Happily, in both cases, they failed. Once again, though, the

9 Robin Maugham, 'Final Release', in Grenfall (ed.), *Gilbert Harding*, 206.

10 Clifford Allen, *Homosexuality: Its Nature, Causation and Treatment* (London: Unwin, 1958), 34.

11 See Reyburn, *Gilbert Harding*, ch. 12 (taking care to filter out Reyburn's homophobic interpretations). John Freeman obviously knew about Harding's experiences with psychoanalysis, hence certain questions on *Face to Face*—another part of the project to unmask Harding's queerness.

point is that Harding set the precedent for later traditions of journalistic interest in the private lives of the famous. An 'exposé' of Harding's sexual tastes would have been the scoop of the 1950s. His fear of this, and of blackmail, coupled with a more general feeling of guilt and failure pumped into him by priests and psychiatrists, conspired to leave him sexually unfulfilled: the first, but not the last, homosexual television personality to be imprisoned by fame.

Harding, Television, and Cinema

One of the best ways of understanding just how central Harding was in embodying the *televisual* in the 1950s is by looking at the feature films in which he appeared. It's odd that while many of the biographical pieces and reminiscences mention Harding's aspirations to acting, none of them refer to these films. This is a notable oversight, but in a way it's curiously appropriate, because in those roles he is not so much acting in any conventional sense, but *signifying*, and what he signifies is television.

Feature films of this period have an ambivalent attitude towards the younger, threatening medium.[12] To begin with, in the days of the BBC monopoly and its concomitant addiction to blandness, a 1949 film like *Train of Events* can treat TV with ridicule. One scene in a television studio begins with two penguins walking out of shot, while a very BBC voice says: 'Well, Charlie and Mabel, a remarkable exhibition of ballroom dancing. I'm sure Victor Sylvester has nothing to teach you.' This shrewd jibe at the novelty-at-all-costs magazine programme is followed by a swipe at the corporation's tendency to foist high culture on to its audience—the next item 'televised' is a pretentious discussion about classical music. Clearly, at this stage the cinema wasn't troubled by competition from quickstepping penguins.

That confidence wavered, inevitably, as the popularity of TV grew. Performers who had made their names on the small screen were turned into film stars, most notably Norman Wisdom. Harding did not have the performing talents to carry a whole film, but he was a name—in television terms the biggest name—and his potential as a box-office draw proved an irresistible temptation. With the exception of *The Gentle Gunman*, a deeply confused drama about the IRA that uses Harding, in scenes outside the main narrative, as a symbol of stubborn Englishness,[13] it's notable that

12 See Charles Barr, 'Broadcasting and Cinema: Screens within Screens', in Barr (ed.), *All Our Yesterdays: Ninety Years of British Cinema* (London: BFI, 1986) for the definitive survey of films that addressed television.

13 For a full analysis of this film, see John Hill, 'Images of Violence', in Kevin Rockett, Luke Gibbons, and John Hill, *Cinema and Ireland* (London: Croom Helm, 1987).

the films he appeared in are all comedies. It is as if film was trying to use him as a joke about television.

The Oracle, for example, skits Harding's bizarre reputation as social commentator, his voice used as a supernatural predictive force that rises up from the bottom of a well (perhaps a joke about the small, dim picture produced by 1950s TV technology). More significantly still, three films released in 1955 were part of the Rank Organization's conscious attempt to woo audiences away from TV by offering big-budget colour spectacle. *An Alligator Named Daisy* and *As Long as They're Happy* are, as their titles indicate, ferociously winsome concoctions, and they each simply wheel on Harding for one scene and one joke. *Daisy* climaxes at a large fête-cum-alligator-show (it's a weird film), in which a number of personalities from radio and television are present. They include Frankie Howerd Jimmy Edwards, the flamboyant racing tipster Prince Monolulu, and Harding. All he is required to do is walk around and be 'rude' in response to a couple of questions. In *Happy* he is incongruously included in an audience for a visiting American pop singer (the film centres on a parody of Johnny Ray). An elderly fan of the singer asks Harding if he 'digs' the singer. 'I'd bury him,' scowls Harding in response. 'Oh you rude man,' she replies. Again, it is the easy, obvious deployment of Harding-equals-rudeness. (By the singer's third song Harding is sobbing along with the rest of the audience—with hindsight this slight gag becomes a teasing foretaste of the tears at the Freeman interview.)

The third and by far the best of these Rank films is *Simon and Laura*. Based on a hit stage play, it tells of two actors who are offered a daily television serial. Simon, played by Peter Finch, is at his gentleman's club when he meets a fellow member, Harding. Seeking his advice about the wisdom of regular television work, he gets this reply:

> Do you know what happens to you when you allow yourself to be regularly exhibited in that glass rectangle? You become public property. Your face, electronically distorted, is huddled round and gawped at by three-quarters of the population of the United Kingdom, and within a month every wrinkle, every wart and pustule, has become part of our British way of life. Start speaking your mind, they'll say you're rude. Stop speaking your mind, they'll say you're namby-pamby and you're slipping. Mind you, I'm not saying that the British public isn't warm-hearted and generous. They are. Terrifyingly so. You have but to clear your throat and the next day you'll be inundated with linctuses, pastilles, pills and potions . . .

That, in a nutshell, is the Harding philosophy. What's so noteworthy about this appearance of it is that it's part of a fiction film, but with the obvious double-bluff assumption that the film's audience is supposed to recognize it as an authentic Harding tirade. By this stage of the 1950s, even those without televisions would have read Harding pieces or interviews in the press. In the film's next scene Laura (Kay Kendall) meets Isobel Barnett, another *What's My Line* fixture, at the hairdresser's and asks her advice. She gets some words of wisdom on earrings and necklines, these two points of fashion also by this time part of general folklore about television.

Four years later, in 1959, the satirical musical comedy *Expresso Bongo* includes, as part of its attack on pop music, a scene where the TV documentary series *Cosmorama* (no prizes for guessing the real series parodied here) visits a Soho coffee bar to film the new teenage craze. *Cosmorama* is fronted by Gilbert Harding, who makes bluffly disparaging comments about 'teenage rebellion' and 'plastic palm trees'. In a later 'studio discussion' Harding has the show stolen from him by the unscrupulous manager of the pop singer at the centre of the plot. *Expresso Bongo* was released less than a year before Harding died, and, brief as his appearance in it is, it does raise questions about what might have happened to Harding's career if he had lived.

Putting it bluntly, wouldn't he have seemed embarrassingly out of place? In a television culture dominated by *Z Cars* and *That Was The Week That Was*, Jimmy Tarbuck and *Steptoe and Son*, Harding would have been stranded, an unlikely rebel from the generation before last, his claims to once-upon-a-time innovation going unheard, as boys in Beatles suits laughed at his elderly colonel appearance. What *Expresso Bongo* does is to expose Harding as old hat, an emblem of a superseded cultural moment, the sad sight of a subversive voice co-opted beyond redemption into the establishment he had once (however unintentionally) scandalized. The cruellest blow of all: by having him front *Cosmorama*, *Expresso Bongo* turns him into Richard Dimbleby.

TV Star or TV Personality?

To conclude then, Harding, as well as being a fascinating character in his own right, draws together in an exemplary way all the key discourses about television in the 1950s. He was not the only hugely popular television performer of that era, but it would not be possible to write an essay such as this centred on Jeanne Heal or Mary Malcolm or Philip Harben. They lack the extra layers of meaning, the added clusters of contextual relevance, that make Harding so absolutely central.

Is it possible to sum up what it was that made him so

monstrously, freakishly popular? Which public nerves did he touch with such electrifying accuracy that he became the Elephant Man of British television? It could be that he matched closely one of the cultural archetypes the British have liked to see as peculiar to their national identity—the brusque, dyspeptic, plain-speaking, short-fused, common-sense archetype that led many of Harding's contemporaries to compare him to Dr Johnson. (It speaks volumes, I think, that such a literary comparison was felt appropriate; few, if any, of today's television favourites would merit such an accolade.) The *Gilbert Harding by his Friends* collection was explicitly conceived to fill the gap left by a Johnson with no Boswell to pen the official record.[14] More recently, in a *tour de force* of cultural-historical analysis, Raphael Samuel has constructed a typology of British archetypes, in which he too places Harding in the Johnsonian camp.[15]

If we accept that it was 'rudeness' that was the key to Harding's success, it was highly fortunate that he was offered a place on *What's My Line.* After all, if a man has delusions of intellectual grandeur, nothing is more liable to trigger a fountain of frustrated spleen than being asked to identify correctly a Theatre Fireman's Night Companion, a Pepper-Pot Perforator, or a Wuzzer.[16] It was, undoubtedly, a trivial way to earn a living, and the sense of wasted time was clearly what lay behind Harding's irresistible volcano of pique. He belonged to the generation of broadcasters who saw documentary reporting as the highest possible calling. He might be an exact inversion of Richard Dimbleby, but deep down it's more than likely that Dimbleby was exactly who he wanted to be.

If the exasperation at ending up in light entertainment was one of the sources of the Great Rudeness, then the other was the way the public, inexplicably but wholly in love with this cantankerous man, laid claim to his time and his person. Every time we hear a soap star today lament the fact that they can't go shopping in peace, they are but an echo of Harding, and at least they know they have to expect it. He didn't—it was all new, unexpected, and thus immeasurably less welcome:

14 See Grenfall (ed.), *Gilbert Harding.* Fanny Craddock's contribution is specifically titled 'The Johnson who Lacked a Boswell'. In the BBC tribute programme broadcast a few days after Harding's death, Sir Compton Mackenzie had employed the Johnson comparison.

15 Raphael Samuel, 'Introduction: The Figures of National Myth', in Samuel (ed.), *Patriotism: The Making and Unmaking of British National Identity,* iii: *National Fictions* (London: Routledge, 1989). Samuel also, intriguingly, links Harding with another crucial 1950s TV figure, Tony Hancock. There's more work to be done here, especially given Hancock's treatment on *Face to Face* (he stated there that he thought happiness was impossible—a very Hardingesque sentiment).

16 A Wuzzer, according to Dicky Leeman, *What's My Line*, worked in a Yorkshire woollen mill and described his job thus: 'you gets t'wool and you wuzzes it'.

Lowering the car window to ask a simple question can either cause obstruction, so great is the crowd of only-too-willing but inarticulate helpers, or provoke immediate insults . . . 'Gilbert!' they mutter convulsively and somewhat familiarly, clutching their tie. 'It's Gilbert!' It is, and all I want to know is where the ill-lit, badly signposted road to some confounded parish hall is.[17]

The bitterest irony of all was that the angrier he got with this kind of public response, the more they loved him for it: getting more angry meant getting more *Gilberty*. It was a bonus, a double help-ing, an encore. He really couldn't win. Which is why he could never convince anyone that it wasn't all an act. If he tried and was dis-believed, his temper would boil over and there was the 'act' all over again. Long before the novel was published, Harding was forced to live out a Catch-22.

There remains the question of the distinction between a televi-sion star and a television personality. Using John Ellis's basic defini-tion of a star as 'a performer in a particular medium whose figure enters into subsidiary forms of circulation, and then feeds back into future performances',[18] Harding would seem to qualify. All those headlines were subsidiary forms of circulation, while one news-paper ran a *daily* column called 'Gilbert Harding—Day by Day', such was the insatiable appetite at one time for Hardingiana. Then there were all the books: many TV performers have written autobiographies, occasionally members of their family will add a second volume (such as Mabel Pickles's irresistibly titled *Married to Wilfred*), but the Harding collection would fill a small shelf. Add to this all the extra radio, stage, film, and public appear-ances, all the journalism and the records and the advertising, and Harding looks like a classic star. Besides, all the things I have attributed to his career as firsts were only firsts in terms of TV— the journalistic prying and public hysteria were nothing new to film stars.

And yet . . . something still pulls me back from calling him a star. I think it's something to do with the fact that most film stars have an aura of mystery, of otherworldliness, of sexual desirability, that is enhanced by the size of the screen and the darkness of the cinema. To visit a cinema in the golden decades of Hollywood was to enter a palace, a temple, a sacred site of surrender and completion. To watch television is to enter the living room. Television performers are too available, they're on too often. If in the 1950s you wanted to see Marilyn Monroe's new film or gasp again at the beauty of James Dean, you had to wait months. Gilbert was yours at the flick of a

17 Harding, *Master of None*, 174.
18 John Ellis, *Visible Fictions* (London: Routledge & Kegan Paul, 1982), 91.

switch every Sunday night. No mystery. Not a lot of sexual desirability either, though he did apparently have one or two exceptionally devoted female fans.[19]

Gilbert Harding, then, was the first paradigmatic television personality. He wasn't, after all, enacting a fictional role, but trading on an aspect (however heightened) of his own personal attributes. He unwittingly inaugurated a tradition which has included Patrick Moore, Barbara Woodhouse, and Keith Floyd (Harding and Floyd might, I'd like to think, have enjoyed the odd glass or two together). They, even at their best, aren't much more than flavour-of-the-month eccentrics, but Harding meant more than that. He occupied the historically pivotal role of undergoing the first-ever public baptism of small-screen adulation. He was typecast as himself, a part he could scarcely unlearn.

On a more personal level he fascinates and means a lot to me because those tensions between private and public lives overlap with a larger struggle over definitions of sexuality. The 1960s, as I have said above, would not have suited Gilbert, and I suspect he'd have regarded gay politics as unduly exhibitionistic. He'd have been wrong, of course, but that wrongness would be due to the lies about his own sexuality that he was coerced into internalizing. Still, fortunately, there are enough alternative images of Harding to combat that trapped, goaded, sweating man on *Face to Face*. I like to think of him shaking with laughter, three whiskies down the road to oblivion, plotting and bitching with Nancy Spain.

19 Both Storey and Reyburn document examples of this.

12

Framing 'the Real': *Oranges, Middlemarch, X-Files*

Robin Nelson

For a text to be popular it must be both accessible and enjoyable [and] . . . in popular narratives realism continues to be the dominant form.

(Marshment and Hallam 1994: 145)

EACH OF THE three programmes addressed in this chapter, *Oranges Are Not the Only Fruit*, *Middlemarch*, and *The X-Files*, deals with well-defined central characters set in solid, identifiable locations inviting from the audience credibility in their worlds as a basis for identification and sympathy with character. Nevertheless each blurs at the same time, though in different ways, the fact–fiction divide. The dramas employ a range of devices (musical, filmic, special effects, poetic, frame-shaking) which go beyond strict naturalism and the norms of TV formulaic realism to open up perspectives at best eliciting an active and complex seeing from readers.

The two serials invite viewers to be detached and involved, even to laugh and cry in the same moment, but neither ultimately allows sentiment to dissipate a critical perspective on the contemporary historical world. *The X-Files* draws viewers into its narratives to chill and thrill ('Don't watch it alone'), but other aspects of the series evince a reflective detachment, at least gesturing at philosophical speculation.

The British serials invite an initial comparison and I shall discuss them first before turning to *The X-Files*. Both are set in the regions

First published in Robin Nelson (ed.), *TV Drama in Transition: Forms, Values and Cultural Change* (London: Macmillan, 1997), 126–8, 139–50.

of England, *Middlemarch* in the Midlands and *Oranges* in a Lancashire mill town. Both are concerned with social reforms in the name of liberation from a stagnant and stultifying tradition which offers itself as the natural way of life. In their settings and major characters they thus reflect oppositional strains of resistance to entrenched power. *Oranges*, particularly, locates its anchor-point of view with a lesbian subculture underrepresented (until recently)[1] in British (let alone transnational) television. Indeed, in so far as history is identified with the law of the father, *Oranges* invites an escape for young women from history in Jess's rejection of patriarchy, represented more in the church through the figure of the pastor than by her virtually silenced adoptive father. *Middlemarch*, in contrasting parallel, illustrates the experience of an idealistic young woman frustrated, both sexually and politically, by a stultifying, hegemonic male order. Both television serials thus connect with the tradition of social realism identified as distinctive of the history of British TV drama, but they also break from it, making no claims to documentary truth. They are imaginative fictions which intersect with aspects of their respective contemporary historical actualities.

The television version of *Middlemarch*, transmitted more than 160 years after the period in which the novel is located, raises interesting questions of relevance to a (post)modern epoch. George Eliot, writing in the realist mode, offers in her novel a reflective commentary on social progress in the nineteenth century. A similar referentiality, though differing in detail, is an important aspect of the TV drama from the point of view of Andrew Davies, the adaptor, but with reference to the 1990s as well as 1830s social context. There are resonances for Davies between Lydgate's frustrated attempts to introduce a health service to Middlemarch and the erosion of Britain's National Health Service in the 1990s.[2] More generally, as evidenced in the rise and fall of Bulstrode, there is a correlation to be drawn between the hypocrisy of moralizing financiers today whose material success, like that of their nineteenth-century predecessors, is sometimes based on moral graft and corruption. But, as the discussion below reveals, a range of forces in the production and reception of *Middlemarch* in 1994 militate against the television text as social critique.

Nevertheless, both *Middlemarch* and *Oranges* potentially have

---

1 In the past three years lesbian relationships have been represented in the mainstream British soaps, *Brookside*, *EastEnders*, and *Emmerdale*. Otherwise overt treatment of particularly physical lesbian relationships in TV drama is rare, but see e.g. *Portrait of a Marriage* (BBC2, 1990), a biography of Vita Sackville West. See also the discussion of *Between the Lines* (Nelson, 1997, ch. 8)

2 For the views attributed to Andrew Davies and insights into the adaptation process, I am indebted to a lecture he gave about making *Middlemarch* in the department of arts education, University of Warwick, 9 Mar. 1994.

something to say about contemporary politics, sexual or civic. *Oranges* confronts more overtly a mainstream audience in sympathetically representing a lesbian perspective and thus giving a voice to a historically marginalized group. Both television serials, however, pick up on their source novels' interrogation of the yet dominant viewpoint of Western society—that of the Caucasian, heterosexual, male, middle class.

Above all, each serial situates agency in structure, dealing with the experience of individuals whose lives are threatened to be constrained and diminished by social forces. They thus challenge social conventions, political orthodoxies, and habitual ways of seeing in the name of freedom for the typical individual imbricated in resistible, and possibly mutable, social forces. Whilst the main characters, that is to say, are individuated and realized dramatically, the focus of interest is not solely upon their distinctive psyches but also on their representativeness of a social group or class. Thus *Middlemarch* and *Oranges* treat seriously issues concerned with the lives of ordinary people in the socially extended tradition of realism, and draw viewers into their possible worlds to make them care about the characters. But, in doing so, neither is lacking either in entertainment value or in a range of perspectives to invite a complex seeing.[3]

Both serials achieved critical acclaim but were also relatively popular. *Middlemarch* achieved 5 million viewers on average per episode. In full awareness of the challenging nature of *Oranges*, Jeanette Winterson (1994: 81) was more pleased by its 'street success' than by critical accolades.

The dramatization of George Eliot's novel *Middlemarch* on BBC1 in the spring season of 1994 brings into sharp focus a range of issues, including: (dis)continuities in dramatic form and narrative tradition; the debate about the codes and conventions of television realism in relation to 'adequating the real'; questions of canonicity and ethical seriousness as criteria of value; and the capacity of 'serious' television drama to succeed aesthetically or commercially in the (post)modern production context.

In screening *Middlemarch*, the BBC extended its tradition of adapting the classics of English literature for the small screen by taking on a work dubbed by A. S. Byatt 'the greatest novel in the

---

3 Brecht sought a theatrical strategy to invite 'complex seeing'. He famously disputed with Lukács the best means by which this might be achieved. As Nichols (1991: 194) summarizes, 'Lukács located the beginnings of this process in experiential qualities of narration, which offer both pleasure and recognition, involvement and awareness simultaneously. Brecht held out for reason joined to passion, Lukács for insight embedded in classic narrative structure. In either case, ideological struggle and political change follow from the changes of habit that art . . . can provoke.'

English language' (BBC 1994: 5). Produced by Michael Wearing and with a screenplay by Andrew Davies, the serialization had a budget of £6 million for the 300 minutes' running-time of its six episodes. By any standards of TV drama production *Middlemarch* was expensive to make, as befitted its status as a flagship production for the BBC at a time when the future of the institution was in question. Such funding is made possible by the world sales potential of a prestigious British period drama with established actors such as Robert Hardy, Peter Jeffrey, Michael Hordern, and Patrick Malahide to draw the audience. Motives other than profit might, however, inform the serialization. For, in a number of respects, the *Middlemarch* project surpasses in ambition and audience reach 'BBC classic drama', which, as designer Gerry Scott observes, 'used to be a studio production, mainly broadcast on Sunday afternoons at children's tea-time, and seen largely as being educational' (BBC 1994: 30).

Middlemarch, in its contrasting novel and television serial forms, offers an excellent example for discussion of linguistic codes and conventions. Two issues are of particular interest in the context of this study: constructed mythologies (in Barthes's sense; see Barthes 1973: 117–74) seeking to naturalize themselves as 'reality'; and the relative decline in (post)modern TV drama of a sense of history. The theoretical question of the facility of languages, and of the realist form in particular, to 'adequate the real' has a particular contemporary relevance to the televisual dramatization of classic literature. For if a television serial could afford unmediated access to the past, it would be possible for the viewers to adjudge the quality of life and its ethical seriousness or otherwise in comparison with modern society. There is, however, no possibility of such unmediated access since all reconstructions cannot but be constructions ideologically shot through with modern ways of seeing.

There is, then, a primary question of the ability of the written language in the form of George Eliot's novel to give a full account of English society in the 1830s, which it consciously professes to do. Questions then follow about the capacity of any language to re-create—as opposed to construct—myths of the past in visual and verbal imagery. Even assuming positive answers about the capacity of the written word or the medium of television, the ability to translate George Eliot's thousand-page prose fiction into a television drama serial of six fifty-minute episodes would remain for consideration. The issue of adaptation as translation will be the focus of this discussion.

The conventions of realism are homologous with the methodology of empirical science in that an attempt is made to transcend the subjective point of view to take a broader, more objective view of the world. As Nagel has noted, however, objectivity and subjectivity are themselves relative to different fields of enquiry:

> A standpoint that is objective by comparison with the point of view of one individual may be subjective by comparison with a theoretical standpoint still farther out. The standpoint of morality is more objective than that of private life, but less objective than the standpoint of physics. We may think of reality as a set of concentric spheres, progressively revealed as we detach gradually from the contingencies of the self. (1986: 5)

A realist novel such as *Middlemarch* advances precepts of how the social world operates, paralleling the hypotheses of science about the physical world. In some respects like a sociological study, it documents in detail its observations of lived experience in support of its way of seeing. The range and breadth of *Middlemarch*'s coverage of provincial town life in the 1830s approximates to a more objective view than is possible in a first-person narrative. With regard to human intercourse, for example, an attempt is made to embrace both the inner and the outer perspectives of the characters and their lives, as it were the physical reality and the subjective experience of it.

Whilst Nagel acknowledges that the idea of objectivity 'applies to values and attitudes as well as to beliefs and theories' (1986: 5), the novel might be seen, in relation to his concentric spheres, to take the standpoint of morality, less objective than the physicist but well outside the personal. In contrast with the presumed scientific objectivity of Flaubert,[4] however, the authorial commentary of *Middlemarch* evidently presents the personal views of George Eliot (Mary Ann Evans) throughout. But, unlike the self-conscious mode of the writers of postmodern fiction, the viewpoint is not reflexively acknowledged. The relative suppression of point of view is important in varying fictional modes in terms of their apparent truth-claims. Though ultimately, as Nagel points out, 'we can't forget about those subjective starting points indefinitely: we and our personal perspectives belong to the world' (1986: 6).

In the dramatization of the novel the viewpoint of the novelist and dramatizer, following the conventions of TV drama's realism, are suppressed. The world of Middlemarch is presented apparently unmediated, thus authenticating its presumed objectivity. It is not until the summary at the very end of the serial when the later

---

4 As Auerbach (1953: 486) observes, in Flaubert's novels 'His opinion of his characters and events remains unspoken; and when the characters express themselves it is never in such a manner that the writer identifies himself with opinion or seeks to make the reader identify himself with it. George Eliot is a much more intrusive author not sharing so fully with Flaubert the belief that 'the truth of the phenomenal world is also revealed in linguistic expression' (cited in Auerbach 1953: 486).

histories of the characters and George Eliot's observations on the significance of the lives of ordinary people are recounted over the visual images (in the voice of Judi Dench as George Eliot), that the authorial voice is overtly heard. This does not mean that the viewpoints of either George Eliot or Andrew Davies are absent from the serial—indeed there are interesting conflicts between them—but that their perspectives remain unacknowledged in accord with the conventional aspect of critical realism.

The process of dramatization for screen of a weighty and densely textured novel inevitably means selection, condensation, and most significantly transposition from the medium of the written word to that of visual images with a soundtrack, bound, moreover, by the conventions of television drama. Inevitably in that process of translation Davies both reads (in Barthes's sense) and rewrites *Middlemarch* in part from his own point of view but with an eye to George Eliot's way of seeing. The notion of fidelity to the original, so often raised when a film or TV serial is made of a novel, is misplaced precisely in its failure to recognize that the process of dramatization is one of translation between languages which are not wholly commensurable. It reveals, furthermore, something of a characteristic 'high cultural' reification of a work implied in the conception of aura which, Benjamin (1992: 211–44) famously notes, mechanical reproduction displaces.

To take a specific example where the difference of viewpoint between Davies and Eliot informs the serial, Davies reads Eliot as being unable to resist revealing her views of characters even to the detriment of her narrative. She reveals, he argues, too much antipathy to Casaubon even before he appears in the novel such that his attraction for Dorothea is almost incomprehensible. Similarly, Davies feels that George Eliot cannot bear her readers to like any of her characters more than she does and that she is severe with characters such as Will Ladislaw and Rosamund Vincy whose physical attractiveness and shallow natures afford them, as she sees and presents them, too easy a life.

Davies's attempts to redress the balance—or tell the story from his point of view—were not entirely successful. Whilst his writing of a weighty and intelligent political speech for Ladislaw to deliver on Brooke's husting served successfully to lend a depth to his character—which Davies perceived to be necessary to make him worthy of Dorothea—his attempts conversely to lighten Casaubon prior to the marriage were to some extent foiled by Malahide's performance. The actor played his own reading of George Eliot's authorial viewpoint portentously against the grain of Davies's intended dramatization.

With regard to the process of translation, a televisual way of seeing and storytelling informed changes to the language and narrative structure of the prose fiction novel. Thinking in filmic language, producer Michael Wearing saw Middlemarch—and Lydgate's arrival in it—in terms of the iconography of a Western: Lydgate as the pioneering individual, the outsider riding into town to make his mark. Thus the reworking of generic tropes may be seen to endorse Baudrillard's sense that media languages recycle themselves in a loop divorced from any historical reality. This kind of thinking also brings out the way in which the balance of a novel can be shifted by the very nature of translation between mediums governed by differing generic conventions.

The two stories centrally informing *Middlemarch* are those of Lydgate and Dorothea, two young idealists committed to progress through social reform. In the novel the two narratives are given roughly equal weight, Dorothea's if anything taking precedence. In the serial, however, it is Lydgate's story which seems stronger. The reason for this might be accounted for simply in terms of the different media. People who do things and make things happen suit the characteristically action-driven plotting of drama—particularly in realist forms—much better than thinkers, whose contemplations are more adequately expressed in the verbal medium of the novel, which affords time and space for reflection. In the narrative Dorothea is frustrated by being a woman constrained by social convention and by her repressive husband from actively engaging in projects. There is literally little she can do. In contrast, Lydgate, with the liberty of masculinity, is afforded the opportunity to visit his patients in and around the town, open a new hospital, and engage in his practical medical research. This difficulty is emphasized by television producers' conception of an affective order and viewing conditions which takes as too slow the kind of pace of cutting which might afford reflection on the part of the audience. A tension between the demands of (post)modern television and the measured reflection demanded by the density and complexity of George Eliot's novel is played out in the process of dramatization.

Taking up Michael Wearing's perspective, the title sequence—cut at sufficient pace to suggest a progressive dynamic—does show Lydgate approaching Middlemarch aboard a stagecoach. He observes the building work of the railway on its outskirts and merely remarks, 'the future'. Lydgate's bright disposition suggests a man ready for action in contrast with some of the more sleepy rural imagery of the shepherd driving the sheep with his dog and the slow traffic of carts in town. The music underscores this juxtaposition, increasing in tempo as Lydgate arrives on the scene. The serial's first sequence proper also involves horse-riding, though ironically in the light of the comments on action versus reflection above, featuring not Lydgate but Dorothea.

Whereas the novel opens with a discussion of religion which might have yielded visual imagery but would scarcely have provided a dynamic opening likely to hook the casual television viewer, Dorothea's horse ride with her sister through the woods affords cinematic dynamism with tracking shots and action close-ups intercut to establish both character and location in a visually interesting way. Making a further contribution to the economy of condensation from weighty novel to the television serial, the ride attempts in addition to solve a problem of the characterization of Dorothea as Davies wished to construct her. He recognized that the incidents of the narrative afforded opportunities to bring out her spiritual and intellectual zeal but that the passionate dimension of her nature—in Davies's view a repressed sexuality—was more difficult to convey through the plot action. The horse-riding sequence was intended to imply Dorothea's wilful suppression of a potent aspect of her personality. Women riding can connote an active sexuality through the associations of physical exertion and close sensual proximity to—and perhaps control over—a powerful animal. The heat of the chase was intended to throw into relief Dorothea's immediate announcement as she dismounts that she will give up the activity. That the sequence may not entirely have conveyed such an implication does not negate the point of the illustration, namely that an attempt was being made to translate an aspect of Dorothea's character which is dealt with obliquely in authorial commentary in the novel into a mainly visual language.

Another aspect of transposition affected by the differing mediums is the mode of storytelling. Although *Middlemarch* was originally serialized for publication by George Eliot, its intertwined narratives needed restructuring for a television version. Where the novel traces one story across a considerable span before moving to the next, the conventions of television drama—accelerated in pace in developed TV practice as illustrated—demands a much faster cutting between shorter narrative segments. The danger of this pacy mix when a number of stories are being told is that it gravitates towards the soap format. Segments are intercut so rapidly that no one narrative can be developed with any subtlety and viewers are afforded no time to engage deeply with, in emotional terms, and/or reflect upon, the experience depicted. That this is a tendency rather than formally determined, however, is evidenced below.

Whilst the serialization of *Middlemarch* avoids the worst superficiality of soaps in terms of representing the textures of lived experience, it does suffer to an extent from the traction of the range of forces noted, which tend to pull George Eliot's densely textured and reflective fiction into the action narrative mould of modern TV formulaic realism. Furthermore, the central couples and their personal relationships, particularly that of Dr Lydgate and Rosamund Vincy, tend to predominate. As a consequence, formulaic realism's disposition to efface history to focus on decontextualized personal relationships in the present moment comes into play. The broader historical context (two years prior to the 1832 Reform Act) of *Middlemarch*, the novel, whilst evident in traces, is minimalized in the television version. It remains in the narrative of Brooke's pretensions to stand for Parliament, in Lydgate's wish to open the hospital, and in Dorothea's reforming zeal. But formulaic realism's privileging of clearly—because two-dimensionally—drawn characters, and action over complexity and reflection, exacts a cost in the television adaptation of *Middlemarch*. The loss is precisely that of situated practice. The reforming zeal of Dorothea and Lydgate comes to seem more a matter of quirks of personality than part of a historical tendency, since their personal relationships, with Casaubon and Rosamund respectively, are made in their immediacy to seem the very stuff of life, in the manner of soaps and popular series.

For all the influences recounted above involved in the reshaping of *Middlemarch* from page to screen, some features of the experience of reading the novel are successfully transposed and carry its capacity, in Wittgenstein's terms, to make its object stand still for apprehension and reflection.

A great strength of George Eliot's novel in suggesting the textures of experience is her ability to convey the complexity of motivation. At its best the dramatization is comparably successful. The moment of Lydgate's visit to the Vincy household with a message for Mr Vincy, when his conscious mind, had it been fully engaged, would tell him that in working hours Vincy would be at the warehouse, illustrates that success. As he perhaps unconsciously expected, Lydgate finds Rosamund, whom he suspects has fallen in love with him, alone and unhappy in her passive predicament of awaiting his move. In a trice he finds himself kissing away her tears and engaged to the mayor's daughter without ever consciously making a decision about his relationship with Rosamund.

The serial's capacity to convey the complexity of such moments was aided by fine performances, in particular from Douglas Hodge as Lydgate. Comparable moments show him in close-up reacting at his wife's bedside after Rosamund, having rejected his specific advice, has fallen whilst riding and suffered a miscarriage. The mixture of anger, pity, and love for his wife, sorrow at the avoidable loss of their child, frustration at that part of his marriage which strikes him as folly are all conveyed by subtle televisual 'face-acting' caught in a series of reaction shots. The complexity arises here from situated practice: Lydgate's positive social dynamic in the tide of a progressive history is set in tension with his equally powerful private passions, which are undermining his project. The depth of emotion evoked arises from a felt complexity within—and potentially through empathy beyond—the diegesis. Screen time constructed through a series of intercut looks and glances affords viewers a more profound engagement than is characteristically offered in formulaic realism.

To succeed in affording viewers time to respond to and reflect on emotional and intellectual complexity, the rhythm of the editing of *Middlemarch* is at such moments very much slower than that of a typical soap or popular series. An example is the sequence in which, having deferred a decision overnight on bowing to Casaubon's will by agreeing to follow his bidding in the event of his death, Dorothea seeks to join her husband on the following morning in the garden where he is reading, only to find him slumped dead over his books. The thoughts and emotions that might be running through her head are complex. Her marriage has been miserable and not at all what she consciously anticipated in terms of her spiritual and intellectual development or, unconsciously perhaps, in terms of sexual satisfaction. She recognizes, however, that Casaubon, despite his apparent emotional rejection of her, has had a frustrated inner emotional and intellectual life of his own. Physically spurned by her husband, she has felt an attraction to Will Ladislaw though she is not as yet—at least consciously—aware of the strength of her feeling. In one sense Casaubon's death is liberating for her; in another it is a great loss and sadness. A complex web is George Eliot's central metaphor for the book as a whole and each of its parts. It is an apt metaphor to describe Dorothea's feelings at this moment, and the lingering camera demanded that viewers reflect on its complexity.

In modern TV screenplay terms the sequence which treats this moment is very slow. Two minutes at the end of the episode are afforded to Dorothea from her entering the garden to the fade to black and the credits at the end of the episode. Almost half of that time is taken up with a close two-shot, foregrounding the top of her deceased husband's head, but showing Dorothea full-face to camera speaking just a few words slowly and softly in a fruitless effort to rouse him as the truth of the situation slowly dawns on her. This is an exceptionally long time for a TV camera to linger on inaction involving no further plot information or dialogue. It demands an active and imaginative response from viewers to engage with the complex web of Dorothea's thoughts and feelings. It is this aspect of the series which, with some success, attempts to retain the textures and moral seriousnesss of the novel, whatever the motivations of the production overall and the difficulties of the transposition of codes. The weakness of the dramatization, as the discussion above of its better moments illustrates by contrast, is that the focus has ultimately been shifted from the broader historical and intellectual context of the action of the novel on to the interpersonal romantic relationships.

There is real value, in the terms advocated in this book for the engagement of deeper feelings for other human beings in a world which tends to desensitize, in the way those relationships are treated. The characters are drawn more fully than the stereotypes characteristic of popular format TV drama. The complexity of the characters' motivation; the sense conveyed that the interplay between mind and body, decision and action, is elusive and that the notion of interest-free, rational action is thus in question; the demonstration that the best-intentioned of actions can result in unhappy effects; the sense conveyed that social circumstances constrain human potential—all contribute to an imaginative viewing experience increasingly rare in the TV drama schedules. It is in this kind of TV drama that the emotional aspect of the ethic of truth-telling comes into play. For a human truth—in marked contrast with a positivist, instrumental truth—is established through a mixture of thought and feeling, albeit in accordance with recognized norms of plausibility and credibility.

The demands consequently made on viewers to watch intently and actively to work out the implications of the internal drama because they are obliquely presented mainly through visual images unsupported by an explanatory dialogue is in marked contrast to the often overwritten popular formats in which, at worst, the dialogue fully articulates the motives of two-dimensional characters, and the visual images merely reinforce the words. The slow pace affords, as noted, time for a mixture of thoughtful and deep emotional responses. In short, there is some potential in the dramatization of *Middlemarch* for the kind of rich reading experiences offered by the novel. The forces of modern TV production and reception have tended, however, to pull the serial towards the narrative structure of a soap and, furthermore, to an overemphasis on love interest. It is unjust to say that the dramatization has reduced the novel to a soap, but equally unjust to claim it has translated the novel fully into the television medium.

It remains briefly to place the dramatization of *Middlemarch* in its historical moment. The production by the BBC at a time when its charter was under review, and when the justifiability of its very independent existence as an institution had been called in question by government ministers, might appear to bear the traces—if only of guilt by association—of serving to (re)construct and popularize a national heritage tradition allegedly inscribed in literary and dramatic high culture. The effective, if unintentional, reassertion of a perennial 'Englishness' in *Middlemarch*, the serial, thus has political resonances in the mid-1990s. The title sequence is interesting when viewed from this perspective. Carved in roman capitals in stone with gold infill, the graphic depiction of 'MIDDLEMARCH' is underscored by measured orchestral soundtrack which strongly evokes the 'England' connoted in the music of Vaughan Williams.

As Andrew Davies acknowledges, one reading of the serial—notwithstanding the context of its historical setting just prior to the 1832 Reform Act—serves to remind a modern audience of a time when Britain was confident of its values and people knew where they stood—subservient to their 'betters'. Much of the action of the plot develops through time to restore misfortunes and redress injustices: Bulstrode's downfall leading to Fred Vincy's ultimate success, for example. When set against visual imagery of the countryside which evokes the 'Englishness' of Constable, the serial—through the very quality of its composition and its technical facility with lighting and photographic apparatus—is lent a sense of national geographic permanence. Indeed, at worst, the skeleton of the narrative might be taken to illustrate that the zeal for reform, differently pursued by Dorothea Brooke and Will Ladislaw, is no more than a diversion from the true course of their lives, their personal relationship in love.

At worst, following postmodernism's dehistoricizing tendency, the history of George Eliot's *Middlemarch* becomes the heritage of the BBC's *Middlemarch*. The past is dislocated and, in place of history, 'free-floating signifiers' are attractively packaged and recirculated. The work and expense to reconstruct the environment of Middlemarch, stressed in the pre-publicity, serves less as empirical realism to authenticate that dynamic process of historical formation valued by Lukács in the historical novel, than as spectacle. It may even serve to reify a reactionary sense of endurable 'Englishness'.

Period drama is increasingly seen worldwide to be the area of British television expertise. Indeed the 'quality' status accorded British television rests in part on the longevity of British (European) cultural traditions. The established reputation of the canon of English (European) literature is augmented in its television version by valued features of more recently established traditions. The dramatization adds actors with international reputations but exhibiting a peculiarly British acting style. Britain provides in addition a wealth of historic locations. There may also be general associations of cultural myths such as those of stability, democracy, and fair play.

High production values are demanded for spectacular imagery. Foremost this entails shooting on film with a budget comparable with that of modern feature film production. Money is needed to find and restore locations 'authentically' and to construct a world which ultimately convinces, not by a history grounded in human experience, but by the depth and richness of its textures. In a medium where landscape is restricted, the sumptuous interior settings and costumes are in themselves a feature of popular spectacle on television.

To raise money, the BBC, wearing its new commercial livery, took full advantage of pre-publicity in all available media to build an audience for a popular project with 'high art' association—ideally suited to the taste of the new social configuration. Following the broadcast of the series, an educational 'resource pack' (jointly prepared with the BFI education department) was produced on a commercial basis for educational institutions to extend interest in the series and potentially to prepare a young audience for future BBC period serials. To amass the budget necessary for a production of this kind, however, world sales—and probably co-production money—are needed, and these have implications for the product.

Attractive imagery of 'the past' is required for the American market, but there must be no dirty fingernails to puncture the myth. In the account above of the dramatization of *Middlemarch* the tension between the *mise-en-scène* as historically grounding context and as heritage backdrop may be seen in play. When contemplating the implications of the ethical seriousness of a television dramatization such as *Middlemarch*, the pleasures taken by some viewers which militate against a critical consciousness can be neither underestimated nor overlooked.

References Auerbach, Erich (1953), *Mimesis: The Representation of Reality in Western Literature*, trans. W. R. Trask (Princeton: Princeton University Press).

BBC Education (1994), *Middlemarch: A Viewer's Guide* (London: BBC).

Barthes, Roland (1973), *Mythologies*, trans. A. Lavers (London: Paladin).

Benjamin, Walter (1992), 'The Work of Art in an Age of Mechanical Reproduction', in *Illuminations*, ed. Hannah Arendt (London: Fontana).

Marshment, Margaret, and Hallam, Julia (1994), 'From String of Knots to Orange Box: Lesbianism on Prime Time', in Diane Hamer and Belinda Budge, *The Good, the Bad and the Gorgeous: Popular Culture's Romance with Lesbianism* (London: Pandora).

Nagel, Thomas (1986), *The View from Nowhere* (Oxford: Oxford University Press).

Nelson, Robin (1997), *TV Drama in Transition: Forms, Values and Cultural Change* (London: Macmillan).

Nichols, Bill (1991), *Representing Reality* (Bloomington: Indiana University Press).

Winterson, Jeanette (1994), *Great Moments in Aviation and Oranges Are Not the Only Fruit* (London: Vintage Books).

13

Broadcast Comedy and Sitcom

Steve Neale and Frank Krutnik

The Sitcom as
Trap

STEPTOE AND SON ran for four series in the 1960s and then returned from 1970 to 1974; when selected episodes were repeated in 1988 they managed consistently to make the top ten weekly TV ratings.[1] The show began in 1962 as one of a series of ten 'comedy playlets' programmed under the title *Comedy Playhouse*. Ray Galton and Alan Simpson were commissioned to write these when their long-running partnership with Tony Hancock was terminated. Galton and Simpson first wrote for Hancock on the radio comedy-variety show *Happy Go Lucky* in 1951, and they continued to work for him both on radio and in the West End revues *London Laughs* (1952) and *The Talk of the Town* (1954–5). With Hancock's reputation growing through the early 1950s, he was eventually offered a starring show on BBC radio, to be scripted by Galton and Simpson. *Hancock's Half-Hour* (1954) is particularly interesting for the ways in which it developed as a situational comedy structured around a comedian.

Hancock was not a conventional stand-up comedian like Bob Monkhouse or Bob Hope, but rather his act came increasingly to emphasize his *reactions* to situations. He was not a joke-teller—and was reputedly a bad ad-libber—but rather presented himself to be *laughed at*. As Freddie Hancock and David Nathan have remarked of his post-war stage performances:

> His idea of comedy was to stand in front of a microphone and work himself into a situation. He did imitations, not in the meticulous manner of an impersonator, but in the style of a clown

First published in Steve Neale and Frank Krutnik, *Popular Film and Television Comedy* (London: Routledge, 1990), 247–61.

1 Unless otherwise noted, the episodes of *Steptoe and Son* referred to here are drawn from the 1970s shows, repeated in 1988, and also available on home video releases.

imitating an impersonator, the funny thing being not the accuracy of the mimicry but the fact that he was doing it at all. In this way he could impersonate people his audience had never heard of . . .[2]

Hancock's Half-Hour represented an accommodation of Hancock's performance skills to the demands of repeatable situation comedy. The situation of the show was firmly centred round the persona developed by Hancock and his writers, and it deviated from the bourgeois family norm of domestic sit-com. 'Hancock' was an 'outsider': a 'belligerent, pompous, frequently childish and petulant',[3] middle-aged bachelor who not only was forever seeking to better himself but believed at the same time that he was already superior. When the show started on radio, Hancock functioned—in quite conventional fashion—as the star performer in an ensemble context, with Bill Kerr, Kenneth Williams, Sid James, and Hattie Jacques among his regular supporting players. However, in time Sid James became increasingly prominent, and the show shifted to a two-man comedy format (this becoming entrenched when the TV version started in 1956).

The early radio shows tended to include moments of fantastical exaggeration of the type particularly suited to the sound medium—for example, in 'The Television Set' (June 1955), Sid sells Hancock a build-it-yourself TV which when constructed is so large that it occupies the whole of the living room. Many of these early episodes also relied upon conventionalized plots in which Hancock is the dupe of one of Sid's elaborate swindles[4]—involving, for example, the sale of Lord's cricket ground as a farm ('Agricultural 'Ancock', February 1957). During the course of the show's run on radio and TV Galton and Simpson moved increasingly from such devices—and such standbys as catchphrases and funny voices[5]—towards a more firmly 'naturalistic' form of situation comedy which centred upon the 'Hancock' character. 'Sunday Afternoon at Home' (April 1958) is frequently cited to illustrate the development of the show, and is an episode from the fifth radio series in which, as Roger Wilmut has noted, 'there was no plot to speak of, and much use was made of long pauses'.[6] Indeed, Barry Took sees Galton and Simpson's distinctive contribution to broadcast comedy as 'their knack of reproducing mundane conversation and lifting it to the level of high art'.[7] The 'Sunday Afternoon' episode was deliberately 'experimental' in terms of the current context of radio comedy in

---

2 Freddie Hancock and David Nathan, *Hancock* (London: Coronet, 1975), 34.

3 Ibid. 83.

4 Roger Wilmut, *Tony Hancock, 'Artiste'* (London: Methuen, 1978), 64.

5 Ibid. 45.

6 Ibid. 72.

7 Barry Took, *Laughter in the Air* (London: Robson/BBC, 1981), 130.

that it represented a move away from tightly constructed plots and gags and towards a low-key 'naturalistic' style which capitalized upon boredom and inactivity, with Hancock and his friends sitting around at home seeking various diversions from the monotony of a Sunday. In the sixth and final radio series Galton and Simpson developed this minimal-plot technique, and the series was also significant in replacing comedians like Kenneth Williams with straight actors.[8]

Hancock's Half-Hour, although it placed increasing emphasis upon 'Hancock' as a *character*, still incorporated moments of specialized performance (indeed, the 'Hancock' character is usually located as a professional comedian): as in 'The Economy Drive' (TV, September 1959), where he impersonates W. C. Fields; 'The Missing Page' (TV, March 1960), where he performs an intricate mime in order to explain the plot of a thriller to Sid; and in 'The Baby Sitters' (TV, April 1960),[9] where he does characteristic impersonations of Winston Churchill, George Burns, and Groucho Marx. Such routines, although frequent, are by no means the major source of the comedy. 'The Bedsitter' (June 1961), the first show of the final TV series, makes this explicit, for the whole episode is a solo performance by Hancock, an extended piece of in-character acting. As in the 'Sunday Afternoon' episode, this show hinges around nothing actually happening, upon precisely how the character reacts to a boring evening—although this time Hancock is on his own (for by the time of this series Sid James had been dropped). This is the episode of the Hancock show which most resembles a one-act play, not just in its continuity of action but also in the use of such 'dramatic' devices as the monologue and 'stage business'.

Hancock ended his partnership with Galton and Simpson before his 1963 series with ATV, but in *Steptoe and Son* the writers were able to extend many of the techniques which had interested them in *Hancock's Half-Hour*. One of the major differences, however, was that the lead roles in *Steptoe* were played by two straight actors— Harry H. Corbett as the son, Harold, and Wilfred Brambell as his father, Albert. The situation was furthermore much more rigidly defined than that of the Hancock show, which occasionally departed from its traditional setting (as in 'The Bowmans' (June 1961), where Hancock is a long-running soap opera star). The situation in *Steptoe and Son* resembles the middle phase of *Hancock's Half-Hour* in that it centres upon a relationship between two men which—as in other two-man sitcoms like *Bootsie and Snudge*, *The Odd Couple*, *Chico and the Man*, and *The Likely Lads*—oscillates between friendship and antagonism. However, unlike these other

8 Wilmut, *Tony Hancock*, 73.
9 Ibid. 112–13.

shows, the two men are united by blood rather than friendship or custom (and the situation further unites familial and working relations, for the Steptoes run a small rag-and-bone business from their home).

In *Steptoe* there is a marked non-correspondence between its *situational* 'normality'—the stable situation to which each episode returns—and the bourgeois-familial 'normality' which is the ideological touchstone of the traditional domestic sitcom. In fact, in its lack of regular female characters, its emphatic squalor, and its verbal and physical crudity (and sometimes cruelty), *Steptoe and Son* is the *inverse* of such shows: the show's situational 'inside' is the conventional 'outside', and vice versa. But at the same time, unlike many of the British 'alternative' sitcoms of the 1980s, the show was aimed at a broad family-based peak-time audience. The key to its notable success seems to be the way in which it represents a *spectacle* of inverted bourgeois decorum for a bourgeois audience: one has to know the 'rules' in order to recognize and to find funny the ways in which they are broken. As such a spectacle, the show works precisely because the Steptoes are *not* the average middle-class family (otherwise their behaviour would be problematic). They are marked out, in other words, as a special case, and the disordered, junk-cluttered setting of the Steptoe home is very much a 'world apart', isolated from the norms of middle-class existence and only occasionally and reluctantly visited by such representatives of the bourgeoisie as the vicar and his wife, a doctor, a tax officer, and Harold's short-lived bohemian acquaintances. Whereas Albert blatantly, often aggressively, rejects middle-class codes of behaviour and sensibility, Harold is continually attempting—like Hancock—to 'better' himself, to adopt bourgeois attitudes, and to impress bourgeois figures. Where Hancock's pretensions are frequently undercut by the ignorance behind his pedantry, Harold's doomed aspirations are marked particularly in his use of language: his attempts at a higher-class discourse are not only patently affected but they are also sabotaged either by Albert's crude jibes or by Harold's own lapses into his 'natural' (as the show implies) vulgarity. His high-flown, somewhat nervous rhetoric always seems to run out of steam and to run aground on such colourful 'non-U' expressions as 'I don't give a toss' and 'you little toerag'. Integral, then, to the show's situation and logic is a deterministic class ideology: Harold, despite his aspirations, cannot escape what he is—a lower-class Steptoe, like Albert.

The plots of most episodes tend to centre upon an attempt by Harold to escape from his frustrating circumstances—either directly, or through 'self-betterment'—and his inevitable failure to do so. At the end, each episode returns the situation to 'normal', at the cost of Harold's continuing frustration. This process is similar to that found in many episodes of *Hancock's Half-Hour* which, as John Fisher has noted,[10] tend to contain circular plot structures, with the end representing an emphatic return to the beginning; 'The Economy Drive' and 'The Lift' (June 1961) are exemplary in this respect. Just as Hancock is perpetually frustrated in his attempt to escape from his 'character', so too is Harold, and both characters similarly are marked by a tendency to fantasize. In 'The Ladies' Man' (April 1960), an episode of his TV show, Hancock's lack of success with women motivates him to enlist in a charm school; but once there he spends most of his time daydreaming that he is a debonair, talented, and sought-after bachelor. Most often, however, the fantasies of both Hancock and Harold Steptoe are expressed through monologues. Militating against Harold's articulation of his wishes—marking them out precisely as fantasy—is the very setting itself (the squalid, cluttered home) and also the pathos-inducing comments and very presence of his father. During these mono-logues, Harold will often be standing in medium close-up to one side of the foreground while, in the background, Albert sits and scowls. Each of Harold's fantasies represents a potential (though often markedly unrealizable) chance to escape from the trap he finds himself in: a career as an actor ('A Star is Born'), or a doctor ('Upstairs, Downstairs; Upstairs, Downstairs'), or a writer ('Men of Letters'), or, particularly, a chance to 'escape' through a hetero-sexual relationship (as in 'And so to Bed' and 'Loathe Story').

The sense of a trap is much more emphatic in *Steptoe* than in the Hancock show, and this is not solely the result of Harold's lower-class status as a rag-and-bone man but also because in his relation-ship with the disgusting 'dirty old man', Albert, family obligation exerts a more complex and pressurizing force than exists in the Hancock–James friendship. As we have noted above, the sitcom as a form conventionally asserts stability at the expense of change: the recurring situation is *reinstated* rather than re-formed. Barry Took has suggested that 'all successful comedies have some trap in which people must exist—like marriage' and that the 'perfect situation' for a sitcom is 'a little enclosed world where you have to live by the rules'.[11] And Mick Eaton has elaborated upon the dramatic logic of the sitcom form:

> The necessity for the continuity of character and situation from week to week allows for the possibility of comedy being generated by the fact that the characters are stuck with each

10 John Fisher, *Funny Way to Be a Hero* (London: Muller 1973), 268.
11 Quoted by Francis Wheen, *Television* (London: Century, 1985), 205.

other. . . . It is as if the formal necessities of the series provide the existential circle from which the characters cannot escape.[12]

Whereas in the majority of sitcoms the implications of this structural necessity are played down, in *Steptoe* they are frequently made explicit—as in the following extract from one of Harold's monologues, inspired by a row over decorating:

> We seem to have reached our usual impasse, don't we? . . . You won't give way on anything, will you? You don't give a toss what colour we 'ave. You just try and go against me, don't you? . . . Whatever I want, you don't. . . . I mean, it's not just the decorations, it's—it's everything. I mean, every idea I have for improvement—I mean, improvements to the house, improvements to the business—you're agin' it. You frustrate me in everything I try to do. You are a dyed-in-the-wool, fascist, spoiled, little know-your-place, don't-rise-above-yourself, don't-get-out-of-your-hole, complacent little turd. (from 'Divided We Stand')

Harold's inability to escape from his 'trapped relationship' with his father becomes the very principle of the comedy, and the often overtly combative nature of the relations between them stems from the fact that the characters are 'stuck with each other'. As the psychiatrist tells Harold of his attempt to kill Albert in 'Loathe Story':

> It's a classical case of subconscious wish-fulfilment. These things are quite often the result of the hyper-tension when two people live in close proximity, in claustrophobic conditions, unable to pursue their outside interests. Happens all the time with married couples.

As this remark highlights, this is not the conventional relationship between father and son, for it displaces the more 'normal' relationship between husband and wife, and the aggression and outright violence are marked at all stages by the fact that women are excluded from the situation.

The Steptoe household is devoid of women—Harold's mother, Albert's wife, has been dead for over thirty years. As Crowther and Pinfold have remarked:

> The absence of a woman in the family was not merely a one-off joke, it was the solid core of the piece. . . . To have brought a woman into this all-male family would have been not only to

12 Michael Eaton, 'Television Situation Comedy', *Screen*, 19/4 (1978/9), 74.

jeopardise the relationship between the two principals but to cause the characters themselves to collapse.[13]

In such domestic sitcoms as *No Place Like Home* and *Bless this House* women play an integral role as the mainstay of the home, cementing family unity. The absence of women in *Steptoe* lends to the situation a fundamental *instability*. Women represent a direct threat to the Harold–Albert relationship. Generally, the danger comes from Harold's attempts to secure a girlfriend—endeavours which are always thwarted by Albert. In 'And so to Bed', for example, Harold's pursuit of the 'sex-starved' cinema usherette Marcia comes to a disastrous end after Albert accidentally punctures his son's new waterbed. And in 'Loathe Story' Harold's sexual and class aspirations are united in the figure of the upper-middle-class Bunty Kennington-Stroud (Joanna Lumley): Albert scuppers the affair in characteristic fashion through his deliberate vulgarity. In an earlier episode, 'The Stepmother' (1964), this situation is reversed in that the threat arises from Albert's plan to remarry, and it is Harold who sets in motion a scheme to break up the 'threatening' relationship. Thus women are here the 'outside' elements which have to be ejected to preserve the stability of the recurring situation. They are the object of Harold's fantasy, but they tend to be held obsessively at bay. It is worth noting that in Galton and Simpson's work for Hancock women also tend to occupy a rather problematic place; according to Roger Wilmut, the team could not write particularly well for women, and female performers tended not to remain with the show very long because of the insubstantial nature of their roles.[14]

Harold and Albert remain locked within an exclusively male circuitry: the very shabbiness of their home is a testimony to its lack of a female presence (compare the *Steptoe* set with the order and cleanliness of the bourgeois home in domestic sitcoms). Under their domestic–business arrangement, Albert is supposed to do the housekeeping and prepare meals while Harold is out on the rounds. However, the old man's activities represent a parody of the maternal, nurturing role since he does as little as he possibly can get away with and is always on the lookout for his own pleasure. Another consequence of *Steptoe*'s exclusion of 'femininity' is the way in which the two men shy away from any overt acknowledgement of their emotional interdependency. There is a nervousness concerning 'sentiment', and it tends to be restricted to Harold's guilty stuttering when he articulates one of his plans to break away, or to one of Albert's pathetic, wounded looks which function as a ploy to

---

13 Bruce Crowther and Mike Pinfold, *Bring me Laughter: Four Decades of TV Comedy* (London: Columbus, 1987), 65.
14 Wilmut, *Tony Hancock*, 40.

generate such guilt. Sentiment and femininity tend, however, not to be merely *absent* but they are rather *replaced* by a comically aggressive 'masculine' conflict through which any problematic emotional and plot complications can be discharged.

The two men are continually fighting, to assert and consolidate their position within the family in regard to each other. This state of conflict, indeed, represents the 'normality' of their relations—and it is customary for the show to conclude with a violently comic chase or fight. The perpetual competition between them also tends to be marked by instances of game-playing: scrabble in 'Men of Letters', chess in 'Cuckoo in the Nest', badminton in 'Loathe Story'. Albert is generally the winner, and in the process he affronts Harold's sense of how the game should be played (for example, by the use of obscenities in Scrabble). What is at stake in these games, as in the competitive 'routines' around which the show as a whole is constructed, is the position of masculine authority: Harold attempts to make Albert aware that he is dependent upon his son and should thus be grateful, whereas Albert schemingly uses various below-the-belt tactics to prevent Harold from deserting him. As David Nathan has commented:

> the old man walks a shaky path between belligerence and fear. His paternal authority is a relic of his younger and stronger days. He knows he is utterly dependent on Harold and that Harold could, if ever he took it into his head, push him into an old people's home or just walk out and leave him helpless. He takes refuge in a cunning pathos[15]

This situation is strikingly similar to the *Arabian Nights* story 'The Old Man of the Sea', where, out of pity, a young man agrees to carry on his back an elderly and infirm man, only to find that the latter is a parasite he cannot shake off. In his novel *Beware of Pity* Stefan Zweig discusses this story in terms which are remarkably close to the dramatic core of *Steptoe*:

> He has become the beast of burden, the slave, of the old rascal; no matter if his knees give and his lips are parched with thirst, he is compelled, foolish victim of his own pity, to trot on and on, is fated to drag the wicked, infamous, cunning old man for ever on his back.[16]

Whenever Harold is on the verge of leaving him, Albert will fake a heart attack or underline his infirmity by reminding his son of his war wounds. And even though Harold is aware of the old man's

15 David Nathan, *The Laughtermakers* (London: Peter Owen, 1971), 129.
16 Stefan Zweig, *Beware of Pity*, (Harmondsworth: Penguin, 1986), 184.

guile, he still finds that he is prevented from leaving because of the pressure of his emotional obligation to his father, and the feeling of guilt that this gives rise to.

What are at stake, then, in the 'serious', dramatic core of *Steptoe and Son* are familial obligation and allegiance in relation to the needs and desires of the individual. Because the situation is never allowed to be resolved, Harold's frustration is emphatically replayed. An episode entitled 'The Desperate Hours' (which is structured like a one-act play, with temporal and scenic continuity) contains what is perhaps the most markedly 'serious' treatment of these issues. The episode—which borrows and inverts the plot of the 1955 film of the same title—draws a dramatic parallel between the Steptoes and the relationship between two escaped convicts who shelter in their home: Johnny (Leonard Rossiter) and the elderly Frank (J. G. Devlin). The Steptoes are here at their most desperate, for they are destitute and hungry in the middle of winter, and the entry of the convicts establishes a comparison between their situation and the more literal trap of prison life; the convicts find the latter to be relatively luxurious! The conflict between obligation and independence which is continually articulated in the *Steptoe* series is here duplicated in the conflict of allegiances faced by Johnny, whose career in crime, imprisonment, and aborted escape attempt are all the result of his friendship with Frank. The Steptoes take sides: Harold tries to convince Johnny that he stands a better chance on his own, and Albert says that he cannot leave Frank to fend for himself. The argument becomes heated, for both Harold and Albert realize that they are in fact defending their own respective positions. Underlining the 'inevitable' resolution—Johnny returns to prison, taking Frank with him—is the familiar truth that Harold cannot escape his own prison of obligation. This episode is unusual in the degree of its dramatic seriousness: it illustrates how the situation is not *in itself* funny but rather is *made* funny.

Crowther and Pinfold have described the problematic of the *Steptoe* series as follows:

> The bonds that hold Harold to his father were those that hold children to ailing parents; that keep men and women locked in loveless marriages; that doom thousands of lives to quiet desperation from which escape is . . . impossible for the average person.[17]

It is the process of the conversion of this 'serious' situation into the terms of comedy which gives the show its particular charge. Often behind the broadest comedy in the show are actions which would

---

17 Crowther and Pinfold, *Bring me Laughter*, 64.

ordinarily be branded disturbing or cruel: for example, in 'Loathe Story' Harold is so upset by Albert's dominating influence that while sleepwalking he attempts to cut off the old man's head with a meat cleaver.

The relations between drama and comedy are particularly clear in the episode 'Upstairs, Downstairs; Upstairs, Downstairs', in which the parallel between the *Steptoe* situation and 'The Old Man of the Sea' is most emphatic. This episode begins in a markedly serious fashion: rather than the customary extended scene between Albert and Harold there is a long sequence between Harold and a doctor. The doctor tells him that Albert is very ill and that he will be bedridden, perhaps for several months. However, Harold does not react sympathetically to the threat of this long-term disability—he is concerned overtly with how this new development represents a further imprisoning of himself to the demands of the old man. This inversion of the 'normal' reaction to such an illness is quite typical of the show. The comic effect of the scene derives from Harold's lack of decorum in front of the doctor, from his exaggerated selfishness, and from the way in which sentiment is undercut in a comically brutal fashion. Harold suggests to the doctor that Albert is only seeking attention, and that he shove the old man in hospital so that he can be off his hands:

> Oh look doctor—I *know* 'im. 'E's not as bad as 'e makes out. You think 'e's ill—believe me, you bung 'im in 'ospital, stretch 'im on the floor, and 'e'll make the quickest recovery known to medical science.

The doctor, emissary of the bourgeoisie, is shocked by this competitive plea for attention: but, of course, we, the 'eavesdropping' audience who are familiar with the Steptoes' situation, know the 'true nature' of their relationship and do not share his reaction.

When the doctor leaves, Harold is called upstairs by Albert—whose nerve-racking, demanding screech of "Arold! 'Arold!' persists throughout the show—and he proceeds to 'wind up' the old man. First of all, he does an impression of a head waiter—a mockery of his service to Albert, and, like many other such moments in the series, perhaps a legacy of the writers' years with Hancock—and then he implies that Albert is on the verge of death. The old man becomes increasingly worried until he realizes what Harold is up to, and accuses him of being a 'callous little toerag'. Harold's cruelty is funny here precisely because of the way in which it makes light of the supposed seriousness of Albert's illness and the way in which it inverts bourgeois decorum (respect for the old, the infirm, human dignity, and so on). The two men then become engaged in one of their perpetual competitive rows, with the restoration to this 'normal' state of affairs serving to siphon off the serious implications of the doctor's sober announcement. Harold pretends that he will not be able to look after Albert because he is going away on holiday; however, when 'victory' is in sight, and the old man seems on the verge of tears—'I won't be a burden to you,' he pleads— Harold backs down from the 'game' and signals a truce by confessing that he was 'just muckin' about'. Such games can only go *so far* without overbalancing the comedy with its serious underpinnings: Albert further highlights the truce by delivering one of the show's recurring catchphrases—'You're a good boy, 'Arold'. But following this moment of relative quiet, Albert is once more shouting out for Harold to come and cater to his wishes, the extent of Harold's imprisoning obligation being highlighted when he has to carry him down to the outside lavatory (one of the key settings of the show).

The situation that Harold had feared comes about: when he has finished his daily round, he spends the rest of his time running and fetching for Albert. And, in the meantime, the old man makes the most of his stay in bed, inviting friends round, drinking beer, and watching the racing on TV, while Harold grows weaker and more exhausted. Whenever Harold falters, Albert produces one of his pained, sorrowful looks and laments about being a burden to him. By this stage in the show the enslavement of Harold is on the verge of turning into a 'melodramatic' problem, but this is sidestepped by means of a markedly comic plot reversal. Twisting his back in bed, Albert finds himself suddenly cured; however, rather than informing Harold of the fact, he proceeds to use the situation to his own advantage and carries on the pretence of being ill. Harold, however, noticing that the fridge has been raided in his absence, hides away in the larder and observes Albert scavenging around in the kitchen. So now a conventional comic plot of deception and counter-deception is in operation, a plot based on discrepancies of knowledge: Albert thinks that Harold is ignorant, Harold allows Albert to think he is ignorant.

Harold goes upstairs to tell Albert that he will give him a blanket bath. Albert is aghast at the prospect—being a 'dirty old man' in every way—and Harold's punishment of his father takes the form, first, of an over-vigorous flannelling, and secondly in pouring astringent surgical spirit over his groin. In a twist reminiscent of the conclusion to one of Boccaccio's stories, Albert screams 'Aaaah! Me goolies!' and leaps out of bed, with Harold proclaiming a 'miracle cure'. Harold laughs exuberantly and follows Albert about the house and yard as the old man seeks to quench the burning in his groin, eventually parking his backside in the kitchen sink. This ending is typical of the series in its combination of crudity, cruelty, and revenge, and in the physical knockabout character of its comedy. As in many other episodes, the dramatic undercurrents of the show and the concomitant emotional tensions are discharged through 'low' farce—which signifies both the restoration of 'stability' and the turning of aggression into 'masculine horseplay'. There is, in other words, no actual solution to the problems bound up within the situation itself, but rather a restoration of the competitive instability–stability of the relationship between the two men (that is, the restitution of instability *as* stability). Finally, it is worth noting that this principle of the 'discharge' of tension marks not only the way in which the plots of the individual episodes tend to be resolved, but it operates also at particular moments, whenever, in fact, the stability of the male relationship is threatened by sentiment or division.

Albert Steptoe, like Alf Garnett (Warren Mitchell), the central figure in the show *Till Death Us Do Part* (1964–74), is a 'monstrous' figure who disturbs the conventional family order and expresses opinions which run counter to accepted middle-class decorum: both characters are markedly racist, for example. However, with both shows, particularly because the family is carefully distinguished from the norm, the implications of their claustrophobic representation of family relations tend to be held in place. Although deviating in terms of their content, what is integral to these shows is a conventional use of the sitcom format—the situation is perpetually restored, and in the process it is both maintained and contained. Their very separation from the situational 'normality' of the traditional domestic sitcom localizes their deviations. As such, they function as further reminders of the ways in which institutional forms of comedy operate as vehicles for dealing with and making acceptable that which is aberrant or potentially threatening.

14

The Lads and the Gladiators: Traditional Masculinities in a Postmodern Televisual Landscape

Garry Whannel

FOR MUCH OF ITS HISTORY the television industry has conceived its audiences in heterogeneous terms; that is, it has assumed that most audiences are relatively mixed in terms of class, age, regional location, and gender. This has been especially true of large audiences. But ever since the establishment of Channel Four there has been a growing interest in identifying and winning more specifically defined target audiences, and advertisers too have paid closer attention to the demographic profile of audiences. The launch of Channel Five, the growth of satellite and cable television, and the advent of digital television are producing a growing fragmentation and demographic segmentation of audiences (see Seymour-Ure 1991).

In the heartland of popular television the major channels still conceive of large audiences in general terms and attempt to win viewers across the spectrum. However, two types of popular programme tend to win a somewhat gender-specific audience. Most soaps are watched by more women than men, and most sport by more men than women. Even in these two programme types, however, the gender balance is often no more uneven than 60–40.

Sport in itself is a distinctly male-dominated institution, whether assessed in terms of those who play, watch, or administer sports. But on television the efforts made to win an audience for sport broadcasting have always focused on the marginal viewer; and in the case of sport this marginal viewer is perceived as female. Various strategies are mobilized in the effort to build audiences. The narrativization of sport places star personalities centre-stage as a potential hook for viewers; contributors are chosen with an eye to their supposed appeal to women (Des Lynam, Alan Hansen in *Match of the Day*; BBC, 1964–); an exclusivist discourse of expertise drawing on masculine cultural capital is discouraged, by making sure that discussion never becomes excessively detailed or 'technical' (see Whannel 1992).

Audiences have been won most effectively where sport as subject-matter is repackaged in the form of 'quasi' sports-programmes like *Superstars* (BBC, 1975–80) and *A Question of Sport* (BBC, 1970–). The most effective strategy for regularly winning a large audience for sport has been that of *A Question of Sport*, which for many years drew much bigger audiences than any other regular sport-related television programme. *Gladiators* (LWT, 1992–), with its 'quasi' sport appearance, has also had some success in winning an audience. More recently, though, the growing fragmentation of audiences, a consequence of the growth in number of channels, has fostered a more precise targeting of demographically specific audiences. In the wake of the emergence of 'new lad' culture an alternative strategy, rooted in a resolutely laddist masculine tone, has been utilized with some success in *Fantasy Football League* (BBC, 1994–6) and *They Think It's All Over* (BBC, 1995–).

These new programmes can simply be seen as new variants of old forms produced by the constant pressure to compete for audiences, but they can also be located within the intersection of other factors such as the changing nature of gender relations, the supposed 'crisis' in masculinity, the growth of fitness chic and body culture, and the increasing self-referentiality of cultural products. Since 1970 the rise of feminism and the evolving place of women in society, marked by legislative reform, social change, and shifting employment patterns, has placed a focus on gender relations in which some entrenched masculine practices have come into question. Forms of sexual discrimination, sexist imagery, and macho behaviour have become more commonly contested, where they had formerly been taken for granted (see Barrett 1980; Rowbotham 1989; Segal 1992).

Changing gender relations, like any social transformation, produce adjustments and tensions. The emergence of 'new man' and 'new lad', the supposed 'crisis in masculinity', and the idea that there is 'trouble with boys' can be seen as manifestations of the tensions around gender relations. The process of recasting gender relations and contesting sexism that grew out of 1970s feminism has produced both responses and reactions (see Mort 1996; Nixon 1996; Edwards 1997).

Responses include challenges to sexist behaviour and imagery, changing patterns of male behaviour, the emergence, in discourse if not in social practices, of the figure of the 'new man', and the reduction of some overt forms of sexism and sexual discrimination. In *Gladiators* it is notable that both men and women compete in very similar ways, whereas in the 1980s programme *The World's Strongest Man* (ITV, 1980–1; BBC, 1982–96), only strong men competed, whilst women watched. The growth of fitness chic during the 1980s has in turn produced a narcissistic body culture in which muscularity and fitness are foregrounded. Where men in *The World's Strongest Man* were in a sense presented as freakish and excessively muscular, the male and female contestants in *Gladiators* are presented as 'ordinary people'.

Reactions include the anti-feminist backlash, discussed by Susan Faludi (1991), the re-emergence of sexist imagery into the cultural mainstream, especially via the covers of the new men's magazines, and the reassertion of sexist masculinities, as best exemplified by the magazine *Loaded*. Lad television—*Men Behaving Badly* (ITV, 1992; BBC, 1995–), *Fantasy Football League*, and *They Think It's All Over*—are all part of the process whereby this reactive laddism has moved into the mainstream. But lad television is not cast in the mould of body culture. Indeed, in its dogged anti-health hedonism it represents a reaction against the dominance of body culture.

The programmes I am discussing here, *Gladiators*, *Fantasy Football League*, and *They Think It's All Over*, all have strong elements of self-referentiality and intertextuality. They refer not so much to some non-televisual 'actuality', but rather to other media forms and conventions. *Gladiators* draws on the structure of sport broadcasting and the iconography of cartoon superheroes. *Fantasy Football League*'s jokes are largely based on the conventions of media sport coverage. *They Think It's All Over* borrows the format of *A Question of Sport* and reduces it to absurdity. These programmes exhibit many features that have been characterized as postmodern: parody, pastiche, and self-referentiality, the absence of any external 'reality', the foregrounding of surface appearance and apparent depthlessness.

From a different perspective, however, they can be seen as a continuation of a media-driven society of spectacle, in which culture is commodified and stars are transformed into celebrities. While the cinema produced stars, it can be argued that television produces personalities (Langer 1981); certainly a great many successful television formats are rooted in the audience appeal of well-established celebrity personalities. Such figures are frequently able to project their fame beyond the field in which it was originally established. Personalities become commodities, whose mere presence helps to win and hold audiences. Before pursuing the implications of these themes, however, I want to look in more detail at the elements of each programme and the conventions through which they are combined.

Gladiators   *Gladiators* employs the well-established elements of the game show format: presenters, contestants, setting, games, and audience involvement. In addition, *Gladiators* is built round the role of the gladiators themselves, whose menace presents the challenge and the threat that is central to the programme. The programme is set in an indoor arena and staged very like a sports event. The use of elaborate lighting effects, outlandish props, and bright, primary colours, and the orchestrating of the crowd by stage managers and cheerleaders give the show the feel of a mainstream light entertainment show. The genealogy of *Gladiators* can be traced back to *It's a Knockout* (BBC, 1966–82) and *Jeux Sans Frontières* (Eurovision–BBC, 1967–), shows that first brought together the iconography and competitive structure of sport and the controlled spectacle of light entertainment (Whannel 1982).

The manipulation of the audience, who are encouraged to participate in organized chants and gestures, and to respond to audio cues (for example, the Queen song 'Another One Bites the Dust'), a common device in audience-oriented television, is becoming a more common feature of sport itself. At Wembley Stadium the spontaneous celebrations of victory are now commonly written over and structured by the playing of music tracks like Queen's 'We are the Champions'. (It is ironic that the macho and homophobic terrace culture should have derived some of its key anthems from gay icons such as Freddie Mercury and the Village People, associated with the muscular macho-ization of gay culture.)

In *Gladiators* ordinary contestants compete against the gladiators, whose costumes, designed in the style of cartoon superheroes and villains, have echoes of science fiction, cyborgs, and mythical beasts. In their physical prowess the gladiators are sporting heroes mythologized. Their mythic status is underlined by the single, fictitious name they each adopt. Although they are thus rendered anonymous, readers of tabloid newspapers will also be aware that at least one, Nightshade, is an ex-international athlete. The gladiators are stern, fierce, individual, and terse in interview. They have no history, no background, and no associates. As menacing figures they combine elements of the new individualism, cyborg technology, and the threat of the streets. By contrast, the 'ordinary' contestants who must encounter the gladiators are, precisely, 'ordinary'. They have jobs, families (who are often visibly present in the audience), supporters, and last names. Details of their lives are revealed in interview. They are ordinary, but fit; they work, but they also find time for jogging or the gym.

Television presenters always have a privileged access to the television audience, controlling the discourse of the show, starting and finishing it. They are the only participants with a licence to talk directly to us, the television audience. The presenters in their pivotal role are a link between sport and show business, the ordinary and the mythic, the spectacle and the audience, and they act as an interface between the ordinary everyday of the contestants and the show-business glamour of the gladiators. In *Gladiators* the presenters are also star personalities: ex-footballer John Fashanu, and Ulrika Jonsson, who also appears on another manifestation of lad television, *Shooting Stars* (BBC, 1995–7).

The games are structured as combat sport events, involving physical challenge and risk. The skills required are rooted in fitness chic, workouts, and gym and body culture. The assault course echoes similar devices in *It's a Knockout* and *The Krypton Factor* (Granada, 1977–93). In *The Krypton Factor*, however, the assault course was only one element in a show that tested mental and physical abilities, whereas *Gladiators* represents the privileging of physical development over mental development, with echoes of neo-Darwinism. In a series of mythical battles in a controlled visual spectacle 'ordinary' people are pitted against mythical beasts in a series of encounters in which the odds seem stacked against them.

The programme offers an apparent model of gender equality. There are two male and two female contestants, in separate events; the games for men and for women are identical or similar; there are female and male gladiators. Yet traditional stereotypes do resurface, as in the contrast between the tough muscularity of John Fashanu, and the girly-babe-ness of Ulrika Jonsson. Jonsson's combination of blonde bombshell looks and her willingness to be simultaneously one of the lads, a good sport, the butt of jokes, and a babe makes her appear as a woman on male terms: the perfect star for the new lad culture. In *Shooting Stars*, where she is endlessly made the butt of crude and cruel verbal and physical jokes from Vic Reeves and Bob Mortimer, she keeps on smiling and playing along, acting out the amused tolerance that 'babes' are supposed to display in the face of laddish excess. Even when her apparently bruised face appeared on a full-page spread in the tabloid press after an incident in Paris involving footballer Stan Collymore during the 1998 World Cup Final, the 'babes and lads' frame was only temporarily dislodged.

How do you win and what do you win? Even though they are commonly defeated by the encounters, the structure of the show dictates that the 'ordinary' people survive. It is the gladiators who are eliminated before the last game. They are not defeated, but the structure of the show determines that in the final contests the two 'ordinary' contestants race each other. The programme constructs a world full of physical challenge, an urban jungle. It's dangerous out there, a world full of threatening figures and obstacles to overcome, but the 'ordinary' people come through OK. So contestants win survival and safety, along with their fifteen (fifty) minutes of fame, and a brief induction into the world of celebrity. As in *Blankety Blank* (BBC, 1979–89) and other game shows, players win time in the limelight.

Although bigger, tougher, fitter, and menacing, the gladiators cannot win; the 'ordinary' people always survive to the end, so the programme offers a validation of ordinary people and their ability to prepare themselves for the rigours and challenges of life. It is noteworthy that the programme was scheduled immediately before *Blind Date* (LWT, 1985–)—which also features 'ordinary' people encountering the world of celebrity and winning a date.

Fantasy Football League   This programme takes football as its subject, but filtered through the device of fantasy leagues, a significant emergent cultural form of the 1990s, in which (mostly) men are able to be fantasy managers, assembling their own virtual football teams. The theme is echoed by the use of football-type songs, scarves, and replica shirts amongst the audience. The format enables the plundering of the sport archives for clips framed by the irreverent and ironic perspective of the programme.

The programme is flip and anti-analysis in tone; there is little pretence at serious discussion of how these fantasy teams might work in an actual game. Indeed as the programme grew into its format, the fantasy league has become progressively less central, and is now largely a prop around which the humour of the programme can unfold.

The programme is set in a parodic version of a laddish flat, with echoes of *Men Behaving Badly* and *The Young Ones* (BBC, 1982, 1984), with sofas, coffee-table, a kitchenette, and football artefacts everywhere. Although clearly stylized, it is easy to imagine it as not too far in appearance from the real-life flat that presenters Frank Skinner and David Baddiel shared for some years. In the programme the presenters share the 'flat' with supernerd Statto, played by gambling pundit Angus Loughran.[1] As presenters, Skinner and Baddiel combine the traditions of variety double acts, the critical irreverence of alternative comedy, and the self-conscious vulgarity of new laddism.

Each week two celebrity guests are ushered in to a jingle in which their names are sung by Skinner and Baddiel. They arrive like guests to a dinner party and are sat on the sofa. Thereafter, however, they function largely as props, pretexts, and butts for the humour of the presenters. Appearing as mere tokens of themselves and their own celebrity, they are given only limited scope to contribute to the humour of the show. Women are more often presented as 'one of the lads' than as babes, although the supposed tenuousness of their involvement in the football culture of the lads is often exposed and used as the pretext for humour. The programme's strategies here reveal a masculine unease about women in relation to football culture; it is unsure whether to embrace them or exclude them. Indeed, it is with the appearance of guests like Birmingham City managing director Karen Brady or Norwich City director (and celebrity cook) Delia Smith, both figures with a stronger link to the real world of football than either Skinner or Baddiel can claim, that masculine unease with women is most apparent. Even when armed with the cultural capital of football knowledge, women are still only, at best, admitted as 'honorary' lads.

The humour of the show draws on the fans and football culture as opposed to the buttoned and blazered traditions of the more po-faced mainstream sport presentation. Some of the humour is effective, bringing out some of the irreverent banter of football, and this contrasts nicely with the formal stiffness of football interviews in football coverage elsewhere. Frank Skinner, the funnier of the two presenters, has a genuinely easy wit, and, like most good comics, much of his humour is rooted in an ability to spot and identify life's absurdities. The programme takes pleasure in its own laddish silliness; for example, in the regular feature 'phoenix from the flames', in the use of ex-footballer Jeff Astle in a series of ever more absurd costumes to sing the final song, and in the joke

1 Frank Skinner and David Baddiel both emerged through the alternative comedy circuit during a period in which the original anti-sexist, anti-racist impetus of alternative comedy itself was beginning to be seen by some as *passé*. Baddiel had particular success, with his performing partner Rob Newman, in a tour which played in larger venues than most acts, culminating in a rowdy farewell at Wembley Arena, after which the pair dissolved their collaboration. Frank Skinner has pursued a solo stand-up act with growing success. Neither would see themselves as 'politically correct'. Angus Loughran made an effective counterpoint to Skinner and Baddiel with his portrayal of the banal, facts-and-figures-oriented football fan Statto; but Loughran is also a newspaper tipster and is rumoured to be a successful gambler.

appearances by emblematic football figures like David Pleat.[2] In particular, 'phoenix from the flames' works because the whole project (to re-enact famous football moments, with one of the original participants, in a public park) is so inherently absurd, and the execution is so carefully inept.

Much of the humour, though, is poorly directed, undisciplined, and immature. Rooted in the laddish culture shaped and defined by new men's magazines like *Loaded* and *FHM,* and in the television programme *Men Behaving Badly,* sexist vulgarity and dumbed-down crudity tends to win out against real focused satire. Women, except when they are babes or surrogate lads, or ideally a combination of the two, are marginalized like Ulrika, and all too readily become the targets of the humour. The programme offers women the limited options of being a 'babe' or a surrogate lad; any other modes of femininity can only be performed against the grain of the programme's conventions and with resultant unease.

Homophobia and racism always seem to be lurking close to the surface. In particular, the parodies of black footballer Jason Lee, rooted firmly in the mainstream tradition of 'coon' imagery, were unforgivable. Just like women, blacks, gay people, foreigners with 'funny' names, and those with physical peculiarities are all potential targets for jokes. As with much laddish culture, this is excused as postmodern irony; and postmodern irony, as Leon Hunt has commented, means never having to say you're sorry.

The humour is also exclusive and excluding, depending upon possession of football knowledge, that alternative form of cultural capital acquired and stored almost solely by boys. Girls may be following football in increasing numbers, but few seem to develop that train-spotter fanaticism that permits the squirreling away of information that can then be flourished to prove credentials. Football's cultural capital acts as a handy currency expended in the project of defending the castle of masculinity against incursion by the feminine. One of the ironies of fantasy league is that football itself is something of a fantasy—set up as a world of its own (sports news, stadiums that exclude the real world) in which men have historically immersed themselves as an escape from work and family.

Clearly, a case could be made for these programmes as prime evidence for the postmodern argument that culture now is characterized by surface appearance, gloss, self-referentiality, parody, and depthlessness. But there is a 'real' referent, football, that has been

2 David Pleat is an English football manager who became famous through an oft-repeated clip of him racing across the Wembley pitch to embrace his players after their triumph in the FA Cup Final. From the perspective of the 1990s, his tight-fitting 1970s-style suit appears highly risible.

undergoing a wave of dramatic commercialization in which the audience is being redefined, prices rising dramatically, the lure of exclusivity attracting a new young male élite, replica kit prices extorting huge sums of money. A lot of the pretensions of the new breed of football club owner are so manifestly laughable that they provide fertile ground for comedy. Yet on these issues Skinner and Baddiel, supposed champions of the fans, are largely silent.

So what is the significance of this intervention of a further level of fantasy, in which people trade in virtual players to build virtual clubs? Can it be an imaginary resolution of that uncomfortable knowledge that the clubs people attach themselves to are in fact no more 'theirs' than the nearest branch of Burger King?

They Think It's All Over

In *They Think It's All Over* the form is that of a celebrity game show in which *A Question of Sport*'s format is reduced to absurdity by the use of games and questions in which any notion of 'knowledge' or 'correct answers' has been abandoned. The set follows the conventions of celebrity game shows, and the contestants are star personalities: two comedians and two ex-sportsmen as regulars, and two celebrity guests each week.

Like Frank Skinner, presenter Nick Hancock has good comic timing and an apparent instinct for the absurd. As with *Have I Got News for You?* (BBC, 1990–), the chair can be made fun of by the panellists, but through his control of the discourse and the presence of a script the presenter is able to appear at most times the most witty. The programme offers parody, in postmodern ironic mode, of *A Question of Sport*, and as with *Fantasy Football League* the flip irreverence and fundamental silliness of *They Think It's All Over* contrasts nicely with the over-serious pomposity of mainstream sport coverage.

However, in similar fashion to *Fantasy Football League*, the humour is irreverent and vulgar rather than truly satirical. It is players and managers more often than owners or administrators who are the target of humour. In particular the two sport stars on the panel, cricketer David Gower and footballer Gary Lineker, are the butt of jokes, focused on Gower's supposed affluent upper-class dilettantism and Lineker's goody-two-shoes image. The need of sport stars to prolong their careers after their playing days drives many into the celebrity trade, and the spectacle of Gower and Lineker in such a format has more than an edge of embarrassment. By contrast footballer Allie McCoist and snooker-player John Parrott on *A Question of Sport* are at least effective producers of humour and not merely the targets of it.

They Think It's All Over draws heavily on banter, that form of social cement central to male camaraderie (see Easthope 1990), and it is very much a boys' club, with comedian Jo Brand one of the few women contributors. As with *Fantasy Football League*, the roots of the humour in the masculine cultural capital of sporting 'knowledge' functions to marginalize women. The tone is set by banter and laddishness, in which crudeness and vulgarity often tends to be a substitute for real wit rather than an organic component of it. Much of the humour, especially Lee Hurst's, draws on physical peculiarities, and the humour of the show is redolent with a giggly embarrassment about sexuality. Minor sports are framed as eccentricities and dismissed as jokes. On the regular item 'feel the sportsman',[3] which does have an inspired dottiness, whole sports, such as judo, become no more than the pretext for the humour of the item. It wouldn't matter except that this is probably the only glimpse of judo on mainstream television in the whole year.

How do you win and what do you win? On one level, winning is unimportant; indeed, as on many contemporary panel games, such as Reeves and Mortimer's *Shooting Stars*, it becomes a joke so that the notion that winning is important is itself mocked. But, on another level, it is the wittiest responses that 'win', and the programme is the site of a tussle between Lee Hurst and Rory McGrath to see who can top the other fastest. The show rewards a quickness of wit in which the professional comedians always excel over the resident sportsmen, whilst the guests are there to be mocked (as in *Have I Got News for You?*).

The show also has elements of dumbing down; a crude depoliticized class antagonism is writ large in Hurst's constant digs at Gower, whilst Lineker is mocked as the good boy, the 'earhole', who never does anything bad, and is represented as scared of hard-man footballer Vinnie Jones. Hurst can be very funny, but the humour constantly imparts closure instead of opening up and revealing the world. 'Crap' functions as the universal dismissive restricted-code word that ends all arguments.

Postmodern Television

So are these programmes examples of postmodern television, and if so does any element of their content really matter? Does it constitute a problem if the sporting simulacrum of *Gladiators* is more popular than 'real' sport? Does it matter that neither *Fantasy*

---

3 The item involves two members of the panel, blindfolded, attempting to guess the identity of a sports star, or on occasion a whole team, by touch. It is played for laughs, is manifestly absurd, but is also the pretext for rather uneasy sexually coy innuendo, especially where the person/s to be guessed are female.

Football League nor *They Think It's All Over* attempt through their humour to unmask, challenge, or confront the machinations of the powerful? Aren't the elements of sexism and racism all in inverted commas and hence essentially playful and harmless?

None of the three have a real referent; they are not, in the manner of early television, relaying in relatively unmediated form cultural practices that have their real roots elsewhere. They are fundamentally televisual forms. Stuart Hall has commented on the hybrid character of television form (Hall 1975), and all three are hybrid in this sense, appropriating and transforming elements both from outside and from within television. They all feature a high degree of intertextuality and self-referentiality, and a degree of pastiche and parody. Thus they match some of the features of postmodernist cultural form.

Gladiators, though, differs in taking itself seriously; the competition is 'for real'. It displaces sport with something 'better'—more dramatic, more spectacular—in which drama is built in, structured, and controlled to a greater degree than would be possible with the television representation of sporting actuality, in which uncertainty is more heavily etched into the practice.

They Think It's All Over is not 'real'; nothing matters, nothing is at stake, anything can be said or done, and the irreverence and dumbing down, and the strong streak of misogyny and homophobia that lurk within the discourses of the programme, are, it must be assumed, looking to be excused as depthless surface gloss with no real effectivity. *Fantasy Football League* notionally refers to the 'real' world of football, but only as the raw material for surreal jokiness and absurdity. The programme conjures up its own world out of its basic elements: the flat, the inhabitants, the guests, the audience, and the video inserts.

Part of the difference lies in the relation of the programmes to masculinity. *Gladiators* grows out of the 1980s obsession with fitness, individualism, and self-improvement, is rooted in body culture, and within its format the notional gender equality means women are validated to the extent that they can work out, build muscle, and perform challenging physical tasks in the same manner as men.

By contrast, *They Think It's All Over* and *Fantasy Football League* grow out of the lad culture of the 1990s, in which hedonism resurfaces in reaction to body culture, and sexism resurfaces in reaction to feminism. This culture has involved a transformation and re-presentation of elements of 'traditional' masculinity—drinking, lechery, and promiscuity—through which new lads may be constructed as an imaginary resolution of the critique of masculinity by gender politics. New lads are 'men behaving badly', but are also attempting to excuse such behaviour by a degree of distance, putting it in quotation marks as ironic. The misogynist spin thereby imparted means that if the sexism of the lads is just a joke, those who, unlike Ulrika Jonsson, choose not to play along are reckoned to have no sense of humour and can be dismissed as reincarnations of that 1970s ogre the 'humourless feminist'.

Although postmodern irony can be a valid description of the forms of *Fantasy Football League* and *They Think It's All Over*, as an excuse or justification it won't wash. The sexist, racist, and homophobic undertones do matter, do have an effect, and need to be combated. The anti-intellectual vulgarity does contribute to dumbing down. Just as the 1990s generation have turned the word 'sad' into a term of abuse, so they have adopted the dismissive 'crap' as a system of closure, negating argument, debate, discussion, and reflection. Lad culture and lad television have contributed significantly to this process.

There have to be ways of producing humour that is life-affirming and which takes as its targets rich and powerful institutions and individuals rather than those who are their pawns and victims. Politically directed and focused satire has a long pedigree, but it is a frail plant that needs nurturing. Cultural producers concerned with representations of sport should reflect more carefully about both their subject-matter and its audience. Sport is being transformed dramatically by powerful commercial interests, driven by television and sponsorship. In the case of football these transformations are marginalizing the concerns of those who have historically sustained the sport—its fans. *Fantasy Football League* would work more effectively with a greater organic link with its audience, which might force the humour to become a little more focused. Properly directed, comedy can be a weapon too. *They Think It's All Over* is in the end locked into a prison of its own construction. Starting as an attempt to debunk and mock *A Question of Sport*, it succeeded all too well, winning a big audience, and becoming the *Question of Sport* for the 1990s. Born in the spirit of the back row in the class, giggling at teacher, the programme, for all its fun, remains trapped in this irreverent, but ultimately juvenile, mode, as funny as the class clown and with no more power or substance.

In comparison with *Fantasy Football League* and *They Think It's All Over*, *Gladiators* appears a more grounded cultural product, albeit one that takes itself too seriously. Beneath the postmodern gloss of its bright shiny surfaces lies a cleverly disguised core of rational modernity. There is little trace of ironic self-parody and more than a hint of rational recreation about its self-important worthiness. This rationality, though, is directed at improvement and cultivation of the body rather than the mind. *Gladiators* is the meeting-ground of the society of spectacle and the culture of narcissism. It offers an entertaining spectacle, but its combination of hearty muscularity and ultimate vacuousness prompts me to recall a slogan heard on the alternative comedy circuit: 'burn down a gym, visit a library'.

References   Barrett, Michele (1980), *Women's Oppression Today* (London: Verso).

Easthope, Antony (1990), *What a Man's Gotta Do: The Masculine Myth in Popular Culture* (London: Unwin Hyman).

Edwards, Tim (1997), *Men in the Mirror: Men's Fashion, Masculinity and Consumer Society* (London: Cassell).

Faludi, Susan (1991), *Backlash: The Undeclared War against Women* (London: Chatto & Windus).

Hall, Stuart (1975), 'TV as a Medium and its Relation to Culture', CCCS Stencilled Paper, (Birmingham: Centre for Contemporary Cultural Studies), 95.

Langer, John (1981), 'Television's Personality System', *Media Culture and Society*, 34.

Mort, Frank (1996), *Cultures of Consumption: Commerce, Masculinities and Social Space* (London: Routledge).

Nixon, Sean (1996), *Hard Looks: Masculinities, Spectatorship and Contemporary Consumption* (London: UCL Press).

Rowbotham, Sheila (1989), *The Past before US: Feminism in Action since the 1960s* (London: Pandora).

Segal, Lynne (1992), *Slow Motion: Changing Masculinities, Changing Men* (London: Virago).

Seymour-Ure, Colin (1991), *The British Press and Broadcasting since 1945* (London: Blackwell).

Whannel, Garry (1982), 'It's a Knock-Out: Constructing Communities', *Block*, 6.

—— (1992), *Fields in Vision: Television Sport and Cultural Transformation* (London: Routledge).

15

The International Circulation of British Television

Tom O'Regan

When I was in Form 6 at a Catholic boys' school in 1976, all the smart kids loved Monty Python's Flying Circus. *Eagerly banding together the morning after each broadcast, they would retell scenes, recite lines, imitate gestures. They were the true cultural élite of the school; as fiercely as they revelled in absurdist British culture (they were Goons fans as well), they already knew how to heap scorn on 'American trash': pop songs, TV shows, films. In the years to come, one member of this Python fan club became a prolific and respected poet; another flirted briefly with the Brotherhood before opting for a career in TV news.*

(Adrian Martin, *Phantasms*)

Robert Hardy was also the star of one of the ABC's [Australian Broadcasting Corporation] earliest BBC serials, the 26-part dramatization of David Copperfield, *which I remember—and I do remember it—as a wonderful actualisation of the book. We hear a lot of sneering about the middle-class ABC around but I remember how much this kind of television meant to my parents then in their twenties and fresh from childhoods of some poverty, and how powerfully it worked to pass on a sense of a shared literary inheritance.*

(Peter Craven, 'The ABC's Us')

BETWEEN THE COMMENTS of film critic Adrian Martin and of literary journalist Peter Craven on their Australian television viewing experience, we get a sense of the depth and diversity of the impact of British television in its international circulation. The different programmes mentioned—*Monty Python's Flying Circus* and *David Copperfield*—produce mixed responses

Published here for the first time by permission of the author, copyright © Tom O'Regan 2000.

originating in wider systems of cultural evaluation and hierarchies of taste, underwriting, in part, the distinction between public broadcasting and commercial broadcasting, between high culture and popular culture. We can find here one international brand image of British television content as a provider of a certain kind of content: middle-class fare skewed in various ways towards the maintenance and reproduction of a literary and cultural heritage. This international image persists, despite its contrary as evidenced in the broad farce of *The Benny Hill Show*, the soap opera of *Coronation Street* and *EastEnders*, innumerable sports broadcasts, adventures, and police series, children's television, documentary series, news services, and so on.

For both Martin and Craven British television is part of the very furniture of their television experience. Its role in social and cultural reproduction, in organizing cultural and social cleavages, is completely naturalized. *Sections* of the international audience do have a loyalty to and intense enthusiasm for particular British television programmes, whether it be the British soccer telecasts on prime-time Malaysian television schedules, the cult following of *Absolutely Fabulous* internationally, or the homage to the Teletubbies in a recent Gay and Lesbian Mardi Gras parade in Sydney. British television is not the distanced, cool, and unemotional television of lore but quite the opposite. It is television that enters people's personal and group calendars, shaping their interactions with others, organizing their taste in culture, their memories of television, and even their very appreciation of the fact of television.

Yet any assessment of British television in international circulation should not stop with exported programmes. The British television presence is not confined to the international circulation of its programmes. It also involves a history of overseas investment in British television and British investment in television production outside the United Kingdom; the indigenizing of British formats and productions by foreign producers; the adaptation of British policy models; the use of British precedent and programming to organize public discussion and debate; and the role played by British television in supplying personnel and training for other television systems. These too are part of the British television story internationally: a story dependent on the cultural resonance its programming, formats, and policy-making have for those who import them.

Britain's Screen Presence

Other producers like the French may provide more programme exports into Arab countries. Germany may supply Austria with more of its programmes, Hong Kong and Japan may export more of their product into South and East Asian markets, and Brazil and Mexico may supply more to Latin American markets. But British television circulates globally in ways no other European or Asian or Latin American producer can cumulatively match. This is paralleled by the revenues it receives from its international production and circulation. Using 1985 data, analysis by the European Institute for the Media noted that the UK obtained much more money from its television exports than did any of its European rivals (187 million ECUS compared to France's 1.6 million and Italy's 9.6 million).[1] Of course, if we compare its presence and revenues with that of its English-language counterpart, the United States, British television looks like a minor presence. Whereas the UK was easily the most dominant European supplier of programming into Western Europe,[2] providing 16 per cent of imported programmes in 1984, by contrast the US provided 44 per cent; where the UK provided 5–7 per cent of non-Arabic imported programmes in Arab countries, the US supplied 32 per cent.[3]

British television's international circulation is dependent on a host of interacting factors such as language and heritage, cultural proximity, market size, the presence or absence of public broadcasters, and the opportunities provided by multi-channel environments. Unsurprisingly British television's best markets are in other English-speaking countries, in Europe, and in the leading industrialized nation in Asia, Japan. Language and a common heritage facilitate British programme circulation in the US, Australasia, and Canada, societies which have been formatively shaped by British immigration. Language also helps explain its presence on South African television schedules under apartheid; Tapio Varis found that in 1983 South Africa imported one-third of its programmes and of these 30 per cent were from the UK (compared to 54 per cent from the US).[4] The Netherlands and the Scandinavian countries also have the highest levels of English literacy in continental Europe, a fact which undoubtedly facilitates the circulation of English-language product. Sharing the English language and British-derived legal and political frameworks can also be the basis for the circulation of some British programming amongst Commonwealth countries in Africa and Asia.

1 European Institute for the Media, European Cultural Foundation, *Europe 2000: What Kind of Television?*, Report of the European Television Task Force, Media Monograph, no. 11 (Manchester: European Institute for the Media, 1988), 82.

2 For an extended discussion of the West European television market-place see Preben Sepstrup, *Transnationalization of Television in Western Europe*, Acamedia Research Monograph no. 5 (London: John Libbey, 1990), 33.

3 Tapio Varis, 'The International Flow of Television Programmes', *Journal of Communication* (Winter 1984), 143–52; 148–9.

4 Ibid. 149.

Some factors facilitating circulation, like a common language and cultural heritage, can be partially cancelled out by other factors such as market size. As a rule smaller countries will import more than larger countries, since the resources for local production are fewer. So, as Preben Sepstrup observes, within Western European television markets 'the British share of supply is rather substantial in the small countries, but insignificant in the large countries'.[5] But the same logic helps explain the relatively insignificant British presence on US television schedules.

The presence or absence of public broadcasting systems can also be a factor in the circulation of British programming. British television is more likely to have a greater market share where there are public broadcasters than where there are none. Most of its significant markets have developed public broadcasting systems which now exist alongside commercial broadcasters in mixed environments. Prior to the advent of the loose network of Public Broadcasting Service (PBS) stations in the mid-1960s British television had made hardly any sustained structural inroads into the USA; with it in place there was a ready-made venue for the delivery of British drama and documentary programming. The Japanese television market, like its US counterpart, is massively dominated by local products. But it does have a stronger tradition of public broadcasting than does the USA. Consequently, it reserves a minor space for British product alongside that of American and other Asian product. The widespread break-up of monopoly public broadcasters has had an impact on the percentages of British programmes in circulation. Just prior to the partial privatization and deregulation of New Zealand broadcasting which saw the NZTV monopoly broken up in 1989, British television accounted for 17.1 per cent of the overall broadcast schedule; four years later its share had slipped to 12.5 per cent.[6]

Similarly, the greater the extent of multi-channel free-to-air and pay-TV environments, the greater the opportunity for exports and for international co-productions with British producers. This expansion has been critical to the UK's increasing involvement with North American partners in public and pay-TV at the pre-production phases of television development; and to its long-standing association with Australian, Canadian, and New Zealand broadcasters.

Within this context the European Institute for the Media estimated that in 1985, 50 per cent of UK television export receipts

5 Sepstrup, *Transnationalization of Television in Western Europe*, 33.

6 Geoff Lealand, 'New Zealand', in Stuart Cunningham and Elizabeth Jacka (eds.), *Australian Television and International Mediascapes* (Oakleigh, Vic.: Cambridge University Press, 1996), 218.

were from North America, with a further 23 per cent from Australia, New Zealand, and Japan, and 24 per cent from Europe.[7] On this reckoning, the rest of East and South-East Asia, South Asia, Africa, and Latin America play very minor roles in British television thinking. British television is largely an English-language, European, and neo-European (Australasian, North American, white South African) event and these markets provide, unsurprisingly, its principal focal point. Indeed, as Jeff Hazel, the then BBC director of channel sales and marketing, told *TV World* in 1995, the BBC's opportunity in Asia lay in its news, not its entertainment programmes. British entertainment does not travel 'that well'; rather 'Our research around the world suggests that our name is linked to news.'[8] Nowhere was this more evident than in the international dominance of the BBC coverage of the death and funeral of Princess Diana in 1997.

Within its best export markets British television can expect a selective but significant presence. Take the highly regarded and successful crime drama series *Prime Suspect III*. It may have only got a 3.7 per cent broadcast share in Boston in 1995 on the PBS station WGBH and a 4.6 per cent share in Japan on the public broadcasting NHK network, but these figures were gauged as resounding successes by the respective broadcasters.[9] Indeed, WGBH was a co-production partner on this season of the programme. Kiko Ito claimed that the series was well received by Japanese viewers 'as a powerful and interesting modern drama from the UK, and viewers were very impressed with the programme'.[10] Now this was, of course, nowhere near its 37.2 per cent share when first screened on the Australian 7 Network (a commercial network) or its 54 per cent share when first broadcast on Granada in the UK, but in the Australian and home markets it was expected to do well.[11] And the larger markets such as the USA can translate a small share into revenues which outweigh the larger share of smaller markets such as Australia.

The British presence is often found in the schedules of public broadcasters within a mixed system. In the Australian television market the principal purchasers of British product are the national public broadcasters, the ABC and, after 1980, the Special Broadcasting Service (SBS). Occasionally the commercial networks pick up

7 European Institute for the Media, *Europe 2000*, 82.

8 Jeff Hazel, quoted in Neal Weinstock, 'Guide to Networks', *TV World Guide to Satellite in Asia* suppl., *TV World* (Dec. 1995), 7–14.

9 See Louise Fancey, 'Suspect Case', *Moving Pictures Television*, 4 (Apr. 1995), 76–81: 79 (Boston), 81 (Japan).

10 Ibid.

11 Ibid. 79 (Australia), 76 (UK).

and show British product on first release, as with *Prime Suspect III*, but mostly they rely on acquiring successful British product such as *Absolutely Fabulous* after its ABC screening. The ABC as the principal public broadcaster has had long-standing agreements with its British counterpart, the BBC, and regularly picks up ITV product too. It is the principal screening venue for mainstream British series, serials, documentaries, and feature films as part of its normal schedules.

Between 1968 and 1994 UK-sourced programmes accounted for 22 per cent of ABC-TV content, consistently outstripping the US share at 15 per cent and other overseas programmes at 7 per cent, and second only to the Australian content share of 56 per cent.[12] (The children's programme *Sesame Street* accounts for a significant portion of the US share.) The percentage of British programmes, coupled with their often strategic prime-time location, has led to positive and pejorative identifications alike of the ABC with the BBC. With the advent of Channel Four at the end of 1982 SBS-TV became a regular Australian outlet for its alternative documentary and drama programming.

This international presence reaches back into the heart of British television itself. With long-standing output agreements with sister Commonwealth public broadcasters in Australia and elsewhere, the BBC was able to gain the benefits that their Hollywood and US network counterparts gained from similar output and affiliation agreements with Australian commercial broadcasters. They had access to a steady and reliable revenue stream not tied into the vagaries of the unpredictable and chaotic global film and television markets for individual programmes.[13] They also had to hand ready co-production partners for series they might initiate. An example of one such series is the BBC–ABC co-production *Sylvania Waters*, which was a project initiated from the UK. The Australian relationship was probably more significant to British television in the 1960s and early 1970s than it is today. Then the ABC spent more on imported programmes than it did on local programme production, with a good proportion of this expenditure going to British producers in the BBC and ITV.[14]

The growing importance of sales to the USA through the devel-

12 These calculations are based on various *ABC Annual Reports*, 1969–95/6.

13 Muriel G. Cantor and Joel M. Cantor, 'American Television in the International Marketplace', *Communication Research*, 13/3 (July 1986), 509–20; 514. They describe the international marketing environment as 'chaotic, unruly, and unpredictable, with no one really in charge and no one knowing, for example, why certain programmes sell one year and do not move off the shelves the next'.

14 See Federation of Australian Commercial Television Stations, *Facts of Australian Content in Television Programme Schedules*, Submission made to the Australian Broadcasting Control Board (Sydney: FACTS, 17 Sept. 1970), 16.

opment, first of the American Public Broadcasting System in the mid- to late 1960s, then subsequently pay-TV and syndicated television services over the 1980s and 1990s, meant that North American preferences increasingly came to shape British television content. Indeed, there has been public disquiet in the UK about the distorting effect that producing for international, usually North American, circulation has had on British television. It is claimed that this has encouraged British television to overemphasize costume dramas that exploit British cultural heritage, and to prefer documentary topics which would appeal to North American and European production partners.[15] With the advent of more television stations in the UK and the consolidation of varieties of pay-TV, this international integration of its production is accelerating. Consequently, international considerations are increasingly impinging on production decisions.

Yet these arrangements are no more than a contemporary variation on an older theme of Anglo-American complementarity, competition, and integration in the audio-visual industries. While we might see Britain and America as offering two different and apparently unreconcilable models for television, there is also a sense in which they are contiguous and connected systems. For the most part British television does not compete directly with American commercial television in international exports but offers a complementary package to it. It is known for its authoritative news and current affairs, with the BBC satellite–cable news service both a competitor to and a complementary service for CNN International. It is known for its documentary series, its recycling of the British literary heritage in costume dramas of Shakespeare, Dickens, or Austen (increasingly supported over the 1980s and 1990s by American finance), its 'quality' contemporary productions like *Prime Suspect*, and its distinctive traditions of soap opera, police series, comedies, and children's television. These very comparative advantages are what attracts American PBS and speciality pay-TV support for British programme production, although this support is itself contingent on their own constructions of mandates to 'educate, inform, and entertain'.

The British presence on international screens is additionally underwritten by some important characteristics both of the domestic British television market and of the English language as a cultural and commercial system. First, British television has historically had proportionately more money available to it than its European and Japanese counterparts, courtesy both of its international presence and of its move in the 1950s to develop a commercial television system alongside the BBC. Using 1984 figures, David Waterman estimated that UK television system revenues as a percentage of gross domestic product (GDP) were 0.47 per cent compared with France's 0.24 per cent, Japan's 0.4 per cent and West Germany's 0.26 per cent. This difference was maintained when he looked at television advertising as a percentage of GDP, noting that the UK had 0.3 per cent, France 0.11 per cent, West Germany 0.08 per cent and Japan 0.3 per cent. While these figures were below that of the USA (0.55 per cent and 0.53 per cent respectively), they none the less indicate that the UK has consistently spent more on its television on a per capita basis than its non-US competitors.[16] While new television services have been eating into this British lead in Europe and beyond, these countries still have a long way to go before they have the infrastructures and expenditures characteristic of the British system.

An additional advantage to British television is that its best markets in other English-speaking countries have also spent proportionately more on television advertising and television system expenditure overall than have their competitors, a fact which has sustained premium price levels for British programming in these markets. Canada simply had to keep pace with its neighbour the USA in order for its own broadcasters, particularly in English-speaking Canada, to maintain access to their audience. Australia had three commercial television networks and a public broadcaster in the five major capital cities by 1965, which ensured a volume presence of British programming not only on the public broadcaster but also in a minor way on the commercial television networks, particularly the 7 Network.

Coupled with this is the very character of the English language itself. The English-language countries, particularly the European (UK and Ireland) and neo-European variants (USA, Canada, Australia, and New Zealand), make up a highly organized and coherent cultural and economic system. There have been few obstacles to symbolic goods trade between them, to investment in each other's markets, and they have substantially harmonized legal, political, and administrative systems. This also has benefited British television.

English is also 'the language of advantage' in international film and television.[17] It is the dominant audio-visual language because it possesses a critical mass of language-speakers and it is on GDP measures the wealthiest language. British television, in producing

---

16 David Waterman, 'World Television Trade: The Economic Effects of Privatization and New Technology', *Telecommunications Policy* (June 1988), 141–51: 143.

17 See Richard Collins, *Television: Policy and Culture* (London: Unwin Hyman, 1990), 52–73.

for wealthy and populous English-language speakers, thus has immediate access to a critical mass of fellow speakers often without recourse to subtitling or dubbing. The combination of numbers and wealth enables higher production budgets, puts it at the cutting edge of technological development and imaging standards, and allows its members to participate at inception in programming and marketing innovations. Wildman and Siwek argue that there is an enormous and continuing gap between the English-speaking market and other language markets. The problem facing competitor language markets is that these either possess the language but not the wealth, or the wealth but not the numbers. Using data collected in the early 1980s, they estimated that Hindi–Urdu had 86 per cent of the population of English-speakers but only 5 per cent of English-speakers' gross national product (GNP); Spanish had 64 per cent of the English-speakers' population but only 15 per cent of its GNP; whilst Japanese, German, and French had a greater proportion of English-speakers' GNP but did not have as many speakers.[18]

Wildman and Siwek argue that film and television produced in 'languages with large and wealthy native-speaking populations' will, because of their large budgets, have 'greater inherent audience appeal' than product in other languages.[19] Thus television producers in the wealthier and more populous languages will be able to have even higher budgets and therefore higher production values than their rivals because they can count on other linguistic populations as part of their export market. Among these large and wealthy language groups, the English language has significant comparative advantages. According to Wildman and Siwek, the poorer and less populous language groups are the prime recipients of the product of the largest and wealthiest language group; so too the largest and wealthiest language market is consequently substantially closed off to product from the poorer and less populous languages. Clearly the English language must by this logic make cultural incursions into weaker languages (as witnessed by the increasing use of English expressions, particularly American English, in languages other than English). They do not argue that English-language, particularly but not exclusively Hollywood, product circulates in spite of cultural differences, but that it circulates so powerfully because of these cultural and linguistic differences.[20] They find the English-language producer's advantage not so much in the exercise of corporate power but in the economic logic of cultural markets.

When Jeremy Tunstall wrote his 1977 classic *The Media are*

---

18 Steven Wildman and Stephen Siwek, *International Trade in Films and Television Programmes* (Cambridge, Mass.: Ballinger, 1988), 86.

19 Ibid. 8.

20 Ibid.

American,[21] he was writing not simply about the USA but about Britain as well. His subtitle more accurately reflected the tenor of his book: 'Anglo-American Media in the World'. Here the British and Americans, the 'Anglo-Americans', are synonymous with international dominance and have largely set the terms for television and the media internationally:

> Without the century-long dominance of Anglo-American media products and styles, many aspects of life in most of the world's countries would be different: consumption patterns, leisure, entertainment, music, and arts and literatures.[22]

For Tunstall, British television is part of an international Anglo-American hegemony that is variously rooted in the history of the British empire, economic and political dominance, and technological advantage. French minister Toubon located a 'modèle unique Anglo-marchand' (the Anglo-Saxon mercantile standard model) 'spreading throughout an increasing number of countries' at an alarming rate.[23] Its very existence has called forth reaction in the shape of proactive French policy (and French pressure on European policy) to identify 'francophony' as 'a possibility for preserving independence in the face' of this imperializing model. The British become here surrogate Americans and the British participation in this trade part of a continuing and expanding cultural imperialism.

More than Programmes The British television presence internationally is, as Tunstall suggests, not confined to the circulation of its programmes internationally. As noted above, it also involves overseas investment in British television and British investment in television production outside the UK. This presence also involves the indigenizing of British formats and productions by foreign producers, the adaptation of British policy models, the use of British precedent and programming to organize public discussion and debate, and the role played by British television in supplying personnel and training for other television systems. On this last point a steady stream of people from Commonwealth countries have received their training in the UK, just as UK personnel have made careers with the public broadcasters in any number of Commonwealth countries.

21 Jeremy Tunstall, *The Media are American: Anglo-American Media in the World* (London: Constable, 1977).

22 Ibid. 18.

23 Marcel Machill, 'Background to French Language Policy and its Impact on the Media', *European Journal of Communication*, 124 (1997), 479–509: 494.

British television invests in local productions in North America, Europe, Africa, and Australasia. For the last decade British partners have become a routine feature of Australian television drama series, with some Australian producers having long-standing relationships with particular British broadcasters. Just as US companies like WGBH in Boston have built up associations with the BBC for British-based documentary (*The People's Century*) and drama programming (*Prime Suspect*), this same relationship forms the basis for BBC involvement in projects initiated by them. International producers in Europe are keen to gain such British investment since this is often important in getting pre-sales deals in other markets.

One of the important and often underrated aspects of British television has been its effect on the productions of the receiving culture, which indigenizes and adapts imported British texts. In television this involved taking up where radio had left off. Wilfred Thomas, an Australian radio compère, talks of how Australian broadcasters in the 1940s 'listened on short-wave to the big American and British comedians . . . and in the mornings we sun-baked by our swimming pool and adapted their best jokes for our audience'.[24] Similarly, two ABC employees, Michael Charlton and Robert Raymond, developed the concept for the long-running current affairs programme *Four Corners* in 1961 out of 'their conversations in the Williams Street wine bars', where they 'kicked around the [BBC] *Panorama*–CBS [Ed Murrow's *See It Now*] concepts'.[25] Such informal borrowing is a signature of the combinatory character of much television drama development and documentary, where programme concepts for stories, or styles of documentary-making, are adapted to local environments.

While this informal route is still taken, today it is more likely to be accomplished through a formalized concept sale route. It is contemporary fashion to date the advent of concept sales to the late 1970s and 1980s, but such sales were already a feature of 1950s and 1960s television. At that time there was a formalized exchange of scripts among broadcasters, in everything from television variety skits and jokes through to scripts for 'live plays', with British television acting as a major supplier and minor importer. After the USA, British television is today the largest provider of programme concepts internationally.

The BBC, for example, regularly produces and markets concept prospectuses for sale to their international counterparts. These prospectuses offer various formats, from educational television to quiz shows, soaps, and news and current affairs concepts, for foreign

24 K. S. Inglis, *This is the ABC: The Australian Broadcasting Commission, 1932–1983* (Melbourne: Melbourne University Press, 1983), 89.
25 Robert Pullan, *Four Corners: 25 Years* (Sydney: ABC Books, 1986), 15.

broadcasters to turn into their own local or parochial programmes. The programmes available for sale are typically those that are not expected to travel much beyond British borders but as concepts offer foreign television producers a short cut for programme development and delivery.

Easily the most significant exports of British television to North America have been programme concepts. While the originals have been available on USA television since the advent of the public broadcasting service in the USA, the American version of British situation comedies is the primary way British television circulates before mass audiences in the USA. So it is that the classic British television shows of the 1960s *Steptoe and Son* and *Till Death Us Do Part* were remade in the 1970s as the hit series *Sanford and Son* and *All in the Family* respectively. *Man about the House* of the 1970s was remade in the 1980s as *Three's a Crowd*, while *Absolutely Fabulous* and *Men Behaving Badly* in the 1990s became *High Society* and *Men Behaving Badly* respectively. This remaking of formats is not confined to the USA: *Steptoe and Son* was remade in Sweden as *Albert and Herbert*.

British television shows have inevitably shaped domestic tastes for certain kinds of programming. ABC's success with the absurdist humour of *Monty Python's Flying Circus* paved the way for the Australian *Aunty Jack* series a couple of years later. British situation comedies are often direct precursors to series in Australia, South Africa, the USA, and Canada. Post-apartheid comedies in South Africa like *Going Up III* drew on American and British precedent to construct their message.[26] Sometimes this influence can be seen more broadly, for example in a wider market for humour:

> This country [Australia] and the city of Melbourne in particular
> has a high and mighty tradition of comedy which is not
> unrelated to the ABC as both a buyer of the local product and as
> a disseminator of the British variety.[27]

A British presence can also be seen in the adaptation of British policy models and broadcasting practice to local circumstance by foreign governments. In his study of communication in the Third World Geoffrey Reeves[28] notes how television throughout Africa is 'substantially dependent on the technology, organisational arrangements and professional values and practices, and pro-

---

26 See Dorothy Roome, 'Transformation and Reconciliation: "Simunye", a Flexible Model', *Critical Arts*, 11/1–2 (1997), 66–94.

27 Peter Craven, 'The ABC's Us', in Morag Fraser and Joseph O'Reilly (eds.), *Save our ABC: The Case for Maintaining Australia's National Broadcaster* (South Melbourne: Hyland House, 1996), 82.

28 Geoffrey Reeves, *Communications and the 'Third World'* (London: Routledge, 1993), 55.

grammes, of countries such as the United States and Britain'. British television policy reports are regularly drawn upon by policy-makers internationally, such that British precedent is sometimes central to the learning cycles of television policy-making. Avril Bell writes of how New Zealand policy-makers adopted the funding model first laid out in the British Peacock Report (1986) when they created New Zealand On Air as an 'Arts Council of the Air' to fund 'programme production on a competitive and transparent basis separate from the business of broadcasting itself'.[29] Similarly, the SKE review of the Irish public broadcaster RTE sought 'the free market remedies for the problems of public service television already put forward by the London consultants Peat Marwick for implementation within the BBC'.[30]

British television is also a public presence internationally as a point of reference for domestic discussion of television, both the programmes and the current and future shape of the television service. A handful of British series have excited much public comment in other countries: *The Avengers* (the *X-Files* of the 1960s) attracted the kind of extended commentary its contemporary equivalent has generated.[31] British television's close relation to varieties of social realism and social problem film-making can mean that its programmes are used as pretexts for domestic social comment and critical commentary, and as spurs for the local television industry. Ken Loach's *Cathy Come Home* (1965), in which the eponymous Cathy loses her home, husband, and child through the British welfare system's inflexibility, defined new vistas for television drama which entered into subsequent feature, television drama, and documentary production internationally. A later moment is provided by Alan Bleasdale's *The Boys from the Blackstuff* (director, Philip Saville) in 1982. This series provided a way of talking about social changes which were also happening at the same time in Australasia, North America, and Europe, where changing gender roles, de-industrialization and restructuring, regional deprivation, structural unemployment, and limited horizons combined to produce a tragedy of working-class masculinity.

Domestic television systems are often measured and held accountable for their failure to match the British system. Writing in the *New York Times* in 1992, television critic John J. O'Connor criticized US television for its 'inability even to consider that

29 Avril Bell, 'An Endangered Species: Local Programming in the New Zealand Television Market', *Media, Culture and Society*, 17 (1995), 181–200.

30 Desmond Bell and Niall Meehan, 'Cable, Satellite and the Emergence of Private TV in Ireland: From Public Service to Managed Monopoly', paper delivered to the International Television Studies Conference, London, July 1988, 27.

31 See Toby Miller, *The Avengers* (London: BFI, 1997).

concepts like culture and national heritage might be too important to hinge almost entirely on corporate interests'. By contrast, in the UK broadcasting was recognized as being 'at the heart of British society', with the BBC maintaining an enviable commitment 'to reflect and nurture the UK's rich cultural heritage . . . fostering and nurturing the national talents, originating and commissioning new works and developing excellence in the arts'.[32] In the late 1980s there were unsuccessful calls for the Australian SBS to be more like the British Channel Four model.[33]

In some of the English-speaking Commonwealth countries and Scandinavian countries, where English literacy levels are high, the multifaceted character of the British presence has shaped the very definition of their public service broadcasters and what such broadcasters mean to their audiences and domestic critics. Peter Craven remarked: 'The [Australian] ABC to me is *The Avengers* (remember Emma Peel?) and *The Goons* and *Steptoe and Son* and Pete and Dud'; only after listing these did he mention some Australian programmes which had also defined for him his national public broadcaster.[34] In this fashion British television is directly invoked in international debates over the scope, orientation, and value of public broadcasting. So it is that Craven, to defend the Australian ABC against draconian budget cuts in 1995–7, makes much of the importance of the British components of its television schedules and the importance to Australian cultural life of this experience.

Equally British television models can be held in disrepute. BBC example and practice is often thought to have cast too long a shadow over the public broadcasters of Australia, New Zealand, and Canada. Multicultural critics in Australia claim that the Australian ABC has been slavish in its adoption of British models, its preparedness to employ English migrants at the expense of those of a non-English-speaking background, and its implicit devaluation of local life experiences not drawn from a particular middle-class and Anglophile cultural experience.

British Television and Cultural Value

The rejection of British television can be visceral. A dear friend once described to me how upon hearing the distinctive Rank gong at the start of the television movie slot as a child she was filled with trepidation as to what was about to follow; she knew she was going

32 Cited in Monroe E. Price, *Television, the Public Sphere and National Identity* (Oxford: Clarendon Press, 1995), 154–5; John J. O'Connor, 'Television View: Still Trapped in a Vast Wasteland', *New York Times*, 13 Dec. 1992, sect. 2, p. 1, col. 2.

33 See Huw Evans, 'Prospects for the SBS', *Media Information Australia*, 46 (1987), 17–22.

34 Craven, 'The ABC's Us', 83.

to be disappointed. British television is simultaneously praised and derided internationally. It is the bastion of quality and high culture (as opposed to the commercial low culture of Hollywood), or out of touch with audiences who reject such élite, class-bound fare. This mixed reaction is part of the very definition of British television internationally. Craven's endorsement of British television's cultural value and Martin's implied criticism of its implication in the denigration of popular culture, particularly American popular culture, have their counterparts in British debates, in which the country's television is associated with prestigious, innovative, quality programming and at the same time with a restrained, stuffy, literary, class-conscious, even paternalist, system designed as much to drive out as to attract viewers.

Such estimations of British television are tied up with the very standing of public television. Whether it is produced for the BBC, Channel Four, or commercial channels, British television in international circulation is typically wed to notions of public broadcasting and its attendant notions of cultural and social capital. It is also tied up with the idea that national public broadcasters like the BBC should be an important, even pre-eminent, means to, as Avril Bell puts it, construct and reconstruct the 'national imaginary within the geographical borders of the nation state'.[35] Indeed, it is still common for British commercial broadcasters to refer to themselves as 'public broadcasters'. Certainly this perception is shared internationally. It makes for an international market niche for British television as a purveyor of 'quality programming', a keeper of an English literary and cultural inheritance, a flagship internationally for the documentary, given the documentary's close alliance 'to the major aspirations of public service broadcasting: the desire to inform, educate and entertain',[36] and a standard against which to measure local output.

In these circumstances, then, it is easy to either underestimate or overestimate the importance of British television in the international system. The legacy of British colonialism and the unequal character of cultural exchange which sees British programming circulating so extensively (including securing so apparently a privileged relation with the USA), leads nationalists from Malaysia to Africa, from Australia to Ireland, to proclaim publicly the need to build a local culture felt to be submerged under the weight of British and American cultural imports. Local content-makers play the anti-British card in seeking to find a place for their programmes on local TV schedules. We can also overvalue the British contribution

35 Bell, 'An Endangered Species', 195.
36 Kilborn, 'New Contexts for Documentary Production in Britain', 141.

because we encounter it so readily in international public discourse as 'the least worst television system in the world'. As a token in larger political games for control over broadcasting policy agendas, it makes a regular appearance. It is a particularly strong reference-point in Commonwealth countries. Here being too British and not British enough is part of the fabric of domestic debates. These debates can be about any number of things: the degree of independence, the kind of public broadcasting, the styles of broad-casting including speech, the ratio of broadcasting imports to exports, the extent and character of the control over commercial broadcasting, and the countries of origin of those imports. They are rarely strictly about the actual British system.

Indeed exposure to this kind of public record can, as it did in my case, create fantasy images of British quality which a dose of actu-ally watching television in Britain did much to dispel. We also over-estimate its impact because we see the flow of cultural materials from Britain to other cultures and, noting its largely one-way char-acter, we underestimate the mutual attraction that had to exist for these imports to take place. We can also underestimate what audi-ences do with these programmes: how they customize them and turn them to their own purposes. All this international attention produces its own imaginary 'Britishness', which, like its 'American' counterpart, may have little to do with the real Britain and more to do with foreign imaginings of it conducted for other purposes. David Thomson once claimed that someone like himself should never have been let loose in America, knowing as he did so much on the one hand and so little on the other. Much the same point could be made about the mismatch between the British television image and the UK itself.

We also have a tendency to undervalue the British television con-tribution by confining it. British television is more than quality television, more than a model for public broadcasting, more than heritage television, more than serious informational and edu-cational television. For every *Brideshead Revisited* there is a *Benny Hill Show*; for every *Absolutely Fabulous* there is an episode of *Tele-tubbies*. To an extent its reputation can be something of a burden for British television producers, critics, policy-makers, and audi-ences alike. There is probably nothing more irritating than the complacent self-regard that comes with supposing one has the 'best television' in the world. Nor is there anything so unctuous as those assuming the responsibility to protect not just British television but television itself from the barbarians. It can too often get in the way of British people interrogating their own system, and even getting their facts right, as happened in the Annan Report. As Ken Inglis notes, Lord Annan and his colleagues' 'inability' to get their facts right about a particular incident involving the ABC and the government of the day in 1970 'demonstrated the dogmatic resistance of English liberal opinion to the idea of any source of revenue for national broadcasting other than a licence fee'.[37]

Conclusion   We hear constantly now that British television is at the crossroads and is about to undergo significant mutation; the end of British television as we know it, and a diminishing domestic and international authority for the British public service broadcasting ethos. The prospects of such change have led to deep pessimism, with titles like Michael Tracey's *The Decline and Fall of Public Service Broadcasting*[38] proclaiming an end to the system of public broadcasting.

And yet the evidence for this is still mixed. The British television system can still attract at any one time 50 per cent of the television viewing audience for particular programmes; such command of the audience is now unheard of in other television jurisdictions with a greater fragmentation of channel choice. It is certainly true that this situation will, over coming years, become less and less possible. It is also clear that the expansion of multi-channel environments, the maturing of pay-TV as a mass distribution system, and the addition of free-to-air television stations within Britain are reshaping the economics of local programme production and international programme purchase alike. But in a sense British television is also already used to operating in these environments. It is something British television has been taking advantage of in its lucrative North American market and in some Asian and European markets for some time now. It will certainly mean that more of the current television programming staples will be internationally integrated at a programme inception level than ever before. And there will be an expansion and consolidation of the already close relation between UK television and its US partners.

Whatever the shape and form changes in British television make, some things will not change. The British command as a nodal point of the English language will not be lessened, despite the challenge from Canada and Australia.[39] The linkages with Australasian and

37 Inglis, *This is the ABC*, 328.

38 Michael Tracey, *The Decline and Fall of Public Service Broadcasting* (Oxford: Oxford University Press, 1998).

39 For a discussion of this challenge, see Paul Attallah, 'Canadian Television Exports: Into the Mainstream', and Stuart Cunningham and Elizabeth Jacka, 'Australian Television in World Markets', in John Sinclair, Elizabeth Jacka, and Stuart Cunningham (eds.), *New Patterns in Global Television: Peripheral Vision* (London: Oxford University Press, 1996).

European broadcasters will not be diminished so much as reconstructed, since they too are undergoing the same changes of environment. The connections with European broadcasters are likely to increase, not lessen. The changes will be both large in some areas and small in others. There are as many different futures as there are programme types and multi-channel, multimedia environments. Certainly there will be changes in its principal markets, with an increasing importance of overseas input into British television programme production at inception. This brings with it both risks and opportunities.

Richard Kilborn has recently discussed some of the implications of this for the documentary. Noting the active interest in co-productions involving European and US partners, he writes:

> The BBC has clearly decided that one of its best hopes for making a mark in the field of documentary is to enter into partnership agreements with other broadcasters to make large-scale documentary series which will command world-wide attention. The most recent of these projects is *The People's Century*, a series of 26 programmes about the mass experience of ordinary people over the last 100 years. This series, which the BBC is making in conjunction with the American company WGBH, is one of the most ambitious the BBC has ever undertaken.[40]

If the one-off documentary is looking more endangered, the future for documentary series production is probably enhanced, not lessened, in this international environment. As Kilborn observes, the BBC itself is placing a major emphasis on projects based on 'the world-wide sales prospects of the series and the possibilities of other kinds of commercial exploitation for the education market, including CD-ROMs and linked-in book publications'.[41] With English-language pay-TV outlets for documentaries such as the Discovery Channel and the prospects of sales through dubbed versions in other language territories, this prospect is no longer restricted to free-to-air television. Documentary production is increasingly linked to publishing, interactive education, and entertainment consumption internationally, and the convergence of media this represents might result in fewer documentaries, but the value and longevity of documentary productions is increased, not lessened.

In such environments there can be no doubt that the British television industry will increasingly integrate pay-TV and free-to-air and be increasingly linked to the cinema and video rental

40 Kilborn, 'New Contexts for Documentary Production in Britain', 148.
41 Ibid.

industries, the publishing industry, and the computing industry. A variety of futures looks possible. One, based on British television as it has currently and historically existed, promises more of the same. Another, based on the experience of the British film industry, promises a lesser screen presence overall internationally than at present. Another future, based on international book publishing, promises a strong British presence in certain markets and an established and managed relation to others, as currently exists with North American and Australasian publishing. And still another future based on the computing industry promises a criss-crossing of all of these.

Whatever is the case, it is hard not to see British television as a significant beneficiary (alongside the USA of course) of the economic benefits stemming from the co-ordination and separation of distribution media that is implicit in the new release sequences for product. An increasingly integrated media ensemble of cinema, video rental, sell-through, pay-per-view, premium pay, basic pay-TV, free-to-air, and product spin-off in CD-ROMs, interactive games, and books should on balance benefit British producers in their international markets.[42]

42 For a discussion of this sequencing, see Eli Noam, *Television in Europe* (New York: Oxford University Press, 1991), 30.

Select Bibliography

ALVARADO, MANUEL, and BUSCOMBE, EDWARD, *Hazell: The Making of a TV Series* (London: BFI, 1978).

——and COLLINS, RICHARD, 'The *Viewpoint* Controversy', *Screen Education*, 19, (1976), 74–81.

——GUTCH, ROBIN, and WOLLEN, TANA, *Learning the Media* (London: Macmillan, 1987).

——and STEWART, JOHN (eds.), *Made for Television: Euston Films Limited* (London: BFI Publishing, 1985).

——and THOMPSON, JOHN O. (eds.), *The Media Reader* (London: BFI Publishing, 1990).

——and TULLOCH, JOHN, *'Doctor Who': The Unfolding Text* (London: Macmillan, 1983).

ANNAN COMMITTEE, *Report of the Committee on the Future of Broadcasting*, Cmnd. 6753 (London: HMSO, 1977).

ARTHUR, C. (ed.), *Religion and the Media* (Cardiff: University of Wales Press, 1993).

ARTHURS, JANE, 'Technology and Gender: Women and Television Production', *Screen*, 30/1–2, (1989), 40–59.

——'Women and Television', in Hood (ed.), *Behind the Screens*.

AUBREY, CHRISPIN (ed.), *Nukespeak: The Media and the Bomb* (London: Comedia, 1982).

BAEHR, HELEN, and GRAY, ANN (eds.), *Turning it On: A Reader in Women and Media* (London: Arnold, 1996).

BAKER, SIMON, and TERRIS, OLWEN, *A for Andromeda to Zoo Time: The TV Holdings of the National Film and Television Archive* (London: BFI Publishing, 1994).

BAKEWELL, JOAN, and GARNHAM, NICHOLAS, *The New Priesthood: British Television Today* (London: Allen Lane, Penguin Press, 1970).

BALLANTYNE, JAMES, *The Researcher's Guide to British Film and Television Collections*, 4th edn. (London: BUFVC, 1993).

BARNETT, STEVEN, *Games and Sets: The Changing Face of Sport on Television* (London: BFI Publishing, 1990).

——(ed.), *Funding the BBC's Future* (London: BFI Publishing, 1994).

——and CURRY, ANDREW, *The Battle for the BBC: A British Broadcasting Conspiracy?* (London: Aurum Press, 1994).

BARR, CHARLES, 'Broadcasting and Cinema: Screens within Screens', in Charles Barr (ed.), *All Our Yesterdays: 90 Years of British Cinema* (London: BFI Publishing, 1986).

——'Television on Television', *Sight and Sound*, 55/3, (1986), 157–9.

——'They Think It's All Over: The Dramatic Legacy of Live Television', in John Hill and Martin McLoone (eds.), *Big Picture, Small Screen: The Relations between Film and Television* (Luton: John Libbey Media, 1996).

——HILLIER, JIM, and PERKINS, V. F., 'The Making of *Upstairs, Downstairs*, a Television Series', *Movie*, 21 (Autumn 1975), 46–53.

BARRY, ANGELA, 'Black Mythologies: Representations of Black People on British Television', in John Twitchin (ed.), *The Black and White Media Book* (Stoke-on-Trent: Trentham Books, 1988).

BAZALGETTE, CARY, 'Reagan and Carter, Kojak and Crocker, Batman and Robin?', *Screen Education*, 20 (1976), 5–14.

——and BUCKINGHAM, DAVID (eds.), *In Front of the Children: Screen Entertainment and Young Audiences* (London: BFI Publishing, 1995).

——and PATERSON, RICHARD, 'Real Entertainment: The Iranian Embassy Siege', *Screen Education*, 37 (1980–1), 55–67.

BEHARRELL, PETER, and PHILO, GREG (eds.), *Trade Unions and the Media* (London: Macmillan, 1977).

Bell, E., 'The Origins of British Television Documentary', in Corner (ed.), *Documentary and the Mass Media*.

BENNETT, TONY, BOYD-BOWMAN, SUSAN, MERCER, COLIN, and WOOLLACOTT, JANET (eds.), *Popular Television and Film* (London: BFI Publishing, 1981).

BEVERIDGE COMMITTEE, *Report of the Broadcasting Committee, 1949*, Cmnd. 8116 (London: HMSO, 1951).

BFI/BAFTA Commission of Inquiry into the Future of the BBC (London: BFI Publishing, 1994).

BLACK, PETER, *The Biggest Aspidistra in the World: A Personal Celebration of Fifty Years of the BBC* (London: BBC, 1972).

——*The Mirror in the Corner: People's Television* (London: Hutchinson, 1972).

BLANCHARD, SIMON (ed.), *The Challenge of Channel Five* (London: BFI Publishing, 1990).

——and MORLEY, DAVID, *What's this Channel Fo(u)r? An Alternative Report* (London: Comedia, 1982).

BOLTON, ROGER, *'Death on the Rock' and Other Stories* (London: W. H. Allen, 1990).

BONDEBJERG, IB, 'Intertextuality and Metafiction: Genre and Narrative in the Television Fiction of Dennis Potter', in Michael Skovmand and Kim Christian Schrøder (eds.), *Media Cultures: Reappraising Transnational Media* (London: Routledge, 1992).

BONNER, PAUL, with LESLEY ASTON, *Independent Television in Britain, v: ITV and the IBA, 1981–92: The Old Relationship Changes* (London: Macmillan, 1998).

BOURNE, STEPHEN, *Black in the British Frame: Black People in British Film and Television, 1896–1996* (London: Cassell, 1998).

BOWES, MICK, 'Only When I Laugh' in, Goodwin and Whannel (eds.), *Understanding Television.*

BOYLE, ANDREW, *Only the Wind will Listen: Reith of the BBC* (London: Hutchinson, 1972).

BRAKE, COLIN, *EastEnders—The First Ten Years: A Celebration* (London: BBC, 1994).

BRANDT, GEORGE (ed.), *British Television Drama* (Cambridge: Cambridge University Press, 1981).

——(ed.), *British Television Drama in the 1980s* (Cambridge: Cambridge University Press, 1993).

BRIGGS, ASA, *The History of Broadcasting in the United Kingdom*, i: *The Birth of Broadcasting* (Oxford: Oxford University Press, 1961).

—— *The History of Broadcasting in the United Kingdom*, ii: *The Golden Age of Wireless* (Oxford: Oxford University Press, 1965).

—— *The History of Broadcasting in the United Kingdom*, iii: *The War of Words* (Oxford: Oxford University Press, 1970).

—— *The History of Broadcasting in the United Kingdom*, iv: *Sound and Vision* (Oxford: Oxford University Press, 1979) (extract: Ch. 3 in this volume).

—— *The BBC: The First Fifty Years* (Oxford: Oxford University Press, 1985).

—— *The History of Broadcasting in the United Kingdom*, v: *Competition, 1955–74* (Oxford: Oxford University Press, 1995).

BRUNSDON, CHARLOTTE, '*Crossroads*: Notes on Soap Opera', *Screen*, 22/4 (1981), 32–7.

—— 'Television: Aesthetics and Audiences', in Mellencamp (ed.), *Logics of Television*.

—— *Screen Tastes* (London: Routledge, 1996).

—— and MORLEY, DAVID, *Everyday Television: 'Nationwide'* (London: BFI, 1978).

BRUNT, ROSALIND, 'The Spectacular *World of Wicker*', *Working Papers in Cultural Studies*, 3 (1972), 7–32.

—— 'Points of View', in Goodwin and Whannel (eds.), *Understanding Television*.

BRYANT, STEVE, *The Television Heritage* (London: BFI, 1990).

BUCKINGHAM, DAVID, *Public Secrets: EastEnders and its Audience* (London: BFI, 1987) (extract: Ch. 6 in this volume).

—— *Children Talking Television: The Making of Television Literacy* (London: Falmer Press, 1993).

—— *Moving Images: Understanding Children's Emotional Responses to Television* (Manchester: Manchester University Press, 1996).

BURNS, TOM, *The BBC: Public Institution and Private World* (London: Macmillan, 1977).

BUSCOMBE, EDWARD, *Films on TV* (London: SEFT, 1971).

—— '*Match of the Day*', *Screen Education Notes*, 3 (1972), 10–11.

—— '*The Sweeney*: Better than Nothing?', *Screen Education*, 20 (1976), 5–14.

—— 'The Representation of Alcoholism on Television', in Cook and Lewington (eds.), *Images of Alcoholism*.

—— 'Creativity in Television', *Screen Education*, 35 (1980), 5–17.

—— 'All Bark and No Bite: The Film Industry's Response to Television', in Corner (ed.), *Popular Television in Britain*.

—— (ed.), *Football on Television* (London: BFI, 1974).

—— (ed.), *Granada: The First 25 Years*, BFI Dossier, no. 9 (London: BFI, 1981).

BUXTON, DAVID, *From 'The Avengers' to 'Miami Vice': Form and Ideology in Television Series* (Manchester: Manchester University Press, 1990).

CAIN, JOHN, *The BBC: 70 Years of Broadcasting* (London: BBC, 1992).

CAMPAIGN FOR QUALITY TELEVISION, *The Purposes of Broadcasting* (London: CQT, 1998).

CARDIFF, DAVID, 'Code-Breaking in Television', *Screen Education*, 14 (1975), 14–20.

CARPENTER, HUMPHREY, *Dennis Potter: A Biography* (London: Faber & Faber, 1998).

CAUGHIE, JOHN, 'Progressive Television and Documentary Drama', *Screen*, 21/3 (1980), 9–35.

—— 'Rhetoric, Pleasure and "Art Television"', *Screen*, 22/4 (1981), 9–31.

—— 'Scottish Television: What Would it Look Like?', in McArthur (ed.), *Scotch Reels*.

—— 'Television Criticism: "A Discourse in Search of an Object"', *Screen*, 25/4–5 (1984), 109–20.

—— 'Before the Golden Age: Early Television Drama', in Corner (ed.), *Popular Television in Britain*.

CLARKE, ALAN, and TAYLOR, IAN, 'Vandals, Pickets and Muggers: Television Coverage of Law and Order in the 1979 Election', *Screen Education*, 30 (1980), 99–111.

COHEN, PHIL, and GARDNER, CARL (eds.), *It Ain't Half Racist, Mum: Fighting Racism in the Media* (London: Comedia, 1983).

COHEN, STAN, and YOUNG, JOCK (eds.), *The Manufacture of News: Social Problems, Deviance and the Mass Media* (London: Constable, 1973; rev. 1981).

COLLEY, IAN, and DAVIES, GILL, '*Pennies from Heaven*: Music, Image, Text', *Screen Education*, 35 (1980), 63–78.

COLLINS, RICHARD, 'Television and the People: Access, Participation and Assimilation', *Screen Education*, 14 (1975), 8–13.

—— *Television News* (London: BFI, 1976).

—— *Television: Policy and Culture* (London: Unwin Hyman, 1990).

—— 'Public Service versus the Market Ten Years On: Reflections on Critical Theory and the Debate on Broadcasting Policy in the UK', *Screen*, 34/3 (1993), 243–59.

—— GARNHAM, NICHOLAS and LOCKSLEY, GARETH, *The Economics of Television* (London: Sage, 1988).

CONNELL, IAN, 'Broadcasting: Democracy or Pluralism', *Screen Education*, 30 (1979), 69–74.

—— 'Television, News and the Social Contract', *Screen*, 20/1 (1979), 87–107.

—— 'The Political Economy of Broadcasting: Some Questions', *Screen Education*, 37 (1980–1), 89–100.

—— 'Commercial Broadcasting and the British Left', *Screen*, 24/6 (1983), 70–80.

—— and CURTI, LIDIA, 'Popular Broadcasting in Italy and Britain: Some Issues and Problems', in Drummond and Paterson (eds.), *Television in Transition*.

COOK, JIM (ed.), *Television Sitcom*, BFI Dossier, no. 17 (London: BFI, 1982).

—— '*Out* and *Fox*: Better Television than we Deserve?', in Alvarado and Stewart (eds.), *Made for Television*.

—— and LEWINGTON, MIKE (eds.), *Images of Alcoholism* (London: BFI, 1979).

COOK, JOHN, *Dennis Potter: A Life on Screen*, rev. edn. (Manchester: Manchester University Press, 1998).

CORNELL, PAUL, DAY, MARTIN and TOPPING, KEITH, *The Guinness Book of Classic British TV*, 2nd edn. (Enfield: Guinness Publishing, 1996).

CORNER, JOHN, 'Documentary Voices', in Corner (ed.), *Popular Television in Britain*.

—— *Television Form and Public Address* (London: Edward Arnold, 1995).

—— *Documentary and the Mass Media* (London: Edward Arnold, 1986).

—— (ed.), *Popular Television in Britain: Studies in Cultural History* (London: BFI, 1991).

—— (ed.), *The Art of Record: A Critical Introduction to Documentary* (Manchester: Manchester University Press, 1996).

—— HARVEY, SYLVIA, and LURY, KREN 'Culture, Quality and Choice: The Re-regulation of TV, 1989–91' in Hood (ed.), *Behind the Screens.*

—— (eds.), *Television Times: A Reader* (London: Edward Arnold, 1996).

CRAWFORD COMMITTEE, *Report of the Broadcasting Committee*, Cmnd. 2599 (London: HMSO, 1926).

CREEBER, G., *Dennis Potter, between Two Worlds: A Critical Reassessment* (London: Macmillan, 1998).

CRISELL, ANDREW, 'Filth, Sedition and Blasphemy: The Rise and Fall of Television Satire', in Corner (ed.), *Popular Television in Britain.*

—— *An Introductory History of British Broadcasting* (London: Routledge, 1997).

CURRAN, JAMES, GUREVITCH, MICHAEL, and WOOLLACOTT, JANET (eds.), *Mass Communication and Society* (London: Edward Arnold, 1977).

—— MORLEY, DAVID, and WALKERDINE, VALERIE (eds.), *Cultural Studies and Communications* (London: Arnold, 1996).

—— and SEATON, JEAN, *Power without Responsibility: The Press and Broadcasting in Britain*, 4th edn. (London: Routledge, 1991).

DANIELS, THERESE, 'Programmes for Black Audiences', in Hood (ed.), *Behind the Screens.*

—— and GERSON, JANE (eds.), *The Colour Black: Black Images in British Television* (London: BFI Publishing, 1989).

DAVIDSON, ANDREW, *Under the Hammer: The ITV Franchise Battle* (London: Heinemann, 1992).

DAVIS, ANTHONY, *Here is the News* (London: Severn House, 1976).

—— *Television: The First Forty Years* (London: Severn House, 1976).

—— *TV Laughtermakers* (London: Boxtree, 1989).

DAY-LEWIS, SEAN (ed.), *One Day in the Life of Television* (London: Grafton, 1989).

—— *TV Heaven: A Review of British Television from the 1930s to the 1990s* (London: Channel Four Television, 1992).

—— *Talk of Drama: Views of the Television Dramatist Now and Then* (Luton: University of Luton Press, 1998).

DENNINGTON, JOHN, and TULLOCH, JOHN, 'Cops, Consensus and Ideology', *Screen Education*, 20 (1976), 5–14.

DINSMORE, SUE, 'Strategies for Self-Scrutiny: *Video Diaries*, 1990–3', in Colin MacCabe and Duncan Petrie (eds.), *New Scholarship from BFI Research* (London: BFI Publishing, 1995).

DOCHERTY, DAVID, *Running the Show: 21 Years of London Weekend Television* (London: Boxtree, 1990).

—— MORRISON, DAVID E., and TRACEY, MICHAEL, *Keeping Faith? Channel Four and its Audience* (London: Broadcasting Research Unit/John Libbey, 1988).

DONALD, JAMES, 'Anxious Moments: *The Sweeney* in 1975', in Alvarado and Stewart (eds.), *Made for Television.*

DOVEY, JON, 'Access Television in the UK', in Dowmunt (ed.), *Channels of Resistance*.

DOWMUNT, TONY (ed.), *Channels of Resistance: Global Television and Local Empowerment* (London: BFI Publishing, 1993).

DRUMMOND, PHILLIP, 'Structural and Narrative Constraints in *The Sweeney*', *Screen Education*, 20 (1976), 5–14.

——and PATERSON, RICHARD (eds.), *Television in Transition: Papers from the First International Television Studies Conference* (London: BFI Publishing, 1986).

——and PATERSON, RICHARD (eds.), *Television and its Audience: International Research Perspectives* (London: BFI Publishing, 1988).

DYER, RICHARD, *Light Entertainment* (London: BFI, 1973).

——'"There's nothing I can do! Nothing!": Femininity, Seriality and Whiteness in *The Jewel in the Crown*', *Screen*, 37/3 (1996), 225–39.

——GERAGHTY, CHRISTINE, JORDAN, MARION, LOVELL, TERRY, PATERSON, RICHARD, and STEWART, JOHN, *Coronation Street* (London: BFI Publishing, 1981).

EATON, MICHAEL, 'Television Situation Comedy', *Screen*, 19/4 (1978–9), 61–89.

ELDRIDGE, JOHN, *Getting the Message* (London: Routledge, 1993).

——'Ill News Comes Often on the Back of Worse', in Arthur (ed.), *Religion and the Media* (Ch. 10 in this volume).

ELLIOT, JOHN, *Mogul: The Making of a Myth* (London: Barrie & Jenkins, 1970).

ELLIOTT, PHILIP, *The Making of a Television Series: A Case Study in the Sociology of Culture* (London: Constable, 1972).

ELLIS, JOHN, 'Broadcasting and the State: Britain and the Experience of Channel 4', *Screen*, 27/3–4 (1986), 6–22.

—— *Visible Fictions*, 2nd edn. (London: Routledge, 1992).

ELSAESSER, THOMAS, 'TV Through the Looking Glass', *Quarterly Review of Film & Video*, 14/1–2 (1992), 5–27.

——SIMONS, JAN, and BRONK, LUCETTE, *Writing for the Medium: Television in Transition* (Amsterdam: Amsterdam University Press, 1994).

EMMETT, B. P., 'The Television and Radio Audience in Britain', in McQuail (ed.), *Sociology of Mass Communications*.

FERGUSON, MARGARET (ed.), *Public Communication: The New Imperatives* (London: Sage, 1989).

FRITH, SIMON, 'The Pleasures of the Hearth: The Making of BBC Light Entertainment', in *Formations of Pleasure* (London: Routledge, 1983).

FROST, DAVID, and SHERRIN, NED, *That Was the Week That Was* (London: W. H. Allen, 1963).

GARDNER, CARL (ed.), *Media, Politics and Culture: A Socialist View* (London: Macmillan, 1979).

——and SHEPPARD, JULIE, 'Transforming Television. Part I: The Limits of Policy', *Screen*, 25/2 (1984), 26–38.

——and WYVER, JOHN, 'The Single Play: From Reithian Reverence to Cost-Accounting and Censorship', *Screen*, 24/4–5 (1983), 114–29.

——and YOUNG, ROBERT, 'Science on TV: A Critique', in Bennett *et al.*, *Popular Television and Film*.

GARNHAM, NICHOLAS, *Structures of Television* (London: BFI, 1973).

—— *Capitalism and Communication: Global Culture and the Economics of Information* (London: Sage, 1990).

GAUNTLETT, DAVID, *Video Critical: Children, the Environment and Media Power* (Luton: University of Luton Press, 1996).

——and HILL, ANNETTE, *TV Living: Television, Culture and Everyday Life* (London: Routledge, 1999).

GERAGHTY, CHRISTINE, *Women and Soap Opera: A Study of Prime Time Soaps* (Cambridge: Polity Press, 1991) (extract: Ch. 7 in this volume).

GILBERT, W. STEPHEN, 'The Television Play: Outside the Consensus', *Screen Education*, 35 (1980), 35–44.

——*Fight and Kick and Bite: The Life and Work of Dennis Potter* (London: Hodder & Stoughton, 1995).

GILLESPIE, MARIE, *Television, Ethnicity and Cultural Change* (London: Routledge, 1995).

GLAESSNER, VERINA, 'Gendered Fictions', in Goodwin and Whannel (eds.), *Understanding Television*.

GLASGOW UNIVERSITY MEDIA GROUP, *Bad News* (London: Routledge & Kegan Paul, 1976).

——*More Bad News* (London: Routledge & Kegan Paul, 1980).

——*Really Bad News* (London: Writers and Readers, 1982).

——*War and Peace News* (Milton Keynes: Open University Press, 1985).

GODDARD, PETER, '*Hancock's Half Hour*: A Watershed in British Television Comedy', in Corner (ed.), *Popular Television in Britain*.

GOLDIE, GRACE WYNDHAM, *Facing the Nation: Television and Politics, 1936–76* (London: Bodley Head, 1977).

GOODWIN, ANDREW, KERR, PAUL, and MACDONALD, IAN (eds.), *Drama-Documentary*, BFI Dossier, no. 19 (London: BFI, 1983).

——'TV News: Striking the Right Balance', in Goodwin and Whannel (eds.), *Understanding Television*.

——and WHANNEL, GARRY (eds.), *Understanding Television* (London: Routledge, 1990).

GOODWIN, PETER, *Television under the Tories: Broadcasting Policy, 1979–1997* (London: BFI Publishing, 1998).

——and STEVENSON, WILF (eds.), *Responses to the Green Paper* (London: BFI Publishing, 1994).

GRAHAM, ANDREW, and DAVIES, GAVYN, *Broadcasting, Society and Policy in a Multimedia Age* (Luton: John Libbey Media, 1997).

GRAY, ANN, 'Behind Closed Doors: Women and Video Recorders in the Home', in Helen Baehr and Gillian Dyer (eds.), *Boxed In: Women and Television* (London: Pandora, 1987).

——*Video Playtime: The Gendering of a Leisure Technology* (London: Routledge, 1992).

GREENE, HUGH CARLETON, *The Third Floor Front: A View of Broadcasting in the Sixties* (London: Bodley Head, 1969).

GREGORY, CHRIS, *Be Seeing You . . . Decoding 'The Prisoner'* (Luton: University of Luton Press, 1997).

GROOMBRIDGE, BRIAN, *Television and the People* (Harmondsworth: Penguin, 1972).

GUNTER, BARRIE, and HARRISON, JACKIE, *Violence on Television: An Analysis of the Amount, Nature, Location and Origins of Violence in British Programmes* (London: Routledge, 1998).

——and WAKSHLAG, JACOB, 'Television Viewing and Perceptions of

Crime Among London Residents', in Drummond and Paterson (eds.), *Television and its Audience*.

GUREVITCH, MICHAEL, BENNETT, TONY, CURRAN, JAMES, and WOOLLACOTT, JANET (eds.), *Culture, Society and the Media* (London: Methuen, 1982).

HALL, STUART, 'Deviance, Politics and the Media', in P. Rock and M. McIntosh (eds.), *Deviance and Social Control* (London: BSA, Tavistock, 1974).

—— 'Encoding/Decoding', in Stuart Hall, Dorothy Hobson, Andrew Lowe, and Paul Willis (eds.), *Culture, Media, Language* (London: Hutchinson, 1980).

—— 'The Whites of their Eyes', in Alvarado and Thompson (eds.), *The Media Reader*.

—— CONNELL, IAN, and CURTI, LIDIA, 'The "Unity" of Current Affairs Television', *Working Papers in Cultural Studies*, 9 (1976), 51–93.

—— CRICHTER, CHAS, JEFFERSON, TONY, CLARKE, JOHN, and ROBERTS, BRIAN (eds.), *Policing the Crisis* (London: Macmillan, 1978).

HALLAM, JULIA, and MARSHMENT, MARGARET, 'Framing Experience: Case Studies in the Reception of *Oranges Are Not the Only Fruit*', *Screen*, 36/1 (1995), 1–15.

HALLORAN, JAMES, *The Effects of Television* (London: Panther, 1970).

—— ELLIOTT, PHILIP and MURDOCK, GRAHAM, *Demonstrations and Communications* (Harmondsworth: Penguin, 1972).

HARTLEY, JOHN, *Understanding News* (London: Methuen, 1982).

—— *Tele-ology: Studies in Television* (London: Routledge, 1992).

HARVEY, SYLVIA, 'Channel Four Television: From Annan to Grade', in Hood (ed.), *Behind the Screens*. (Ch. 4 in this volume).

—— and ROBINS, KEVIN (eds.), *The Regions, the Nations and the BBC* (London: BFI Publishing, 1994).

HAYWARD, PHILIP (ed.), *Picture This: Media Representations of Visual Art and Artists* (London: John Libbey, 1988).

HEATH, STEPHEN, and SKIRROW, GILLIAN, 'Television, a World in Action', *Screen*, 18/2 (1977), 7–59.

HELLER, CAROLINE, *Broadcasting and Accountability* (London: BFI, 1978).

HILL, JOHN, 'Television and Pop: The Case of the 1950s' in Corner (ed.), *Popular Television in Britain*.

HINDS, HILARY, '*Oranges Are Not the Only Fruit*: Reaching Audiences Other Lesbian Texts Cannot Reach', in Sally Munt (ed.), *New Lesbian Criticism: Literary and Cultural Readings* (Hemel Hempstead: Harvester Wheatsheaf, 1992).

HOBSON, DOROTHY, '*Crossroads*': The Drama of a Soap Opera* (London: Methuen, 1982).

HOLLAND, PATRICIA, *The Television Handbook* (London: Routledge, 1997).

HOLLINS, TIMOTHY, *Beyond Broadcasting: Into the Cable Age* (London: BFI Publishing, 1984).

HOOD, STUART, *A Survey of Television* (London: Heinemann, 1967).

—— 'The Politics of Television', in McQuail (ed.), *Sociology of Mass Communications*.

—— (ed.), *Behind the Screens: The Structure of British Television in the Nineties* (London: Lawrence & Wishart, 1994).

——and O'LEARY, GARRET (eds.), *Questions of Broadcasting* (London: Methuen, 1990).

——and TABARY-PETERSSEN, THALIA, *On Television*, rev. edn. (London: Pluto, 1997).

HORRIE, CHRIS, and NATHAN, ADAM, *L!ve TV. Telebrats and Topless Darts, The Uncut Story of Tabloid Television* (London: Simon & Schuster, 1999).

HORSMAN, MATTHEW, *Sky High: The Inside Story of BSkyB* (London: Orion Business Books, 1998).

HOWKINS, JOHN, *New Technologies, New Policies?* (London: BFI Publishing, 1982).

HUGHES, PATRICK, *British Broadcasting: Programmes and Power* (Bromley: Chartwell-Bratt, 1981).

——'Today's Television, Tomorrow's World', in Goodwin and Whannel (eds.), *Understanding Television*.

HURD, GEOFFREY, '*The Sweeney*—Contradiction and Coherence', *Screen Education*, 20 (1976), 5–14.

——'The Television Presentation of the Police', in S. Holdaway (ed.), *British Police* (London: Edward Arnold, 1979); repr. in Bennett *et al.* (eds.), *Popular Television and Film*.

ISAACS, JEREMY, *Storm over Four: A Personal Account* (London: Weidenfeld & Nicolson, 1989).

JAMES, CLIVE, *Visions before Midnight: Television Criticism from the 'Observer', 1972–76* (London: Cape, 1977).

——*The Crystal Bucket: Television Criticism from the 'Observer' 1976–79* (London: Cape, 1981).

——*Glued to the Box: Television Criticism from the 'Observer', 1979–82* (London: Cape, 1983).

KEANE, J., *The Media and Democracy* (Cambridge: Polity Press, 1991).

KELLY, RICHARD (ed.), *Alan Clarke* (London: Faber & Faber, 1998).

KERR, PAUL, '*Gangsters*: Conventions and Contraventions', in Bennett *et al.* (eds.), *Popular Television and Film*.

——'Classic Serials: To be Continued', *Screen*, 23/1 (1982), 6–19.

——'F for Fake? Friction over Faction', in Goodwin and Whannel (eds.), *Understanding Television*.

KIDD-HEWITT, DAVID, and OSBORNE, RICHARD (eds.), *Crime and the Media: The Post-modern Spectacle* (London: Pluto, 1995).

KILBORN, RICHARD, 'New Contexts for Documentary Production in Britain', *Media, Culture and Society*, 18 (1996), 141–50.

——and IZOD, JOHN, *An Introduction to TV Documentary: Confronting Reality* (Manchester: Manchester University Press, 1997).

KING, ROGER, 'Drinking and Drunkenness in *Crossroads* and *Coronation Street*', in Cook and Lewington (eds.), *Images of Alcoholism*.

KINGSLEY, HILARY, and TIBBALS, GEOFF, *Box of Delights* (London: Papermac, 1989).

KUMAR, KRISHAN, 'Holding the Middle Ground: The BBC, the Public and the Professional Broadcaster', in Curran *et al.* (eds.), *Mass Communication and Society*.

LAING, STUART, 'Banging In Some Reality: The Original *Z Cars*', in Corner (ed.), *Popular Television in Britain*.

LAMBERT, STEPHEN, *Channel Four: Television with a Difference* (London: BFI Publishing, 1982).

LEALAND, GEOFFREY, *American Television Programmes on British Screens* (London: Broadcasting Research Unit, 1984).

LEAPMAN, MICHAEL, *The Last Days of the Beeb* (London: Allen & Unwin, 1986).

LEMAN, JOY, 'Wise Scientists and Female Androids: Class and Gender in Science Fiction', in Corner (ed.), *Popular Television in Britain.*

LEWIS, JUSTIN, 'Decoding Television News', in Drummond and Paterson (eds.), *Television in Transition.*

—— 'Are you Receiving Me?', in Goodwin and Whannel (eds.), *Understanding Television.*

LEWIS, PETER, *Community Television and Cable in Britain* (London: BFI, 1978).

—— *Whose Media? The Annan Report and After: A Citizen's Guide to Radio and Television* (London: Consumers' Association, 1978).

LOGAN, PAMELA W., *Jack Hylton Presents* (London: BFI Publishing, 1995).

McARTHUR, COLIN, '*Days of Hope*', *Screen*, 16/4 (1975–6), 139–44.

—— *Television and History* (London: BFI, 1978).

—— (ed.), *Scotch Reels: Scotland in Cinema and Television* (London: BFI Publishing, 1982).

MACCABE, COLIN, '*Days of Hope*: A Response to Colin McArthur', *Screen*, 17/1 (1976), 98–101.

—— 'Memory, Phantasy, Identity: *Days of Hope* and the Politics of the Past', *Edinburgh '77 Magazine*; repr. in Bennett *et al.* (eds.), *Popular Television and Film.*

—— and STEWART, OLIVIA (eds.), *The BBC and Public Service Broadcasting* (Manchester: Manchester University Press, 1986).

McCANN, GRAHAM, *Morecambe and Wise* (London: Fourth Estate, 1998).

MacDONALD, BARRIE, *Broadcasting in the United Kingdom: A Guide to Information Sources*, 2nd edn. (London: Mansell, 1993).

McDONNELL, JAMES (ed.), *Public Service Broadcasting: A Reader* (London: Routledge, 1991).

McGRATH, JOHN, 'TV Drama: The Case against Naturalism', *Sight and Sound*, 46/2 (1977), 100–5.

MacMURRAUGH-KAVANAGH, M. K., 'The BBC and the Birth of *The Wednesday Play*, 1962–66: Institutional Containment versus "Agitational Contemporaneity"', *Historical Journal of Film, Radio and Television*, 17/3, (1997), 367–81.

McNAIR, BRIAN, *News and Journalism in the UK* (London: Routledge, 1994).

McQUAIL, DENIS (ed.), *Sociology of Mass Communications* (Harmondsworth: Penguin, 1972).

—— BLUMLER, JAY G., and BROWN, J. R., 'The Television Audience: A Revised Perspective', in McQuail (ed.), *Sociology of Mass Communications.*

McRON, ROBIN, and MURDOCK, GRAHAM, 'The Television and Delinquency Debate', *Screen Education*, 30 (1979), 51–67.

MADDEN, PAUL (ed.), *Keeping Television Alive: The Television Work of the National Film Archive* (London: BFI, 1981).

MADGE, TIM, *Beyond the BBC: Broadcasters and the Public in the 1980s* (London: Macmillan, 1989).

MASTERMAN, LEN, 'Football on Television: Studying the Cup Final', *Screen Education*, 19 (1976), 14–27.

—— (ed.), *Television Mythologies: Stars, Shows and Signs* (London: Comedia/ MK Media Press, 1984).

MEDHURST, ANDY, 'Every Wart and Pustule: Gilbert Harding and Television Stardom', in Corner (ed.), *Popular Television in Britain* (Ch.11 in this volume).

MEECH, PETER, 'The Lion, the Thistle and the Saltire: National Symbols and Corporate Identity in Scottish Broadcasting', *Screen*, 37/1, (1996), 68–81.

MELLENCAMP, PATRICIA (ed.), *Logics of Television: Essays in Cultural Criticism* (Bloomington: Indiana University Press, 1990).

MILLER, TOBY, *The Avengers* (London: BFI Publishing, 1997).

MILLINGTON, BOB, and NELSON, ROBIN, *'Boys from the Blackstuff': The Making of TV Drama* (London: Comedia, 1986).

MORLEY, DAVID, *The 'Nationwide' Audience* (London: BFI, 1980).

—— '*The "Nationwide" Audience*: A Critical Postscript', *Screen Education*, 39 (1981), 3–14.

—— *Family Television: Cultural Power and Domestic Leisure* (London: Comedia/Methuen, 1986).

—— *Television Audiences and Cultural Studies* (London: Routledge, 1992).

MORRISON, DAVID E., *Television and the Gulf War* (London: John Libbey, 1992).

MULGAN, GEOFF (ed.), *The Question of Quality* (London: BFI, 1990).

—— and PATERSON, RICHARD (eds.), *Reinventing the Organisation* (London: BFI Publishing, 1994).

MURDOCK, GRAHAM, 'Understanding Television Drama Production' *Screen Education*, 26 (1978), 59–67.

—— 'Authorship and Organisation', *Screen Education*, 35 (1980), 19–34.

—— 'Money Talks: Broadcasting Finance and Public Culture', in Hood (ed.), *Behind the Screens* (Ch. 5 in this volume).

NEALE, STEVE, and KRUTNIK, FRANK, *Popular Film and Television Comedy* (London: Routledge, 1990) (extract: Ch. 13 in this volume).

NEGRINE, RALPH, *Politics and the Mass Media in Britain*, 2nd edn. (London: Routledge, 1994).

NELSON, ROBIN, *TV Drama in Transition: Forms, Values and Cultural Change* (London: Macmillan, 1997) (extract: Ch.12 in this volume).

NOBLE, GRANT, *Children in Front of the Small Screen* (London: Constable, 1975).

NOWELL-SMITH, GEOFFREY, 'Television–Football–The World', *Screen*, 19/4 (1978–9), 45–59.

O'MALLEY, TOM, *Closedown? The BBC and Government Broadcasting Policy, 1979–92* (London: Pluto Press, 1994).

O'SHAUGHNESSY, MICHAEL, 'Box Pop: Popular Television and Hegemony', in Goodwin and Whannel (eds.), *Understanding Television*.

O'SULLIVAN, TIM, 'Television Memories and Cultures of Viewing, 1950–65', in Corner (ed.), *Popular Television in Britain*.

PAGET, DEREK, *No Other Way to Tell It: Dramadoc/Docudrama on Television* (Manchester: Manchester University Press, 1998).

PALMER, JERRY, *The Logic of the Absurd* (London: BFI Publishing, 1987).

PATEMAN, TREVOR, *Television and the February 1974 General Election* (London: BFI, 1974).

PATERSON, RICHARD, '*The Sweeney*: A Euston Films Product', *Screen Education*, 20 (1976), 5–14.

PATERSON, RICHARD, 'Planning the Family: The Art of the Television Schedule', *Screen Education*, 35 (1980), 79–85.

—— '*Gangsters*: The Pleasure and the Pain in the Text', in Bennett *et al.* (eds.), *Popular Television and Film*.

—— 'A Suitable Schedule for the Family', in Goodwin and Whannel (eds.), *Understanding Television*.

—— 'Friends, Fools and Horses: British Television Fiction in 1996', in Milly Buonanno (ed.), *Imagining Dreamscapes: Television Fiction in Europe* (Luton: University of Luton Press, 1998).

—— (ed.), *Organising for Change* (London: BFI, 1990).

PAULU, BURTON, *Television and Radio in the United Kingdom* (London: Macmillan, 1956; rev. 1981).

PEACOCK COMMITTEE, *Report of the Committee on Financing the BBC*, Cmnd. 9824 (London: HMSO, 1986).

PETLEY, JULIAN, 'Fact Plus Fiction Equals Friction', *Media, Culture and Society*, 18/1 (1996).

PETRIE, DUNCAN, and WILLIS, JANET (eds.), *Television and the Household: Reports from the BFI's Audience Tracking Study* (London: BFI Publishing, 1995).

PILKINGTON COMMITTEE, *Report of the Committee on Broadcasting 1960*, Cmnd. 1753 (London: HMSO, 1962).

PINES, JIM (ed.), *Black and White in Colour: Black People in British Television since 1936* (London: BFI Publishing, 1992).

POOLE, MIKE, 'The Cult of the Generalist: British Television Criticism 1936–83', *Screen*, 25/2 (1984), 41–61.

—— and WYVER, JOHN, *Powerplays: Trevor Griffiths in Television* (London: BFI Publishing, 1984).

POTTER, J., *Independent Television in Britain*, iii: *Politics and Control 1968–80* (London: Macmillan, 1989).

—— *Independent Television in Britain*, iv: *Companies and Programmes, 1968–80* (London: Macmillan, 1990).

PRIOR, ALLAN, *Script to Screen: From 'Z Cars' to 'The Charmer'* (St Albans: Ver Books, 1996).

PURSER, PHILIP, *Done Viewing: A Personal Account of the Best Years of Our Television* (London: Quartet, 1992).

PYM, JOHN, *Film on Four: A Survey, 1982–91* (London: BFI Publishing, 1992).

REITH, JOHN, *Into the Wind* (London: Hodder & Stoughton, 1949).

ROBINS, KEVIN, and WEBSTER, FRANK, 'Broadcasting Politics: Communications and Consumption', *Screen*, 27/3–4 (1986), 30–44.

ROOT, JANE, *Open the Box: About Television* (London: Comedia, 1986).

SCANNELL, PADDY, 'Public Service Broadcasting: The History of a Concept', in Goodwin and Whannel (eds.), *Understanding Television* (Ch.2 in this volume).

—— and CARDIFF, DAVID, *A Social History of British Broadcasting*, i: *1922–1939: Serving the Nation* (Oxford: Basil Blackwell, 1991).

SCHLESINGER, PHILIP, *Putting 'Reality' Together: BBC News* (London: Constable, 1978).

—— 'Princes' Gate, 1980: The Media Politics of Siege Management', *Screen Education*, 37 (1980–1), 29–54.

—— DOBASH, R. EMERSON, DOBASH, RUSSELL P., and WEAVER, C. KAY, *Women Viewing Violence* (London: BFI Publishing, 1992).

—— MURDOCK, GRAHAM and ELLIOTT, PHILIP, *Televising Terrorism: Political Violence in Popular Culture* (London: Comedia, 1983).

—— and TUMBER, HOWARD, *Reporting Crime* (Oxford: Oxford University Press, 1994).

SENDALL, BERNARD, *Independent Television in Britain*, i: *Origin and Foundation, 1946–62* (London: Macmillan, 1982).

—— *Independent Television in Britain*, ii: *Expansion and Change 1958–68* (London: Macmillan, 1983).

SEYMOUR-URE, COLIN, *The British Press and Broadcasting since 1945*, 2nd edn. (Oxford: Basil Blackwell, 1996).

SHAW, COLIN (ed.), *Rethinking Governance and Accountability* (London: BFI Publishing, 1994).

SHUBIK, IRENE, *Play for Today: The Evolution of Television Drama* (London: Davis-Poynter, 1975).

SHULMAN, MILTON, *The Least Worst Television in the World* (London: Barrie & Jenkins, 1973).

SILJ, ALESSANDRO (ed.), *East of Dallas: The European Challenge to American Television* (London: BFI Publishing, 1988).

SILVERSTONE, ROGER, *The Message of Television: Myth and Narrative in Contemporary Culture* (London: Heinemann Educational Books, 1981).

—— *Framing Science: The Making of a BBC Documentary* (London: BFI Publishing, 1985).

SIMON OF WYTHENSHAWE, *The BBC from Within* (London: Gollancz, 1953).

SIMPSON, PHILIP, ' "Presentness Precise" — Notes on *The History Man*', *Screen*, 23/1 (1982), 20–30.

—— (ed.), *Parents Talking Television: Television in the Home* (London: Comedia, 1987).

SKIDMORE, PAULA, 'Telling Tales: Media Power, Ideology and the Reporting of Child Sexual Abuse in Britain', in Kidd-Hewitt and Osborne (eds.), *Crime and the Media*.

SKIRROW, GILLIAN, '*Widows*', in Alvarado and Stewart (eds.), *Made for Television*.

SMITH, ANTHONY, (ed.), *The Shadow in the Cave: A Study of the Relationship between The Broadcaster, his Audience and the State* (London: Quartet, 1976).

—— *Books to Bytes: Knowledge and Information in the Postmodern Era* (London: BFI Publishing, 1993).

—— *British Broadcasting* (Newton Abbott: David & Charles, 1974).

SPARKS, COLIN, 'The Impact of Technological and Political Change on the Labour Force in British Television', *Screen*, 30/1–2 (1989), 24–38.

—— 'Independent Production', in Hood (ed.), *Behind the Screens*.

SPARKS, RICHARD, *Television and the Drama of Crime: Moral Tales and the Place of Crime in Public Life* (Buckingham: Open University Press, 1992).

STEVENSON, WILF (ed.), *All our Futures* (London: BFI Publishing, 1994).

—— and SMEDLEY, NICK (eds.), *Responses to the White Paper* (London: BFI, 1990).

STONEMAN, ROD, 'Sins of Commission', *Screen*, 33/2 (1992), 127–44.

STRINATI, DOMINIC, and WAGG, STEPHEN (eds.), *Come On Down? Popular Culture in Post-war Britain* (London: Routledge, 1992).

STUART, CHARLES (ed.), *The Reith Diaries* (London: Collins, 1975).

SUTTON, SEAN, *The Largest Theatre in the World: Thirty Years of Television Drama* (London: BBC, 1982).

SWALLOW, NORMAN, *Factual Television* (London: Focal Press, 1966).

SYKES COMMITTEE, *Broadcasting Committee Report*, Cmnd. 1951 (London: HMSO, 1923).

TAYLOR, D., *Days of Vision* (London: Methuen, 1990).

TAYLOR, JOHN RUSSELL, *Anatomy of a TV Play* (London: Weidenfeld & Nicolson, 1962).

—— *Anger and After: A Guide to the New British Drama* (London: Eyre Methuen, 1969).

—— *The Second Wave: British Drama of the Seventies* (London: Methuen, 1971).

TAYLOR, LAURIE, and MULLAN, BOB, *Uninvited Guests: The Intimate Secrets of Television and Radio* (London: Chatto & Windus, 1986).

THOMAS, LYN, 'In Love with *Inspector Morse*', *Feminist Review*, 51 (1995), 1–25.

THOMPSON, JOHN O., 'Tragic Flow: Raymond Williams on Drama', *Screen Education*, 35 (1980), 45–58.

—— (ed.), *Monty Python: Complete and Utter History of the Grotesque* (London: BFI Publishing, 1982).

THUMIN, JANET, ' "A Live Commercial for Icing Sugar". Researching the Historical Audience: Gender and Broadcast Television in the 1950s', *Screen*, 36/1 (1995), 48–55.

TRACEY, MICHAEL, *The Production of Political Television* (London: Routledge & Kegan Paul, 1977) (extract: Ch.1 in this volume).

—— *The Decline and Fall of Public Service Broadcasting* (Oxford: Oxford University Press, 1998).

—— and MORRISON, DAVID, *Whitehouse* (London: Macmillan, 1979).

TRIBE, KEITH, 'History and the Production of Memories', *Screen*, 18/4 (1977–8), 9–22.

TULLOCH, JOHN, 'Gradgrind's Heirs: The Quiz and the Presentation of Knowledge', *Screen Education*, 19 (1976), 3–13.

—— 'Television and Black Britons', in Goodwin and Whannel (eds.), *Understanding Television*.

—— *Television Drama: Agency, Audience and Myth* (Routledge, 1990).

TUMBER, HOWARD, *Television and the Riots* (London: BFI Publishing, 1982).

TUNSTALL, JEREMY, *The Media are American: Anglo-American Media in the World* (London: Constable, 1977).

—— *The Media in Britain* (London: Constable, 1983).

—— *Television Producers* (London: Routledge, 1993).

ULLSWATER COMMITTEE, *Report of the Broadcasting Committee* Cmnd. 5091 (London: HMSO, 1936).

VAHIMAGI, TISE, *British Television: An Illustrated Guide*, 2nd edn. (Oxford: Oxford University Press, 1996).

VAUGHAN, DAI, *Television Documentary Usage* (London: BFI, 1976).

WALKER, JOHN A., *Arts TV: A History of Arts Television in Britain* (London: John Libbey, 1993).

WAYKINS, GORDON (ed.), *Tonight*, BFI Dossier, no. 15 (London: BFI, 1982).

WAYNE, MIKE, 'Television, Audiences, Politics', in Hood (ed.), *Behind the Screens.*

WEDELL, E. G., *Broadcasting and Public Policy* (London: Michael Joseph, 1968).

—— (ed.), *Structures of Broadcasting: A Symposium* (Manchester: Manchester University Press, 1970).

WHALE, JOHN, *The Politics of the Media* (London: Fontana, 1977).

WHANNEL, GARRY, 'Winner Takes All: Competition', in Goodwin and Whannel (eds.), *Understanding Television.*

—— '*Grandstand,* the Sports Fan and the Family Audience', in Corner (ed.), *Popular Television in Britain.*

—— *Fields in Vision: Television Sport and Cultural Transformation* (London: Routledge, 1993).

WILLIAMS, RAYMOND, *Communications* (Harmondsworth: Penguin, 1970).

—— *Television, Technology and Cultural Form* (London: Fontana, 1974).

WILLIS, JANET, and WOLLEN, TANA (eds.), *The Neglected Audience* (London: BFI Publishing, 1990).

WILSON, H. H., *Pressure Group* (London: Weidenfeld & Nicolson, 1961).

WINSTON, BRIAN, 'Public Service in the "New Broadcasting Age"' in Hood (ed.), *Behind the Screens.*

WINTERBOTTOM, MICHAEL, 'In Production: *Minder*', in Alvarado and Stewart (eds.), *Made for Television.*

WOLLEN, TANA, '*The Flame Trees of Thika*', in Alvarado and Stewart (eds.), *Made for Television.*

WORSLEY, T. C., *Television: The Ephemeral Art* (London: Alan Ross, 1970).

WYVER, JOHN, 'Representing Art or Reproducing Culture? Tradition and Innovation in British Television's Coverage of the Arts (1950–87)', in Hayward (ed.), *Picture This.*

Index

(Note: The UK terrestrial broadcasters the BBC, ITV, and Channel Four have not been indexed since references to them occur on almost every page.)

Corbett, Harry H. 280
Corner, John 202
Coronation Street 9, 146, 148, 149,
    150, 153, 154, 156, 160, 173–83,
    185–8, 190–4, 303
Cosby Show, The 109
Cosmorama 261
Cotton, Bill 146
Cracker 14, 216
Craddock, Fanny 248
Cranston, Maurice 70
Craven, Peter 303, 304, 316, 317
Crawford Committee 28, 29, 47
Crime Monthly 219
Crimestrike 107
Crimewatch UK 197, 204, 215, 219,
    222
Critical Eye 109
Crossman, R.H.S. 43, 67
Crossroads 146, 156
Crowther, Bruce 284, 286
Crowther, Geoffrey 78
Cullen, Alma 200
Culture and Anarchy 56
Cutting Edge 109

Dad's Army 14, 18
Daily Express 180
Daily Herald 81
Daily Mail 30, 84
Daily Sketch 64
Daily Telegraph 78, 218
Daily Worker 78
Dallas 15, 153, 156, 161, 173, 192
Dangerfield 216
Darkest England 110
Darling, George 87
David Copperfield 303
Davidson, J.C.C. 31, 34, 36, 37, 40,
    41, 42, 237
Davies, Andrew 266, 268, 270, 272,
    276
Days of Hope 8, 20
Days of Our Lives 15
Dazzling Image 110
Dean, James 263
Dear Viewer 64
Dearden, Basil 215
Dell, Edmund 107
Demme, Jonathan 217
Dempsey, John 218

Dench, Judi 270
Derby, Lord 65, 72, 74, 81, 91
Desperate Hours, The 286
Devlin, J.G. 286
Dexter, Colin 200, 201
Dhondy, Farrukh 110
Dickens, Charles 9, 309
Dietrich, Marlene 256
Dimbleby, Richard 252, 261, 262
Discovery Channel 320
District Nurse 149
Dixon of Dock Green 215
Double Your Money 252
Doyle, Tony 210
Dr Finlay's Casebook 149
Dream On 107
Drop the Dead Donkey 110
Dunkley, Chris 210
Dyer, Richard 173, 181, 185, 202
Dynasty 15, 153, 156, 173, 192, 194

EastEnders 15, 16, 145–72, 173–6,
    179–85, 187–94, 303
Eaton, Mary 209
Eaton, Mick 282
Eco, Umberto 6
Economist, The 66, 68, 69, 70, 78, 79,
    83, 89, 124, 133
Eden, Anthony 73
Edinburgh Television Festival 103,
    127
Edwards, Jane 232
Edwards, Jimmy 260
Eldridge, John 18
Eliot, George 267–74, 276
Elliot, Walter 65
Elliott, Philip 166
Elstein, David 99, 105
Elstree Studios 151
Emmerdale Farm 146, 160, 161
Equal Opportunities Commission
    199
European Institute for the Media
    305, 306
Evening Standard 66, 180, 218, 244
Expresso Bongo 261

FA Cup Final 48
Fabian Society 87
Face to Face 254, 264
Fairlie, Henry 68